1985

QADDAFI AND THE
UNITED STATES SINCE 1969

QADDAFI AND THE
UNITED STATES SINCE 1969

P. Edward Haley

PRAEGER

PRAEGER SPECIAL STUDIES • PRAEGER SCIENTIFIC

New York • Philadelphia • Eastbourne, UK
Toronto • Hong Kong • Tokyo • Sydney

Library of Congress Cataloging in Publication Data

Haley, P. Edward.
    Qaddafi and the United States since 1969.

    Includes index.
    1. United States—Foreign relations—Libya.
2. Libya—Foreign relations—United States. 3. Qaddafi,
Muammar. I. Title.
E183.8.L75H34   184   327.730612   83-26993
ISBN 0-03-070587-8 (alk. paper)

Published in 1984 by Praeger Publishers
CBS Educational and Professional Publishing,
a Division of CBS Inc.
521 Fifth Avenue, New York, NY 10175 USA

©1984 by Praeger Publishers

456789   052   987654321

Printed in the United States of America
on acid-free paper

In Memory of My Father

ACKNOWLEDGEMENTS

This is a book about U.S. foreign policy toward the revolutionary government of Libya during the decade and more since a spottily educated, vaguely Westernized young signals captain, Muammar Qaddafi, who idolized Gamal Nasser, overthrew the frail monarchy of King Idris on September 1, 1969. It is based on numerous interviews conducted over a period of two years with U.S. policy-makers, diplomats, and others who were and are directly involved in Libyan-U.S. relations. In addition, I examined thousands of pages of documents declassified under the Freedom of Information Act, along with numerous books, U.S. government documents, journals, and miles of newspaper microfilm and microfiche.

For their generous assistance the author wishes to thank David Newsom, William Quandt, James Blake, Harlan and Linda Robinson, Ellen Laipson, Clyde Mark, John Cooley, W. Alan Roy, Lillian Harris, Frances Avila, Andrew Terrill, Elaine Rossi, William Moses, a number of U.S. diplomats and intelligence officers who spoke to him off the record, and the students in Political Science 137, The Middle East in World Politics. The late Malcolm Kerr of American University, Beirut, arranged a seminar at UCLA, at which I was able to present an early version of the book before an informed audience. Mary Anderson used a word processor in magical ways to prepare the manuscript through its successive drafts, and her cheerful, untiring efforts were of great assistance.

CONTENTS

LIST OF TABLES

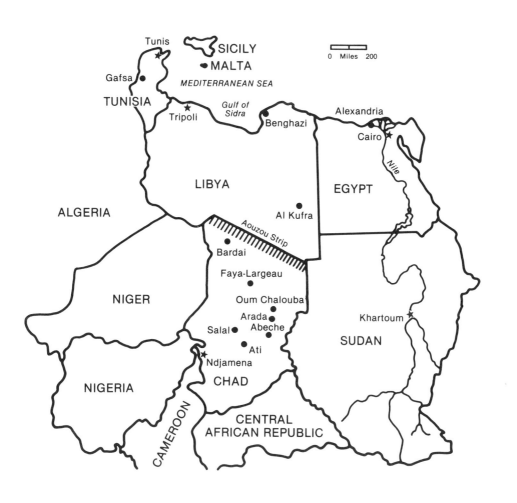

I
THE FAILURE OF
CONCILIATION, 1969-1973

1
INTRODUCTION:
THE SEARCH FOR A POLICY

The objectives of the United States in regard to Libya resemble those that have guided U.S. policy toward most of the nations in the Middle East and Africa. These objectives have strategic, regional, and commercial dimensions. The strategic objectives of the United States are, minimally, to deny the military use of the territory and resources of Libya to the Soviet Union. This has been a major strategic goal of the United States in its relations with Libya since 1969. However, in the years immediately following World War II the United States and Britain maintained a number of military bases in Libya and utilized Libyan territory for their own strategic ends. After Qaddafi's seizure of power both Western governments evacuated their bases. They did so to avoid inflaming the already substantial anti-U.S. prejudice of the new, highly nationalistic leadership of Libya and out of a belief in the declining utility of such outposts as the bases at Wheelus and Tobruk. The quick, easy evacuations were also intended to hold out the prospect of friendly relations between Libya and the United States and, by removing the irritant of foreign "occupation," to free Libyan nationalism to oppose any new Soviet military and political presence.

Before Qaddafi took power the regional objectives of the United States in the Middle East centered on reducing the likelihood of a major Arab-Israeli war and maintaining the flow of oil from the Gulf to Europe, Japan, and North America. These objectives have expanded as Soviet influence has increased in the Middle East and North Africa. Under the monarchy, Libya played no part in the major regional issues. Libya was not an active player in the contest between "revolutionary" and conservative governments, which

3

Nasser had proclaimed. It took no position on the Arab-Israeli conflict. The latter was deeply resented inside Libya during the 1967 War and helped undermine Idris's rule. In short, before 1969 Libya was passive internationally and conservative internally. Qaddafi has reversed both orientations. His international activism is of most concern to other governments, of course, and has contributed to a significant expansion of U.S. regional objectives. The Libyan attacks against Chad, Sudan, and Tunisia, and its support for Polisario against Morocco, for example, have drawn the United States more deeply into the struggles of these countries for sovereignty and internal stability than ever before.

Until the Reagan administration broke all ties to Libya, the safeguarding of the dominant position of U.S. oil companies in Libya was the principal commercial objective of the United States. The mutual advantages of this relationship are very strong. It has withstood the nationalization of the oil industry by Libya and the imposition by the United States of a total embargo on the importation of Libyan oil, not to mention a variety of scandals, scares, and skirmishes. High on such a list would be the Billy Carter affair, the Libyan hit-team allegedly sent to assassinate President Reagan, and the "shoot-out" between United States and Libyan aircraft in 1981 over the Gulf of Sidra. However, another important U.S. objective grew directly from the presence of U.S. oil companies. This was the obligation to protect the American community of some 2,000 people living and working in Libya. While it was always in the minds of U.S. policymakers, the seizure of the hostages in Teheran and Qaddafi's record of sudden, violent actions, turned the welfare of Americans in Libya into a major concern.

All these objectives are obvious; none are unusual. In fact, there has been much less controversy about the objectives of U.S. policy toward Libya than about the means chosen to realize those objectives. The United States has adopted four sets of methods to achieve its objectives in Libya since the mid-1950s. The first method, adopted before the revolution, required the United States to defend Libya against external attack but not to intervene to save the monarchy against internal upheaval. This position was communicated frankly to King Idris by David Newsom, the last U.S. ambassador to serve under the monarchy, in 1967.(1) Newsom returned to Washington in August 1969 to become assistant secretary of state for Africa. His successor, Joseph Palmer, with whom he was exchanging assignments, arrived well after Qaddafi had overthrown the old king.

Ambassador Palmer was, therefore, a principal architect of the first set of methods by which the United States would attempt to achieve its objectives in regard to Qaddafi's Libya. Palmer's method was conciliation. He stressed the long-term compatibility of Libyan and U.S. interests. He and his principal political assistant at the embassy argued that Qaddafi was a sincerely religious man and an intense Arab nationalist. Accordingly nothing should be done to interfere with what they saw to be Qaddafi's "natural" anti-Soviet bias. There is some evidence that Jalloud, one of Qaddafi's closest associates, encouraged Palmer in these views. Inspired by these ideas, the United States agreed quickly and easily to evacuate its large Wheelus air base and even agreed to sell weapons to the new regime. The blunders of the United States in dealing with Nasser and Castro were not to be repeated. The British followed suit and evacuated their base at Tobruk at the same time. The approach ended in failure. Once the evacuations had been carried out in 1970 Jalloud suddenly told Palmer that as long as the United States supported Israel it could never have good relations with Libya. Next, the highest Libyan officials were ordered not to have anything to do with the U.S. embassy. Finally, Ambassador Palmer asked for his own recall because no one would discuss any serious matters with him. He was ordered back to Washington in 1972. His departure brought representation at the ambassadorial level to an end.

For the next ten years the United States chose to pay little attention to Libya. During this time Qaddafi pushed his policies to an extreme: strident opposition to Israel and the United States, heavy financial and logistical support for Palestinian and European terrorism, and significant covert and, increasingly, overt armed intervention in Arab and African countries, such as Tunisia and Chad, and even an Asian country, the Philippines. By the early 1980s Qaddafi had also made Libya a close political ally of the Soviet Union and had purchased a huge arsenal of Soviet arms, far in excess of his own armed forces' capabilities to use.

While all this was going on the United States imposed a few mild restraints on its dealings with Libya. The United States refused to sell arms or military aircraft of any kind to Libya and opposed the export of civilian equipment — heavy trucks, for example — that might have military applications. Generally the State Department was successful in preventing the export of such "dual use" items; sometimes it was not. But the attitude of the U.S. government was clear. In 1975 the Ford administration took the policy of indirect opposition to Libya one step further. Anwar Sadat had grown more and more impatient with Qaddafi, with his opposition to Egypt's peace policy, with his various subversive plots, with his funding of terrorism, and with his increasing cooperation with the Soviet Union. Resolved to teach Qaddafi a lesson Sadat obtained from the Ford administration a commitment to deter Soviet intervention if Egypt went to war with Libya. This was a step toward a policy of direct U.S. opposition to Qaddafi's external adventures. However, the Carter administration withdrew the commitment immediately after taking office. The main reason for the withdrawal apparently was a concern in the White House that the promise to Sadat could deprive the United States of control of its own policy in circumstances that might end in a military clash with the Soviet Union.(2) The withdrawal of the promise to Sadat was also consistent with the administration's overall determination, which was especially strong in the early months, to deemphasize military methods in the Third World and to avoid treating every incident there as a manifestation of a larger Soviet-U.S. competition. In regard to Libya this approach represented a return to the diplomacy of restraint, with occasional efforts by high U.S. officials, including David Newsom, who was now in Washington as undersecretary of state for political affairs, to discover if there was any possibility of a normalization of relations with Libya.

The attempts to achieve U.S. objectives by paying little or no attention to Qaddafi were not the products of oversight or carelessness. Instead, they came from a series of judgments about the feasibility at home and abroad of resorting to sterner military and economic measures and about the damage Qaddafi was capable of inflicting on the interests of the United States and its allies. At home, in the wake of Vietnam and Watergate, there was little support for foreign military intervention by the United States. Moreover, the Nixon, Ford, and Carter administrations were convinced that the United States' Western European allies would oppose the imposition of military and economic sanctions against Libya. Without European support, U.S. policymakers concluded, the sanctions would fail and the consequences would be worse than the ostensible cure. Qaddafi would be strengthened in power because of the backlash in Libya and the Arab world produced by U.S.-led sanctions. The position of the Soviet Union in Libya and the Middle East would be strengthened. Moreover, the status of the U.S. oil companies and the well-being of the large American community would be put at risk. It was also argued that Libya's capacity for mischief was slight – essentially a small, poorly trained army and some terrorists. But perhaps the most important reason for disregarding Qaddafi was that to provoke a military or economic showdown with Libya would have run exactly contrary to the "step-by-step" peace policy of Henry Kissinger in the region from 1973-75 and the Camp David diplomacy of the Carter administration from 1977-80.

Despite the truth of these observations, restraint was as much a failure as the earlier conciliatory method had been in realizing U.S. objectives with regard to Libya. Ignoring the mild sanctions imposed by the United States against Libya and the general indifference with which he was treated, Qaddafi continued to use all his resources to oppose the chief Middle Eastern goals of the United States. He fought against every U.S. plan for an Arab-Israeli peace settlement, and purposely assumed the role of the most shrill and nasty Arab critic of Sadat's peace initiatives. Libya was a founding member of the Steadfastness and Rejection Front and paid large subsidies to Palestinian factions opposed to any form of negotiations with Israel. During every period of tension in the area Qaddafi could be counted on to urge the Arab oil producers to turn the oil weapon against the United States. The accumulation of massive amounts of Soviet weapons continued. Qaddafi was implicated in numerous plots and conspiracies to overthrow the governments of the neighboring states, such as Tunisia and Sudan. Sadat repeatedly charged Qaddafi with sponsoring terrorism inside Egypt.

In addition, Qaddafi proved to be a more potent troublemaker than U.S. policymakers had thought he could be. The Libyan-sponsored attack on Tunisia and the invasion of Chad were eyeopeners, and Qaddafi's support for Polisario against Morocco was especially unwelcome. Morocco had grown in importance in the eyes of U.S. policymakers because of United States' plans for the defense of the oil in the Arabian Peninsula by a Rapid Deployment Force. These plans, of necessity, require the use of Moroccan bases for the movement of troops and supplies to the Gulf. Qaddafi heightened his own international isolation by sending assassins to kill Libyans opposed to his regime and to frighten the Libyan exile community from joining any would-be coup makers in toppling him from power. As the numbers of Libyans murdered in Europe mounted and an attempt was made to kill a Libyan living in the United States, the stage was set for a change in U.S. policy. Qaddafi ordered the invasion of Chad just before the Carter administration's term expired. This was final proof, if any were needed, of the inadequacy of the "arm's-length" methods. A much more direct and aggressive U.S. policy toward Libya would have been adopted, regardless of the outcome of the 1980 presidential election. That the victor was Ronald Reagan, a proponent of massive increases in arms spending and the vigorous assertion of U.S. power abroad, made the abandonment of the old approaches certain.

Under Reagan the United States applied a "bare-knuckle" approach of all-out opposition to Libya. A systematic plan to increase all kinds of pressure on Libya was formulated and put into action in the first months of the new administration. The plan was comprehensive and multifaceted. The United States sought the help of its European allies against Qaddafi. However, unlike previous administrations the Reagan White House had decided in advance not to allow European reservations to stalemate strong, aggressive U.S. action against Qaddafi. In fact, the Europeans took only those actions against Qaddafi that they regarded as appropriate, such as Britain's demand to halt the assassination campaign and France's opposition to the invasion of Chad. They did not join Reagan in the other steps he took and rejected the administration's view of Qaddafi as a devil somehow "larger than life." Almost from the moment it took office the Reagan administration began to brand Qaddafi as a maniacal terrorist and an international outlaw. The purpose was not merely to tarnish the Libyan leader's reputation but to isolate Qaddafi and deprive him of aid in the event of a showdown with the United States, or one of its allies, such as Egypt. Other steps taken by the

Reagan administration were the formal rupture of diplomatic relations with Libya, the withdrawal of all Americans from Libya, and a ban on Libyan oil imports and on the export to Libya of all items containing advanced technology. After the Iranian hostage crisis no U.S. president would take diplomatic risks with another country that might result in the imprisonment of U.S. citizens. More than any other step, therefore, the withdrawal of Americans sent a signal that the United States was "clearing the decks," and was ready for any kind of political and military developments.

This message was reinforced by the trap laid for Libya in the Gulf of Sidra. Elaborately planned on the U.S. side, the plan was to assert the U.S. claim that the Gulf is an international waterway by sailing a naval task force across the line claimed by Libya as its territorial limit. This had been done often in the past, and there had been reports, leaked by the U.S. government, that Libyan fighters had fired on U.S. planes probing this air space. The difference was that in August 1981 the U.S. task force and, in particular, its naval aviators and their commanders had been meticulously prepared to destroy any Libyan aircraft that behaved in a menacing way. When two Libyan jets fired first at a U.S. air patrol, as Qaddafi admitted they had, they were both shot down.

Nor was pressure against Libya on the covert side overlooked. During the summer of 1981 there were a number of leaks, ostensibly from the Congress, and counterleaks from the administration about a covert plan organized and funded by the CIA to overthrow Qaddafi. Simultaneously, the United States supported France in its effort to bring about Libya's withdrawal from Chad and covertly aided the anti-Libyan movement in Chad led by Hissene Habre. Working closely with the governments of Egypt and Sudan, the administration reinstated President Ford's pledge to deter Soviet intervention if Egypt went to war with Libya. The U.S. commitment was renewed just before Sadat's assassination in support of Egyptian and Sudanese plans to attack Libyan forces in Chad.(3) Finally, the Reagan administration engaged in an ostentatious military and economic strengthening of Morocco, Tunisia, Egypt, and Sudan. In part, the administration was merely exploiting the "Libyan menace" in order to win support for steps it wished to take in pursuit of Secretary Haig's "strategic consensus" against the Soviet Union, and as an element in the arrangements necessary for the creation of a Rapid Deployment Force. But the outcome was exactly the opposite of what Qaddafi desired. These countries were being made stronger instead of weaker and U.S. influence and presence were being increased instead of lessened. The administration took pains to make clear that they owed much of the political feasibility for the outpouring of funds and defense commitments to Qaddafi's aggressive behavior in the Arab world, and northern and central Africa, not to mention inside Europe and the United States itself.

With these observations in mind one can form a clear picture of the nature and development of U.S. policy toward Libya since 1969. There have been three phases: conciliation, restraint, and opposition. Put in other terms the United States has tried friendship, indifference, and hostility. Friendship and indifference led nowhere. Worse, in the final stages of the diplomacy of restraint, Qaddafi took a number of steps that harmed important interests of the United States and its allies. By a prolonged and systematic effort involving a number of Arab, African, and European governments the Reagan administration brought Qaddafi's Libya under severe diplomatic, military, and, to a lesser extent, economic pressures. The changes in Qaddafi's foreign policy once these pressures began to bite were startling and easy to observe. Most notable was Libya's withdrawal from Chad. However, it is much more difficult to make a sure connection between the resort to hostility by the United States and the changes in Libyan policy. A number of factors appear to have come together in Chad that influenced the Libyan decision to withdraw. Some were beyond the ability of the administration to control. One of these was a worldwide decline in demand for oil, which cut heavily into purchases of Libya's premium-priced crude. This struck at the financial basis of Qaddafi's aggressive foreign policy. A second was the failure of the Chadian factions dependent on Libya to unite in effective coalition against Habre. A third was France's opposition to Libya's expansion into central Africa. A fourth was Egypt's and, in particular, Sadat's animosity toward Qaddafi's schemes. Egypt actually went to war against Libya on one occasion and was ready to attack again in October 1981. A fifth was the widespread African opposition to Qaddafi, which found symbolic expression in opposition to the seating of Polisario as a member of the Organization of African Unity, although it was strenuously sought by Algeria and Libya, and to Qaddafi's assumption of the presidency of the African organization. Given these circumstances, a U.S. policy of open hostility toward Libya had its own impact multiplied and certainly contributed to the alteration of Libyan policy.

These considerations give rise to two questions of major importance to U.S. policy. First, would an earlier turn to hostility by the United States have produced a comparable effect on Libyan policy? Might it, in other words, have helped forestall the invasion and attempted annexation of Chad or the attempted uprising in Tunisia? Second, now that a major change in Libyan policy has been achieved, should the hostility be tempered with some form of conciliation? This has been the French approach since the Libyan withdrawal from Chad. Must U.S. policy, in other words, have only one note to play, whether friendship, indifference, or enmity? The analysis returns to these questions and others in the concluding chapter.

A study of U.S. policy toward Libya requires as its foundation an interpretation of the goals and means of Libyan foreign policy, as formulated and carried out by Qaddafi and his fellow officers. Although a number of basic studies have appeared recently on Libyan internal politics and economic development since the revolution, suprisingly little has been written about Libyan foreign policy. Therefore, I have devoted a good deal of space to the description of the principal foreign actions of the Libyan government since 1969 as these may be known from interviews with policymakers, newspapers, journals, U.S. government documents, and other publicly available sources. The purpose is to provide a portrait of Libyan foreign policy, an accurate, necessarily impressionistic rendering of the essence of Libyan policy rather than an exhaustive anatomical chart. Without this the reader will neither be able to fathom the analysis of U.S. foreign policy that accompanies the account of Libya's adventures abroad nor judge the merit of that analysis.

Of course, it is impossible even to describe anything as complex as another nation's foreign policy — even by portraiture — without forming an overall opinion about it. When the personalities involved are as vivid as Qaddafi's and the issues as spectacularly controversial as terrorism, oil, and the Palestinian question the reader has all the more claim to know the author's fundamental opinions about his subjects. In my view Qaddafi's vision and actions are neither crazy nor haphazard. Indeed, what gives his goals as wide an impact and audience as they have had is precisely their representative nature. They are widely shared in the Middle East and the Third World, even if some of the governments there would shrink from the extreme form or unscrupulous implementation Qaddafi has given them.

At the most general level, Qaddafi is "non-aligned" in what has come to be the characteristic distorted sense of that term. In other words, Qaddafi is rhetorically neutral but in fact is willing to work closely with and rely only on the Soviet Union among the major external powers. There are differences between Libya and the Soviet Union: for example, the Soviets accept the existence of Israel and regard as admissible and even desirable a final, negotiated settlement of the Arab-Israeli conflict; Qaddafi will do neither. But he is determined to emphasize the elements of agreement between Libya and the Soviet Union and to work with the Soviets wherever possible in foreign policy.

Qaddafi also sees himself and Libya as charged with a prophetic and revolutionary role in world affairs. He uses Libya's oil wealth to proselytize on behalf of Islam and to support revolutionary movements around the world. His vision is anti-Western in a general and also in a specific sense. That is, he rejects the primary philosophical, religious, and political teachings of the West, and he opposes all forms of Western influence in whatever ways he can, usually by striking at Israel and the United States. An elaborate expression of Qaddafi's view of the world appears in his Green Book. The message of the Green Book, which Qaddafi regards as a "gospel" for the Third World, is anti-Western in this fundamental sense: reject "East" and "West," he exhorts the reader; disregard communism and capitalism; the truth lies in neither but in a "Third Way," which Libya is following.

The translation of this general orientation into specific goals and actions gives Qaddafi's policies their anti-Western and anti-Israel bias. Beyond a concern for assuring the continuation of Libya's internal economic development and the survival and security of the regime, Qaddafi has formulated two foreign policy goals. They are: to achieve a wider role for Libya and Libyan ideas of the proper international order in the Middle East, Africa, and the Islamic countries, the three spheres of Libyan foreign policy; and to weaken the West and, if possible, destroy Israel. In a sense, these are opposite sides of the same coin: by weakening the West the possibility of a wider role for Libya is enhanced. Even so, the two are distinct from one another because they appear to be pursued for their own sake. For example, it is enough, or so it seems, that a course of action will reduce French influence in central Africa for it to be seriously considered in Tripoli and often adopted.

In pursuing these goals Qaddafi has relied on three principal means: foreign intervention, terrorism, and outside assistance. Libya is too small and backward to achieve its ends without major foreign help in practically every area. In his practice of foreign intervention and terrorism Qaddafi has stirred a hornet's nest of resentment, hatred, and opposition. Under Qaddafi's control, Libya has recognized no moral bounds on its willingness to use force, deceit, or cunning to advance toward its goals. No terrorist acts have been too odious, no boundaries too sacred, no project too vast or dangerous — the "Islamic bomb" — to be denied Libyan participation. But two reservations need to be made and remembered when considering the means Qaddafi has chosen for his foreign policy. First, they are not unique or extraordinary instruments. Outside aid and foreign intervention are common practices among nations, great and small. Only in his wholesale subsidy of terrorism does Qaddafi depart from the customary practice of nations. However, even here Qaddafi's behavior does not strike me as out of keeping with the culture and history of the Middle East, where, after all, the society of Assassins flourished from the eleventh to the thirteenth century, and the Barbary pirates lived off Mediterranean commerce 500 years later. Nor does it appear to me as alien to the customs of Europe at various periods in the distant and not-so-distant past, whether one thinks of the character of statecraft during the wars of religion, the dynastic competitions of the seventeenth century, or the ideological and atavistic mayhem of Stalin and Hitler.

In short, Qaddafi's use of foreign policy is at once familiar and strange. We recognize much about his goals and the means he has chosen to reach them, but at the same time, he strikes us as peculiar, as uniquely incomprehensible, and as exceptionally menacing. There is reason for this. Qaddafi controls huge oil reserves; he is a bitter opponent of Israel and the West; he is a radical, violent supporter of Palestinian statehood; he is a devout, proselytizing Muslim; and he is a willing friend of the Soviet Union, a recipient of huge supplies of Soviet weapons, someone who has said he would not hesitate to seek membership in the Warsaw Pact, if that were necessary to protect Libya against Western intervention. One is at a loss to imagine a combination of policy stands that would press on more neuralgic spots in North America, Western Europe, and Japan.

As fundamental as these differences are and justified as it is to oppose Qaddafi's efforts to achieve many of his goals, there is a sense in which the fascination with and hatred of Qaddafi exceed the undeniably real provocation he gives. In the international media, and therefore in the consciousness of many people around the world, Qaddafi has become a mythical figure, larger than life, inhuman or perhaps only partly human, a twentieth-century Mediterranean Minotaur, half man, half beast. Some nations in the West, especially the United States and Israel, have encouraged this interpretation. Qaddafi realizes this, of course, and exploits it, drawing down on himself the anger and frustration of an entire civilization and, in this way, aggrandizing his person and his views. If the vehemence of denunciation exceeds the reason for it, this disproportion itself needs explaining. Libya is a small country. Whatever its wealth or the ruthlessness of its leaders it has not and will never play a leading role in Middle Eastern and African affairs. The description of Qaddafi's foreign policy in this book will in itself lay to rest many of the exaggerated fears of Qaddafi. At most Qaddafi has been a nuisance. Therefore, something more is involved in the "Mything of Muammar" than his deeds and intentions, which are, to repeat, fundamentally opposed to the West.

As this inquiry proceeded it became increasingly clear that part of the explanation of the portrayal of Qaddafi as Frankenstein's monster lay in a failure of cultural and political imagination in the West. In this failure lies the cause of the inability of the West, particularly the United States, to understand and anticipate major developments in the Middle East, such as the Lebanese War, the Iranian Revolution, and the attack on the Grand Mosque in Saudi Arabia. There is, first of all, an unwillingness to treat Qaddafi and, more generally, the developing world, as really possessed of a valid history and cultural and religious tradition. Qaddafi and other leaders like him thus appear to be mutants, ahistorical outlaws, rather than genuine, representative figures thrown up by forces and aspirations long present in their societies, however foolish or malign they might be as individuals. The result of this outlook is that even the most critically important views – such as Qaddafi's rage at

Israel and his commitment to the Palestinian cause – are devalued as the quirks of an irrational dictator. The dialogue between Qaddafi and Oriana Fallaci during an interview published in the New York Times in late 1979 offers a perfect example of this.(4) Fallaci condemned Qaddafi for disregarding the consequences of giving Libyan arms to radical Palestinians. She attacked him beause the Palestinians gave some of the Libyan weapons to Italian terrorists, who made war in Italy, a country at peace with Libya. Fallaci disregarded Qaddafi's answer. She had already concluded he was despicable. But his answer was instructive all the same. Does the West think of the harm that befalls Palestinians as a result of its aid to Israel, he asked? No. But that harm is a consequence that I set beside the consequences in Italy when I arm the Palestinians. In effect Qaddafi was saying that he took the Palestinian cause as seriously as the West took its devotion to Israel. But Fallaci was not prepared to credit this and accused him of behaving like a modern Saladin! Qaddafi answered with a denunciation of Western civilization.

Edward Said has suggested two other factors that help explain the unwillingness of the West, and particularly the United States, to treat Qaddafi as something other than an outlaw or maniac. There is a deep cultural antipathy to Islam, Said has argued, that derives from centuries-old images of the conflict between Christian and Muslim civilization. Western experts have not by and large enabled the West to adjust its images of the Islamic world away from the polarity of the Middle Ages to a bewilderingly complex modern reality. Echoing the French Orientalist Maxime Rodinson, Said pointed out that one must deal with Islam on at least three different levels: as doctrine, as the doctrine is interpreted, and as the interpretations are put into practice in concrete, widely differing political, cultural, and geographic conditions. Said detected in the West's unwillingness to alter its obsolete images of Islam a longing to reestablish the domination of the Muslim world achieved by the West in the nineteenth and early twentieth centuries, and a reluctance to face the implications for its views of development and "modernization" that are posed by a leader like Qaddafi, or even more powerfully, by one like the Ayatollah Khomeini.

In addition, Said observed, there are strong government and corporate interests that affect not only what is presented in the media but, through research grants and endowments, what is studied, and even what questions are asked about Libya and the Middle East. Wishing to strengthen its military capabilities in the Mediterranean and the Middle East, the U.S. government has exaggerated the erratic menace in some of Qaddafi's behavior as a way of preparing opinion in Congress and the country at large to accept and approve huge increases in military spending. Large amounts of this money are to go for additions to conventional weaponry, for use, as it was openly suggested in the budget debates, primarily against Libya and other maverick states, and in defense of friendly governments in the Gulf. The effects of corporate censorship on the accumulation of knowledge about the Middle East can be readily perceived by asking what kinds of problems and sensitivities firms would have which were either already in business in Libya and the Gulf in a big way or hoped soon to be.(5)

The point is not to minimize Qaddafi's hostility to the West or his desire to reduce Western influence in the Middle East. These are all too obvious, and, as this account of Libyan foreign policy makes clear, Qaddafi has repeatedly struck at the West: at France by his military interventions in central Africa, at the United States by his opposition to the Camp David process, at Israel by his massive subventions of the most uncompromising and violent elements of the Palestinian resistance. But it would be as grave an error to exaggerate the significance of these actions as it would be to minimize it.

2
THE UNITED STATES AND REVOLUTION IN LIBYA

Libya is an international Cinderella. Her story since independence in 1951 matches folktale: a sudden transformation from poverty and colonialism, out of the dim mists of British power politics and UN paternity, to oil riches beyond anyone's wildest dreams; her politics and foreign policy firmly wedded to Muammar Qaddafi, her Prince Charming, apparently happily ever after.

If this were the only story to be told there would be interest enough, for Libya offers a unique study in economic and political development. The population is small, around 3 million, great wealth flows from the oil, and the political leadership is reformist and has been continuous since Qaddafi came to power by a military coup on September 1, 1969. Moreover, substantial social and economic progress has occurred in Libya in the last decade. While in these ways the country departs from the norms of underdevelopment — overpopulation, poverty, and political instability — in other ways Libya conforms to them: there is a significant lack of indigenous skilled labor and professionals in the work force; illiteracy is a continuing problem; by hiring everyone the government has solved the welfare problem while saddling the state with a surplus of underemployed unqualified enlistees; traditional culture obstructs progress, particularly for women; and there are too many foreigners at work in Libya, especially at skilled and managerial tasks. Understandably, these aspects of Libyan life, together with the regime's enforcement of a rigid Islamic and political orthodoxy, suppress individual initiative and encourage large numbers of young Libyans to avoid not only political opposition but, perhaps more importantly, the kinds of hard, long-term development of their own

15

attitudes, skills, and talents that cannot be bought or imported and that will alone make their country truly self-sufficient and self-respecting.

For fifty years after 1900, Libya's relations with the outside world were shaped by world war and the clash of the interests of the European colonial powers. At the end of the First World War Germany was shorn of her overseas possessions in Africa and Asia, which were divided among the victorious Allies. At the end of the Second World War, therefore, it was natural for the numerous countries of Western and Central Europe which has been dismembered or subjugated by Germany to resume their identity as independent sovereign nations, however brief and fictive that guise might prove for those nations bordering the Soviet Union.

Italy's case was different. Among the victors in 1918, she chose the losing side in the next war and lost her large colonial holdings, Ethiopia and Libya. Liberated and administered by British and Free French forces Libya entered the postwar era an international basket case: occupied, partitioned, impoverished, with no apparent economic prospects whatsoever, soon to be a ward of the fledgling United Nations. Stalin's claim to a share of Libya's territory as part of the peace settlement in North Africa is as well known as it was without meaning for the eventual nature of that settlement. The Soviet dictator's bid, nonetheless, serves to illustrate the character of the calculations on which Libya's future would be decided. Those calculations would be based on considerations of power and interest not of the Libyans themselves but of Britain and her allies, the United States, France, and before long, Italy herself. The concerns of the British government were to arrange Libya's future in a way that would protect her imperial interests in Egypt, the Suez Canal, and the Middle East, and, at the same time, would foster harmony in Western Europe, or at least not give gratuitous offense. Long before 1953, when Libya received independence, a third concern had intruded itself, the need to prepare for a possible conflict with the Soviet Union, to be fought on lines similar to those followed in the war just ended. This required major overseas air and naval bases. In the eyes of the United States, the leading power in the Western coalition, Libya was an ideal military outpost. The outbreak of the Korean War only served to underline Libya's desirability. Under U.S. pressure to settle the political defects of Libya's sovereignty the British first sought to strike a bargain with Italy and France that would have effectively partitioned the country among the three of them. When this proposal failed by one vote in the General Assembly, Britain and the United States resolved on independence for Libya. Although the UN commissioner, Adrian Pelt, managed to prevent the formal conclusion of international agreements between King Idris and Britain before independence, Libya's future orientation was a foregone conclusion.(1)

Under the rule of the Sanusi leader, Idris, the independent kingdom of Libya would be established. Libya would then join in alliance with Britain and the United States in agreements that made available the airfields that both nations desired for somewhat different purposes, the British primarily to supplement their Middle Eastern role, the Americans to provide added reach as they began to organize a diplomatic and military coalition against the Soviet Union. Because of Libya's extreme poverty Britain began to supply substantial amounts of economic aid, an activity in which the U.S. joined after Libyan independence because of its presence at Wheelus Air Force Base. Thus, from the end of World War II through Libyan independence and into the early 1960s, the bases of U.S. relations were clear, and it was a simple matter to reconcile the diverse strains of policy and interest that had converged on Libya. Libya's poverty, British imperial interests, the U.S. strategic design against the Soviet Union, and the preservation of harmony among the members of the Western alliance had merged to create a country dependent on Western economic aid whose territory had become a pawn in the global strategic contest and whose economy was open to Western trade and investment.

By the late 1960s, when Qaddafi seized control of Libya, the basis of U.S. strategy and diplomacy in the Eastern Mediterranean was anything but clear. In fact the entire diplomatic, political, and military situation of not just Libya but the United States, Britain, France, the Soviet Union, and all the nations of the Middle East had changed so drastically as to create a novel and unfamiliar international scene. British imperialism was either gone from the Middle East or, in the southern Arabian peninsula where it remained, it was on the way out. Much of Britain's need for bases in Libya had disappeared with the failure to overthrow Nasser in 1956 and the fall of the Hashemite dynasty in Iraq two years later. The other face of the decline of British imperialism was, of course, the rise of Arab nationalism throughout the region, personified in Gamal Abdel Nasser, whose ideals of Arab unity and flamboyant and seemingly invincible anti-Western actions had made him a hero of Qaddafi and his fellow revolutionary officers. In Arab eyes, Israel was a creature of Europe and the United States. Resentment of Europe and the United States had been sharpened to razor's edge by Israel's crushing defeat of the Arabs in 1967, and the seemingly permanent Israeli occupation of Sinai, Golan, West Bank, and Gaza. The Palestinian question and the Arab-Israeli dispute had become major obstacles to good relations between Arab states and the United States. That oil, of which an abundance had been discovered in Libya, had become crucial to the burgeoning economies of Europe and Japan and was of increasing importance to the United States, only served to heighten the importance of Arab opinion to the West.

The Nixon administration, in its first year in office, was eager to put an end to the U.S. role in the war in Vietnam, to open relations with China, and to fashion a more traditional kind of relationship with the Soviet Union, one which did not deny the probability of collisions of interest and policy, but which featured jointly accepted limits and rules of behavior as well as much higher levels of trade, a responsiveness to one another, and a civility of discourse usually enjoyed by the great powers of European civilization in times of peace for a thousand years. The other factor in the Soviet-U.S. equation was the steadily increasing naval, land, and strategic strength of the Soviet Union, some of which quickly translated into augmented Soviet military and economic aid and diplomatic support for the Arab nations that rimmed the Mediterranean. In its more formidable stance the Soviet Union presented a major alternative source of weapons and technical assistance for a nationalist revolutionary like Qaddafi. It was an option that both restrained Western reactions to Arab decisions — for fear of driving the nationalist leaders toward the Soviets — and at the same time added real strength to the Arabs in the form of arms, expertise, and freedom to maneuver. Meanwhile, the maintenance of harmony between the United States and Western Europe had become a much more complex task than it had been in the late 1940s. It was no longer simply a matter of decisive leadership and military and economic guarantees. The European nations now felt it was both sensible and possible for them to move in different directions than the United States wished to move not only in dealing with Eastern Europe and the Soviet Union on security questions but also in their economic and political relations with the nations of the Middle East, Africa, and Asia. This was of a particular importance in regard both to the Arab-Israeli conflict and the oil negotiations in Tripoli and Teheran in the early 1970s. U.S. leadership was no longer accepted automatically in these areas, and there was an obvious and growing belief among the Europeans that they knew better and could do a better job — in diplomacy or oil-well drilling — if they were given or could contrive the appropriate opportunity.

Qaddafi thus initiated his rule when the substance and nuance of world politics was changing and unfamiliar. The implications of the growth of Soviet military power were unclear. The "politics of oil" were still a few years away, although the rehearsal during the 1967 war should have been more closely heeded. Above all, U.S. concerns both domestic and foreign were increasingly dominated by the public revulsion caused by the war in Vietnam. Already the "post-Vietnam" arguments were heard on all sides: it was time for the United States to do less, to stop policing the world, to rely on Third World nationalism to block Soviet expansion, to reap the benefits of the Sino-Soviet conflict in the form of the reduced defense budgets and hedged commitments that were justified by the disappearance of a monolithic world communist movement, to recognize and act on the growing irrelevance of military power and the transcendent importance of economic concerns; finally, to be convinced that in a nuclear missile age there was nothing that could imperil the physical survival of the United States and, therefore, there was no longer any need to keep military bases in hand or to keep friendly regimes in place in far-flung places like Libya, Taiwan, South Vietnam, or the Panama Canal.

The change in the status of Wheelus Air Force Base in Libya was symptomatic of the evolution of U.S. opinion, in and out of government. In the autumn of 1969 few in the Nixon administration would express any strong interest in Wheelus. Certainly no high official would say publicly that Wheelus was essential to have as a strategic outpost from which to attack the Soviet Union. After all, Polaris submarines and carrier-launched aircraft could do that without encountering nationalist mobs. Nor was Wheelus seen to be necessary as a means of projecting U.S. power into the region in order to block Soviet expansion or to keep the Arab-Israeli conflict under control. No one argued in favor of the use of force to protect Middle East oil, most of which was in the hands of the conservative monarchs of the Arabian Peninsula who were indifferent to the Palestinians and who had more money than they could possibly use. At best, U.S. generals and diplomats thought of Wheelus as a convenient place to train fighter pilots: there are so many cloud-free days, so many hours of uninterrupted training flights. But the same flying weather could be found in the southwestern United States.(2) It was at this moment in the evolution of U.S. politics, strategy, and diplomacy that Qaddafi and his fellow officers overthrew Idris and seized control of Libya.

Since coming to power in 1969 Muammar Qaddafi and his government have acquired reputations as violent, xenophobic, and capricious Muslim zealots in charge of a precious source of fabulous wealth. They are seen simultaneously as unable to comprehend the responsible, constructive role they ought to be playing in world affairs as heirs to oil fortune, and as unscrupulous militant opportunists willing to practice and subsidize terrorism or invade a neighboring country whenever it suits their whim.

To Anwar Sadat, Qaddafi was "100% sick and possessed of the devil."(3) To the Israelis he is a hated foe. To the oil company directors he is a formidable nationalist with whom, nonetheless, it is possible to make a deal that will stick. To the CIA, Qaddafi is a religious zealot with some pathological tendencies, notably in his dependence on the existence of an external threat.(4) Devil, zealot, or just enfant terrible? Regardless of one's opinion of him Qaddafi has made himself and his country a center of attention, controversy, and conflict.

Given all the attention and controversy, it is not surprising that the origins of Qaddafi's takeover in Libya and the manner in which he has stayed in power, despite having angered and damaged the interests of virtually every government in the region and the West, have also become topics of interest and speculation.(5) There appear to be two general explanations of Qaddafi's success in seizing power and holding on to it. They are: Qaddafi was put in power and was kept there, at least in the early years, by the United States and the oil companies; and, he took power and kept it because of a series of awful blunders by the oil companies and the United States. The two may be described as the conspiracy and blunder explanations. Proponents of conspiracy say that the United States put Qaddafi in power and protected him. Advocates of blunder say that the United States was surprised by the coup and then adopted a series of inadequate policies that failed to impose any serious restraints on Qaddafi until the resort to all-out hostility by the Reagan administration in 1981. Qaddafi has been so hostile to the United States and to Western interests in the Middle East that it may seem strange to begin an account of Libyan-United States relations with a conspiracy theory of U.S. assistance in his seizure of power. It is necessary because the conspiracy explanation is widely believed in the Middle East and is taken seriously in some books written about Libya.(6)

The conspiracy theorists depend on what inevitably must be circumstantial evidence. They make good use of "who benefits" logic to buttress their point of view. Their argument is that Qaddafi came to power with the blessing and even the assistance of the United States and Great Britain, whose intelligence agencies then protected him by warning of coup plots and supplying arms and "mercenary" advisors. Proponents of this explanation of the coup disagree as to how long U.S. protection lasted. Some believe it endured through 1976. Others suggest a divorce occurred after the 1973 war, with the Arab oil embargo and the drastic rise in oil prices. In this view Qaddafi was aided and protected chiefly because the United States hoped he would be an anti-Soviet Arab nationalist. This view of the coup fits into the school of thought that sees U.S. foreign policy as anti-Soviet above all else. Because Qaddafi also played a critical part in major oil price increases some Europeans believe that the United States helped him to power as part of an attempt to allow significant oil price rises to occur. This would have increased the energy costs of Europe and Japan and thus have blunted their industrial efficiency vis-à-vis the United States, a major oil producer. Higher oil prices would also have augmented the revenues of the Shah of Iran in order to enable him to pay for the weapons he needed to turn his country into a pro-U.S. regional fortress.(7) To advocates of the conspiracy idea, the benefits of higher oil prices explain the curious softness of the U.S. government during the Tripoli-Teheran negotiations, and particularly its willingness to back the oil companies in resisting the oil producers' demands before 1973. Some advocates of the conspiracy interpretation say that the United States played a crucially important part in Qaddafi's seizure of power. Some say flatly that the United States installed Qaddafi in power and must accordingly share the blame and responsibility for the harm he has done since 1969.(8) Others soften the verb a bit and say "helped to install" or "didn't prevent" Qaddafi from coming to power. Ruth First collects this kind of explanation and then lets the reader choose, after making it clear she believes the worst but can't prove it.(9)

Obviously, there is a great deal of difference between "installed" and "didn't prevent," but in all their ambiguity and post hoc reasoning the conspiracy theorists are getting at something important. What was the United States' knowledge of, involvement in, and responsibility for the Qaddafi coup? Did anyone in the U.S. government know about the coup before it took place? Did anyone on the U.S. side speak to anyone in the Qaddafi group or leaders of other coups-in-the-making about the Qaddafi effort? John Cooley, former Middle East correspondent of the Christian Science Monitor, argues, for example, that U.S. Ambassador David Newsom met with Qaddafi at least once before the coup. Cooley cites an account in the New Yorker of Newsom's unannounced visit to an oil camp in the Libyan desert as proof of the contact. In the New Yorker article Newsom is described as arriving at the camp alone, "dusty and dishevelled," during a fifteen-day solo trip in the desert.(10) Newsom, of course, denied having any contact with Qaddafi or his officers and maintained that although he visited an oil camp at about the time alleged, he did so as a member of a larger party on a normal visit.(11) If contact occurred, what was promised or said or implied? Was there contact before the coup between Qaddafi and the foreign oil companies? Other Libyans? With the U.S. or British governments?

In 1969 Newsom left his post as U.S. ambassador in Tripoli not long before the coup. He returned to Washington to become assistant secretary of state for Africa, the bureau then responsible for relations with Libya. His replacement, Ambassador Joseph Palmer, exchanged jobs with him, leaving the post of assistant secretary for Africa to go to the embassy in Tripoli. In 1974, Newsom became ambassador to the Philippines. Even in Southeast Asia, according to press reports, there was Qaddafi's support for Muslim rebels to deal with.(12) Newsom returned to Washington in 1977 to become undersecretary of state for political affairs in the Carter administration, which made him the highest ranking Foreign Service officer in the State Department. He kept important duties in regard to Libya, as indicated, for example, in his appearances before Congress in regard to the Billy Carter affair.

According to Newsom, "There isn't a shred of evidence to suggest that the United States had prior knowledge or associated with Qaddafi and his coup."(13) While this is not necessarily a flat denial, Newsom clearly meant it to be one. In support of his position, Newsom offered some evidence and a number of arguments. None of them are fully persuasive, although when they are taken together they make an interesting brief that the U.S. govern-

ment adopted a "hands-off" orientation toward the Qaddafi revolution. The foundation of Newsom's argument against the conspiracists
is that they assume a "U.S. ability to manipulate a number of
elements that simply doesn't exist."(14) Lacking this manipulative
power the United States must "react rather than act" in situations
such as the coup of September 1. If the United States sets out to be
active and decisive — to shape events — then it must almost
immediately commit to specific countries and specific individuals.
"There are very real [costs]," Newsom added, "because of the
reaction of others to this."(15)

The conspiracists also ignore, according to Newsom, the strong
opposition in Congress in the late 1960s to the assumption of new
foreign commitments of the kind that would have been required if
the United States had decided either to support King Idris or to aid
Qaddafi and his fellow officers. Widespread public opposition to the
war in Vietnam together with the Symington committee's investigation of national commitments and Senator Fulbright's outrage over
what he termed the "routine" acceptance of foreign entanglements
had created a policy environment hostile to an activist policy in
Libya. The nature of the coup itself also argues against U.S.
involvement in Newsom's view. The circle of conspirators was quite
small. There were only a few officers, and none were well known.
Very few civilians joined Qaddafi before his success. Qaddafi chose
most of the civilian members of his first government after he had
seized power.

Aiding Qaddafi is, of course, only one side of the coin of
activism; the conspiratorial opposite would be defending the Libyan
monarchy. On this Newsom had much of interest to add to the
record. The existence of Wheelus Air Force Base in Libya and a long
history of U.S. and British aid to Libya both suggest an implied
Western commitment to protect King Idris and to keep him in
power. Because of the growing sensitivity in Congress about U.S.
commitments, particularly military commitments, that were
accepted without legislative consultation, Newsom sought and
received instructions in 1967 — well before the coup — to say to King
Idris that the United States had no obligation to defend any
paticular regime in Libya.(16) The king was told that the U.S. interest
in Libya was in the preservation of the country's independence and
territorial integrity, not its existing government. Thus when Omar
Shalki appealed to Idris to seek U.S. help in defeating Qaddafi the
king declined, apparently because he doubted the U.S. would come
to his aid.(17)

Newsom's instructions did not prevent a reconsideration of
intervention within the U.S. government when the coup occurred.
The argument was made by military and other participants in the
deliberations that the resources and location of Libya in the
Mediterranean were important to U.S. and allied security. "What
does that mean," Newsom asked, "in terms of U.S. action?" No one

favored military intervention to protect U.S. interests. Newsom's formulation of U.S. interests in Libya was: (1) protection of the large American community in Libya; (2) preservation of the pro-Western orientation of the government to the extent possible; prevention of the domination of Libya by an adversary power; (3) minimization of the degree to which Libya can frustrate U.S. peace efforts in the Middle East.(18) Congressional support for military action was doubtful. Few Arabs would have supported intervention. There was no demonstrable threat to the supply of oil to the West. Military intervention would have been opposed by the Western European allies of the United States. There were talks with the British but never a formal offer of joint or unilateral action to save Idris's throne. Of course, Newsom admitted, the U.S. decision might have been different if the king had come back to Libya to fight for his throne, if he had found strong popular support there, and if the Cyrenaican Defense Force had rallied to his defense instead of staying quietly in their barracks.(19)

The conspiracy theories have a second side to them. Not only did the United States put Qaddafi in power, but initially, at least, the United States protected him. As experienced an observer of the Middle East as John Cooley of the Christian Science Monitor has argued that in the early 1970s Qaddafi was widely believed in the Middle East to be under U.S. protection.(20) Newsom admitted that the United States twice "protected" Qaddafi, but in pursuit of U.S. national interests, not out of a desire to make a client dictator secure. The first "protection" was given when the U.S. government informed Qaddafi of a coup building against him. The coup and its revelation by the United States are described in The Hilton Assignment by Patrick Seale and Maureen McConville, a book Newsom said is "factually based."(21) Newsom admitted that the United States warned Qaddafi of the plot and "tried to turn it off," because it was going to be a total failure, and in its failure would have been attributed to the United States. This in turn would have endangered the American community in Libya. There was no desire to save Qaddafi.(22)

In regard to the second form of protection Newsom was asked: "Has the United States discouraged Egypt from attacking Qaddafi's Libya?" He replied: "Yes. Particularly since Camp David." In explanation he again made clear that a desire to serve larger American interests rather than any love of Qaddafi had informed U.S. policy in this matter.

> An Egyptian attack on Libya would not be confined to (the battlefield between) Egypt and Libya. There would be repercussions throughout the Maghreb. The Algerian reaction is uncertain. Tunisia might be threatened. An Egyptian action of this kind would harm U.S. efforts to create a comprehensive peace settlement of the Arab-Israeli conflict. Moreover,

it would be wrong to say that the U.S. had stopped an Egyptian attack on Libya. It's far from clear that the Egyptians have ever decided to do this. It is not a case of Sadat deciding to invade only to be stopped by the United States. It's a level below that. We expressed opposition to an invasion when we learned it was being considered inside the Egyptian government.(23)

Newsom's denial of a U.S. role in Qaddafi's coup was echoed by James Blakely, charge in Tripoli after Newsom's departure, and later Newsom's deputy in the Africa bureau. Trouble was brewing in Libya, Blakely said. Anyone could see that. There was too much oil money floating around, too much obvious corruption. The king was too uninterested in ruling for the country to escape serious problems. But no one was looking for a coup by junior officers. Every one was asking, "What will happen when the King dies?" Blakely said. "That's how wrong we were."(24)

Moreover, Blakely added, if the United States contrived to put Qaddafi in power, it was a ludicrously bad decision, because Qaddafi never acted in accord with U.S. interests. He promptly demanded the evacuation of Wheelus Air Force Base and overthrew the previous relationship with the international oil companies. No friend of the United States would have done either. There were strong suspicions in Washington, Blakely said, that Qaddafi would prove to be hostile to U.S. interests. Despite these misgivings, Ambassador Palmer was given permission to make every plausible effort to establish a normal, mutually beneficial relationship with the new Libyan government. Palmer argued strongly from Tripoli that a U.S. decision to quit the base at Wheelus was necessary and was perhaps even sufficient to create good relations. In making this argument he was encouraged by Major Jalloud, second only to Qaddafi in power among the revolutionary officers. Jalloud dangled friendship as bait until the United States evacuated the base. Then he sprang the trap and told Palmer that Libya could never have friendly relations with the United States because of U.S. support for Israel.

After this, relations between the two countries soured so badly that in 1972 Palmer asked to be recalled from Tripoli because the Libyan government refused to deal with him and was wasting his time. From Palmer's departure until the formal break in relations by the Reagan administration nine years later the United States enjoyed no ambassadorial representation in Tripoli. Again, this is not the behavior of a government in any sense friendly to the United States. The war of attrition against Egypt, the Rogers plan, and above all the role of the United States in protecting Israel and Hussein during the assault by the Palestinians on Hussein's government in 1970 undoubtedly contributed to the Libyan decision to refuse to deal with the United States.

If the conspiracists are wrong about the situation in Libya, their critics add, they are even more grievously wrong about what was possible in U.S. foreign policy in the first years of the Nixon administration. King Idris received no U.S. military or diplomatic assistance not because the Nixon administration had fashioned a covert plan to help Qaddafi to power in Tripoli, but because many in Congress and among the U.S. people in general were deeply opposed to the assumption of any new military and political commitments abroad. The powers of the "imperial Presidency" were being sharply curtailed. Senator Fulbright, in particular, had launched a personal crusade against what he termed the secret, seemingly inexorable, and unconstitutional expansion of foreign aid agreements into binding obligations on the part of the United States to defend even the most oppressive regimes against internal upheaval.

There were other factors to consider in addition to congressional and public opinion. Perhaps the most important was that any intervention in Libya would instantly poison U.S. relations with Egypt and Syria and ruin any hopes of leading the nations in the area toward a settlement of the Arab-Israeli conflict. A peace settlement was the first concern of the State Department, and Secretary William Rogers made this one of his chief projects.

Other telling arguments could also be made against intervening to help the king. No appreciable support for the king developed, and there was no organized opposition to the coup. It was also held that the loss of Wheelus deprived the United States of nothing more than hundreds of days of good flying weather every year for NATO pilots, something nice to have, but not essential and available elsewhere. In the missile age, bases like Wheelus were unnecessary militarily and were a lightning rod for nationalist anti-U.S. agitation. The several thousand American citizens living in Libya were an added concern. They would be vulnerable in the event of military action against Qaddafi. And finally, neither Britain nor France favored an intervention. Britain had already begun to eliminate virtually all its political and military commitments "east of Suez," while France was deep in the trough of one of its anti-U.S. cycles and could be counted on to take advantage of any miscues in U.S. policy to drive out U.S. commercial and political influence in Libya and the rest of the Arab world.

On the political question, in short, the anticonspiracists make a convincing case that the United States did not put Qaddafi in power. But what about oil prices and, in particular, the two kinds of negotiations that occurred from 1969-1975?(25) These were the negotiations with the Libyan government over revenue (price), control of production levels, and "participation" (nationalization); and the coincident negotiations with OPEC on price and participation. The conspiracy argument about these two sets of discussions runs as follows. The United States had three objectives in its encounters in Tripoli and Teheran: (1) to raise the price of energy for Europe and Japan, huge oil importers, thereby blunting their alarming industrial efficiency because the United States is such a large domestic producer of oil; (2) to preserve the positions of U.S. oil companies in the Middle East; and (3) to provide the Shah of Iran the revenues he needed to turn his country into the leading military, economic, and political power in the Gulf, and a pro-Western fortress or "hedgehog" vis-à-vis the Soviet Union.(26) If these were their objectives, the Nixon administration had little reason to oppose the demands for higher prices at Tripoli and Teheran. In 1970 and 1971 no one expected the quadrupling of prices that would occur in just three years, and the price explosion doesn't necessarily count against the conspiracists. Even James Akins, who was one of the few U.S. officials to warn that an oil crisis was at hand, spoke in those days of a rise to a price of no more than five dollars for a barrel of high-grade crude petroleum.(27)

Moreover, the conspiracists argue, by declining to back the oil companies against Qaddafi and OPEC the United States was getting the somewhat higher oil prices it desired and was preserving the position of most of the U.S. companies. Qaddafi's early anti-Soviet actions were a bonus. In other words, the picture in regard to oil is, if anything, even more tantalizing and obscure than the political reaction of the United States to Qaddafi's coup. The obscurity is compounded in regard to the oil question because so much of the information is held in private hands and is not open for study. The main controversy is over the reasons for U.S. refusal to support the international oil companies in their price negotiations in Teheran and Tripoli in 1970 and 1971.

One must begin by recognizing that the conspiracists are correct in suggesting that the United States was less troubled than its allies at the prospect of higher oil prices. An increase to a price in the three to four dollar range or even five dollars over several years would not have been regarded as cause for great alarm in Washington. The United States, unlike most of its allies, was a large domestic producer of oil, and would have to send less money abroad to pay for the more expensive fuel. The cost advantage for U.S. industry grew substantially when President Nixon controlled domestic U.S. oil prices, sharply limiting domestic price increases while allowing the price for imported oil to rise to the world level.

There are several very strange aspects to the behavior of the U.S. government during the negotiations in Teheran and Tripoli between the international oil companies and OPEC. In brief, Qaddafi threatened the independent oil companies in Libya with nationalization of their principal source of crude oil unless they agreed to a substantial increase in the amount of money they paid the Libyan government and therefore in the price they charged for their oil and oil products. The major oil companies whose chief sources of oil lay in the Gulf area, feared that they would be "leap-frogged." If they conceded the Libyan demands, the Gulf producers would raise their

claim; a concession in the Gulf, which was of overwhelming importance to them, would then bring an even higher Libyan demand,
which would produce in turn an even higher demand in the Gulf, and
so on. In retrospect it is clear that the oil companies feared
uncertainty more than they feared the price rises themselves, but at
the time the oil companies appeared willing to resist the demands of
both Libyan and Gulf producers.

To plan and execute a successful campaign of resistance, however, the companies had to cooperate with one another in ways –
such as a "safety-net" for Libyan independents – that violated
antitrust statutes, particularly in the United States. Accordingly
they sought and received authorization from the U.S. Justice
Department to ignore antitrust laws and to cooperate in planning
their response to "leap-frogging." To judge from what is known in
the public record the companies decided to fight. They would
demand a single negotiation whose results would be binding on all
the parties, Gulf and Mediterranean. Any country seeking a higher
price unilaterally in violation of the agreement could be punished by
oil company boycott and legal action, and implicitly, by U.S.
military and political pressure. Then, at the critical moment in the
negotiations U.S. Undersecretary of State John Irwin appeared in
Teheran and informed the companies' representatives that the U.S.
government would not support them in their quest for a single,
binding negotiation. Incredulous, defeated before the battle was
joined, the companies accepted defeat and agreed to major price
increases under terms that did not prevent leap-frogging. "Having
faced down a serious effort to achieve industry solidarity at the
beginning of 1971," one bitter independent oil company executive,
George Schuler of Bunker Hunt later said, "the producing states
recognized that industry had no other card left to play. It was
merely a question of time before this recognition was acted
upon. . . . If a political and economic monster has been loosed upon
the world, it is the creation of Western governments and companies."(28)

Libya is central to those developments because Libya's demands
for higher prices and its threats of nationalization established the
leap-frogging dilemma and revealed to the Gulf producers that there
would be no Western military reprisal for such behavior. If Libya had
been treated as Iran was in the early 1950s – a total boycott by the
oil companies and military as well as covert political intervention by
Britain and the United States – the showdown at Teheran would have
had quite a different outcome. It is Libya's immunity that raises the
eyebrows and hypotheses of the conspiracists. Qaddafi was put in
power and allowed to push prices up, they conclude, because this
would make it possible to establish new energy prices that would
favor the United States more than the Europeans and the Japanese.

The analytical problem is clear. Why did the United States
permit prices to rise as they did? In particular, why did the U.S.

government desert the oil companies at precisely the moment they appeared to have laid the groundwork to defeat both Qaddafi and the Gulf producers? Three factors appear to account for U.S. behavior. First, the U.S. government simply failed to understand what was at stake and never coordinated its actions internally. That the Justice Department waived antitrust jeopardy, implying endorsement of the oil company hard-line, and that the State Department reneged in Teheran, is evidence not of conspiracy but of confusion and lack of coordination. It also suggests that for domestic political reasons the Nixon administration was obliged to achieve its ends without the threat or use of force. Second, the Iranian and Saudi governments exerted strong pressure on Washington to avoid a showdown in Teheran. The Saudis and Iranians argued that the financial costs of leap-frogging would be slight compared with the chaos that might ensue if the companies were to be allowed to try to break OPEC in order to subject the oil producing countries back to the old kinds of controls and subordination. Third, what the public record shows the major international oil companies to have said and done shouldn't be taken at face value. Things are not always what they seem. In particular the independents and majors had fundamentally different economic and crude-source positions. The majors put the preservation of their concessions in the Gulf above all else. The independents relied heavily on Libyan crude. This had led to bitter clashes in the past. It is not at all certain that the two could have held a united front, even if the U.S. government had chosen to support the single-negotiation strategy.

There is another piece of the oil puzzle which, looked at alone, strengthens the possibility that a "deal" of some kind was struck in 1969 and 1970 between the Libyan revolutionaries and the Western governments and major oil companies. To grasp the full plausibility of the conspiracy interpretation it is necessary to go back to 1968. Libya's apparently radical behavior in forcing cutbacks in oil production in 1970, which immediately produced a rise in international prices for crude and for shipping space, was exactly the remedy the major oil companies needed in order to avoid having to curtail production in and therefore the income of the Gulf countries.(29)

By 1968 the major oil companies were deeply worried that the rapid growth in Libyan production, caused chiefly by the independent companies and therefore out of control of the majors, would force them to cut Gulf production severely. As John Blair observed, it was not simply a matter of offsetting Libyan increases with corresponding decreases in Mideast countries (Iraq, Iran, Kuwait, Saudi Arabia). Rather, "the question was whether the latter would accept the reduction necessary to prevent the appearance of a price-destroying surplus . . . and if it proved impossible 'to satisfy' them, the companies could lose their concession."(30) Then, wonder of wonders, at precisely the moment of crisis and panic, the revolutionary government of Libya cut production: from 3,318 million barrels a day in 1970 to 2,761 in 1971 to 2,239 in 1972. "In its 1972 Forecast Exxon promptly revised its Middle East (Gulf) growth rate (in crude production) upward from 4.2 to the historical rate of 10 percent."(31) Was it all a coincidence? Meanwhile, the Qaddafi government used the greater vulnerability of the independents to loss of access to Libyan crude supplies as a wedge to divide the oil companies. One by one the independents accepted lower production levels and agreed to make higher payments to Libya. It was in this context that the negotiations in Teheran and Tripoli took place and the mysterious retreat by the U.S. government occurred.

It is plausible that the Iranians and Saudis wished to avoid a single all-encompassing negotiation because it would be dominated by extremist demands. Iran's foreign minister warned Undersecretary Irwin that in such a negotiation the companies would be forced to accept "the highest common denominator."(32) The shah threatened Irwin with a total production halt if the United States insisted on a single negotiation. As for Libya it is easy to understand the determination of the Libyan government to have separate negotiations. Only in this way could Libya derive maximum benefit from the high quality of the oil and the country's proximity to Europe. In other words if Libya and the Gulf producers were certain to reject a single negotiation why didn't the companies and the Western governments have ready a forceful contingency plan whose implementation would compel the producers to come to the table?

The standard explanations are, essentially, the twins already suggested: conspiracy or blunder. "The only conclusion to be drawn," as John Blair put it, "is that the abortive effort toward a 'joint approach' was either an incomprehensible blunder or elaborate charade, deliberately designed to divert attention away from policy decisions that had already been made at higher levels.(33) George Schuler's testimony to the Church committee is an example of an explanation based on the blunder hypothesis. As already noted the conspiracy explanation is put forward by Ruth First and Peter Odell.(34) There are difficulties with both explanations.

The blunder hypothesis holds that the U.S. government in general and the State Department in particular are simply ignorant of the extent to which other governments politicize economic questions. While the economic negotiators of other countries — who happen to be government employees — routinely draw on the diplomatic and military power of their national governments to get their way, the United States foolishly declines to support its economic envoys, who often happen to be private businessmen, with its great military and diplomatic power.(35) The trouble with this interpretation is that it is contradicted by the content of State Department recommendations on Middle East oil and the Arab-Israeli conflict, which are marked by an intense awareness of the political and military dimensions of those issues. If anything, the opposite charge would seem to have merit — that the U.S. government was so acutely conscious of the region's military and political problems that it overlooked the essential economic parts of the picture: the steady growth in oil consumption and the growing dependence of the industrial world including the United States on Middle East oil. The oil conspiracy interpretation also overlooks the conflicts and fundamentally different interests of the major oil companies and the independents; and it assumes an ability on the part of the U.S. government to control the international oil companies, which is not supported by the history of the international oil industry. An alternative explanation is, therefore, essential, one that relies neither on blunder or conspiracy to explain the behavior of the United States.

One must begin with the fundamentally different interests of the major and independent oil companies. The majors could afford to be indifferent to Libyan oil. It was a nuisance to them; their situation would actually have improved if Libya and its oil had simply vanished from the face of the earth. The majors' great concerns were the protection of their existing dominance over Gulf crude reserves, prices, and production and, if worse came to worst, the assurance of preferential access to what was, after all, nearly two-thirds of the world's non-Communist oil.(36) Thus, the majors were extremely sensitive to the desire of the governments of Iran and Saudi Arabia to split the negotiation. The independents would react in exactly the same way in regard to the Libyan government's determination to have separate talks, for Libya was their principal and, in some cases, sole supplier of crude petroleum. At the least, one could safely say that the cards were stacked in favor of separate negotiations from the very start.

From the oil companies' standpoint, however, this was just the beginning of the problem. What was really at issue in the Teheran and Tripoli talks was not primarily what price would be charged but who would set the price. It was a political rather than economic question, a test to determine who was strongest, comparable in a way to the early corporate battles against the union movement. Both sides realized this. The minimum oil company objective was, of course, to retain exclusive rights to Gulf crude. But what was the maximum objective? Wouldn't it have been to retain not just access but also their historical control over price and production levels? Since 1960, OPEC had denied the companies the power to lower posted prices, the price used to calculate payments to host governments. But the companies still hoped to maintain their power to set market prices and production levels and to check the drift toward nationalization of their concessions. If they were to do this they needed to compel the governments of at least the Gulf producers to change their position and accept a single all-encompassing negotiation whose outcome would be regarded as binding on all producers, Libya included. If Qaddafi objected and shut down his nation's petroleum operations, the majors would be in the driver's seat. They

would use part of their Gulf production to keep the Libyan independents afloat – making them, in effect, captives of the majors – and,
by boycotting Libya, as Iran had been boycotted, bring Qaddafi to
heel or even bring him down. The key was to get the U.S.
government in on the side of a single negotiation, in a word to
mousetrap the United States by creating a situation in which the
United States would end up having to back the companies as they
strove to make Saudi Arabia and Iran back down, and to isolate and
coerce Libya. Even if the majors and independents doubted this
approach would succeed, in order to be taken seriously by the Gulf
producers and the U.S. government, they had to behave as if they
preferred it to all others and expected it to work. If in the process
the independents were crippled or destroyed or forced to live on the
majors' crude, so much the better.

The objectives of the U.S. government were quite different from
those of the companies and the Gulf producers, although the policies
of all three intersected at various points. To begin with, the existing
governments of Iran and Saudi Arabia were friendly to the United
States, not hostile as Mossadegh's regime had been two decades
earlier. The extremes of coercion and subversion used against
Mossadegh were inappropriate. Moreover, in the 1950s the shah had
been friendly to the West, an ideal alternative to Mossadegh. In the
1970s the shah's opponents were hostile to the West, hardly an
alternative to be seized. Second, under the Nixon Doctrine, it was
U.S. policy to build up regional powers and rely on them to oppose
the Soviet Union under a nuclear guarantee from the United States.
Third, the state of public opinion in the United States ruled out any
showdowns that required the use or threat of force. This meant that
the shah's threat to "shut down" the entire Gulf had to be taken very
seriously.(37) In any case, at the State Department, the producers'
demands for higher prices were regarded as reasonable and appropriate. James Aikens, then "Mr. Oil" at State and later ambassador to
Saudi Arabia, regarded the initial demands of the Qaddafi government for a price rise of 40 cents a barrel as too low, and later said
so publicly.(38) State wanted higher prices in order to strengthen the
position of the "moderates," such as Iran, Kuwait, and Saudi Arabia,
against the assaults of the "radicals," such as Algeria and Libya, and
to blunt criticism of Western exploitation. The U.S. government saw
an additional advantage in higher prices: higher oil revenues would
allow Iran and Saudi Arabia to step up expenditures for economic
development and military expansion. Both were important goals of
U.S. foreign policy. Moreover, the transfer of funds achieved in this
manner would in the end be far more reliable and less controversial
(at foreseeable price levels) than U.S. military or economic grants
or other forms of foreign aid.(39) Finally, the actions of the United
States were affected by at least two other factors. The diffusion of
authority in the government undoubtedly explains why the Justice
Department would grant business review letters authorizing a

collaborative oil company effort only to have the State Department torpedo the fruits of that collaboration a few days later. It is also unlikely that the government would refuse from the outset to back the oil companies, for this would have appeared as an "antibusiness" action.

The tidiness of the oil situation in Libya and its insulation from the poor political relations between Tripoli and Washington may also be explained on grounds other than conspiracy. The explanation is a special form of symbiosis (a higher price benefits country and company alike) that has allowed the majors to retain exclusive access to Gulf crude, despite a complete reversal of control over price and production level. In Qaddafi's Libya, as John Blair observed:

> The curtailments on the independents and crude-long majors meant the attainment of greater revenues with lower output. To the major oil companies, they meant the end of the Libyan danger to the world price structure and to this threat to their prized Middle East concession. . . .
>
> To the majors and (oil producing) governments alike, the reduction in Libyan output was the necessary prerequisite to the staggering price increases of late 1973 and early 1974. Had Libyan production by the independents and crude-long majors been running at the rate anticipated five years earlier by Exxon, the supply in 1973 would have been increased by some 1,500,000 b/d. Had it been necessary to find a market for such a quantity, the chances of making the 1973-74 price increases stick would have been exceedingly remote.(40)

The Teheran and Tripoli price rises and the cooperative although radically changed producer-oil company relationship in Libya (and the Gulf) were not caused by conspiracy but by symbiosis. It is one of the world's choicest ironies that Qaddafi and the oil companies do each other's work. The major oil companies could happily do without Qaddafi provided his successor was equally committed to shutting in Libyan production. For his part Qaddafi would surely be glad to replace the U.S. oil companies, but only if the newcomers were as compliant with his wishes and able to keep as much oil off the world market as effectively as the Americans have been.

II
THE FAILURE OF
NON-COOPERATION, 1973-1980

3
QADDAFI TURNS TO TERROR

Qaddafi failed to extend his influence and win agreement with his ideas in 1973 in the two critical areas of oil and the Arab-Israeli conflict. Sadat, Faisal, and Assad shut him out of the October War, and he was unable to stop Egypt and Syria from entering direct negotiations with Israel. In regard to oil diplomacy, it was the Gulf producers that called the tune both as to the imposition of the embargo and its termination, which plainly was in preparation as the year ended. As humiliating as it must have been for him to be forced aside and ignored in this way on the main issues, Qaddafi nonetheless possessed other weapons that could be used in other policy arenas. He had toyed with them from the beginning of his regime; now he turned to them in earnest. The policy arenas lay for the most part in Africa, Asia, Europe, and even the United States, places far from the cockpit of the Eastern Mediterranean and the Gulf. The weapons on which Qaddafi began increasingly to rely were those of terror, subversion, and intervention. It was not simply that Qaddafi had been denied a more conventional role. His passionate hatred of Israel and the West and his strong convictions about Islam, not to mention his exalted conception of his own role in the scheme of things, would undoubtedly have pushed him into opposition sooner or later. He had, nonetheless, begun by attempting to operate within the system primarily according to the rules – in dealing with Egypt, Sudan, and Syria, for example – while admittedly attempting to make drastic changes in both system and rules. Rebuffed in a humiliating way, he turned all the more wholeheartedly to the dark sides of power and politics and clung to his ambitions and expectations.

35

There are some examples of more or less conventional Libyan diplomacy in 1973, and these should not be overlooked. Qaddafi took a very active part in the Arab effort, which fitted Sadat's war plan, to isolate Israel by persuading African governments to break diplomatic relations with the Jewish state. At the annual summit of the Organization of African Unity (OAU) in Addis Ababa, May 24-29, 1973, for example, Qaddafi demanded the rupture. He even attempted to have the headquarters of the organization moved from Addis Ababa to Cairo as a slap at the Ethiopian government, which maintained ties with Israel. In April the New York Times reported that Qaddafi had also promised the government of Chad to end support for the National Liberation Front of Chad in exchange for Chad's agreement to break relations with Israel.

Qaddafi reached farther into Africa in his support for the regime of Idi Amin in Uganda. In April and again in July the London Observer reported that Qaddafi had paid France to ship major combat equipment to Uganda. The Observer said that 80 armored personnel carriers equipped with missiles were to be sent to the brutal Ugandan dictator who was under sporadic military pressure from exile forces led by Milton Obote operating out of sanctuaries in Tanzania. At the OAU summit Obote had accused Libya and Palestine liberation groups of sending troops to help Amin stay in power. It was publicly known that since the previous January Libya had been training several hundred of Amin's troops in Libya.(1)

An incident that bridged the gap between conventional diplomacy and subversion occurred during a state visit by Qaddafi to Tunisia, December 13-18, 1972. In a public speech couched in words that hardly disguised his meaning, Qaddafi called for the immediate establishment of Arab unity, the overthrow of monarchical regimes, the establishment of similar forms of government in all Arab lands, and war against colonial powers, such as that waged by Libya against Britain through its aid to the IRA. President Bourguiba of Tunisia, surprised by the tenor of Qaddafi's remarks, changed his plans and also addressed the crowd to refute Qaddafi's arguments as utopian and immature.

Qaddafi was only meddlesome on this occasion in Tunisia, as he had been little more than a nuisance during the summer of 1973 as Sadat, Assad, and Faisal prepared war against Israel and an oil embargo of the United States. However, the trend of Qaddafi's diplomacy was clear. It became obvious in the reports from Morocco of Libyan support for an attempted overthrow of King Hassan. On April 2, the Moroccan government announced the suspension of the Rabat branch of the leftist party Union nationale des forces populaires (UNFP) and the arrest of a number of the party's most important leaders. According to government statements members of UNFP had led an attempt to destabilize Moroccan society by staging bombing and terrorist attacks in the cities and had tried to initiate guerilla warfare in the Atlas Mountains by infiltrating men and weapons into Morocco from Algeria and Libya. The government brought 156 Moroccans to trial before a military court on June 25. They were charged with plotting the overthrow of King Hassan with the aid of Qaddafi. Some members of the group, the government charged, had been trained in Algeria in 1967 and Syria in 1969 and had been armed for guerrilla warfare in Morocco by Libya.

Amidst those reports of Libyan support for guerrillas in Morocco, Qaddafi reached halfway around the world to give aid to a Muslim secessionist movement in the Philippine islands of Mindanao and the Sulu archipelago. Libyan arms and money apparently reached the rebels through Sabah (eastern Malaysia), whose chief minister, Tun Datuk Mustapha bin Datuk Harun, was a native of the Sulu Islands. Security on Mindanao vanished as a result of the fighting. Toward the end of April, Philippine President Ferdinand Marcos, who had placed the entire country under martial law the previous September, announced that "nearly a million people" had abandoned their homes in Mindanao to escape the hostilities.(2) It was in keeping with Qaddafi's desire for significant influence in the Muslim world that the World Islamic Conference, meeting in Benghazi on March 26-27, appealed to the Philippine government to end "the reported repression and mass extermination of Moslems." The conference also named a delegation of the foreign ministers of Afghanistan, Libya, Saudi Arabia, Senegal, and Somalia to discuss the matter with the Philippine government in Manila. Four of the delegates actually made the trip – the foreign ministers of Libya, Saudi Arabia, Somalia, and Senegal – and toured some of the Muslim areas in four provinces August 17-18.

Although it is a violation of international law to intervene in the domestic affairs of another country, governments regularly support armed rebellions in other states. This support certainly falls within accepted international diplomatic and military practice, and Qaddafi's backing of revolutionaries in Morocco and the Philippines accords with it. But Qaddafi did not stop with this kind of aid. He went on to give money, arms, and sanctuary to terrorists who committed random acts of horror. The question, therefore, is at what point does the support given to foreign revolutionaries by an internationally recognized government become criminal? The activists in every cause will claim to represent the "will of the people," and in the absence of a supervised plebiscite the validity of their competing claims is difficult to assess. The appropriate standard, in my view, is whether or not the assistance is used directly in support of the revolutionary cause on behalf of which it was given in the first place. The critical responsibility of the donor is to ensure that the recipients of his aid are not swept away by the fanaticism and moral relevatism that permeate desperate life-and-death struggles in every part of the world. If they are the donor must stop the aid or become an international outlaw. It is difficult to make simple judgments because of the unavoidable dependence of most revolutionaries on outside help. What is difficult to judge in the abstract becomes far easier to discern when one examines specific concrete cases. As one considers example after example of the uses made by revolutionaries of outside government assistance, it becomes clear that the use is sometimes so tenuously connected with the original revolutionary cause as to be merely criminal. When the donor government declines to halt its aid and in fact even increases it in face of the obvious criminality and irrelevance of the violence it has helped unleash, then the government has become no less an outlaw than the terrorists it has nourished.

In addition to passing the standard of directness – that aid be used in a fashion recognizably connected to the cause for which it was given – donors and recipients must accept certain moral restraints on their actions, as well. The relevant moral standards against which one measures the actions of revolutionaries and the governments who aid them are obviously not what Arnold Wolfers termed a "perfectionist" ethic. Revolution, like war and, in fact, much of politics as a whole, require the taking of life and the commission of deeds that in ordinary times would not be countenanced. There are limits, nonetheless, beyond which revolutionaries, soldiers, and political leaders may not go or they will cease to act legitimately and will become outlaws.

The essence of these limits is conveyed by the words prudence and proportion. The political meaning of prudence and its political use are as old as political philosophy. Critical to both is the avoidance of the evils against which activists supposedly revolt in the first place. It is too simple to say that a movement is an imprudent failure and deserving of both moral and political censure if the lives taken and sacrifices endured on its behalf produce effects that are the opposite of its announced goals. The heroic efforts of virtuous men and women in a good cause may be twisted by an evil regime into a pretext for heightening repression. They are still legitimate and praiseworthy. Even so, activists unavoidably incur a heavy moral responsibility to avoid causing greater damage to their cause than would have occurred had they not acted outside the law. Thus, activists who murder and steal mercilessly and irrationally on behalf of "the workers" may end by causing a loss of freedom to the working class and to many other groups in their society.

To meet the test of proportion, acts that violate the norms of an established society must be logically suited to the revolutionary, military, or political goals of the activists. The calculated murder of innocent people – the dozens of murders perpetrated by terrorists at the airport near Rome or the machine gunning of tourists at Lod Airport in Israel – are without political proportion and exhibit only the madness of destruction for its own sake. Apparently the realization of the depravity of their actions began to prey on the minds of some of the most destructive terrorists of the 1970s and contributed to their decisions to surrender to the authorities or to forswear their commitment to revolutionary violence. "You begin by giving up your humanity, and end by renouncing your political ideals. The relation between your objective and the means used to reach it becomes insane," said a former member of the German Revolutionary Cells. In the words of a former member of the strategic command of the Red Brigades, "I wanted to do what I could to stop this massacre, because we were going beyond every conceivable political strategy toward madness. . . ."(3) Judged by these standards Qaddafi has become an international outlaw, not because he has supported revolutionaries but because he has refused to end his support even when it was turned to irrelevant criminality and had no recognizable connection with Palestinian or Libyan causes.

Beginning in the early 1970s Qaddafi began to support terrorist and revolutionary groups and to initiate terrorist violence without regard for prudence or proportion. There was, of course, a consistent pattern to the acts. They were anti-Western and anti-Israeli, and they were designed to weaken the democracies of Western Europe and North America, to reduce their international influence, and to destabilize the countries bordering the Mediterranean. No acts of terror were launched or sponsored by Qaddafi in Eastern Europe or the Soviet Union. For a year or two before the October 1973 War Qaddafi criticized the Soviet Union for allowing Jews to emigrate to Israel. Once he decided to seek massive Soviet military aid even this feeble criticism stopped, and Qaddafi began to align Libyan foreign policy with that of the Soviet Union. This was particularly noticeable on matters of great importance to the Soviet Union, such as Soviet intervention in Ethiopia or, later, the invasion of Afghanistan.

A strong connection grew up in the 1970s between Qaddafi and Black September, a hybrid terrorist unit picked from Yasir Arafat's Al Fatah and George Habash's Popular Front for the Liberation of Palestine (PFLP). Qaddafi's ties to Black September may have started as long ago as 1972 when Palestinian terrorists began training for the kidnapping and murder of Israeli athletes at the Olympic Games in Munich. According to Claire Sterling in The Terror Network, Qaddafi provided "the funds, arms, and training for the Olympic Games massacre."(4) Sterling argued that at the outset Qaddafi preferred to pay right-wing anti-Semites to kill Jews. It was for this reason, for example, that he chose Claudio Mutti to found the Italy-Libya Association in 1973. Mutti had been expelled as an extremist from the neo-Fascist Italian Socialist Movement (MSI) in 1964, and was arrested in 1980 as an accomplice in the bombing of the train station in Bologna, Italy which killed 84 people. Mario Tuti, a confederate of Mutti's, took 100,000 lire from the Libyan embassy in Rome just before a shoot-out in which Tuti killed two policemen. He was later imprisoned for life for various terrorist killings.

Sterling added that another Italian fascist organization, Avanguardia Nazionale, was also on Qaddafi's payroll.(5)

Black September had the longest reach, however, and would strike at Jews anywhere in the world. In late December 1972, Black September guerrillas attacked the Israeli embassy in Bangkok, Thailand, and took as hostages three members of the staff, two of their wives, and the ambassador, Dr. Shimon Avimor. They held their prisoners for nineteen hours and finally released them in exchange for safe conduct to Cairo in the company of two members of the Thai government. There is some evidence that Qaddafi disliked the leftist orientation of the Marxist commando organizations such as the Popular Front for the Liberation of Palestine.(6) If a break occurred it was mended after intensive talks in Tripoli in the summer of 1973. According to this interpretation Qaddafi then not only restarted the payments for the Palestinians but also began to make payments in support of the activities of the Soviet terrorist, Carlos, in Western Europe.

According to Sterling's account, which is based on Western newspaper stories, published interviews of Carlos, and briefings by Western intelligence services, Carlos is an agent of the Soviet intelligence service or KGB. He is Venezuelan. His real name is Ilich Ramirez Sanchez, and he claims to have been a pro-Moscow Communist since his teens. Sent to Cuba for advanced guerrilla training in 1966 at the age of seventeen, Carlos returned to Venezuela twice on secret missions before being ordered to Patrice Lumumba University in Moscow for two years. In Moscow he met Mohammed Boudia, one of George Habash's closest collaborators and director of the PFLP's campaign of terror in Western Europe. Boudia, a Communist since the 1950s, was later killed by the Israeli secret sevice for his part in the Munich massacre.(7) Boudia arranged for Carlos to join the forces of Haddad and Habash in the Middle East.(8) In 1970 Carlos was sent to Jordan where he took part on the side of the PFLP in the war against King Hussein. Carlos was then ordered to England where he joined with his KGB control from Cuba, Anton Dager Bouvier. The two spent their time amassing guns and explosives and preparing lists of Jews and others to kill in the name of the Palestinian Resistance. Carlos shot the first man on the list in the mouth in December 1973, but Joseph Sief, a prominent supporter of Israel, owner of the Marks and Spencer stores, survived. Carlos fled England for Paris. The connection between the Palestinian Resistance and the Soviet Union was underlined by the reaction of the PFLP to the attack on Sief. The murder was attempted by "one of our freedom fighters," the PFLP announced in Beirut on December 31.(9) Because Boudia had been killed by the Israelis in 1973, Carlos was put in charge of Boudia's Paris operation. After a visit to Aden to touch base with Haddad, Carlos returned to Paris with "Colonel Qaddafi's promise to foot the bills."(10) According to the statements of an imprisoned German terrorist, Hans-Joachim Klein, the Palestinian leader, Wadi Haddad, acting through the Soviet agent, Carlos, was responsible for many of the terrorist murders, bombings, and kidnappings that were committed in Europe for the next three years. Carlos's job in Paris was to carry out Haddad's orders from Aden. "It is always said that the Baader-Meinhof Gang, the June 2 Movement, and the Revolutionary Cells are totally independent," Klein said in 1978. "That is utterly untrue. Without Haddad, nothing works."(11)

In charge of the Paris operation and bankrolled by Libyan money, Carlos became an active and deadly terrorist leader. He planned the successful seizure of the French embassy in the Hague by Japanese commandos. He attempted but failed to launch similar attacks on diplomats in Stockholm, Copenhagen, and Berne. With French assistants he bombed three Paris newspapers, commenting later: "I got praise for that from Beirut."(12) Carlos supplied the Basque ETA with the explosives they used to kill Franco's chosen heir, Admiral Carrero-Blanco. He provided forged passports to terrorists. He sent two Soviet-made ground-to-air SAM-7 missiles by Greek courier to Rome's Fiumicino airport for use by Palestinian terrorists to shoot down an Israeli El Al airliner. A tip from Israeli intelligence enabled Italian police to capture the missiles and the terrorists before they could act. The missiles had come from Libya on Carlos's instructions. In a total failure of judgment the Italian government allowed all five terrorists to go free and even shipped three directly back to Libya on an Italian military plane. The Italian authorities mistakenly believed they could get in the good graces of the terrorists in this way.(13) Carlos and his men tried and failed to blow up El Al planes on the ground at Orly airport in Paris. And, in his biggest coup, Carlos organized and personally led the kidnapping of OPEC oil ministers who were meeting in Vienna in December 1975. Libya supplied the inside information needed to make the attack succeed.(14)

If he had a brief quarrel with the Marxist guerrillas, Qaddafi was apparently on excellent terms with Black September in the spring of 1973 when eight of their members murdered three diplomats – two American and one Belgian – in the Saudi Arabian embassy in Khartoum, Sudan.(15) The two Americans were George C. Moore, about to end a tour as charge d'affaires in Khartoum, and Cleo Noel, the new U.S. ambassador. Egyptian-born Guy Eid, the third to die, was charge at the Belgian embassy.

On the evening of March 1 the Saudi ambassador was giving a reception in honor of George Moore. The foreign diplomatic community had been invited, and was well represented. About 7 P.M. eight members of Black September drove a Land Rover through the embassy gates and opened fire with revolvers and machine guns. The guests scattered. Many climbed the compound wall and escaped, others hid in the garden and found their way to freedom later. Still others told the terrorists their nationalities and were allowed to leave. Noel, wounded in the ankle by a ricochet, Moore, Eid, and several others, including the Saudi ambassador, Sheikh Abdullah el Malhouk, his wife and children, were taken prisoner. Noel and Moore were tightly bound, and the terrorists beat them and kicked them mercilessly, according to an eyewitness.

After several hours the terrorists, led by Abu Salem, second-in-command at the Fatah office in Khartoum, issued a statement saying they would kill the hostages unless certain demands were met within twenty-four hours. The demands were ambitious but implausible and included: the release of Abu Daoud and other Fatah guerrillas held in Jordan; the release of Major Rafeh Hindawi, a Jordanian officer held for plotting against Hussein's regime; the release of Sirhan Sirhan, the assassin of Robert Kennedy; the release of all Arab women detained in Israel; and the release of the members of the Baader-Meinhof terrorist group imprisoned in West Germany. None of the governments concerned would negotiate with the terrorists in the Saudi embassy, although the Nixon administration attempted to send a high-ranking State Department official to Khartoum. He arrived too late to help. With their ultimatum unanswered, the Black September guerrillas took Noel, Moore, and Eid to the embassy basement and shot them repeatedly about 9 P.M. on March 2.

The terrorists refused to surrender the next day. They announced they would hand over the bodies only if they were given safe conduct to an unspecified Arab capital. This demand was refused. Sudanese Interior Minister Mohammed el Baghir, acting on instructions from an emergency cabinet meeting, gave them until dawn the following day to surrender. They complied and were immediately taken into custody. On June 24, 1974, a Sudanese court sentenced the eight murderers to life imprisonment. President Nimeiry, however, commuted their sentences to seven years and ordered them released to the PLO to serve their time under Palestinian supervision, based on his view that the PLO was "the legal representative of the Palestinian people." The United States immediately recalled its ambassador in protest against this decision. To close the incident, at least temporarily, and to prevent it from damaging his new relationship with the United States, President Sadat put the murderers in jail when their plane arrived in Cairo.(16) Yasir Arafat apparently intervened in the later stages of the siege when it became clear the terrorists had no other way out.

A number of curious facts surfaced after the cold-blooded killings by Black September. At least two pieces of information suggested a connection to Libya, in addition to the role of Black September. The reaction of the Sudanese authorities is the primary piece of evidence. Spokesmen for the Sudanese government stressed their belief that Libya was responsible for the attack and that it had been planned to undermine the regime of President Nimeiry. Not only had the Sudanese president just reestablished good relations with the United States – as Cleo Noel's presence tragically testified – but he had also withdrawn Sudan from the proposed merger with Libya. Sudanese authorities also added two other pieces of information. On March 6 Nimeiry accused Fatah of planning the raid and murders. According to Nimeiry, Fatah's chief representative in Khartoum, Faway Yassin had left Sudan on a Libyan airliner bound for Tripoli several hours before the attack on the embassy began on March 1. Other Sudanese added that the attackers had arrived in Khartoum from Libya on a Libyan plane as well. And on March 9 Sudanese investigators told journalists that the main target of Black September had actually been Ethiopian Emperor Haile Selassie, then in Khartoum on a state visit. The terrorists, posing as Saudi officials, had telephoned the Ethiopian embassy several times to invite the emperor to the reception for Moore. Apparently the emperor was to have been taken hostage and released in exchange for the release of the guerrillas in Jordan. Given the demented standards of the terrorists, however, it is hard to imagine that the emperor would have been allowed to go free, if he had ever been taken prisoner. He surely would have been murdered. What better way to humiliate Nimeiry and plunge Ethiopia into chaos?(17)

No Arab state – not even Libya, Syria, or Iraq – publicly condoned the killings in Khartoum. The exact nature of Qaddafi's involvement in the affair may never be determined, but within a few days, Libya's connection with terrorist activities was once more in the news, and this time there could be little doubt. On March 28, 1973, the Irish navy intercepted the S.S. Claudia, a German-owned, Cyprus-registered vessel, near county Waterford off the southeast coast of Ireland. On board were five tons of weapons and explosives – 250 rifles, 240 small arms, and a large number of antitank mines – all of Soviet or East European manufacture. Joe Cahill, the former commander in Belfast of the Provisional Irish Republican Army, was also aboard. Cahill was arrested, as were five other Irishmen who had sailed out to meet the Claudia from Dungarvan harbor. The ship and its crew were released after the weapons were unloaded. Contacted in Hamburg, West Germany on April 2, Herr Gunther Leinhauser, managing director of Giromar Shipping of Nicosia, was positively gossipy about the whole affair. He was the "middleman" in an arms deal between the IRA and Libya, the German entrepreneur said:

> The IRA contacted me and I arranged the transport. I went to Tripoli and arranged things with the IRA men but I was not present when the ship was loaded . . . . The Libyans dealt directly with the IRA and the IRA paid me half my fee before the loading. The Claudia was loaded outside Libyan territorial waters but the arms came from Tripoli.(18)

Three IRA men had been in Tripoli to supervise the deal, Leinhauser said. But something was wrong. There were supposed to be 100 tons of armaments on the ship. He didn't know what had happened to the other 95 tons. Maybe the crew had panicked and thrown all 190,000 pounds of them overboard, he suggested helpfully. Herr Hans-Ludwig Flugel, master of the Claudia, told reporters that only 5 tons had been loaded on his ship. He had expected 100 tons; nothing had been thrown overboard.

Of course, testimony of people like Leinhauser and Flugel is worth very little in the absence of corroborating evidence. In 1967 Leinhauser had received a suspended nine-month prison sentence for smuggling Czech arms through West Germany, France, and Turkey to Kurdish rebels in Iraq.(19) The main reason Leinhauser was believed was that Qaddafi was boasting publicly about his aid to the IRA. In an interview with the Paris newspaper Le Figaro three weeks after the seizure of Claudia, Qaddafi proudly confirmed that Libya had given aid to the "Irish guerrillas."(20) By one estimate, when the Claudia was taken, Qaddafi had already given the Provisional IRA more than $2 million, and by the late 1970s, according to the terrorist "deserter" Peter McMullen, was giving them $5 million a year.(21) Qaddafi continued to brag about his aid to the IRA, and after 1976 began to allow them to train in Libya with Cuban instructors in demolitions, weapons, and psychological warfare.(22)

The Arab-Israeli war of October 1973 and the subsequent oil embargo preempt our attention and eclipse many of the events that occurred before the Egyptian and Syrian attacks during Yom Kippur. It requires an effort of will to recall just how violent the weeks and months were before the war began. If one starts with the attack on the Israeli athletes at Munich in September 1972, there follows a string of extremely violent and increasingly horrible episodes, to which the Israelis contribute in reprisal and preemption. These attacks become doubly interesting when one recalls that it is now known that Qaddafi initiated and funded a number of them and was linked in obvious if indirect ways to others, such as the murders in Khartoum.

On April 9, 1973, nine Arab guerrillas tried to kill the Israeli ambassador in Nicosia by blowing up his house. Although the explosives detonated and destroyed the first floor of the house, the ambassador's wife and children, who were at home, were on the second floor and were not killed. The terrorists were caught. At the same time as the attack on the ambassador's house, another group of Arab guerrillas in two vehicles drove onto the runway of the Nicosia airport and opened fire on a parked Israeli airliner. The plane was empty save for a security guard who opened fire on one of the cars, killing one Arab and wounding two others. That car crashed. The survivors and the occupants of the other car were captured. Documents on the Arabs identified them as members of the National

Arab Youth Organization. They carried Gulf State and Saudi passports. Their weapons were Soviet and East European.(23) They were released in 1974.(24)

Within twenty-four hours of the Nicosia attacks Israeli paratroops and naval commandos went ashore on a beach near Beirut. Cars hired by Israeli agents were waiting for them. In Beirut on the elegant rue Verdun, they broke into the apartments of three top Palestinian leaders. Blasting the doors open with grenades and explosives they shot dead Mohammed Yussef Najjar, known as Abu Yussef, one of the founders of Al Fatah and regarded as second only to Yasir Arafat in that Palestinian organization. Also killed were Kamal Adwan, Fatah spokesman and member of the executive committee of the PLO; Kamel Nasser, official spokesman of the PLO and close associate of Arafat; and Najjar's wife. While the apartment attacks were underway, other Israeli commandos attacked the headquarters of the Popular Democratic Front for the Liberation of Palestine (PDFLP), a splinter of the PFLP, and killed and wounded a number of guerrillas. After about two hours the Israelis withdrew by car and launch. They lost two dead and carried two wounded.(25) Early in July the Israeli air attache in Washington, Colonel Yosef Alon, was shot dead as he and his wife returned from an embassy party. As soon as the worldwide news services picked up the story the Voice of Palestine in Cairo claimed the killing was in reprisal for the assassination of Mohammed Boudia the previous week. Boudia was blown up as he entered his car in Paris on June 28.

The direct one-on-one attacks didn't stop, but before long they were supplemented by indiscriminate mayhem committed against individuals who had at best an accidental connection with the Palestinian question. Such an attack occurred on August 5 when Black September terrorists killed 34 and wounded 55 when they opened fire and threw grenades in the transit lounge of Athens airport. When the terrorists were arrested after trying unsuccessfully to bargain their way to freedom with the lives of 50 hostages they said they were "sorry"; they had made a mistake. They were supposed to attack an Israel-bound TWA flight. By mistake they had attacked passengers for New York and Geneva. Eyewitnesses said the terrorists joined the line of passengers waiting for baggage inspection. They then threw grenades and opened fire. In an attempt to escape, they herded 50 passengers and airport employees into a corner of the lounge and held them hostage while they negotiated with police. After several hours they surrendered. Athens had been the scene of an unsuccessful attack on the El Al office two weeks earlier. A Palestinian guerrilla armed with a machine gun and grenades had tried to enter the airline office. An alert guard foiled the attack by closing an inner security door. The terrorist turned and ran to a nearby hotel. He captured 17 hostages and demanded to speak to the Greek deputy premier, Stylianos Pattakos, who refused. With the aid of several Arab diplomats the

Greek police arranged for the release of the hostages in exchange for safe conduct for the terrorist out of the country. He left on a Kuwaiti airliner bound for Kuwait.

Just a day after the attack on the El Al office in Athens, terrorists hijacked a Japan Air Lines Boeing 747 en route from Paris to Tokyo via Amsterdam. A female member of the terrorist group was killed and several passengers were wounded when a grenade exploded just before the airliner, carrying 145 passengers and crew, was seized. The pilot was forced to fly to the Middle East. Eventually he was allowed to land in Dubai. The terrorists forced the crew and passengers to sit in the airplane on the ground at Dubai in 100-degree weather for three days. While flying over the Mediterranean the hijackers had radioed Nicosia airport and said their group was composed of Palestinian commandos and members of the Japanese Red Army. They demanded the release of Kozo Okamoto, a Japanese terrorist who had taken part in the shooting of pilgrims at Lod Airport in May 1972 and was now serving a life sentence in Israel.

In Dubai the hijackers said they belonged to an organization called "Sons of the Occupied Territories." Despite the repeated efforts of the Dubai authorities the hijackers refused either to negotiate or to surrender. Finally on July 23, the third day of the ordeal, a message in English arrived for the hijackers. At first authorities thought it was a prank, but when the terrorists heard the message from "13,569 inhabitants of the Federal Republic of Germany" to kill or release the hostages they immediately ordered the plane to fly to Libya. Before takeoff they freed four elderly passengers who were exhausted by the heat and took on board the coffin of their dead female colleague. When they arrived in Benghazi, Libya, the terrorists ordered everyone out and then blew up the plane. The PLO denied involvement, but such denials had become routine since the Israeli raid on Beirut. The Libyan government announced that the hijackers would be tried in accord with Islamic law. Responding to a request from the Japanese government Libyan authorities identified the terrorists: a Japanese, wanted in Japan for preparing the Lod massacre, two Arabs, and an Ecuadorean national whose name was given only as "Carlos."

The reluctance of the Palestinian guerrilla organizations to claim credit for these atrocities derived from their well-founded fear of Israeli reprisal. On July 21, for example, a Moroccan thought to be a member of Black September was shot to death in the Norwegian town of Lillehammer, 115 miles north of Oslo, by two assailants. Norwegian authorities arrested six, including two Israelis, for the killing of Ahmed Bouchiki. Those arrested were members of an Israeli counter-terror group, "The Wrath of God." They were apparently trying to prevent Black September from assembling a team in Norway to hijack an El Al jetliner in Denmark.

On August 10 Israel made another daring — and potentially tragic — strike at the leader of PFLP, George Habash. Israeli fighters forced an Iraqi airliner flying over Lebanon to land in Israel for a "passenger check." After two hours the plane and all passengers were allowed to go on to Beirut. News reports said later that the Israeli government had thought Habash was on the plane. Apparently Habash had intended to take the flight but had cancelled his plans at the last minute. Habash put out the story that he had changed his plans for security reasons. Press reports from Beirut, however, indicated that Habash, who has a heart condition, had felt unwell at the airport. Israel was censured by the UN Security Council on August 15. The whole episode was chillingly reminiscent of the disaster that had occurred the previous February when Israeli fighters had shot down a Libyan airliner flying over occupied Sinai with 123 persons on board. The pilot, a Frenchman, and his Libyan copilot had become confused during their approach to Cairo airport and had drifted east of the Suez Canal. When challenged by Israeli fighters and ordered to land, the pilot, still believing he was over Egyptian territory, had mistaken the U.S.-built Phantoms for Soviet-built MIGs. In other words, as the cockpit recorder confirmed, the pilot had thought he was obeying the Egyptian challenge by continuing to fly west toward Cairo airport. The Israeli fighter pilots were ordered to bring down the airliner, and they opened fire, damaging the plane so heavily that it crashed. Only 15 people on board survived; 108 were killed. In an unusual action the Israeli government admitted error and offered to compensate the families of the victims.(26)

Several terrorist attacks by Palestinians were planned for early September, to coincide with the first anniversary of the Munich Games massacre. Qaddafi played a critical part in one of these, the use of SAM-7 missiles to shoot down an El Al plane at Fiumicino airport, as was noted earlier. The SAM-7 attack was prevented, but an attack on the Saudi embassy in Paris succeeded. On September 5 in mid-morning five armed Arabs entered the Saudi embassy and took fifteen hostages. They called themselves members of "El Eqab (Punishment)," and demanded the release of Abu Daoud, then serving a life sentence in Jordan, and their own safe conduct out of the country. They threatened to kill their hostages and blow up the building if their demands weren't met. A number of Arab ambassadors aided French authorities in the inevitable negotiations. Eventually the terrorists took five hostages aboard a Syrian Caravelle and flew to Cairo, where they were allowed to land and the plane was refuelled. Refused permission to land in Libya, they ordered the plane to Syria, where it circled Damascus, and then flew on to Kuwait and landed. They ordered the plane into the air again on a course toward Riyadh. Over the Saudi capital they threatened to throw out the hostages one by one unless Abu Daoud was released. Their actions evoked no response, and they ordered the plane back

to Kuwait. On the ground again they made more threats, then released the hostages on September 7 and, eventually, surrendered to
Kuwaiti troops.

One week passed quietly, then two, but the string of violence had
not run out. On September 28 two heavily armed Arab guerrillas —
calling themselves "Eagles of the Revolution" — seized six Jewish
hostages and two Austrian customs officials on the Moscow-Vienna
train. The train was the "Chopin Express," which had carried nearly
all of the 70,000 Jews allowed out of the Soviet Union since 1971.
Half the 70 passengers on the train were Soviet Jews bound for
Schoenau transit camp in Austria, which was operated by Israel. The
guerrillas had boarded the train in Bratislava, Czechoslovakia. They
clearly had the consent and cooperation of the Communist
authorities, if not the KGB, for the Czech police passed them
through the ordinarily meticulous searches at the heavily guarded
frontier, without a second glance at the variety of weapons they
carried. With the Communist authorities helping on their side of the
border it was a simple matter for the terrorists to walk along the
passageway once the train crossed into Austria and capture some
Jews. Three of the Jews and one customs official escaped, leaving
four hostages in the terrorists' hands. They left the train with their
captives, commandeered a car, and drove to Vienna's Schevechat
Airport. They demanded an airplane to fly themselves and their
hostages to an Arab country.

Initially, the Austrian government refused to allow the hostages
to be taken out of the country, but offered the terrorists free
passage. Some twelve hours later, Austrian Chancellor Bruno
Kreisky announced that agreement had been reached with the
terrorists. The hostages would be released unharmed and their
kidnappers would be given safe conduct out of Austria. In exchange,
Austria would close the Schoenau camp. In a vain attempt to still
the public outcry that arose in the West against this act of
capitulation Kreisky made two points: to allow a foreign government
to operate an establishment like Schoenau in his country was to
invite acts of terror and violence which Austria was unwilling to
permit and unable to prevent; and, the transit of Jews through
Austria would continue. Meanwhile, the kidnappers were flown
south by two Austrian pilots in a two-engine Cessna aircraft. They
refuelled in Italy and Yugoslavia and tried to land in a North African
Arab country. Denied permission to land in Algeria and Tunisia they
threatened to blow up the plane in mid-air and were allowed to land
in Libya. Tragically, the easy escape of the "Chopin Express"
kidnappers was the rule rather than the exception. According to
official Israeli figures, of 204 Palestinians arrested for terrorism
outside the Middle East from 1968 to 1975, three were in jail in
1975.(27)

Within a few days Egypt and Syria attacked Israel, and their
governments became the purveyors of violence on a massive scale.

But the senseless acts of indiscriminate terror continued. Perhaps the worst was the fire-bombing of a Pan-American airliner at Fiumicino airport in December 1973, as a protest against Egyptian-Israeli peace talks in Geneva. According to Sterling, "The Italian Ministry of the Interior found that the hit-men had acquired their air tickets in Tripoli and were carrying weapons, fire bombs, grenades, and money provided by Libya."(28) In other words, Libya was responsible.

Qaddafi continued his support for terrorism, and within two years vastly increased his involvement. According to the former Libyan minister of planning, Omar el-Meheishi, Qaddafi had set aside $580 million for terrorism and paramilitary activities in 1976. He spent tens of millions on arms for the Palestinians during the Lebanese civil war of 1975-76.(29) Beginning in 1976 he established training camps for ten to twenty thousand foreigners in Libya staffed by Cuban, Soviet, East German, Syrian, and Palestinian instructors. There were the camps for Europeans at Sirte, Sebha, and Az Zaouiah; for Tunisians at Bab Aziza – they were sent to overthrow Habib Bourguiba in January 1980; for some two thousand Egyptians at el-Beida; for Sudanese and Chadians at Maaten Biskara; and for advanced students in sabotage and underwater demolitions, Cuban and East German instructors at Raz Hilal camp near Tokra.(30) At this point, of course, Qaddafi had passed beyond supporting terrorism – although he continued to do this – to the subversion, destabilization, and overthrow of foreign governments. Seven thousand of Qaddafi's African warriors paraded in Benghazi on September 1, 1979, the tenth anniversary of the revolution. "Here are the liberators of the Third World," the loudspeakers blared as the black and Arab troops goose-stepped past Qaddafi on the reviewing stand.(31) Some of those who paraded before the Libyan leader that day in Benghazi – the Tunisians, Chadians, Sahraoui of Polisario, and the Sudanese – would see large-scale action within a year. For the others there was always terrorism. For this Qaddafi provided false passports, money, safe houses in Europe, villas in Libya, and fat contracts for the murder of Qaddafi's opponents living abroad, as the Edwin Wilson-Frank Terpil affair would reveal.

The motives for Qaddafi's extensive support for and practice of terrorism are clear. He wished to strike at Israel, the West, and enemies of his regime, domestic and foreign. It is not necessary and would in any case be incorrect to regard him as a mere puppet of the Soviet Union in order to find his actions abhorrent and detrimental to Western security interests. Qaddafi has publicly aligned Libyan foreign policy with that of the Soviet Union – refusing to condemn the invasion of Muslim Afghanistan, for example, or staging international conferences for and inviting pro-Soviet groups to attend. But this is small payment, indeed, for the huge arms supplies and implicit security commitment Qaddafi receives from the Soviet Union. Moreover Qaddafi's public, rhetorical diplomacy is not the most important problem he poses for the United States and its allies in the Middle East and Western Europe. Terrorism sponsored or initiated by Libya is one part of the problem. The other part is foreign intervention – the systematic training in Libya of thousands of guerrillas to be used to destabilize or overthrow neighboring governments.

There are two reasons why Libyan terrorism was taken seriously and opposed so vehemently by the United States. The first and most obvious reason is that terrorism strikes at the very fiber of decent society, at the hope of ordinary people that their lives can be lived sanely and according to reason and law. This is not an exaggeration of the havoc terrorists can work. In Turkey, terrorists killed four thousand people in 1980, about eleven deaths every day. In Italy in 1979 there was a terrorist attack somewhere in the country every three hours.(32) The disorder fostered by terrorists accordingly hurts much more than the bodies of the immediate casualties of kidnappings, assassinations, or explosions. The very irrationality of terrorism – by defeating the expectation of sanity and reason – sets loose diffuse but strong and irrational currents within society. If the established government cannot cope with the terrorists swiftly and effectively, everything is threatened; all life becomes politicized and, increasingly, militarized. A contest follows between the agents of irrationality, as in El Salvador. Life becomes "nasty, brutish, and short," a war of all against all. Culture and freedom vanish, regardless of which side wins. This is the first and greatest evil that derives from Libyan terrorism, and all other terrorists.

Moreover, while Qaddafi may think that he is in charge of the terrorism he supports or initiates, there is much evidence that Qaddafi and the Palestinian terrorists he pays and uses have been manipulated by the Soviet Union.

> There is massive proof that the Soviet Union and its surrogates, over the last decade, have provided the weapons, training, and sanctuary for a worldwide terror network aimed at the destabilization of Western democratic society . . . there has been a straight transfer of terrorist skills and equipment from Moscow to the Palestine resistance to the terrorists of Europe and beyond, with the knowledge and assistance of the Russians themselves. Soviet-bloc arms were being shipped from Eastern Europe to the Middle East, then transshipped to Western European terrorists through a Bulgarian staging post or via Libya.(33)

In the early 1970s Qaddafi began to assist in the training of Palestinian guerrilla formations, along with Cuba, Algeria, Syria, Lebanon, South Yemen, the Soviet Union, and several East European governments, notably East Germany. These guerrilla formations then offered training and money to terrorists who would strike at

Israel and the West, but never at the Soviet Union or its allies. In these circumstances, to aid Palestinian terrorism was to cooperate in the propagation of irrational violence against the West throughout the 1970s. It was also to render direct assistance to the foreign policy of the Soviet Union. Only the West was under attack; there were no East European or Soviet students in the camps in Lebanon or South Yemen or Libya. Given the extremely close ties between Cuba and the Soviet Union, for Qaddafi to allow Cuban instructors to operate in Libyan and other guerrilla camps is not merely the giving and receiving of assistance between one "non-aligned" country and another. It also exposes the guerrillas and Libyan nationals to subversion and manipulation. It is, in short, to risk becoming a tool of the foreign policy of the Soviet Union, a country that clearly stands to gain infinitely more than Qaddafi or the Palestinians if terrorism can be used, in Sterling's words, "to weaken and demoralize, confuse, humiliate, frighten, paralyze, and if possible dismantle the West's democratic societies."(34)

With the help of the works of John Amos, Brian Jenkins, and other students of the Palestinian movement and international terrorism it is possible to identify Libya's reasons for such close and long-lived support for these murderous organizations.(35) The easiest and most obvious sources of Qaddafi's involvement are his political and religious beliefs in Arab unity and Islam. Terrorists were atacking Israel and the West — the enemies of Islam and Arab unity in Qaddafi's mind — and this made them worthy of support. But terrorism was doubly attractive to Qaddafi because in the short run he lacked the trained terrorists and organizational and intelligence capabilities to attack Israel and the West on his own. As Amos observed:

> Qaddafi's strategy of attacking Western positions in the Middle East, Israel, and all Arab states perceived to be pro-Western, logically led to a theory of targetting Western countries in their "own backyard," meaning attacking them in their own territories. Tactically, this required the creation of an ability to hit targets located in Western countries as well as elsewhere. For this Libya did not possess a sufficiently extensive and sophisticated intelligence organization (at least at the outset) to carry out clandestine foreign operations. This lack plus Libya's oil wealth, led to the obvious conclusion: utilize existing terrorist groups; coordinate, finance, and supply them. . . . The selection of these groups, while seemingly random, was actually very carefully done to further the goals of the larger Libyan strategy. . . . By 1976, the list of groups armed and trained [by Libya] had grown to encompass FROLINAT, Philippine Muslims, Thailand Muslims, Eritrean groups, and a variety of African organizations. . . . The arms supplied were usually Soviet, and Libyan

embassies served as supply and communications centers. Tripoli itself became the meeting place of almost every terrorist or insurgent group in the Middle East, Africa, and Asia.(36)

Thus, Qaddafi's resort to terror derived from his fundamental beliefs and his basic strategies of weakening the West and expanding the role of Libya. However there are two other questions whose answers shed additional light on Qaddafi's commitment to terrorism. First, why was it possible for Libya to find so many terrorist groups ready and willing to cooperate in attacking the West and Israel? And, what groups did Libya support and what were the exact links between Libya and the terrorists?

The rise in terrorism around the world in the late 1960s and throughout the 1970s has occurred because of the interaction of three kinds of conditions. They may be termed social-technical, Palestinian, and global. The technical conditions conducive to terrorism are the most obvious. The present worldwide systems of air transport and new coverage – particularly television – are highly vulnerable to attack and manipulation. Newly developed explosives and lightweight automatic and rocket weapons can give tremendous fire power to small groups. Moreover, there is some evidence that the tightly-knit isolated clandestine terrorist cell is peculiarly attractive to Arabs because it is somewhat similar to longstanding patterns of group loyalty in Arab society.(37)

In the late 1960s and early 1970s several developments took place that turned large numbers of Palestinians to terrorism. By the end of the civil war in Jordan it was clear that the strategic choice of large-scale military confrontation based on analogies to the Algerian and Vietnamese revolutions had failed and was, in any case, far too costly in dead and wounded to be continued. In addition, Syria and Jordan had closed their borders to Palestinian raiders. During the debate over strategy that followed, the advocates of international terrorism won out for at least the years 1971-74. The initial resort to terror was a calculated move. Fatah spun off the Black September Organization. PFLP conducted its own operations and fathered a number of other groups, including the Popular Revolutionary Front for the Liberation of Palestine (1972); the Arab Nationalist Youth for the Liberation of Palestine (1973); Sons of the Occupied Homeland (1973); Arab Armed Struggle Organization (1975); and Organization of Struggle Against World Imperialism (1976). Although the number of terrorists was never large – Israeli intelligence estimated Black September at three to four hundred – their clandestine methods of operation in small isolated cells assembled only just before an attack made them extremely difficult to counter or control. It was not long before the terrorists – young, fanatic, perhaps suicidal – began to select and attack targets on their own outside Israel and Jordan, the initial targets. The attack on the Saudi embassy in Khartoum in March 1973 and some of the attacks in Europe mentioned earlier may have been examples of this.

The dangers to the PLO are obvious. The support of wealthy and influential Arab governments, who understandably saw themselves as potential targets, was put at risk. The risks of internal conflict within the Resistance were both multiplied and rendered potentially fatal; there were a number of terrorist attacks by Palestinians against other Palestinians. This "free-lance" terror also opened the Resistance to manipulation by Libya and Iraq who were willing to back splinter terrorist groups, such as Black June (Iraq) or Arab Nationalist Youth for the Liberation of Palestine (Libya).(38)

Finally, global circumstances favored the rise of terrorism. In the early 1970s there were numerous international conflicts whose origins were arguably similar enough to persuade their various partisans to give support to one another. The PFLP was most active in these transnational contacts; Fatah was much less involved because of its own ideological priorities and its reliance on the financial support of conservative Arab regimes. The PFLP approach, which was imitated by other groups, led to the use of multinational hit-teams – Palestinians, Filipinos, Japanese, Germans, Portuguese – but also to the exchange of intelligence, forged travel documents, weaponry, training, safe houses, escape routes, and asylum. In these latter activities, as well as the use of its own agents (Carlos) to infiltrate and manipulate the attacks, the Soviet Union became much involved. Here the global contest between the United States and the Soviet Union played an important part in the rise of terrorism. To the Soviets these groups offered an evidently irresistible chance to conduct "surrogate warfare" against the United States and its allies. The prospect of non-Soviet combatants fighting and dying to weaken the West must have been highly pleasing to the Kremlin. The terrorist movements were even doctrinally sound in Marxist terms for they could be viewed, as Amos has suggested, as an extension at a lower level of violence of the old Soviet doctrine of wars of national liberation.(39)

For these reasons, when Qaddafi began to look for instruments to attack the West he not only found terrorists ready and waiting for him, but "in the wings" there were the powerful technically advanced nations of the Soviet bloc, which he eventually realized would lend support. The Soviet Union was careful not to openly support such groups, because of the obvious impact on its own foreign relations. However, a number of clandestine training centers in the Soviet Union were set up: at Lumumba University itself, the Lenin Institute in Moscow, and elsewhere on the shores of the Black Sea. East Germany, Bulgaria, Czechoslovakia, and Poland acted as Soviet agents in the training of terrorists. The Soviet Union's prize agent Cuba, trained, armed, or maintained contact with German, Irish, Latin American, and Palestinian terrorists. The Soviet Union also made a number of generally unsuccessful attempts to use Arab Communist parties to penetrate the Palestinian movement. China, North Korea, and North Vietnam were involved in training and arming Middle Eastern terrorists on a significantly lower level than the Soviet Union and Eastern Europe.(40) The high point of multilateral terrorist cooperation – what Amos and Sterling have called "the terrorist network" – was impressive: "An operation can be planned in Germany by a Palestine Arab, executed in Israel by terrorists recruited in Japan, with weapons acquired in Italy but manufactured in Russia, supplied by an Algerian diplomat financed with Libyan money."(41)

Qaddafi moved into the terrorist network in two ways. First he opened his land and his treasury to existing terrorist organizations. In May 1972 the PFLP played host in Tripoli to a terrorist summit attended by representatives of Black September, Fatah, the IRA, Baader-Meinhof, the Iranian National Front, and the Turkish People's Liberation Army. This meeting was followed by others, such as the conferences in Baghdad (sponsored by the Soviet Union) and Trieste in 1974, with Libyan and Algerian officials in November 1976, at Larnaca in July 1977, and in South Yemen in 1978. These meetings are important because they facilitate joint planning and the sharing of organizational, intelligence, material, and intelligence resources. This in turn extends the reach of any single group – using Portuguese terrorists to attack an Israeli official, for example – and makes the attacks harder to anticipate.(42)

Qaddafi also moved to establish his own terrorist organization. In June 1972, in the same speech in which he boasted of arming the IRA and the Black Power movement in the United States, Qaddafi offered to arm and train every Arab who would join the Palestine Resistance. Within twenty-four hours 500 Arabs had allegedly registered at the Libyan embassy in Cairo.(43) The factionalism and constant splintering of the Resistance brought a steady flow of dissident Black September, PFLP, and other militants into Tripoli, where they could be coopted into groups under Libyan control. As early as 1976 there were stories coming out of Libya that Qaddafi had created a special hit-team, a charge revived by the Reagan administration in 1982. The PFLP and Libya were said in 1977 to have established the Palestinian Red Army, whose duties were to assassinate any Arab leader willing to make peace with Israel or work for an overall Geneva-type peace conference.(44) Centrist Palestinian leaders have placed more emphasis on diplomacy and have sought to limit and control terrorism in the years since 1975. However, the debate over the utility of terror has not ended, and the hit-men and hijackers could again come to the fore in the Resistance.(45) Meanwhile, Qaddafi has managed to strike some harsh blows against Israel and the West. Although not all Libyan-supported attacks were great successes, as the fiasco at Entebbe revealed, the terrorist network, of which Libya was and is an integral part, significantly increased instability in the Middle East including Iran and the Arabian Peninsula, and arguably in Western Europe as well. Sadly, there is no argument about how much the terrorists added to human loss and suffering.

4
OUTSIDE ASSISTANCE—
THE SOVIET CONNECTION

Qaddafi has been quick to exploit the willingness of both allies and enemies of the United States to help in his quest for a major role in the Middle East and Africa and his efforts to reduce U.S. influence in the Middle East. Initially the French were eager partners with Qaddafi, and quickly replaced the British and Americans as Libya's arms supplier. They in turn were soon overshadowed by the Soviets, who have shipped huge amounts of sophisticated and heavy weapons to Libya. The French, nonetheless, maintained their Libyan connection and evidently attempted to use the arms sales to buy Qaddafi's cooperation with French policy in Africa. The invasion of Chad, a humiliating defeat for Giscard d'Estaing's Africa policy, showed the weakness and unreliability of this method of dealing with Qaddafi. Shortly after taking office, nonetheless, the Socialist government of Francois Mitterand lifted the Gaullist embargo on arms sales to Libya.

After cancelling a large order for a British air defense system Qaddafi quickly opened arms negotiations with the French government in 1969. There were frequent newspaper stories in December 1969 about negotiations which apparently began in November between France and Libya for the sale of large amounts of armaments, electronic gear, tanks, and Mirage aircraft. Beginning in early January 1970 various French government sources confirmed that some armaments would be sold, but only small quantities were mentioned. Finally, with controversy growing, the French defense minister, Michel Debre, told the National Assembly on January 21 that France had agreed to sell one hundred Mirage aircraft to Libya between 1970 and 1974, of which eighty would be of the latest type,

Mirage-5 and Mirage-III-E fighter bombers, equipped with missiles. The remaining twenty would be Mirage-III-B training and reconnaissance aircraft. The French defense minister and the prime minister, Jacques Chaban-Delmas, defended the sale as a competititve commercial action in which France had beaten out the "Anglo-Saxons." It was consistent with France's embargo of arms sales to the "battlefield countries" of the Middle East, which were Israel, Jordan, Syria, and Egypt. If Libya tried to transfer the aircraft to Egypt or another Arab country where they would be used against Israel then France would embargo subsequent deliveries. The United States and Israel strongly opposed the deal, with the Israelis scathingly critical of French cynicism and the Americans concerned that the sale would disturb the arms balance in the region.(1) In exchange for the arms, Debre told the National Assembly, Libya had agreed to end its support of the rebellion in Chad where France had committed some 3,000 of its troops against the insurgents.

Despite its criticism of the French sale, the Nixon administration was reluctant to cancel an order for eight F-5 jets placed in May 1969 by the old regime and due for delivery in 1971-73. Ten of the F-5s had already been sent under an agreement signed with the monarchy in 1967. U.S. military aid to Libya had not been suspended but was being reassessed, according to a State Department spokesman.(2) Reports from unnamed intelligence agents in Western Europe published in the Times stated that Egyptian officials had initiated and helped to conclude the Mirage deal for Libya. The report was denied by the French government and the Libyan embassy in Paris.(3) If not the first, the Soviet Union was certainly among the first new suppliers of arms to Qaddafi. Two shiploads of T-54 and T-55 medium tanks along with armored personnel carriers, trucks, and other vehicles arrived in Tripoli on July 20, 1970. The United States immediately expressed its concern to the Soviet government, but that did little to slow the shipments, which in subsequent years became extremely large.

The juxtaposition of Soviet and French arms led the Moroccan government to take issue with the United States for its opposition to the French plane sale to Libya. During a visit by Secretary of State Rogers to Morocco as part of an African tour, King Hassan and his ministers stressed that the United States should welcome the French move because it would make it possible for Libya to avoid having to rely solely on Egypt or the Soviet Union for arms.(4) Indeed, for the next three years, with the exception of 25 MIG-21 trainer aircraft from Egypt and the July 1970 shipment of tanks from the Soviet Union — variously estimated from around 50 to over 200 — Libya bought its aircraft, missiles, helicopters, and tanks from France, its ships from Britain, its troop transports from the United States, and its armored personnel carriers from Italy, an American design manufactured in Italy under license. With the exception of what eventually proved to be 110 Mirage aircraft Libya ordered only a few of each of these items. Beginning in 1974, however, two developments appear to have caused Qaddafi to seek very large arms supplies from the Soviet Union. First, he was determined to oppose Sadat's opening to the United States and Egypt's acceptance of step-by-step negotiations with Israel. To do so safely, Qaddafi had to increase his military strength and, above all, the impression that Libya was militarily strong and enjoyed a special relationship with the Soviet Union. Second, Qaddafi's desire to radicalize the Libyan internal political and economic revolution may also have played a part, for the huge arms deliveries – repeatedly displayed on parade – and the ostentatious link with the Soviet Union may have been a way of overawing opponents of his regime.(5)

Qaddafi's condemnation of all sides – Israeli, Arab, Soviet, and American – during the October 1973 War left him with a quandary. Libya does not have the technicians nor the sophisticated equipment it needs to modernize its society and armed forces. The Americans were out, of course. In the long term the criticism of the Soviets could be allowed to be forgotten. But what about the days and months immediately ahead? Yugoslavia was the answer, and Qaddafi made a visit to Belgrade, hurriedly arranged, on November 18. News dispatches on the visit stated that Qaddafi would promise to provide large quantities of oil to Yugoslavia in exchange for Yugoslav assistance in the organization and training of Libya's armed forces. For Qaddafi the purpose of the talks was the development in his country of modern, hard-hitting naval, air, and ground forces. Tito was expected to agree to the exchange of oil for weapons and training.(6) At a news conference at the end of three days of talks with Yugoslav officials Qaddafi seemed to confirm this when he said: "My visit to Yugoslavia marks the beginning of a new phase in even closer relations – political, economic, industrial, and other." He also repeated his objections to the Arab summit, the results of which, he said, would be "nonsense."(7) An agreement between the two countries was announced on November 21. Under the terms that were made public Libya would supply two million tons of crude, or 25 percent of Yugoslavia's oil needs. Yugoslavia agreed to build six oil tankers for Libya; to set up joint national companies in fishing, agriculture, construction, oil, and industry; and to build and staff a hospital in Benghazi.(8)

Qaddafi went from Yugoslavia to France, arriving in Paris on November 23. French authorities expected Qaddafi to ask that the embargo be lifted on the shipment of French arms to "battlefield states" in the Middle East. Because of an article published coincidentally in Cairo by Mohammed Hassanein Heykal, speculation arose that Qaddafi might seek French cooperation in the nuclear field. Heykal, editor of Al Ahram, wrote to urge the Arabs to acquire nuclear weapons by pooling their financial, scientific, and material resources. In the course of the article Heykal stated that Qaddafi had tried unsuccessfully to buy a nuclear bomb in 1970.

Heykal didn't reveal what country or countries Qaddafi had approached.

By far the most important development in Libyan foreign policy in 1974 was the start of foreign economic and military cooperation between Libya and the Soviet Union. Libyan Prime Minister Jalloud went to Paris in early April to attend the funeral of French President Georges Pompidou. A memorial mass in honor of Pompidou was held in Notre Dame cathedral on April 6. Immediately afterward the heads of state and representatives in attendance began to meet one another privately to discuss matters of state. Nixon captured the headlines with an ostentatiously hectic schedule calculated to divert attention from the revelations of the Watergate investigators who were gaining ground on him at home. With Nixon monopolizing the headlines, Jalloud was content to hold a quiet meeting with Soviet President Nikolai Podgorny on April 7. Jalloud's meeting with Podgorny followed by one day an announcement in Tripoli that Qaddafi had given up his administrative and political responsibilities in order to "devote all his time to popular organization and ideological action." Whatever the precise redistribution of duties inside the Libyan government might have been, it is clear that Qaddafi kept a firm hand on all the power that really mattered. It is also clear that this kind of announcement would have been welcomed in Moscow because of Qaddafi's past condemnations of communism and Soviet policy. He had been very critical of Soviet support for India during that country's war with Pakistan, for example, and had attacked the Soviet-Iraqi treaty of April 1972 as "imperialist."(9) His Third International theory was designed to present an alternative to communism as much as to capitalism. It is also possible that Qaddafi had used his repeated attempts at union with Egypt to persuade Sadat to reduce his reliance on the Soviet Union.(10) Qaddafi's apparent demotion, therefore, was meant to signal a fundamental change in direction for Libya and was undoubtedly seen as such by the Kremlin, which publicly welcomed the apparent reduction in the scope of Qaddafi's responsibilities.

The outcome of this judicious signaling and the visit with Podgorny was an invitation to visit the Soviet Union. Jalloud spent May 14-20 in the Soviet Union and was accompanied by a sizable delegation including the minister for industry and raw materials and the deputy minister for the economy. Jalloud was given special treatment. He spoke with Brezhnev, for example, as well as Kosygin and Podgorny. But the communique issued at the end of the visit gave the best measure of the significance of the visit. It announced "the identity or closeness of the positions of the Soviet Union and the Libyan Arab Republic on the most important international problems."(11) They agreed in condemning Israel and the "imperialist forces" supporting her, in other words the United States; they both demanded a complete Israeli withdrawal from all territories occupied in 1967; they both pledged to "continue to give . . . every assistance" to the Palestinian Resistance. In addition to this common ground, the two governments had poor relations with Egypt and, as Qaddafi had stated in an interview published in Beirut on April 28, Libya and the Soviet Union both opposed the efforts of the United States to reestablish its influence in the Arab world.(12)

The relationship established during Jalloud's week-long trip to the Soviet Union gave every appearance of becoming an entente. It is true that the two countries did not conclude an alliance, but they had clearly chosen to emphasize what they had in common rather than their differences, and had begun to identify issues on which they could cooperate, such as assistance to the Palestinians and opposition to Israel and the United States. In addition to these shared objectives, the two also laid out ambitious plans for economic, scientific, technical, and military cooperation. They signed a trade agreement on May 20 and granted one another most-favored-nation status. They agreed the following day to establish a joint commission on trade and economic and technical cooperation. And although the two governments were silent about it after the visit ended, the Iraqi news agency, citing informed sources in Tripoli, reported that Libya had asked the Soviet Union to supply arms and that the Soviet government had agreed to increase its arms shipments. Here was the foundation of what would become a massive Libyan arsenal of Soviet military equipment.(13)

Qaddafi turned to the Soviets despite his past belief that the Soviet Union was an "imperialist power." Presumably he continued to believe this. Why the change? In his speech at the dinner given in his honor by Soviet Premier Kosygin, Jalloud made clear that Libya needed Soviet military and political support in order to escape from the isolation Libya had imposed on itself by alienating most of the Arab world as well as its neighbors in North Africa. In addition, Egypt's turn away from the Soviet Union toward the United States threatened to catch Libya between two fires. Libya found itself, in Jalloud's words, "under pressure from imperialist and reactionary forces." The remedy he proposed was for "all forces of progress and truly revolutionary forces to come out against this situation."(14) The entente made sense for the Soviets, as well. With its large reserves of hard currency and major oil deposits Libya was a highly desirable partner for the Soviet Union. If it was possible to barter Soviet military and industrial equipment for Libyan oil, for example, the Soviet Union could then either use the oil for its own needs or resell it to the West and use the hard currency gained in this way to pay for its increasing imports of Western technology.(15)

From this time on, Qaddafi drew steadily closer to the Soviet Union as a way of breaking his country's isolation and multiplying its strength. When Syrian-Soviet relations cooled during the Lebanese War of 1975-76, Libya and Iraq became the strongest allies of the Soviet Union in the Arab world.(16) However, there are important differences between Libya and the Soviet Union, in regard, for example, to the nature of a just settlement of the Palestinian question. Throughout the 1970s the Soviet Union offered a three-point plan: complete Israeli withdrawal from the territories occupied in 1967; recognition of the legitimate rights of the Palestinian people, including the creation of a Palestinian state; and guarantees of the security of all states in the region, including Israel.(17) Alongside this Qaddafi's position is simplicity itself: destroy Israel. It could be argued that this is a distinction without a difference, since both the Soviet and Libyan stands are unacceptable to Israel and would be regarded as mortally dangerous by any Israeli government. The only difference in Israeli eyes might be that the Libyan plan would result in instant destruction while the Soviet plan would lead to death by agonizing degrees. But this is too pessimistic an interpretation, one that overlooks the important consequences that follow from the Libyan-Soviet differences on this point. The Soviet Union will participate in peace-making efforts in the Middle East, such as the Geneva conference, while Qaddafi remains unalterably opposed to all initiatives of this kind. Whatever differences existed did not, of course, prevent the development of extensive ties between Libya and the Soviet Union. Both governments chose to emphasize what united rather than divided them. As Kosygin put it during Jalloud's visit: "If we were to compare that which unites Libya and the Soviet Union to those things on which our views do not coincide, there would be no doubt that the preponderance would fall on the side of that which unites us."(18)

Judging from the amount of resources committed by Libya and the Soviet Union one of the most important shared objectives is the shipment to Libya of huge amounts of Soviet military equipment. As the recipient of this equipment Libya finds a degree of protection from outside pressures. With its rapidly increasing air- and sealift capabilities the Soviet Union could quickly come to Qaddafi's aid if he were attacked and find a ready source of military supplies already in place and available to its expeditionary force. For Qaddafi the arms not only lend prestige to his endeavors but provide the means he needs to intervene in other countries, such as Chad or Uganda, as well as an inexhaustible reservoir of arms to give to foreign guerrillas and terrorists. The gains for the Soviets are no less real. "An arms agreement with a developing country," as Roger Pajak observed, "has been the point of departure for nearly every major Soviet advance in the Third World, beginning with the first Egyptian accord in 1955." By supplying weapons to nationalist governments the Soviets help to weaken or eliminate Western influence and often acquire a political and military presence in strategic areas. The more a nation comes to rely on the Soviet Union as its only source of weapons, the more dependent it is on Moscow's good will for training and maintenance. Libya is certainly in this category, as are Afghanistan, Algeria, Ethiopia, Iraq, and Syria. Moreover, through its training programs, largely conducted in the Soviet Union, the Soviets establish ties to present and future leaders.(19) That the influence gained by the Soviet Union through its military aid has limits and may even collapse altogether, as it did in Egypt and Indonesia, does not detract from its value or reality.

The amounts of arms that have been transferred to Libya by the Soviet Union are impressive. In the five years 1974-78 Libya increased her arms imports by about 50 percent every year. Although Algeria and Saudi Arabia achieved the largest relative build-up during this period, spending nearly 9 times and 6 times respectively more for arms than they had in the previous five years, Libya spent 3 times more than Algeria and 1.7 times more than Saudi Arabia. Indeed, Libya's build-up during the latter period matched that of Israel (see Table 2). Egypt spent significantly less than the other three from 1974-78: expenditures by Egypt declined from $3,606 million to $1,261 million, a drop of nearly 65 percent. Libya and Israel spent 4 times more on arms than Egypt in these years.

Libya was not only the largest recipient of Soviet arms in this period – 3 times more than Algeria, 8 times more than Egypt – but the Soviets provided Libya with extremely large amounts of advanced offensive equipment, far more tanks and aircraft, for example, than Libya's population of 2.8 million (1978) and armed forces of 50,000 could possibly use. Soviet armor forms the backbone of Libya's armored forces. There are 2,000 T-55, 400 T-62, and 200 T-72 main battle tanks, all delivered from 1974-78. The Soviet Union and Brazil have supplied hundreds of armored fighting vehicles. Libya disposes of an assortment of Soviet and European warplanes. Some two-dozen MIG-21 trainers were sent to Libya through Egypt in 1971 after the United States withdrew from Wheelus Air Force Base. In January 1970 Libya ordered 110 Mirage fighter-bombers from France. Sixty of these had been delivered by May 1974 and, as has been seen, some were given to Egypt for use in the October War. A new order for 38 Mirage F-1 fighters was signed in 1975 for delivery in 1977. One hundred modern MIG-27 fighters were ordered from the Soviet Union in 1978 and delivery began that year. Yugoslavia sold Libya 50 light jet fighters in 1975 and began to deliver them in 1977. Several dozen missile-carrying fast patrol boats and 10 submarines, 6 Soviet, 4 Spanish, and a number of Scud tactical battlefield surface-to-surface missiles with conventional warheads round out the Libyan arsenal.(20)

Egypt and Israel agreed to the limitation of armaments and forces in the Sinai Peninsula on September 4, 1975, in Geneva. Israel pledged to withdraw a further 12 to 26 miles east of the Mitla and Giddi passes and to return the oilfields at Abu Rudeis to Egypt. An American civilian group of no more than 200 would provide early warning from listening posts in the strategic passes. Egypt and Israel would maintain their own listening posts as well. The U.N.

Emergency Force (UNEF) would occupy the buffer zone between Israeli and Egyptian forces, and Egypt and Israel would be allowed to deploy no more than 8,000 soldiers, 75 tanks, and 60 artillery pieces along the front immediately behind their side of the buffer zone. Egypt would allow the passage of nonmilitary cargo through the Suez Canal for Israel, and Israel would receive increased military, political, and economic assistance from the United States. Perhaps most important of all, Egypt and Israel undertook to settle "the conflict between them and in the Middle East" by peaceful means, and not to resort to "the threat or use of force or military blockade against each other."

Progress toward the conclusion of the interim agreement on Sinai had been accompanied by a steady warming of relations between Egypt and the United States, a trend that eventually ended in Egypt's reversal of alliances from the Soviet Union to the United States. There was an Egyptian-U.S. summit in Salzburg, Austria on June 1, for example, involving Ford, Kissinger, and Sisco on the American side and Sadat, Mubarak, and Fahmy on the Egyptian. As Egypt drew closer to the United States its relations with the Soviet Union worsened. The Soviet Union refused to attend the ceremony in September marking the conclusion of the Sinai accord and condemned Sadat for having betrayed the long alliance between Egypt and the Soviet Union. On October 25, on the eve of what proved to be a very successful trip by Sadat to the United States, the Soviet Communist party newspaper Pravda recalled the repeated examples of Soviet support for Egypt, and stressed the military aid given in 1955 and during the wars of 1967 and 1973. In earlier attacks Moscow had rebuked Sadat for resurrecting capitalism in Egypt and for having made secret commitments to the United States in connection with the Sinai agreement. Sadat publicly denied one such report — that he had closed down the Voice of Palestine radio station in Cairo because of a secret promise to the United States — and accused the Soviets of trying to stimulate opposition to him in the Arab world. Sadat also continued to complain that the Soviets had refused to deliver the military equipment Egypt had requested. At one point in mid-September Sadat said publicly that he had ordered four MIG-25 aircraft out of Egypt, ostensibly because their pilots had refused to fly reconnaissance missions near Israeli positions in the Sinai. This proved, Sadat said, that the Soviets were in Egypt for reasons other than protecting Egyptian security.(21)

If there were little but hard feelings between Moscow and Cairo in 1975, Soviet-Libyan relations blossomed. Premier Kosygin visited Libya in May. New agreements were signed. Large shipments of Soviet weapons began arriving, and Libyan policy began to fall into step with Soviet policy in the Middle East and Africa. Understandably, Libya's relations with Egypt and Sudan worsened; they were already bad with Tunisia because of the failed merger and worse with Morocco because of Libyan intervention in the Spanish

Table 1. Value of Arms Transfers and Total Imports, 1969-1978, by Country

Year	1969	1970	1971	1972	1973	1974	1975
Algeria							
Arms Imports	16	46	58	14	53	24	100
Total Imports	1640	1946	1807	2103	3215	5193	6689
Arms Imports / Total Imports(%)	0.9	2.3	3.2	0.6	1.6	0.4	1.4
Egypt							
Arms Imports	178	1004	514	776	1134	280	389
Total Imports	1036	1215	1350	1269	1224	2868	4380
Arms Imports / Total Imports(%)	17.2	82.5	38.0	61.1	92.6	9.7	8.8
Israel							
Arms Imports	259	355	382	381	307	1189	835
Total Imports	2712	3228	3512	3500	5661	6636	6680
Arms Imports / Total Imports(%)	9.5	11.0	10.8	10.8	5.4	17.9	12.5
Libya							
Arms Imports	32	92	146	183	240	402	612
Total Imports	1098	857	1039	1468	2420	3369	3943
Arms Imports / Total Imports(%)	2.9	10.8	14.1	12.5	9.9	11.9	15.5
Saudi Arabia							
Arms Imports	129	46	29	155	106	414	278
Total Imports	1220	1098	1202	1609	2637	3489	4692
Arms Imports / Total Imports(%)	10.6	4.2	2.4	9.6	4.0	11.8	5.9

1976	1977	1978	Total*	1969–1973	1974–1978	1974–1978 1969–1973
338	460	581	1690	187	1590	8.50
5645	7125	7279				
5.9	6.4	7.9				
158	220	214	4867	3606	1261	0.35
4028	4816	6267				
3.9	4.5	3.4				
1058	1100	884	6750	1684	5066	3.01
5996	5787	6891				
17.6	19.0	12.8				
1058	1200	1768	6033	993	5040	5.08
3398	3782	5719				
31.1	31.7	30.9				
497	925	930	3509	465	3044	6.5
9199	14656	21274				
5.4	6.3	4.3				

*Millions of constant 1977 dollars.

Source: World Military Expenditures and Arms Transfers, 1969–1978 (Washington: U.S. Arms Control and Disarmament Agency, December 1980).

Table 2. Total Arms Transfers of Major Suppliers, 1974-1978, by Recipient Country

Supplier	Algeria	Egypt	Israel	Libya	Saudi Arabia
Totals*	1,500	1,200	4,800	5,000	3,000
United States	--	60	4,600	5	1,500
Soviet Union	1,200	430	--	3,400	--
France	10	260	20	270	280
United Kingdom	--	110	60	20	725
Federal Republic of Germany	280	170	--	140	20
Czechoslovakia	--	30	--	180	--
Italy	10	10	30	330	90
Poland	--	--	--	220	--
People's Republic of China	--	40	--	--	--
Canada	--	--	--	--	--
Others	40	50	5	350	380

*Millions of current dollars.
Source: World Military Expenditures, 1969-1978 (Washington: U.S. Arms Control and Disarmament Agency, December 1980).

Sahara. Qaddafi was also active in Lebanon. He spent lavishly during the Lebanese War of 1975-76. Initially he supported the Palestinians and later shifted his backing to carefully chosen Lebanese Muslim factions.

Kosygin arrived in Tripoli on May 12 and stayed for three days. When he left he had laid the basis for extensive economic, technical, political, and military cooperation between Libya and the Soviet Union. The two most notable agreements were for the sale of a very large amount of military equipment to Libya, worth $800 million according to <u>Pravda</u>, worth much more according to Egyptian and U.S. sources, and, two weeks later, a Soviet pledge to build a nuclear research reactor for Libya of 2-10 megawatt capacity and to train Libyan scientists in atomic physics. The nuclear agreement followed by about six weeks a warning by the director of the U.S. Arms Control and Disarmament Agency, Fred Ikle, that Libya was among a group of nations seeking nuclear weapons, a search being conducted under the cover of the peaceful use of nuclear technology.(22)

In 1975 Libyan foreign policy overlapped with that of the Soviet Union because of the start of a massive military aid program and Qaddafi's opposition to Sadat's Egypt. But there was at least one other important area of convergence. Libya had recognized East Germany in June 1973 and North Korea in January 1974. In February 1974 Romania and Libya established diplomatic relations and concluded several bilateral agreements. There followed the April meeting with Podgorny and Jalloud's trip to Moscow. Then in March 1975, two months before Kosygin's visit Libya recognized North Vietnam.(23) Following the major commitment of Soviet military and political support to Libya, these countries, and particularly East Germany and Cuba, another close Soviet ally, would prove to be major sources of instruction in advanced military, police, and intelligence skills.

With Soviet aid increasing so dramatically the United States decided to stop its assistance to Libya. In late August the State Department informed Congressman Les Aspin that the U.S. government had prohibited the sale of eight cargo planes to Libya and had also declined to allow 56 Libyan technicians to come to the United States for training in the maintenance of the C-130 transports already owned by Libya.(24)

Libya and Algeria gave each other promises of political and military support as the year ran out. Presidents Boumedienne and Qaddafi met in southern Algeria on December 29 to coordinate their policies on the Spanish Sahara and the Palestine problem. The communique issued after their meeting stated that Libya and Algeria would regard an attack on one as an attack on both. This stand, presumably, was of some help to Algeria in its efforts to oppose Morocco's annexation of the Spanish Sahara. Morocco and Algeria had recently recalled their ambassadors and, according to news reports, Algeria had called up 100,000 men to strengthen its standing army of 55,000. The Algerian army had been ordered to the border with Morocco.(25)

Libya's search for outside assistance in 1976 revealed an increased reliance on the Soviet Union, although there remained a lingering engagement with France. Of particular importance was the willingness of the French to provide Libya with a nuclear power plant. This acquisition came as part of a group of agreements for economic and technical cooperation between Libya and France signed during the visit of French prime minister, Jacques Chirac, to Tripoli, March 20-22. The usual joint economic and technical commission was established, to meet alternately in Paris and Tripoli once a year, and provision was made to build cement and desalination plants. But the agreement to build one nuclear power plant was the controversial item. It was to be a 600 megawatt facility, but France would provide Libya no facilities for nuclear research and would not build the apparatus needed to produce heavy water, which might be used for nuclear weapons.(26) The United States had also agreed to sell Egypt two nuclear reactors in September 1976.(27) It should be noted that Libya's nuclear agreement with France came within ten days of the public disclosure by the U.S. Central Intelligence Agency that Israel had ten to twenty nuclear weapons "available for use."(28) The disclosure came during an ostensibly off-the-record CIA briefing for the American Institute of Aeronautics and Astronautics in Washington on March 11.

However, it was Libya's increased reliance on the Soviet Union that became most prominent in 1976. The growing Libyan dependency on the Soviet Union was apparent in the greatly increased arms sales, discussed earlier. But much more than arms was involved. On August 30, for example, barely two weeks after Egypt began a military build-up on its border with Libya, the official Soviet newspaper Pravda published an attack against Egypt for dividing the Arab world and urged Arab support for Libya.(29) Three days later, during the revolutionary anniversary parade in Tripoli, Soviet ground-to-ground Scud missiles were displayed for the first time, along with T-62 and T-54 tanks and other modern armaments.

The growing closeness between Moscow and Tripoli served as an alternative to good relations with Egypt for Brezhnev and Qaddafi and, in a sense, was a way of punishing Sadat for his indifference to them both. On March 15, Egypt had abrogated its alliance with the Soviet Union and was clearly determined to move much closer to the United States and Western Europe than it had in the past. For example, Sadat visited the United States, France, Britain, Germany, Italy, and Yugoslavia in late 1975 and early 1976, along with the oil-rich countries of the Gulf, in search of aid and arms. Even China was tapped by the Egyptians and agreed to supply thirty MIG engines and industrial spare parts.

Qaddafi visited Moscow December 6-9 and took his country into an even closer relationship with the Soviet Union. Agreements on shipping, economic and technical aid, and cultural cooperation were signed, and Soviet leaders made much of Qaddafi during his visit. An interesting development occurred during the visit, one that shows a good deal about the manner in which Brezhnev and Qaddafi sought to make use of one another. It is up to the reader to decide who had done what to whom in the high-powered transaction. On December 1 the chairman of Fiat, Giovanni Agnelli, announced that Libya would purchase a 9.6 percent interest in the Italian automobile company. A complicated $415 million deal had been worked out, but in essence, Libya agreed to pay $207 million for 30 million shares of Fiat common and preferred stock; to buy $104 million in convertible bonds maturing from 1978-82; and to loan Fiat $104 on terms well below prevailing interest rates for long-term loans. Agnelli then flew to Moscow December 9 and met Qaddafi. Agnelli denied next day that any of the $104 million loan would be used to finance the extensive Fiat undertakings in the Soviet Union. His denial was contradicted by the Italian Communist party newspaper, L'Unità, which stated that Fiat would not only use the Libyan money to pay for projects in the Soviet Union, but that Soviet officials had participated in the discussions between Qaddafi and Agnelli.(30)

There were two interesting developments in 1977 concerning Libya's quest for outside assistance. Fidel Castro paid a nine-day visit to Libya in March, and Qaddafi appealed to President Carter in June to join him in working for an improvement in U.S.-Libyan relations. Castro's visit was part of a Soviet diplomatic offensive in Africa. It overlapped the African tour of Soviet President Nikolai Podgorny, and Castro ended his travels by going to Moscow, arriving on the day Podgorny returned, for two days of talks with Brezhnev, Kosygin, and other top Kremlin leaders. Podgorny visited Tanzania, Zambia, Mozambique, and Somalia; Castro's itinerary, sometimes improvised at the last minute, was Algeria (March 1); Libya (March 1-10); South Yemen (March 10-12); Somalia (March 12-14); Ethiopia (March 14-16); Tanzania (March 17-21); Mozambique (March 21-23); Angola (March 23-31); Algeria (March 31-April 2); East Germany (April 2-4); Moscow (April 4-6). Little was said in public about the Cuban leader's visit to Libya. Castro and Qaddafi did sign the usual agreements to increase cultural, economic, and technical cooperation. Reporters were also told that the two had discussed the Ethiopian civil war. Their communique condemned "imperialist maneuvers against the Ethiopian revolution." They apparently were referring to Sudan's willingness to give asylum and diplomatic and material help to the rebels in Eritrea in northwestern Ethiopia.(31) Since one of the purposes of Castro's visit was to try to settle the dispute between Somalia and Ethiopia in order for them to form, with South Yemen, a bloc of radical states in the Red Sea area, it seems likely that Qaddafi and Castro spent part of their time trying to concert their policies toward the countries in the Horn of Africa. The plan for a radical coalition along the Red Sea coast of Africa was supported by the Soviet Union but opposed by Egypt, Sudan, Saudi Arabia, and the United States. The feud between Somalia and Ethiopia could not be patched up, and this left a large hole in the coalition.

Qaddafi's overture to the United States was accompanied by a request that the United States allow delivery of the eight C-130 transport aircraft purchased by Libya in 1973. Speaking at a celebration marking the seventh anniversary of the closing of

Wheelus Air Force Base, Qaddafi also proposed that the two countries restore ambassadorial representation at their embassies. The next day the State Department responded that in order for the United States to agree to a renewal of full diplomatic relations Libya would have to halt its support for international terrorism and begin to work for a Middle East peace settlement. The conditions were unacceptable to Qaddafi, of course, but neither side shut the door all the way. Qaddafi wanted the airplanes or at least wanted to outwit and embarrass the U.S. bureaucracy, and continued his pursuit of the planes, even to the point of hiring Billy Carter, the president's brother, as a lobbyist. When this became known a scandal blew up – inevitably known as the Billygate affair. Before Billygate, however, the two countries carried on a series of secret high-level exploratory talks. The United States was represented by Undersecretary of State David Newsom and Libya by its ambassador to the United Nations, Mohammed Kikhia.(32) Libya chose this moment to reach agreement on compensation with Texaco and Standard of California whose Libyan subsidiaries had been nationalized in 1973 and 1974. Each U.S. company would receive about $76 million in crude oil supplies in the ensuing fifteen months. The World Court had ruled earlier that the companies should be given compensation.(33) Libya may have been emboldened to ask for the C-130s by the decisions of the U.S. government to supply them to Sudan, Zaire, and Egypt.

The supply of arms to strengthen the nations on or near Libya's borders, such as Egypt, Sudan, Somalia, and Morocco, revealed one element of the Carter administration's response to Qaddafi. It was part of an overall response to instability and growing Soviet and Cuban intervention in Africa. Another part of the overall response – which would be revealed in the U.S. response to the Libyan invasion of Chad, as well – was shown during the invasion of Zaire's Shaba province from Angola in early March. This was to seek political solutions to disputes primarily through the initiatives of African nations without direct U.S. intervention. Thus, after the invasion when President Mobutu of Zaire appealed for Belgian and U.S. support, the U.S. responded with small amounts of "nonlethal" military equipment. The United States would send no arms and ammunition, and contemplated, according to a White House spokesman, "no dramatic change in the policy of military aid for Zaire."(34) Nigeria offered to mediate and sent its foreign minister, Brigadier General Joseph Garba, to Zaire and Angola. Meanwhile the invaders continued to advance. They were several thousand lightly armed irregulars who claimed to be members of the Congolese National Liberation Front, a remnant of the 1960s secessionist movement of Moise Tshombe. Finding no results from the Nigerian mediation and no answer to his appeal for aid from the OAU, President Mobutu turned to Morocco, Egypt, and Sudan. On April 8 King Hassan of Morocco agreed to send 1,500 troops to

Zaire, and France offered to transport them (short of aircraft France eventually had to ask the United States for help in completing the airlift). On April 10 President Sadat announced he was sending a military mission to Zaire, and the next day Nimeiry promised help from the Sudan to defeat the invasion. Fifty Egyptian pilots and mechanics reached Zaire May 2. Mobutu had accused the Soviet Union and Cuba of launching the invasion, and at the end of April he suspended relations with Cuba, East Germany, and the Soviet Union. Mobutu broke relations with East Germany on May 2. All three Communist countries denied involvement, and the Soviet ambassador in Paris informed French President Giscard d'Estaing of his country's opposition to the French/Moroccan intervention in Zaire. The arrival of the Moroccan contingents quickly reversed the course of the fighting in Shaba province, and the invaders were steadily pushed out of the country. The last towns held by the invaders were recaptured May 25-26.

In addition to the continued build-up of Soviet arms, Libya's quest for outside assistance in 1978 took several interesting turns. The deaths of two prominent East German officials on March 6 in a helicopter crash called attention to the increasing reliance of Libya on the Soviet bloc for technical and managerial help. East Germany in particular supplied advisors for Qaddafi's police and intelligence organizations. The dead Germans were Werner Lamberg and Paul Marhowski, both important figures in the ruling party of East Germany, the Socialist Unity Party. Lamberg was a member of the party executive, the Politburo. They died, according to Western press accounts, in what was meant to be an assassination attempt against Qaddafi. A number of arrests were made in the Libyan air force after the crash. The assassins apparently believed Qaddafi would also ride in the helicopter with the two Germans.(35)

The most intriguing development concerned the Soviet commitment on October 4 to supply Libya with a center for nuclear research. The deal included a 300,000 kilowatt reactor and a research center. Presumably there would be training for Libyan physicists in the Soviet Union. This arrangement came at a time of an escalating arms race in the region and increased awareness of Israel's possession of nuclear weapons and the likelihood of nuclear proliferation to its Arab neighbors. On January 26, for example, the U.S. Central Intelligence Agency declassified a document under the Freedom of Information Act which indicated that as early as 1974 the United States believed Israel possessed nuclear weapons. There had been repeated stories about Israel's nuclear arsenal over the years, notably a Time magazine report after the 1973 war, and a 1976 CIA briefing for American scientists, which had been leaked to journalists afterward by one of the audience. The declassified document was apparently the first official confirmation of Israel's possession of nuclear weapons. The document carried the date September 4, 1974, and was headed "Prospects for Further Proliferation of Nuclear Weapons." It also predicted that Egypt, among a number of other countries, would not acquire nuclear weapons in the next ten years, that is, not before 1984.(36)

5
ORGANIZING OPPOSITION TO PEACE

Within a week of taking office in late January 1977 the Carter administration responded to the desire of Syria, Egypt, and Saudi Arabia for a peace settlement in 1977. Putting his prestige and political future on the line, Carter was to spend the next eleven months attempting to fashion a set of agreements acceptable to all the parties to the Arab-Israeli conflict, including the Palestinians, and broad enough to allow a general conference to succeed.(1) Carter took a number of domestically costly steps, such as endorsing a "homeland" for the Palestinians, and for a time it looked as if he might pull it off. At one point, apparently, Carter even received word that the PLO was ready to accept Resolution 242, which could not be done without recognizing Israel.(2) The Carter administration was urging the PLO to accept 242 and then make the acceptance subject to whatever conditions it wished to raise. It was not to be. A warning came in March at the thirteenth session of the Palestine National Council (PNC), meeting in Cairo, when the Palestinian representatives once again endorsed the National Charter or Convenant of 1964, which condemns Israel's existence as illegal, and calls for its destruction by armed struggle. The PNC also adopted a new program, which rejected Resolution 242 and all negotiations based on it. Resolution 242 formed a cornerstone of both U.S. and Israeli policy for the settlement of the Arab-Israeli conflict, although the two allies interpreted it differently.

The essence of the U.S.-Israeli disagreement was over how far Israel had to withdraw in the West Bank, Gaza, and Golan in order to comply with Resolution 242. Israeli Labor governments had envisioned substantial withdrawals, but the newly-elected Begin government took a very different stand and was not prepared to withdraw nearly as far as its predecessors.(3) Nor was it prepared to negotiate directly with the PLO. However, by October the United States and Israel had agreed on most of the procedures for the peace conference at Geneva. According to the document read in the Knesset by Foreign Minister Dayan on October 13 Palestinians would be allowed to participate in the peace conference, but only as members of a united Arab delegation and a working group on the West Bank and Gaza. Egypt reacted to this by demanding that the PLO be specifically included in the guidelines for the conference. The PLO flatly rejected any procedure that excluded its representatives who alone, in its view, had the right to speak for the Palestinian people. Syria declared it would "never go to Geneva without the PLO" and called for an Iraqi-Syrian-Palestinian alliance against Israel. Qaddafi attacked the U.S. plan and, predictably, voiced the most extreme protest by calling on Lebanon, Syria, Jordan, and Egypt to allow the Palestinians to attack Israel across their frontiers.(4) In an effort to disrupt the movement toward a peace conference the PLO fired Katyusha rockets into the northern Israeli village of Nahariya, on November 6 and 8, killing three. This prompted the inevitable Israeli reprisal on November 9, which on this occasion took the form of severe air bombing against targets in and around Tyre and two small towns to the south, Hanniye and Azziye. Over 100 people were killed in the Israeli attacks. It was all too familiar. There would be more fighting, more death, and barring a miracle, all the progress toward peace of the past year would be lost. At this point Sadat announced his willingness to go to the Israeli parliament itself if that would make it possible to hold a Geneva peace conference. Israel responded with a formal invitation, and the historic visit took place.

Sadat took his remarkable decision primarily because he had assumed the role of peacemaker and was convinced that peace would serve the best interests of his people and the entire Arab world. This is clear in his words before the Knesset. "Ring the bells for your sons," he said:

> Tell them that those wars were the last of wars and the end of sorrows. Tell them that we are entering upon a new beginning, a new life, a life of love, prosperity, freedom and peace. . . . I have chosen to set aside all precedents and traditions known by warring peoples. . . . Despite all that the decision was inspired by all the clarity and purity of belief and with all the true passions of my people's will and intentions. . . .

Because he saw himself as a peacemaker, Sadat was undoubtedly sincere in his claim not to have decided to visit Israel by calculating what his visit might achieve. In his words: "I announce before you that I have not thought of carrying out this initiative from the precepts of what could be achieved during the visit. And I have come here to deliver a message." At the same time he was acutely aware of what would be lost if the existing momentum toward peace were dissipated. For Egypt a sterile conference in Geneva would be as harmful as no conference at all. There would be no second chance for peace. Sadat had no fall-back position left. Moreover, economic recovery for Egypt would fail, because the conditions necessary to draw massive amounts of investment from the West and the conservative Arab states would not be established. Worse, the heightening tensions would justify still heavier military expenditures and could even lead to another war with Israel. With this in mind, he traveled to Jerusalem.

The visit stunned the watching world. The superpowers disagreed about what Sadat had done. The United States strongly supported Sadat's initiative, and the Soviet Union condemned it as a scheme designed by the United States to divide the Arab world and lead Egypt to a separate peace with Israel. However, virtually all the Arab states were against it. Their reactions ranged from Jordan's faint praise to the Rejectionists' fulminations. Libya belonged to the second group, and the nearly universal negative Arab reaction gave the group a broad stage on which to act. Only Sudan, Tunisia, Morocco, and Oman expressed support for the visit.

Libya's protest was the most extreme in the Arab world. Qaddafi's plan clearly was to attempt to prejudice the reactions of all other Arab governments. On November 18, with an advance party of Egyptians already in Israel to prepare for the visit, Libya demanded the ouster of Egypt from the Arab League. Next day, to coincide with the start of Sadat's visit, Libya broke diplomatic relations with Egypt. The Palestinian Resistance also reacted strongly. Arafat's Al Fatah condemned the visit. The PLO on November 20 called for "maximum sanctions and complete isolation" to be imposed on Egypt. Al Sa'iqah, the Syrian-backed Palestinian group, demanded Sadat's overthrow. Palestinians attacked Egyptian embassies in Beirut and Athens. By contrast, Syria's reaction was measured. Assad rejected Sadat's actions, but put his criticism in less extreme terms. "There are divergences over the methods of working for peace," Assad said. Sadat's visit had made the convening of the Geneva conference more difficult.(5)

Libya's prominence in the organization of Arab opposition to Sadat showed in the choice of Tripoli as the site of a meeting of Rejectionists to concert their policies. Assad of Syria announced plans to hold the meeting on November 27 in response to an Egyptian invitation to all parties to the Arab-Israeli conflict except the PLO to come to Cairo to prepare for the Geneva conference. Ultimately only Israel and the United States accepted the invitation to come to Cairo. Sadat was unconcerned. "If no one is coming, okay, I shall deal with whoever comes," he told CBS television. Even if Egypt were the only Arab nation to go to Geneva, he would reject a separate peace, conclude a comprehensive agreement with Israel, and the Arab nations could then accept or reject it.

The Tripoli meeting opened on December 2. It lasted five days and was attended by the heads of government of Syria (Hafez Asad), Libya (Muammar Qaddafi), Algeria (Houari Boumedienne), and South Yemen (Salem Rubayi Ali). The PLO was represented by its chief, Yasir Arafat, and the leader of the PFLP, George Habash. Iraq sent a lower-ranking delegate, Taka Yassin Tezrawi, a member of the Iraqi Revolutionary Council. The participants took a number of important steps that were outlined in the Tripoli Declaration. They agreed: (1) to establish an Arab "front for resistance and confrontation"; (2) to "freeze" their relations with Egypt (Libya had demanded a total rupture); (3) to boycott all Egyptian individuals and firms dealing with Israel; (4) to challenge Egypt's membership in the Arab League and to seek the removal of Arab League headquarters from Cairo; (5) and to consider any attack on any member of the front as an attack against all.

The silences of this program are eloquent. There is no rejection of a negotiated settlement with Israel, and no decisive and final break with Egypt. Prior to the conference only Assad of Syria had reacted in this measured way, and it is clear that his views were most influential in shaping the Tripoli Declaration. The program as written was an attempt to set terms that would win the widest possible acceptance in the Arab world – across the spectrum from Saudi Arabia to the PLO – and, at the same time, offer the greatest possible incentive for Egypt to turn away from its new course of reconciliation with Israel. If Egypt refused, there would be time later for more severe punishments.

The PLO agreed to this approach, but it was too much for Iraq. Shortly before the end of the conference the Iraqi delegate walked out and refused to join in the Tripoli Declaration. More, much more ought to be done, he told a news conference. At a minimum Resolutions 242 and 338 ought to be rejected as the basis for negotiation and settlement with Israel. It was Assad's responsibility, he added: "He still believes in a policy of peaceful surrender and negotiations."(6) Sadat answered his opponents by breaking diplomatic relations with all five Arab countries, recalling the Egyptian ambassador from Moscow, and closing some of the cultural centers and consulates in Egypt of the Soviet Union, Czechoslovakia, Hungary, East Germany, and Poland. Meanwhile the United States attempted and failed to persuade Syria, Lebanon, Jordan, and Saudi Arabia to support Sadat openly.

The Cairo conference opened on December 14 with only representatives of the United States, Israel, and the United Nations attending along with those of the host country. On December 25-26 Sadat and Begin met in Ismailia, Egypt and agreed to raise the Cairo conference to the level of foreign ministers and to establish two permanent committees – military and political – to be led by the two countries' defense and foreign ministers and to act under the auspices of the larger conference. The military committee would meet in Cairo, and its political counterpart would meet in Jerusalem starting in January. The military committee would deal with the stages of Israeli withdrawal and the measures to be taken – zones that were demilitarized and in which forces were limited, surveillance, grievances – and the political committee would deal with the nature of peace between Israel and Egypt.

Two days after his meeting with President Sadat, Prime Minister Begin announced his plan for the West Bank and Gaza. This step completed the political picture, for Sadat's concerns transcended the peace with Israel and embraced the Palestinian question, as well. Despite Israel's desire to keep the two questions separate, Israeli plans for the occupied territories necessarily became an integral part of the negotiations with Egypt. Begin's plan was to abolish Israeli military administration in the West Bank and Gaza and allow local self-governing institutions to be established by the Palestinians in the two regions. Begin had given the plan to Sadat at their summit in Ismailia.

Most Arab states had condemned the meeting at Ismailia, and Begin's announcement only increased their antagonism and condemnation. Libya announced that Sadat "will sign everything our enemy Israel wants him to." The PLO declared that Sadat had abandoned the Palestinian cause, killed a West Bank mayor it accused of collaborating with Israel, and exploded a bomb in the Israeli town of Natanya, killing two. As 1977 ended, the Rejectionists announced plans to meet in January in Algiers or Baghdad to intensify their opposition to Sadat.

By comparison with the wide-open field Qaddafi gained after Sadat's trip to Jerusalem, the other possibilities for expanding Libya's influence were small and uninteresting. Libya continued to offer Malta political leverage in its dealings with NATO. In late November Maltese Premier Dom Mintoff threatened to sign a defense treaty with Libya unless France and Italy gave Malta the economic and military aid it needed to offset the loss of revenues and support from the closing of the last British and NATO bases in the country in 1979. In February Qaddafi supported the seizure of power by Colonel Mengistu Haile Mariam in Ethiopia, who promptly announced plans to seek aid from the Soviet bloc. Qaddafi later concerted his support for Mengistu with Fidel Castro during a ten-day visit to Libya by the Cuban leader in March. The war between Somalia and Ethiopia over the Ogaden region put the Soviet Union in a bind because it was supplying arms to both countries. By September the Soviets had decided to favor Ethiopia, even if it cost them their formerly close ties to Somalia, which it did. The Soviet Union agreed to send massive amounts of arms to Ethiopia, and Cuba and East Germany contributed military, technical, and medical advisors.(7) Large numbers of Soviet military personnel would soon be sent to Ethiopia, as well.

Early in 1977 Qaddafi obtained the release of Pierre and Francoise Claustre, French citizens who had been held captive by Toubou rebels in northern Chad for months. The rebels, led by Goukouni Oueddei, of Frolinat, had taken Madame Claustre prisoner in April 1974 and had then seized her husband who had come to seek her release in August 1975. Reports in Paris said that the decision of the French government to release the Palestinian terrorist Abu Daoud had contributed to the safe release of the Claustres. The French counterintelligence service, Direction de la surveillance du territoire (DST) had arrested Daoud, who had taken part in the Munich massacre, on January 7, while he was in Paris with a PLO delegation to attend the funeral of Mamdouh Saleh, who had been murdered on January 3. Daoud's release from a Jordanian prison had been demanded by the terrorists who attacked the Saudi embassy in Khartoum and murdered three diplomats. Inexplicably, the French government had found a procedural loophole on which to base its denial of West Germany's request for extradition. The French rejected Israel's request as without legal foundation, and Daoud went free. Other news reports in Paris at this time indicated that Libya had shifted its support away from Hissene Habre and to Goukouni Oueddei, both rebel Frolinat leaders in Chad.(8) In early November Qaddafi offered to mediate the release of six French technicians kidnapped by Polisario guerrillas the previous May.(9) Later the same month, the leaders of Algeria, Niger, and Libya met in Tripoli and established a commission to examine the possible ways of increasing regional cooperation between their countries. The three had made a similar agreement at a meeting in Algeria in April 1976. Government sources in Tripoli indicated that Libya hoped the cooperative relationship would soon include Mali, Chad, and "other brother countries."(10)

Camp David was the main international event of 1978. For once the initiative was in the hands of the peacemakers in the Middle East. As a result of Sadat's visit to Jerusalem a break had occurred in the decades-long build-up of enmity and mistrust between Arab and Jew. The Rejectionists — both within the Palestinian movement and the larger Arab world — could only react to the new shape given reality by the bold Egyptian moves and their sequels from Israel and the United States. But they reacted fiercely, and Qaddafi shared their resolve to destroy the Camp David agreements. Libya's participation in and leadership of the spreading determination throughout the Arab world to isolate and punish Sadat's Egypt and to defeat and overthrow the Camp David agreements were the main steps Qaddafi took in 1978 to weaken the West.

At the Tripoli summit of December 1977 the Rejectionists had decided to meet again to coordinate their moves against Egypt, Israel, and the United States. That meeting took place February 2-4 in Algiers and included the leaders of Syria, Libya, Algeria, South Yemen, and representatives of the PLO. Iraq stayed away. Little information was made public about the discussions that occurred or any agreements that might have been reached by the participants. According to a Palestinian spokesman, the five members of the front of "Steadfastness and Rejection" had agreed the week before the conference to the reopening of Palestinian military camps in Syria, which had been closed two years earlier during the first phases of the Syrian intervention in Lebanon.

Meanwhile, Libya and Syria drew closer to the Soviet Union and increased their supplies of Soviet arms. Jalloud paid an official visit to Moscow in mid-February during which he informed Soviet leaders of the results of the Algiers summit. He then extended his visit for five days in order to be on hand when Assad arrived in Moscow for a two-day visit on February 21. During Assad's visit Soviet leaders agreed to large increases in military aid for Syria. Unconfirmed press reports suggested that Jalloud had offered Assad $1 billion for the purchase of Soviet arms. An arms race was underway in the Middle East, with huge transfers of arms going not only to Soviet clients, Syria, Algeria, and Libya, but also to American clients, Saudi Arabia, Iran, Israel, and, increasingly, Egypt. On February 24, for example, the Carter administration proposed the first sale of military equipment to Egypt (F-5 aircraft) in history. The sale was to be part of a much larger "package" that would send even larger numbers of the more advanced F-15s to Saudi Arabia and F-15s and F-16s to Israel. The package was itself an unintended comment on the arms race in the region. While the Carter administration was sending more arms to Egypt, Sudan, Morocco, Israel, and Saudi Arabia — all opponents of Qaddafi — it rejected Libya's request to ship the eight C-130s ordered in 1973. On February 21, with Jalloud still in Moscow, the State Department announced the denial of export licenses for the transports and the withdrawal of approval of Lockheed's maintenance of the C-130s already in Libya. The decisions were taken, according to the department, because of Libya's "continuing support for international terrorism."(11)

At the semiannual meeting of the Council of the Arab League in Cairo March 27-29 an effort was made to devise a procedure for settling the disagreements in the Arab world caused by Sadat's opening to Israel. The council resolved to convene a summit conference to respond appropriately to Israel's recent large-scale invasion and occupation of southern Lebanon. However, the price of Arab disunity was clear. Given the widespread Arab opposition to Sadat's initiative the council had to recognize that any call for a summit — even to address as grave a question as the invasion of Lebanon — would be rejected by many member governments. Five states had boycotted the current council session: Syria, Iraq, Libya, Algeria, South Yemen. Therefore it was necessary first to establish a "committee of solidarity," which would try to prepare the "necessary climate" for a summit. Sudan's President Nimeiry was chosen to head the committee.

The summer passed without any decrease in Arab opposition to Sadat. But Egypt and Israel worked closely with the United States and continued to narrow their differences. In early July, for example, prior to a special foreign ministers' conference at Leeds castle south of London, the Egyptian government released its response to the Begin plan to grant local autonomy to Palestinians living in the West Bank and Gaza. As might be imagined the two plans were miles apart. The Israeli government envisioned an end not to military control of the two areas but to Israeli military government there and its replacement by representative local Palestinian authorities with severely limited powers of self-rule: education, health, sewers, and the like. Egypt countered with a proposal for total Israeli withdrawal and Palestinian self-determination after a five-year transitional period, which would be supervised by Jordan and Egypt in the West Bank and Gaza respectively.

These differences produced a deadlock in the negotiations, which wasn't broken at Leeds. Still, the two sides were talking to one another. This alone was unbearable to many Arabs. As usual, Libya found a method to take this sentiment to an extreme. After the Egyptian soccer team defeated Libya 1-0 at the African Games in Algiers on July 22, the Libyan team attacked the Egyptians with clubs. The Algerian police had to be called to stop the fighting, in which two Egyptian players were injured. Libya was expelled from the tournament the next day, and on July 24 the Egyptian government announced that in the future it would refuse to allow its athletes to participate in contests held in any of the five Rejectionist states.

The positions of the Arab governments had varied from dismay to defiance in their opposition to Sadat's new dealings with Israel. As a result of their disunity – Iraq's rejection of the Rejectionists is the perfect symbol – little in the way of sanctions had actually been imposed on Egypt by the end of the summer, and no unified Arab stand had been developed that might become the positive side of the rejection of Sadat's peace plans. Camp David gave all Sadat's opponents another chance.

After Camp David the Arabs' outrage and chagrin at the near certainty of a separate Egyptian-Israeli peace carried them further and Egypt was punished diplomatically and economically. The disdain and even arrogance that many Egyptians feel toward Arabs, whom they will refer to in unguarded moments as backward, uncivilized, and helpless (without Egypt), could not disguise the impact of the sanctions. The punishments hurt, not enough to force Sadat to change course, but enough to give pause and to sow a strong desire for reconciliation among many Egyptians in high office. Nonetheless, not even Camp David could bring the Arab governments together. They could only agree on punishing Egypt, and even here they were not unanimous. The essentially negative consensus in the Arab world – agreement on what to be against, not on what to be for – continued, as shown by the failure of Saudi Prince Fahd's peace plan (itself unacceptable to Israel) to win widespread Arab support in 1981.

The Camp David summit began on September 6. On September 7 Syrian Foreign Minister Abdel Halim Khaddam condemned the meeting and urged the Arab governments to sign alliances with the Soviet Union if the U.S. and Israel concluded a defense treaty. The idea of a U.S.-Israeli pact had been mentioned by officials of both countries as a way of encouraging Israel to withdraw from the Sinai and make peace with Egypt. The Camp David summit ended on September 17 with agreement on two documents: a framework for peace between Israel and Egypt and a framework for a general peace in the Middle East, which included a number of guidelines agreeable to Egypt and Israel for the handling of the West Bank and Gaza. In essence, the Begin plan was to be applied to these territories with the exception that at the end of the five-year transitional period Israel, Egypt, Jordan, and Palestinians from the West Bank and Gaza (nominated and elected in ways controlled by Israel) could open the question of who possessed sovereignty over the two areas for negotiation. The five-year transition begins only with the establishment of the local Palestinian self-governing authorities. That clock has yet to run.(12) In support of the agreements the United States undertook to provide major economic, military, technical, and diplomatic assistance to both countries.

With denunciations of Sadat, Israel, and the United States issuing from Arab capitals and Moscow, the five members of the Steadfastness and Rejection Front met in Damascus to lay plans on September 20. At the end of the four-day conference the front announced that all five were breaking all political and economic ties with Egypt. They denounced the Camp David agreements as null and void and pledged to work for their downfall with the cooperation of friendly states, particularly the Soviet Union. They promised to establish joint military and political commands – no details were provided – and requested the Arab League to move its headquarters out of Egypt. Qaddafi played a major part in the conference. Midway through the conference, for example, Qaddafi and Arafat went to Jordan to reinforce Hussein's initial reluctance to join in the Camp David process (bilateral negotiations on peace with Israel and Egypt-Israel-Jordan-Palestinian negotiations about the West Bank and Gaza). Arafat, Hussein, and Qaddafi met in Mafraq, a town in northern Jordan, on September 22. Next day Hussein said he had been "absolutely shattered" by Egypt's unilateral peacemaking. Several days later, after meetings with Assad, Hussein said he and the Syrian leader saw "eye-to-eye" in their opposition to Camp David. Back in Damascus, Qaddafi disagreed with Arafat about funding the military activities of the Steadfastness and Rejection Front. Journalists reported that Qaddafi had rejected a plan for Libya to donate a fixed percentage of its oil revenues for war purposes, and that the Libyan leader had sharply disagreed with Arafat about this.(13)

The reaction to Camp David was so strong it brought Syria and Iraq together, although not for long. After a trip to Saudi Arabia Assad, who had taken a very active part in organizing Arab opposition to Camp David, went to Baghdad October 24-26. The Syrian leader and Iraqi president, Ahmed Hassan al-Bakr, agreed to establish a bilateral defense and foreign affairs committee at the ministerial level, which, obligatorily, was presented as working toward "a full military union." A "joint steering body" meeting every three months would supervise military cooperation. There were to be political, economic, and cultural committees, as well. The communique was silent about Iraq's earlier offer to provide a fund of $9 billion to aid the states bordering Israel. Nor was there any mention of the two countries' ideological disputes with one another, their territorial and riparian claims, or charges and countercharges of terrorism against each other.(14)

The first sanctions against Egypt began to make themselves felt at a summit meeting of the Arab League in Baghdad, November 5-9. Egypt was not invited to attend. All twenty other Arab League members attended. The summit was plainly meant to deter Sadat from making peace with Israel. Therefore, although the Arab leaders agreed to impose political and economic sanctions on Egypt, they kept the resolutions secret, waiting and hoping for the peace negotiations to collapse. If they succeeded, the sanctions would come into effect. The communique issued after the summit reaffirmed the resolutions adopted at Algiers (1973) and Rabat (1974), stated that no government could unilaterally attempt to solve the Palestinian question or the Arab-Israel conflict, maintained that all solutions had to be approved at an Arab summit conference, explicitly rejected the Camp David agreements, and called on Egypt to abrogate them and to refuse to sign any treaty with Israel. The minimum Arab terms for peace according to the document were total Israeli withdrawal from all territories occupied in 1967, including Arab Jerusalem, and the establishment of an independent Palestinian state. The conference also resolved to hold a summit meeting every November.(15) The summit then sent a low-level delegation to Cairo to treat with Sadat. The Egyptian leader refused to see them.

Qaddafi was active at Baghdad. He sided with Arafat, among others, against the moderates led by Saudi Arabia, but failed to win immediate sanctions against Egypt. Libya also joined the Saudis and Iraqis in pledging to establish a $3.5 billion fund to be renewed annually for the use of the front-line states endangered by Egypt's detente with Israel. Implicitly, the funds would be available to Egypt if Sadat were to recant. Thus incentives as well as sanctions were to be used to persuade Sadat to reconsider and break off the talks with Israel.

The other measures taken by Qaddafi in 1978 to weaken the West were less spectacular than his leadership of the effort to isolate Sadat and overturn the Camp David agreements. However, his support for the revolt against the Shah of Iran involved him in an internal upheaval whose outcome cost the West far more dearly than the relatively mild sanctions imposed on Egypt. The developing peace treaty between Egypt and Israel was too firmly rooted in the enduring military and economic interests of both nations to be derailed even by strong external and internal pressures. Such was not the case with the shah's regime, which would collapse before a combination of internal and external destabilization within the next year. Libya's aid to the shah's opponents was administered in cooperation with the PLO, according to European and U.S. intelligence sources. On November 22, 1978, for example, an aide to Qaddafi, Salah el-Din, and the head of the PLO political department, Farouk Khaddoumi, met the Ayatollah Ruholla Khomeini in Paris to offer him Libyan arms and money. Qaddafi also offered the Iranian religious leader the use of Libyan radio facilities for broadcasts to Iran.(16)

Qaddafi also continued his flirtation with Malta, and the flamboyant Maltese Premier Dom Mintoff, continued to try to use his "Libyan option" to coerce the Europeans into sweetening their aid packages for his country. Mintoff asked Algeria, Libya, France, and Italy to ensure the island nation's economic well-being after the departure of the British in 1979 and the expiration of the country's agreements with NATO in 1978. Boumedienne of Algeria visited Malta on January 3, 1978 to discuss aid. Qaddafi went to Malta July 3-4 for the same purpose. In the communique issued after the Libyan leader's visit Qaddafi assured Mintoff that Libya would provide the military, economic, and political assistance needed to make certain that Malta would not have to allow the return of foreign military bases to its soil. Mintoff played the obvious card and threatened to rely solely on aid from Arab governments. But the ace was getting old, and neither France nor Italy took the threats seriously.

For the Palestinian Resistance and, indeed, the entire Arab world, the change in international terrorism in 1978 was an ominous one. There were attacks against Israel, notably the poisoning of shipments of Israeli oranges to the Netherlands and West Germany in January; a Fatah raid near Tel Aviv that killed thirty-seven; an attack on El Al passengers at Orly airport, France; and an attack on an El Al crew bus in London, killing a stewardess and wounding nine. The Arab Revolutionary Army Palestine Command claimed credit for the poisoned oranges, a blow against the Israeli economy, it said, and the Popular front for the Liberation of Palestine Special Operations, a splinter of PFLP, claimed the attack on the bus. But most of the violence by Palestinian terrorists was turned against rival factions of the Resistance or against Arab governments rather than Israel. Because of Libya's entanglement in the terror network this raises the question of Libyan instigation of some of these attacks, particularly in the case of Abu Nidal and his Revolutionary Council and Black June organization. A partial list of the Palestinian and Arab targets struck would include: the murder of Yusuf Siba'i, editor of El Ahram in Nicosia (February 18); the assassination of the PLO representative to Kuwait, Ali Yasin, in Kuwait (June); attacks by the PLO and Fatah on Iraqi diplomatic personnel and installations in Beirut, Brussels, London, Paris, and Karachi, Pakistan (July); the murder of two PLO representatives, Izz al-Din Qalaq and Adnam Hammad in Paris and an attack on the PLO office in Islamabad, Pakistan, killing four (August).(17) Finally, in late August, with the mediation of Mohammed Yazid, Algerian ambassador to Iraq, Abu Nidal, leader of the Revolutionary Council and Black June organizations announced in Baghdad that his followers would halt their attacks on Fatah, which had been strongly supported by the Iraqi government.

> The Revolutionary Council operates as an agent of the Iraqi government, and has been the cutting edges of a series of assassination operations aimed at moderates within Fatah and the PLO. [It] has extensive ties (again growing out of its Black September origins) to both the PFLP and Libya. . . . Abu Nidal's attacks [were] aimed at splitting Fatah leadership . . . in destroying any moderate voices within the Resistance. PLO spokesmen such as Hammami, al-Qalaq, and Ali Yasin . . . who openly argued for some peaceful solution to the Palestine problem, including some accommodations with Israel, were targeted by Abu Nidal's agents. . . .
>
> In the Arab context, Abu Nidal's group functions as a surrogate for Iraqi Arab world strategies. Abu Nidal's headquarters are also those of the Rejection Front (although George Habash is its titular head), and in this sense he plays a pivotal role in Iraqi orchestration of opposition to Arab moderate leaders. Even more, Abu Nidal's men, operating under the name Black June, have carried out a number of attacks on Syrian and Jordanian targets.(18)

Abu Nidal's cessation of attacks against Fatah and the temporary reconciliation between Syria and Iraq should be seen as part of an effort by Iraq and Libya, the paymasters of the vicious Palestinian splinter groups, to create a coalition of all Arab governments to oppose Sadat's peace policy. It certainly was not done for humanitarian reasons. The summer of terror aimed at Fatah and Fatah's terrorist reprisals also served to show the ease with which Libya could use its contacts with Abu Nidal and other groups in the terror network to employ violence against proponents of a negotiated settlement with Israel or closer relations with the West.

The signature of a peace treaty between Egypt and Israel on March 26, 1979 strengthened Libyan and Arab opposition to President Sadat and to Camp David, as the frameworks for bilateral and multilateral peace agreements between Israel and its neighbors were known. Even Morocco joined in the condemnation of the peace treaty, leaving only Oman and Sudan in favor of the Egyptian leader's initiative. King Hussein played an active part in the orchestration of Arab opposition to the treaty. On March 17 he met Yasir Arafat on Jordanian soil at El Mafraq air base 70 kilometers northeast of Amman. They agreed to constitute a Jordanian-PLO committee to organize opposition to the treaty, and the king offered to allow the opening of a PLO office in Amman, the first formal act of this kind since the expulsion of the PLO from Jordan in 1971. On March 22, Hussein went to Saudi Arabia for discussions with the Saudi leadership, and he made similar visits to Damascus and Baghdad on March 26. Thus, the Conference of Foreign and Economic Ministers that opened in Baghdad on March 27 had, in a sense, been organized by Hussein, who had presumably been seeking a common denominator of opposition to Egypt satisfactory to the leading Arab opponents of the peace treaty. Hussein doubtless also meant his actions to convey an unmistakable signal to Washington and throughout the Arab world that Jordan would never be a party to Camp David. Making certain no one misunderstood, Hussein recalled his ambassador from Cairo on March 27; Egypt recalled its ambassador to Jordan two days later. By May, of the eighteen Arab governments which attended the Baghdad conference seventeen had broken diplomatic relations with Cairo; only Somalia had not taken this step. Oman and Sudan (and Egypt) did not attend. Egypt had already broken relations with Syria, Iraq, Algeria, South Yemen, and Libya in December 1977 over the Tripoli conference, called in opposition to Sadat's Israel visit, and the formation of the Steadfastness and Rejection Front. The conference in Baghdad lasted four days, March 27-31. Its purpose was to implement the decisions in principle taken at the November 1978 summit: in a word, to punish Egypt. There were harsh disputes over how severely Egypt should be punished. Libya's approach was two-sided, a combination of "I-told-you-so" and a demand for the most damaging possible sanctions against Egypt, short of going to war.

Qaddafi sang the "I-told-you-so" theme in a message to Arab kings and presidents broadcast by Tripoli radio on the opening day of the conference. When I warned you Sadat was a traitor, Qaddafi told the other rulers, and said he was closer to Israel than to the Arabs, you smiled and declared it was our bilateral differences that made me say that. When I observed that Sadat was more interested in fighting Libya than in defeating Israel you shook your heads and remarked that his main concern was to fight Israel. Well, Qaddafi crowed, the peace treaty shows that we told the truth: "The world bears witness to the prediction of the Libyan revolution. . . . There is still danger in ignoring the predictions of the Libyan revolution, whose correctness time has shown. This is because the Libyan revolution is the conscience and true vanguard of the Arab nation; the vanguard does not lie to his people."(19)

At Baghdad, Libya made common cause with Syria and the PLO, and to a lesser extent with Iraq, in pressing for the severe punishment of Egypt. Their demands, drastic and thorough, divided the conference and threatened to disrupt it. At a critical point on March 28 Yasir Arafat alternately pleaded with and bullied the conferees and then led the PLO delegation in a walkout. They were joined by Syria and Libya, and the evening session of the conference was canceled in order to allow for emergency consultation. "We are against unity of ranks at the expense of our people," said Farouk Khaddumi, head of the political department of the PLO. "A firm stand is a must . . . Save your reputation before the world by adopting a firm resolution."(20)

On March 30 the Libyan government made public the details of the sanctions it wished the conference to endorse. They closely paralleled the "working paper" submitted by the PLO, and broadcast over the clandestine Voice of Palestine.(21) The Libyans demanded that the conference agree to impose punishment on Egypt in all areas, political, military, and economic and seek the overthrow of Sadat and his government. In outline, the Libyan position at Baghdad was as follows:

POLITICAL

- Sever all political relations with Egypt
- Seek Egypt's removal from all Arab and African organizations, such as the OAU, the non-aligned movement, and the Islamic conference
- Support the enemies of Sadat inside Egypt to overthrow his government
- Consider any state not boycotting Egypt as hostile, and any state supporting Egypt as unfriendly
- Strike at U.S. interests in various fields
- Oppose any hostile acts by Egypt against any African or Arab state

ECONOMIC

- Apply the boycott regulations against any Egyptian firms or individuals dealing with Israel

- Deny all aid to Egypt
- Deny oil to Egypt
- Deny all contracts to Egyptian companies
- Withdraw all financial deposits from Egypt
- Prohibit tourism to Egypt
- Stop all forms of economic cooperation

MILITARY

- Suspend all military support for Egypt
- Prevent Egypt from receiving Arab funds for military purposes
- End all commitments to aid Egypt militarily
- Establish no new military cooperation with Egypt
- Transfer the Arab military industrial authority out of Egypt
- Call for the condemnation of Egyptian policy and the overthrow of the Egyptian government

Unlike the PLO, which published its working paper before the negotiations started, Libya chose to release its demands later in the conference presumably after many of the controversial points had been agreed to by the conferees. In other words, Qaddafi was dealing in fulfilled prophecy. He couldn't miss. The most extreme demands, such as calling for the overthrow of the Egyptian government, were included for symbolic and propaganda purposes. Fakery aside, Qaddafi was making the point that the Arab world had taken a position much closer to his own than to Sadat's. The response of Saudi Arabia and the other Arab governments to these kinds of demands was to accept that Egypt should be penalized but to argue that there should not be a complete rupture.(22) To this Syria, Libya, and the PLO replied that an historic turning point had been reached. One was either for Sadat or against him, an ally of Zionism or its enemy. "There is no room for neutrality," as Saddam Hussein declared in his opening address. "There is nothing before us in the Arab homeland except black or white," was the way Qaddafi put it in his message to Arab kings and presidents.(23) This is an old rhetorical and political device, to destroy the middle ground and to equate good with one's own views and evil with any other outlook. At Baghdad, as far as the wording of the sanctions was concerned, it worked.

But there was more to the opposition than just reluctance to make a complete break with Egypt. There was first the problem of strange bedfellows. Saudi Arabia and the other sheikdoms and monarchies had much more in common with Sadat's Egypt than they could ever have with Iraq or Libya or the other members of the Steadfastness and Rejection Front. To break with Egypt totally would be to make the fundamental strategic error of confusing temporary and permanent friends. Second, Libya and the PLO sought much more than sanctions against Egypt. They were out to break the connections between the Arab monarchies and the United States. Both Arafat and Khaddumi urged the conference to face up to the responsibility of the United States for the unilateral peace treaty and to strike back at U.S. interests. In his address to the conference Libyan Foreign Minister Turayki called for a political and economic boycott of the United States.(24) However, such a step would gravely weaken the military and economic security of governments like those of Saudi Arabia, Jordan, and Morocco. If they broke with Egypt and the U.S. they would have no one to depend on if their new-found allies turned against them. None of these governments wanted to run both these risks, and no reference to an anti-U.S. boycott appears in the final communique. While there were risks in going too far with the PLO, Syria, Libya, and Iraq, there were also risks in appearing to be lukewarm about punishing Egypt. For that reason, the conferees whether they were reluctant or determined gave unanimous approval to the PLO-Syria-Libya position. On paper at least the Baghdad conference was their victory, and they described it as just punishment for Sadat and a slap in the face for the United States.

The sanctions agreed on at Baghdad put a heavy burden on Egypt, one that weighed on the collective mind as well as the body of Egypt. The country had become an outcast, condemned by nineteen of twenty-two Arab states for ignoring Arab summit resolutions; for joining forces with Israel; for acting unilaterally in the Arab-Israeli conflict; for violating the Arab nation's rights; and for relinquishing its commitment to the Palestinian cause. As punishment the con- ferees vowed to carry out sweeping political and economic penal- ties.

The political measures were of three kinds: bilateral, Arab, and international. Each of the conferees, officially the Council of the Arab League, undertook to withdraw their ambassadors from Cairo immediately and to recommend that all Arab states sever political and diplomatic relations with Egypt within one month. At the Arab level, the council decided to suspend Egypt from the Arab League, to move the headquarters of the League and all its agencies from Cairo to Tunis within two months, and to suspend Egypt from all specialized Arab organizations.(25) The council also resolved to seek the help of other governments for a number of actions: to suspend Egypt from the OAU, the non-aligned movement, and the Islamic conference; to cooperate with those governments opposed to the Sadat regime; to oppose the Egypt-Israel treaty; and to condemn the U.S. policies of Camp David and support for the peace treaty.

The economic sanctions were more damaging than the political. The council acted mainly in the areas of finance, aid, and trade. It resolved to halt all loans, deposits, guarantees, financial and technical contributions, and aid to Egypt (aid alone amounted to from $600 million to $1 billion); to ban any extension of aid to Egypt from Arab funds, banks, and financial institutions; and to request Arab governments to refrain from purchasing the bonds and public loans of the Egyptian government. In regard to trade Arab governments were to refrain from all trade with Egypt, to provide no oil or oil derivatives to Egypt, and to apply the Arab boycott regulations to all Egyptian organizations and individuals who dealt with Israel. Finally, the council decided to ask the United Nations to move all its regional offices out of Egypt.

Words on pieces of paper never translate directly into action, and Saudi Arabia, Morocco, and the other reluctant parties to the final agreement at Baghdad could console themselves with that small grace. While they would certainly comply with the more obvious political sanctions — such as breaking diplomatic relations — they also knew it would be up to them to decide which of the more or less obscure but most vital economic penalties they would honor, such as the prohibitions on aid, financial transactions, and tourism. In addition, the status of the hundreds of thousands of Egyptian technicians and teachers living and working abroad in Arab countries had been expressly protected. It was a small point, but at least there would be no massive exodus, no disruption caused by their loss. There was solace, too, in the prohibition on oil shipments. It appeared horrible but was meaningless; Egypt had been a net oil exporter since the return of the first Sinai oil fields in 1975. Tourism was not stopped; Egypt remained a popular vacation spot, especially for visitors from the Arabian Peninsula. Saudi Arabia did not withdraw its commercial deposits from Egypt, although it did stop large government-to-government economic and military assistance. Even so, there was no disguising the dominance of the conference by the views of the PLO, Syria, Libya, and Iraq. The Steadfastness and Rejection Front had called the tune.

In the weeks and months that followed the economic and political sanctions were carried out. The Organization of Arab Petroleum Exporting Countries suspended Egypt on April 17 and prohibited sales of oil to it; the next day the Arab Monetary Fund suspended Egypt. At the tenth conference of the foreign ministers of Islamic states meeting at Fez, Morocco, May 8-12, Egypt was suspended. The Arab League held its first meeting in its new headquarters in Tunis on June 28. An extraordinary foreign ministers conference dealt in large part with the transfer of League facilities which had been greatly complicated by Egypt's decisions to freeze League bank accounts and prohibit the transfer of Egyptian employees. Saudi Arabia announced on May 14 that from July 1 the Arab Military Industrial Organization in Egypt would cease to exist. And on July 6 the U.S. government confirmed that the sale of fifty F-5E fighters to Egypt had been indefinitely postponed because Saudi Arabia had withdrawn its original commitment to pay for the aircraft. Egypt was suspended from the Islamic Conference on May

9. Libya and Iraq led efforts to have Egypt expelled from the organization. On November 29 the UN General Assembly voted 75-33 to condemn the Egypt-Israel treaty as invalid and not binding on the Palestinians. Sadat was able to block action against Egypt at the OAU meetings in Morocco, July 17-21, although the Libyans and Algerians staged a walkout during his address. In June, in preparation for its sixth conference, the non-aligned movement's coordinating bureau also refused to recommend Egypt's suspension, although it did issue a statement condemning the peace treaty.

Sadat repeatedly tried to minimize the significance of the lost Arab aid, essentially Saudi and Gulf money, but it hurt Egypt in several ways beyond the sheer loss of the money itself. It made other investors much more wary, and thus cut into Sadat's hopes of internationalizing Egypt's list of donors. Soviet aid had already been lost. The withdrawal of Saudi aid would reduce the European and international sources he had hoped to tap. Egypt was being forced to rely more and more heavily on the United States. It was not a question of generosity. The Carter administration and the U.S. Congress willingly offered Egypt massive amounts of economic aid and were steadily raising the quantities of U.S. military assistance. The lopsided dependence reduced Sadat's bagaining leverage against Israel and cut into his diplomatic and political freedom of action. The Arabs' isolation of Egypt threatened Sadat's hopes to give Egypt rapid domestic economic development and a leading international and Middle Eastern role.

The main Palestinian guerrilla and terrorist actions in 1979 were attacks inside Israel. The PLO increased these attacks after the conclusion of the treaty in late March. Arafat had apparently achieved some success in substituting attacks on Israel for the ferocious and deadly internal feuding that had marked the preceding year. However, there were a number of foreign incidents, and Qaddafi continued to range Libya on the side of the most violent and uncompromising elements of the Palestinian movement.

On March 14, timed to coincide with President Carter's visit to the Middle East, the PFLP and Israel agreed to a prisoner exchange. Sixty-six Palestinian guerrillas were released from jail in Israel and allowed to leave. In return one Israeli prisoner was released. He had been captured in southern Lebanon. The guerrillas boarded a Bulgarian airplane, which had brought the Israeli soldier to Israel from Damascus, and were flown to Tripoli. In late April, Egypt accused Syria of establishing a Palestinian terrorist organization — Eagles of the Palestinian Revolution — and using it for attacks against Egypt. Officials in Cairo blamed Syria and the Eagles group for a package bomb that had exploded in Cairo on April 19, killing a customs officer and wounding three other people and a bomb explosion in a hotel in January that had injured four. Egypt also blamed Syria and Libya for the attack on the Egyptian embassy in Ankara, Turkey on July 13, by four guerrillas claiming to belong to the Eagles of the Palestinian Revolution. Two Turkish guards were killed in the attack, and an Egyptian diplomat died when he jumped from a high window in an attempt to escape. The guerrillas surrendered on July 15 without achieving any of their demands, which reportedly included a plane to take them and their hostages to an Arab country; the severance of Turkish relations with Egypt and Israel; and a denunciation by Turkey of the peace treaty.

Three days before the package exploded in Cairo, four Palestinian guerrillas apparently attempted to hijack an El Al airliner at Brussels airport. Discovered before they could seize the plane, the guerrillas detonated a small bomb in the passenger lounge and began a shoot-out with police and Israeli security guards. Two were captured and two escaped. A successful hijacking occurred in September but it was aimed against Libya. Three Lebanese took over an Alitalia plane in Beirut and ordered it flown to Havana, where the non-aligned conference was underway. The hijackers had seized the plane in order to publicize the disappearance in Libya in August 1978 of Moussa Sadr, the spiritual leader of Lebanese Shiite Muslims. When France refused to allow the plane to be refueled in Nice, the hijackers agreed to a landing in Rome. After discussions with Iranian negotiators at the airport the hijackers agreed to release the hostages in exchange for the broadcast over Iranian radio of their appeal to the non=aligned leaders on Sadr's behalf. Most of the passengers were then released in Rome. The broadcast was made several hours later. The airplane then flew to Teheran where the remaining hostages were released, and the hijackers surrendered to Iranian authorities. Libya denied any knowledge of what might have happened to Sadr who, it claimed, had left the country for Rome. Italian authorities had no record of his entry into Italy. On December 6 a Moroccan newspaper, Al-Muharrir, reported that Sadr had been killed in Libya by an officer who had misinterpreted his orders. The Imam's travel documents were then forged to make it appear he had left Libya. According to the newspaper the Italian ambassador in Teheran had announced that the Italian government had started an investigation of Sadr's disappearance after someone had been found with the religious leader's passport.(26)

In early December there was further evidence of Qaddafi's determination to support an uncompromising stand against Israel. On December 6 Libyan troops surrounded the PLO office in Tripoli. Three days later the head of the office, Suliman al-Shurafa, was expelled from Libya. According to Arab diplomatic sources in Lebanon, Qaddafi had begun a campaign to unify the Palestinian movement into "Libyan-style revolutionary committees." In Qaddafi's view Palestinian disunity prevented the intensification of the struggle against Israel, Egypt, and the Camp David process. Qaddafi had first spoken of the Palestinians' need to form revolutionary committees on November 29, an international day of solidarity with the Palestinian cause. He had also organized Palestinians living in Libya to harass members of the PLO and Fatah, according to Palestinian sources. On December 10, in an interview with the New York Times, Qaddafi called the PLO "a collection of storefronts peddling differing views," not the way to liberate Palestine. Arafat, he said, was on "the road to treason," that is, a negotiated settlement with Israel.(27) A few days earlier Qaddafi had said that Palestinians must never abandon their armed struggle to recover their homeland. If the peace treaty allowed the Suez Canal to be opened, he exhorted his listeners, then the Palestinians must destroy the canal.(28)

The dispute between Libya and the PLO escalated on December 6 when Arafat, speaking during a visit to Jordan, accused Qaddafi of staging the siege of the PLO office in Tripoli with members of Libyan intelligence. If Libya instigated attacks against the PLO by people's committees, he warned, Palestinians would retaliate by occupying Libyan embassies everywhere around the world.(29) Four days later the PLO Executive Committee appealed to Qaddafi to stop the siege of the PLO office and the propaganda attacks against the PLO. The expulsion of the PLO representative in Tripoli followed.

Qaddafi's appeals for Palestinian unity against Israel made clear the rationale behind his attacks on the PLO. In a broadcast on December 7, for example, Tripoli radio argued that a reorganization of "the Palestinian masses" was the only means that could prevent a compromise settlement with Israel. That reorganization ought to be patterned after the Libyan "revolutionary committees, popular congresses, and general peoples' congresses." Qaddafi, "the leader of the revolution," had created the opportunity for such a reorganization to take place inside Libya. In this way alone, would the Palestinians be able to "impose their revolutionary logic over the Arab arena" and overcome the inactivity which had engulfed the Arab world.(30) A subsequent broadcast stated that the siege of PLO offices and the popular committees that had been formed in Libya on the international day of solidarity with Palestine had been undertaken to protest the decision of the tenth Arab summit conference at Tunis to curtail Palestinian military operations against Israel from southern Lebanon. The official Libyan news agency, JANA, announced on December 9 that a delegation of members of the PFLP, Democratic Front for the Liberation of Palestine, and PFLP-Struggle Command had arrived in Tripoli and endorsed Qaddafi's actions. JANA also carried a communique from the "Palestinian committee for coordination between the revolutionary committees in Libya," purporting to speak for "the Palestinian masses in the Jamahariyah." The communique attacked the PLO as high-living capitulators and praised the Libyan revolutionary experience as the way to the salvation of the Palestinian cause.(31) The PLO struck back by suggesting that Qaddafi had attacked the

PLO and closed its Tripoli office as a way of appeasing the United States after the embassy attack and showing that he was genuinely interested in better Libyan-U.S. relations. The director of the PLO office in Rabat, Abu Marwan, accused Qaddafi of trying to force the Palestinians to accept his revolutionary structures and of not living up to the obligations set by the Baghdad summit.(32) The clandestine Voice of Palestine accused Qaddafi, whom it characterized as a "dwarf," and "the author of hollow slogans," of carrying out a role planned by Israel and the United States. If Qaddafi wanted a fight, the broadcast warned, the PLO would give him one.(33)

After an emergency meeting, the Fatah Central Committee on December 11 reasserted its claim to be the sole representative of the Palestinian people and agreed with the PLO Executive Committee on the urgent need for a meeting of Arab states, or at least the Steadfastness states, to oppose Libya's actions. Two days later a Lebanese newspaper reported that Arafat had asked the president of South Yemen, Abd al-Fattah Ismail, to mediate between the PLO and Qaddafi.(34) The PLO denied asking for mediation.(35) Nonetheless, the Libyan leader continued his campaign against the PLO. On December 16, he closed the PLO office in Benghazi and expelled three high-ranking PLO officials from Libya. On the same day JANA reported an anti-PLO demonstration by students in a small town, Baui Walid. The Voice of the Arab Homeland broadcast on Tripoli radio announced that Libya had become what the Palestinian movement had always wanted, "a solid, firm base" for "fedayeen action" against Israel. Why was this dream come true being met by a campaign of lies and distortion, the broadcast asked.

The Voice of Palestine answered with reports of the arrest of two more PLO officials in Libya on December 17 and of continuing efforts by Libyan authorities to form revolutionary committees among Palestinians in Libya. A day earlier, an editorial in the official PLO journal, Al-Thawrah, attacked Qaddafi on three grounds: his actions undermined the PLO's right to represent the Palestinian people; he was attempting to impose on the Palestinians a revolutionary experience and an organizational formula which were not their own and which they had not chosen; and, above all, Qaddafi took these actions in the context of an effort on his part to improve relations with the United States – an apology for a Libyan attack on the U.S. embassy, an unwillingness to cut off oil shipments to the U.S., a call for the release of the hostages in Teheran, an assertion that U.S. Middle Eastern policy was moving toward neutrality. The editorial concluded: "Qaddafi is merely settling a Palestinian bill . . . in return for pleasing Washington."(36)

The PLO's accusations of a "rapprochement" between Libya and Washington in the winter of 1979-80 make little sense in light of the blossoming scandal surrounding Billy Carter and Robert Vesco's attempts to bribe officials in the Carter administration. These measures horrified the administration and wounded it politically. Moreover the embargoed air transports hadn't been released, and high-level talks held by Undersecretary Newsom during the summer hadn't gone anywhere. There had been no agreements on terrorism, Camp David, African intervention. Most obvious of all, Qaddafi sought to escalate violence against Israel by creating his own wing of the Palestinian movement based in Libya. In short nowhere was Libyan policy in line with U.S. goals and objectives in the Middle East or anywhere else. And the PLO knew it. The charges of collaboration with the United States were nothing more than an attempt to contaminate Qaddafi with the most damaging possible poison. In an interview with Der Spiegel at this time, Abu Iyad (Salah Khalaf), accused Qaddafi of wanting to own the Palestinian Resistance and of trying to treat Palestinian militants like paid mercenaries. There had been a long series of quarrels between the PLO and Qaddafi since 1975. But really, Abu Iyad said: "Qaddafi is the modern Don Quixote who fights windmills."(37)

Syria made an effort to repair the split between Qaddafi and the PLO. Syrian Foreign Minister Khaddam flew to Libya and met with Qaddafi on December 20. But instead of improving, relations grew worse. On December 22 the Palestine news service in Beirut announced that Qaddafi had broken relations with the PLO. All dealings on an official level were to be stopped and Libyan financial assistance was to be ended. Qaddafi claimed that this meant a loss of $80 million to the PLO. Salah Khalaf (Abu Iyad), a member of Fatah's Central Commitee, said on December 16, for example, that Fatah had received nothing from Qaddafi since 1975. Most of Libya's support had gone to the more uncompromising groups, such as PFLP, and presumably such organizations would be unaffected by the cut-off in aid.(38)

Despite this development a break in the downward spiral of hostility was at hand and was apparently achieved through the mediation of Syria, Algeria, and possibly Jordan. President Assad met with Arafat and other members of the PLO Executive Committee in Damascus on December 21 and, among other topics, discussed efforts to settle the Libyan-PLO dispute. The PLO Executive Committee promptly released a statement saying it approved of Assad's mediation. Then, on December 24 the Libyan ambassador in Amman, Jordan, Salih-shas-Sanusi, told a press conference that serious efforts were being made to overcome the crisis in Libyan-PLO relations. As reported in the Jordanian paper, Ar-Ra'y, the ambassador also said that the Palestinian and Libyan revolutions were in harmony and that Libya would not change its view that the PLO was the sole legitimate representative of the Palestinian people. The recent differences were just differences of opinion. The Palestinian committees being established in Libya were intended to support the Palestinian revolution. "I assure you," the ambassador added, "that the existing crisis between Libya and the

Palestinian revolution is only a transient one and will be contained through the efforts exerted by the Libyan and Palestinian leadership and the Arab brothers."(39) A news report that originated in Damascus at about this time predicted a summit between Qaddafi, Arafat, and Algerian President Chadli Benjedid in Algiers before the end of the year. While allowing these efforts to go forward, Qaddafi continued to strike at the PLO. For example, a Libyan envoy was sent on a secret mission to Beirut to meet anti-PLO Palestinian groups. In Tripoli on December 25, 26, and 27 Qaddafi met with the heads of the PFLP General Command (Nayif Hawatimah and Ahmed Jibril); the PFLP (George Habash); the Palestine Popular Struggle Front (Samir Qushah); and Saiqa (Majid Hassan). According to PLO sources, Libyan intelligence also continued to arrest, threaten, and harass Palestinians.(40) On this ambiguous note, the year ended.

6
OUT OF UGANDA AND
INTO CHAD AND THE WESTERN SAHARA

Libya's intervention in Chad increased in 1978 and helped reveal the sharp "tilt" toward the Soviet Union that Qaddafi had given his country's foreign policy. The National Liberation Front (Frolinat) opened a campaign at the end of January to capture Faya Largeau, a small but important town in north central Chad. A week earlier the government of President Malloum had reached a settlement with Hissene Habre, who in 1977 had lost control of Frolinat to another faction which had Libyan support. The agreement, signed in Khartoum on January 22, was, nonetheless, a step toward national reconciliation. It provided for the establishment of a government of national union and a constituent assembly, the reorganization of the armed forces, and amnesty for all political prisoners.(1)

When Malloum then was unable to stop the fighting in northern Chad, he suspended diplomatic relations with Libya and ordered the Libyan ambassador out of the country. Malloum accused Libya of aiding the rebels in the north and of taking a direct part in the fighting there. Malloum also canceled a meeting of the Libyan and Chadian foreign ministers in Niger, which was to have opened on February 7, to discuss the Aouzou border dispute. Qaddafi had renewed Libya's claim to this large area along Chad's border with Libya. It had been ceded to Italy by France in the 1930s. However, the treaty of cession was never ratified by the French legislature. The next day Malloum requested the UN Security Council to take up Libya's intervention in Chad, including Libya's seizure of the Aouzou strip, which the Chad government said had never been approved by the OAU. Qaddafi denied the accusations on February 13 at a session of the OAU liberation committee then meeting in Tripoli. In his remarks at the opening ceremonies Qaddafi said he opposed "any foreign interference in the affairs and quarrels of Africa." Fine words, but it became increasingly clear that Qaddafi did not apply them to his country's growing involvement in Chad or to the large-scale involvement of Soviet and Cuban troops on Ethiopia's side in the wars against Somalia and Eritrea.

As relations between Libya and Chad worsened, they improved between Libya and Sudan and, on February 8, the two countries reached agreement on the reopening of diplomatic relations and other steps to bring about a normalization between them. As a result a Sudanese representative participated in talks in Tripoli, February 16-18, with Libyan and Chadian delegates. The communique issued after the talks recorded major concessions by Chad to Libya. Chad promised: to withdraw its complaint to the UN Security Council; to seek a restoration of diplomatic relations with Libya; and to permit the Libyan embassy in Chad's capital, Ndjamena, to operate normally. In this way, Chad enlisted the temporary aid of the Libyans and Sudanese in establishing a cease-fire and working toward an end to the fighting in the country.

On February 18 the town of Faya Largeau fell to the Frolinat. The same day Libya and Sudan issued a statement to the press in which they appealed to Frolinat to accept a cease-fire. They also endorsed the agreement between Hissene Habre and the Malloum government and urged all sides to work for national reconciliation. Their statement added that Libya and Sudan had formed a bilateral commitee of mediation to work with all sides in Chad. Frolinat replied on February 19 and accepted the cease-fire because, in its words, it had achieved effective control of all of northern Chad. The cease-fire applied only in the northern combat area, the announcement added, and Frolinat had no intention of compromising with the government.

Chad-Libyan relations and the civil war were the subject of a summit meeting in Sebha, Libya, among Qaddafi, Malloum, President Kountchi of Niger, and Sudanese Vice-President Major Abou Kassem Mohammed Ibrahim, standing in for Nimeiry who was on a foreign trip. Chad and Libya declared that they would settle their differences in a "new fraternal spirit" and that the Libyan ambassador would return to Ndjamena. Again Chad granted important concessions to Libya, concessions that not only improved the military and political circumstances of Frolinat, but appeared to institutionalize Libyan intervention in Chad. Specifically, the communique of the first Sebha conference declared that a peace conference would be held at Sebha on March 21 between the Chadian government and Frolinat. Vice-President Ibrahim would be chairman of the conference, and Niger and Libya would also attend. In addition, Libya and Niger would establish a military committee "to supervise the situation in Chad until national reconciliation has been achieved."(2) This vague and far-reaching mandate was only partially restrained by subsequent agreements.

The second Sebha conference opened on March 23. The government of Chad was represented by Colonel Mamari Djime Ngakinar, vice-chairman of the Supreme Military Council, and the rebels by Goukouni Oueddei, newly elected (March 16) president of the "revolutionary council" of Frolinat. The foreign ministers of Libya and Niger, respectively Dr. Ali Abdessalam al Turayki and Major Moumouni Djermakoye, represented their governments. Again, Chad gave ground to Frolinat and Libya. In the communique, which was issued in Benghazi, Chad agreed to recognize Frolinat; to abide by the cease-fire (effective April 10); to take every step to facilitate the efforts of Libya and Niger in seeking its implementation; to stop all anti-Frolinat propaganda; to allow freedom of movement throughout Chad; and to help the Niger-Libya military committee to assure there were neither foreign military bases nor any foreign military presence in Chad. The obligations of Frolinat were to abide by the cease-fire; to aid Libya and Niger in implementing it; to stop antigovernment propaganda; to allow free movement within Chad; and to assist the military committee in efforts to stop foreign military intervention in Chad. The agreement was guaranteed by Sudan, Libya, and Niger. A follow-up meeting was scheduled for June 7 in Tripoli.(3)

Part of the explanation of the readiness of the Chad government to relinquish huge chunks of its sovereignty undoubtedly lay in its military weakness. A news report in Western Europe in late March indicated that the Chadian government had lost half its 5,000-man army in the fighting around Faya Largeau and controlled "barely a quarter of the country."(4) The same report stated that the situation was so bad that France had flown 1,000 troops into Chad to defend the capital, Ndjamena. This was denied by the French Foreign Ministry on April 6, although it confirmed that 150 advisors had been sent to Chad to help government forces, bringing the officially admitted numbers to 400 French advisors in Chad.

Within three weeks of the end of the second Sebha conference the fighting started again. According to press reports Frolinat broke the cease-fire by seizing Salal on April 15 and sending its troops southward toward Ndjamena. President Malloum appealed to France for military aid, and on April 26 the French government officially announced that it had sent reinforcements. Some 1,700 soldiers of the Foreign Legion and French advisors supported by 10 aircraft were sent to Chad, and 500 of them took part in battles around Ati, on the main highway 280 miles northeast of the capital, which began May 18. Their intervention defeated the Frolinat offensive, and the guerrillas were driven north behind the lines they had held at the time of the cease-fire. On June 22 Malloum charged that "thousands" of Libyan troops had invaded Chad. His charges were supported by Western diplomats in Ndjamena, who told reporters that 800 Libyan soldiers had entered the northern region of Chad.(5)

Under the circumstances it is understandable that when it finally took place on July 3-6 the follow-up conference which had been planned at Sebha failed to lead to agreement. Frolinat demanded the withdrawal of French forces before agreeing to a cease-fire. The government countered by insisting that Frolinat had to end hostilities first. Although the future of the civil war in Chad thus remained uncertain, Libya's intentions had become all too clear. Under the guise of seeking a peaceful settlement of the conflict and forestalling foreign intervention Qaddafi sought to increase Libyan influence in Chad, and to strengthen Frolinat at the expense of the Malloum government, particularly by making it politically impossible for France to intervene militarily in Chad. Closing his eyes to the large-scale and decisive Soviet and Cuban intervention in Ethiopia he maneuvered and railed against the West, in Chad, where he was directly concerned, and in Zaire. Qaddafi's plans were revealed, for example at the OAU foreign ministers' conference, July 7-15, in Khartoum. Called to precede the annual OAU summit (July 18-22) the foreign ministers' conference immediately erupted in the vehement quarrels and disputes between moderate and radical states that characterized the summit conference as well. The Libyan foreign minister, Ali Abdessalam al Turayki, ignited the disputes at the opening session by stridently denouncing the governments of Chad, Mauritania, and Zaire for asking France to send troops into their countries. Zaire and Mauritania answered in kind, and the discussion became so heated that the session was adjourned shortly after it began. A follow-up meeting was scheduled for June in Tripoli.(6)

The bitterness of the discussions arose in part from the events surrounding the second invasion of Shaba province, Zaire, by the Congolese National Liberation Front. In response to a request for help from Zaire, and alarmed by reports of the deteriorating military situation and increasing attacks on Europeans in Kolwezi, Shaba, the French government sent 800 paratroops from the Foreign Legion base on Corsica into Shaba on May 19. About 1,800 Belgian troops also arrived in Kolwezi on the same day. Some of the French and Belgian equipment and personnel were flown to Zaire by U.S. Air Force C-130s. The paratroops quickly captured the town and the surrounding areas, and the invaders began to retreat into Angola and Zambia. They left behind hundreds of murdered Africans and Europeans. The Belgian units began their withdrawal on May 22. On June 4 the first Moroccan troops arrived in Shaba on U.S. transports, which then carried French troops back to Corsica. In addition to Moroccans, other African nations sent small contingents. These were: Senegal, Central African Empire, Togo, Ivory Coast, Gabon, and Egypt. Zaire charged that the invasion had been planned and supported by the Soviet Union, Cuba, Libya, and Algeria. Although these nations, of course, denied any responsibility for the invasion, it is difficult to believe that the government of Angola, with its strong military and economic backing from the Soviet Union and Cuba, could not have stopped the invaders if they had wished to.

To many Africans the invasion of Zaire from Angola, a nation enjoying significant help from Communist governments — there were some 21,000 Cuban troops in the country — and the quick and effective military response by France and the United States, raised the specter of the division of Africa into battlefields where Africans would fight out the quarrels of the superpowers, as had happened for so many years with such deadly results in Southeast Asia. Even the creation of the African security force for Shaba could not still the fears, because this had been done outside the OAU and in direct support of Western policy and of the policies of African states more or less aligned with the West.(7) This alarmed those African governments with revolutionary objectives just as much as the Soviet and Cuban interventions in Angola and Ethiopia alarmed the more moderate governments. At the same time neither the moderates nor the radicals were willing to renounce the right to call for ouside assistance from whichever nation or bloc they chose to ask. In a sense, intervention lay in the eye of the beholder and was practiced by one's enemies. It was to this viewpoint, and to a widely shared anti-Western bias, that Qaddafi appealed with his calculated attacks on the French presence in Africa and his calculated silences on Soviet and Cuban actions.

Since the departure of Spain from the Western Sahara in 1975 and its division and annexation by Morocco and Mauritania, the leading foreign supporter of Polisario had been Algeria. In late 1977 and early 1978 relations between France and Algeria were strained by a series of incidents stemming from Algeria's support for Polisario. Polisario had enjoyed greater military success against Mauritania, the weaker of its two rivals for control of the Western Sahara. During its attacks, a number of French nationals had been captured and the mining economy of Mauritania disrupted, both because of the fighting and because of the resultant exodus of European technicians and engineers. As a result France strengthened its garrison in neighboring Senegal and began to conduct air attacks against Polisario units threatening to attack Mauritania. During this period two developments of interest occurred. The first was a shift in Libya's position toward the conflict. During a week-long visit to Algeria May 31-Jun 6 Qaddafi announced that Libya, which had favored a negotiated settlement, had decided that a negotiated solution to the conflict was no longer possible, because Polisario had shown that it could win independence. The Algerians were delighted. In the context, this amounted to support for Algeria's alliance with Polisario in its war with Morocco and Mauritania.

The other development eventually took Mauritania out of the conflict altogether. On July 10, the Mauritanian chief of staff,

Lieutenant Colonel Mustapha Ould Mohammed Salek, led a successful coup against the government of President Mokhtar Ould Daddah.
Two days later Polisario declared a cease-fire toward Mauritania,
and invited the new government to reconsider its position on the
Western Sahara. Salek clearly intended to do just that. He sent
delegations to France, Libya, and Morocco. After the Mauritanian
envoys' visit to Paris, French President Giscard d'Estaing began a
mediation effort involving Algeria, Ivory Coast (as a potential go-
between), and Morocco. Mauritania and France were reported to
have agreed on an arrangement to allow Polisario to govern the
southern (Mauritanian) zone of Western Sahara which would be
federated with Mauritania. When King Hassan vehemently rejected
the idea and implicitly threatened Mauritania, the new Salek
government hesitated to go forward with the plan. "We shall never
accept," Hassan said in an address to the Moroccan people, "the
existence on our southern frontiers of a regime which is ideo-
logically different from those of Morocco and Mauritania." However, as 1978 expired, the cease-fire between Polisario and
Mauritania was still in effect, and fighting continued in the
Moroccan sector of the Western Sahara.(8)

The Soviet Union and Libya continued to develop their relations
with Idi Amin of Uganda along similar lines in late 1977 and early
1978. In November 1977, for example, the Ugandan government
announced that two squadrons of Soviet jet fighters MIG 17 and 21,
had been stationed at Entebbe. Their pilots were to be trained by
Soviet advisors. On January 25 Uganda radio carried a report of the
signing of trade and technical cooperation agreements with the
Soviet Union. The previous month Amin had visited Libya and signed
agreements for cooperation in trade, industry, and culture. Part of
the arrangements provided for the exchange of cotton from Uganda
as payment for oil from Libya.(9) In May news reports originating in
Nairobi stated that the Soviet Union had agreed to conduct geo-
logical surveys in Uganda, and that the two governments had signed
agreements on scientific and cultural cooperation for 1978-79.(10)
Both British and French newspapers carried stories about the entry
of a small number of Cuban troops into Uganda. The Observer
(London), on August 6, 1978 spoke of the entry of "a company" of
Cuban soldiers from South Yemen July 15 or 16.(11) Le Nouvel
Observateur in May estimated that there were twenty to thirty
Cuban military personnel in Uganda at that time.(12)

Libya chose to intensify its armed interventions in Africa in
1979. To his support of Frolinat in Chad, Qaddafi added attacks by
Libyan forces in the north and the support of a new secessionist
movement in the south led by Lt. Colonel Wadal Abdel Kadar
Kamougue and drawn from the government forces, Forces armees
tchadiennes (FAT). In what turned out to be a futile and largely
symbolic gesture Qaddafi also sent hundreds of troops to the aid of
Ugandan dictator, Idi Amin, but could not prevent his overthrow by

the combined forces of Tanzania and Ugandan dissidents in a Ugandan National Liberation Front (UNLF).

In August 1978 Hissene Habre had joined the government of Chad as prime minister. His Forces armees du nord (FAN), although in theory integrated into the national armed forces (FAT), remained loyal to him. Fighting erupted between elements of FAN and FAT in Ndjamena in February 1979. The disunity within President Malloum's government was surpassed by the fragmentation of Chad along racial and religious lines – a Moslem Arab north and African Christian or animist south – overlaid by the criss-crossing military lines of the eleven Chadian factions.(13) Confusion and disorder in the country were increased by the murder of large numbers of Muslims in the south and serious disagreements, often resulting in bloodshed, between different rebel groups. For example, thirty people were reported to have died in August 1978 during fighting between factions of Goukouni Ouedde's Frolinat after their defeat by French-Chadian troops at the battles of Ati and Djedda (50 kilometers northeast of Ati).(14) Christian missionaries reported the massacre of at least 10,000 people, mostly Muslims, in the south, with the worst outrages committed in Moudou in March 1979, when 800 people were killed by rioters.(15)

The chaos was such that Chad's neighbors were at last able to convene a conference on national reconciliation in order to attempt to stop the bloodshed and to restore government in the country. Proposed by Sudan in February, the conference idea was taken up by Nigeria, which invited the Chadian factions, neighboring states, and representatives of the OAU to meet in Kano, in northern Nigeria. When the meeting finally began on March 11 it was attended by President Malloum, Hissene Habre, Aboubakar Mahamat Abderaman of MPLT, which was supported by Nigeria and based near Lake Chad, and representatives of Libya, Sudan, Niger, Cameroon, and Nigeria. On March 16 a peace accord was signed, to come into effect a week later.

Given the nearly complete breakdown of civil life and security and the extensive foreign intervention in Chad it is not surprising that this was only the first of four conferences of national reconciliation to be held in Nigeria in 1979. All were failures. At the end of 1979, although the French government had begun to withdraw its troops, foreign intervention in Chad had increased rather than decreased, and there was no sign of peace among the warring Chadian factions. Chad was still in this sad condition four years later; the difference could be measured best in the lives of the people of Chad, lost in untold numbers to the hunger, disease, and anomic violence that flourishes in civil strife and foreign meddling. At the first Kano conference it was agreed that pending the formation of a "transitional government of national union," Goukouni Oueddei would become head of state in a Provisional State Council, made up of two members from four Chadian factions.(16)

The published accord signed at Kano had the following provisions: (1) a general cease-fire in Chad and the provision by Nigeria of a neutral peacekeeping force; (2) the creation of an independent monitoring commission of delegates from all the participants in the conference including the Chad factions, Nigeria to act as chair; (3) the establishment of a "transitional government of national union" composed of representatives of all factions to prepare for free elections; (4) the demilitarization of Ndjamena and its surroundings to a radius of 60 miles; (5) the granting of amnesty to all political prisoners, the release of all hostages, the release of all prisoners of war, and the pardoning of all exiles; (6) the gradual combination of all the different military formations into one army and the break-up of all political organizations. On March 20 the French government announced its intention to begin a gradual withdrawal of its troops from Chad. Three days later President Malloum established the Provisional State Council (PSC) and resigned. So far so good.

But nothing went as planned. The first Kano accord was doomed to remain an outline of one desirable method of arriving at a settlement, and nothing more. In early April, for example, the 800-man Nigerian peacekeeping force was unable to keep order in Ndjamena or to stop looting and attacks on southerners by the guerrilla units there, which refused to withdraw in compliance with the provision in the Kano agreement for a demilitarized zone in and around the capital.(17) A follow-up conference in Kano, April 3-11, ended in disarray. Like the uninvited witch of "Sleeping Beauty" five Chadian factions who had not gone to Kano demanded to participate. When Habre and Oueddei refused, the Nigerians put them under house arrest to force them to change their minds, but then had to release them both because of threats from their supporters to attack the Nigerian peacekeeping force in Ndjamena.(18) Ignoring the five, Oueddei and Habre formed the council in Ndjamena on April 16 and took the Interior and Defense portfolios respectively, sharing the other leading posts with MPLT and FAN.

Libya's response was to step up its intervention. In April, for example, Libya supported a southern secessionist movement led by Lt. Colonel Kamougue of FAT, which fought a bloody engagement with Frolinat and FAN elements south of Ndjamena in late May. In mid-April Qaddafi sent Libyan troops 300 miles deep into northern Chad and along the border with Sudan. Although Libya denied its troops had entered Chad, the purpose of the offensive was apparently to punish MPLT and Frolinat which, having won a good deal of power in the new transitional government, felt strong enough to break with Qaddafi and to demand the return of the Aouzou strip.

A third peace conference was convened May 26-27, this time in Lagos, the capital of Nigeria. In an astonishing twist the four factions in the PSC did not attend but the five "dissidents" did, together with the original five neighboring countries and the Central African Empire, a new participant. Ignoring the irony of the situation, these eleven branded the new government of Chad as unacceptable and unrepresentative, and demanded its replacement by a "legal" transitional regime by June 25. Chad's neighbors threatened to impose an economic boycott on Chad if the PSC rejected this demand. The eleven also called for the immediate withdrawal of all French troops, their place to be taken by a pan-African force.

The PSC reacted on June 1 by requiring Nigeria to withdraw its peace force from Ndjamena, calling them an "occupation army." The Nigerians left June 3-4. Nigeria then stopped oil exports to Chad, and Goukouni Oueddei accused Lagos of trying to "suffocate" his country and to impose a government on Chad. Meanwhile relations worsened between the factions in the PSC. In early June there were several collisions and then a pitched battle on June 11-12 between units of MPLT and Frolinat that took dozens of lives. Ten days later Frolinat troops also fought with several hundred soldiers in FAN.

It would have been too much to expect Qaddafi to have stayed out. While maintaining his support of Kamougue in the south, he sent 2,500 troops supported by Mirage fighters into northern Chad on June 26. They started toward Faya Largeau where they ran into determined Frolinat resistance. Western diplomats in Ndjamena told journalists in early July there wre "at least 800" Libyan troops in Faya Largeau, and that the city was defended by Soviet-made surface-to-air missiles. Hissene Habre controlled about 700 troops. Their arms and equipment were provided by France.(19) After heavy fighting the Libyans retreated into northern Chad. Habre and Oueddei quarrelled about who had done what, with Oueddei claiming the victory belonged to Frolinat and accusing Habre, who denied it, of refusing to fight.(20) According to news reports Frolinat had originally agreed to Libyan annexation of the Aouzou in exchange for help in defeating the Chadian government.(21)

In mid-August a fourth peace conference met in Lagos. It was the largest yet. All eleven Chad factions were present as were delegations from Chad's neighbors. Also present were representatives of Senegal, Benin, Congo, and Liberia. After a week of meetings the conferees signed another peace accord. It differed from the March 16 Kano agreement in several important ways. To supervise a general cease-fire there was now to be established a neutral monitoring commission made up not of Chad's neighbors chaired by Nigeria but of contingents from nations not bordering on Chad to be chaired by the secretary-general of the OAU. It was later decided that Congo, Benin, and Guinea would man this force. As before it was agreed that Ndjamena would be demilitarized, that there would be a general amnesty for exiles and political prisoners, and that all factional armed units would be merged into one national army. In addition, the agreement envisioned the constitution of a transitional government involving all factions in which Goukouni Queddei would be president and Wadal Abdel Kader Kamougue vice-president. The accord also asked for the withdrawal of all French troops whose presence, it was stated, was "an impediment to a lasting solution of the problems of the country."(22)

Although a broad-based transitional government was established on November 10, the fourth peace conference also appeared to have formulated a set of desirable goals rather than a program leading to an end to civil war and foreign intervention and the beginning of peace and an orderly life for the people of Chad. For example, although the forces of FAP, FAN, FAT, and MPLT began to withdraw from Ndjamena in October, they retired only to nearby villages and refused to comply with the demilitarization of the capital to 100 kilometers that had been stipulated in the Lagos accord. French military withdrawal was not completed in 1979. On September 4, Goukouni Oueddei, as head of an interim Provisional Administrative Committee, asked the French to stay in Chad until the neutral pan-African force arrived. In November, although the beginnings of an integrated army were formed, Congo, Benin, and Guinea had still not sent their soldiers to supervise the cease-fire.

Chad was not the only scene of Libyan military intervention in 1979. In late October 1978 Ugandan troops loyal to Idi Amin attacked Tanzania in the area west of Lake Victoria. After claiming he had acted in retaliation for a Tanzanian invasion, Amin announced the annexation of about 750 square miles of Tanzanian territory on November 1. There followed offers of mediation from the OAU, the UN, and various African countries, including Libya. Amin accepted Libya's offer, but Tanzanian President Julius Nyerere rejected all offers, preferring to seek the defeat and overthrow of Amin. Tanzania, joined by various Ugandan rebel organizations living in exile, went on the offensive on November 12. Their operations made slow but steady progress and by mid-February Tanzanian units had advanced several dozen miles into Uganda and were 100 miles from Kampala, the capital.

Qaddafi chose this moment to launch a new mediation, and sent Libyan Foreign Minister Turayki to Kampala and Dar-es-Salaam. The Ugandan leader accepted the Libyan initiative and announced he had ordered his troops to fire only in self-defense. However Nyerere rejected the mediation bid. The matter was before the OAU, he told Turayki, and this made Libyan mediation unnecessary. Moreover, Tanzania would not agree to the Libyan terms, which included a cease-fire, an end to propaganda attacks, and a mutual withdrawal three miles on either side of the border. The OAU indeed attempted to arrange a cease-fire, but failed, primarily because of Tanzanian intransigence. Nyerere knew the Ugandan invasion had given him a chance to finish with his murderous neighbor, and he was determined not to miss it. A decisive battle took place near Lukaya, 65 miles from Kampala, on March 11, and Tanzanian forces, aided by Ugandan exiles and deserters from Amin's army, began to close on Kampala. The Ugandan exiles were organized in two major groups:

Forces of National Revolt, led by former president Milton Obote; and Save Uganda Movement, operating from Dar-es-Salaam. A Ugandan National Liberation Front was formed by eighteen different exile groups which met in northern Tanzania, March 23-25.(23)

Libyan military intervention apparently began in mid-February, according to the eyewitness account of a Norwegian journalist who arrived in Nairobi on February 19. The journalist told of the arrival of hundreds of Libyan soldiers and plane loads of arms and ammunition. News accounts published in Nairobi mentioned 2,500 Libyan soldiers in Uganda equipped with tanks and armored vehicles. The Libyan government denied all military involvement. Then, embarrassingly one of its military transports, a Tupolev 154, was forced to make an emergency landing in northeastern Zaire.

Speaking at the third annual conference of the Libyan-funded Islamic Development Bank for Africa, Amin said that Palestinian guerrillas had joined with his troops to defeat the invaders. He asked the conference for aid, and a grant of $4 million was approved for Uganda.(24) As the Tanzanians and their Ugandan allies approached Kampala, Qaddafi apparently issued a warning to Nyerere: stop the invasion of Uganda or Libya will throw its full military weight on Amin's side against Tanzania. Nyerere ignored the threat. Tanzania shelled Kampala and Entebbe airport with 122 mm artillery on March 28. The day before the shelling started Nyerere rejected the Libyan ultimatum. Foreign diplomats in Kampala said that Libyan troops alone defended the capital and that the Ugandan army had disintegrated.(25) MIG-21 jets of the Tanzanian air force bombed Entebbe airport on April 1 and damaged the main runway. The assault on Kampala began the next day. The strategy of Amin's Libyan defenders was apparently to keep open the road to Jinja, an industrial town 40 miles east of Kampala, as their escape route. On April 4 they quit Kampala and moved east, leaving Kampala defenseless. They were reported by Ugandan exiles to have suffered heavy casualties during their defense of the capital.(26) From Jinja the Libyan troops were apparently ordered to airstrips at Nakasongola and Natisivera, 100 miles north of Kampala. Safely out of the range of the invaders, they were put on C-130s and Boeing 727s and flown to Tripoli on April 6-7. The Libyan ambassador to Uganda fled with his countrymen. With them went Amin's last hope for keeping power.

Kampala fell on April 11, and that night the Ugandan National Liberation Front announced the establishment of a provisional government. The hideous regime of Idi Amin was gone at last. A BBC report on April 14 said that Amin's executive jet, flown by Libyans, refueled at Soroti airfield in northeastern Uganda. Meanwhile, the bodies of dead civilians were collected and buried in Kampala. One hundred dead, many bearing the marks of torture were found at the headquarters of Amin's secret police, the State

Research Center.(27) The smell of the decomposed flesh lingered even after the bodies had been removed and served as a final reminder of the horrors from which the Tanzanian invasion had freed the people of Uganda.

Libya had made a genuine if inadequate effort to help Amin hold on to power. The Libyan government's explanation for this unsuccessful intervention on behalf of an abhorrent regime was given by a senior government official in Tripoli on April 2: "We will not abandon President Amin. We consider him a Muslim revolutionary leader supporting the Palestinian cause and opposing foreign interference in African affairs."(28) This rationale is certainly consistent with Qaddafi's long-range goals for Libya, Islam, and Arab nationalism, and does not require a victory to be plausible. Moreover, the intervention was not necessarily as quixotic as it might seem. The Tanzanian invasion force was small: the figures 4,000-6,000 troops were given in the press, and Tanzania lacked the resources for a long war. Amin disposed of a 20,000-man army, on paper at least. Even allowing for corruption and poor training some portion of these could be counted on to fight hard, if only because they feared to lose, as some Nubian units apparently did in the last days before the fall of Kampala. Among weak combatants a relatively small expeditionary force can have an effect out of all proportion to its numbers. A French contingent of similar size had produced a military stalemate in Chad at very low cost. This outcome, which would have cast Qaddafi as an effective Islamic guardian angel and won him a voice in determining the future of Uganda, may have been his objective all along. It was an approach he continued to follow in Chad.

In North Africa Libya maintained its backing for Algeria's role in the conflict in the Western Sahara in late 1978 and 1979, but found room within this general limit to play an active role as mediator, and in this way to expand Libya's influence. Representatives of Mauritania and the Saharan Arab Democratic Republic (SADR – the governmental arm of Polisario) met September 9-14, 1978 and held further talks in Tripoli, Bamaho (Mali), and Paris during the following months. In late October news reports described a three-point proposal for a peace settlement which had been offered to the combatants by Algeria, Libya, and Mauritania. The plan called for (1) a referendum in Tiris el Gharbia, the Mauritanian sector of Western Sahara, supervised by the OAU, to enable the inhabitants to choose between independence, federation with Mauritania, and full integration with Mauritania; (2) the cession by Morocco to Mauritania of territory along the existing northern border in order to establish Mauritanian sovereignty next to Morocco, as King Hassan had demanded; (3) Moroccan consent for Sahrawi refugees living in Tindouf (southwestern Algeria) and in the Moroccan Sahara to move to Tiris el Gharbia. Neither Polisario nor Morocco would accept this plan. Polisario reportedly also refused a French plan calling for a referendum in the Moroccan sector and a federation of the southern sector with Mauritania.

Polisario continued its military operations against Morocco, and won new diplomatic gains, including the recognition of SADR by Tanzania on November 9 and the passage of a UN General Assembly resolution by 90 votes to 10 endorsing the right of the Western Sahara to self-determination and independence.(29) More than two-thirds of the members of the OAU at the organization's sixteenth annual meeting held in Monrovia, Liberia, July 17-21, 1979, called for a cease-fire and referendum on self-determination in the Western Sahara, supervised by the UN. Mauritania voted in favor of the resolution.(30)

The death of Algerian President Houari Boumedienne became the occasion for a warming of relations between Algeria and Mauritania. Colonel Mustapha Ould Salek then lost power in early April to Lt. Colonel Ahmed Ould Bousseif in Mauritania, although Salek continued for a time as titular head of state. Initially Bousseif appeared to put good relations with Morocco ahead of a settlement with Polisario, and this led to a continuation of the stalemate between the two. However, within three weeks of taking power, Bousseif sent his foreign minister to Tripoli for talks on the Western Sahara with the Libyan government. On April 26 the official Libyan news agency claimed that the Mauritanian and Libyan foreign ministers had signed a protocol stipulating that Mauritania would withdraw from Tiris el Gharbia and would return to Tripoli on May 26 to negotiate a peace treaty with Polisario. Although Polisario agreed with this announcement, the Mauritanian Foreign Ministry publicly differed with Libya, saying that Mauritania had gone no further than to recognize the right of self-determination for the Sahrawi people and the need for further discussions between all parties to the conflict. The situation grew more confused in late May. No Mauritanian delegates appeared in Tripoli on May 26. Then Lt. Colonel Bousseif died in a plane crash on May 27. He was succeeded by the defense minister, Lt. Colonel Khouna Ould Kaydalla.

The summer passed in heavy fighting between Polisario and Moroccan forces and rising tensions between Algeria and Morocco. In mid-July Polisario announced the resumption of military operations against Mauritania because of a lack of progress toward a satisfactory negotiated settlement. Then, the logjam broke. At Monrovia the Mauritanian delegation voted in favor of self-determination in the Western Sahara, and on July 31 Lt. Colonel Kaydalla announced that Mauritania intended to free itself of an "unjust and fratricidal war." He abandoned Mauritania's claims on Tiris el Gharbia, and said his country would do no more than administer the territory pending the realization of self-determination in accord with UN and OAU resolutions. If a general settlement satisfactory to Morocco, Mauritania, SADR, and Algeria could not be achieved, he said, Mauritania was prepared to reach a bilateral agreement with Polisario.

Talks between Polisario and Mauritania followed immediately in Algiers, August 3-5, and led to a peace settlement under which Mauritania recognized Polisario and surrendered all claims to Tiris el Gharbia.(31) On August 10 Lt. Colonel Kaydalla went to Morocco for discussions with King Hassan. The Moroccan foreign minister, Mohammed Boucetta, had condemned the peace treaty as frivolous and incompatible with existing international and bilateral agreements. If Mauritania evacuated Tiris el Gharbia, he warned, Morocco would occupy it. At the end of his talks with the king, Lt. Colonel Kaydalla announced to the press that Mauritania considered itself "definitely disengaged from this conflict." Although he said the two countries promised to respect each other's security and to maintain "privileged relations," a better sign of the state of relations between the two came to light. Before Kaydalla ended his visit the Moroccan government allowed a dissident Mauritanian officer, Lt. Colonel Ould Ba Ould Abdel Kader, to publicize the formation of a "democratic Islamic front of Mauritania" devoted to the overthrow of the Mauritania. Kaydalla correctly viewed this as an insult and left Morocco ahead of schedule. On August 11 Morocco occupied Tiris el Gharbia, and four days later declared it a province of the Kingdom of Morocco with a new name, Oued Eddahab, Arabic for its previous Spanish name, Rio de Oro. In response Polisario vowed to strike into Morocco "as hard and as deep as possible." Polisario found additional diplomatic support for its cause at the conference of non-aligned nations in Havana, September 3-9. The day before the conference opened Egypt announced its "full military support" for Morocco and sent arms shipments to the embattled kingdom. Meanwhile, heavy fighting occurred in the desert, with both sides claiming to have inflicted heavy casualties on the other.(32)

Qaddafi made a number of other efforts to expand Libyan influence in 1979. There was, for example, the agreement in principle announced in September 1978 and confirmed the following January for Libya to invest $300 million in Turkey for joint projects in industrial development. Similar aid agreements were signed by Turkey during this period with Iran, Saudi Arabia, and the World Bank. About this time West Germany and Britain agreed to a rescheduling of Turkish debt payments owed to them. Libya also concluded several agreements for economic, scientific, and cultural cooperation with South Yemen in November 1978 and January 1979.

Libyan assistance to Pakistan was sizable throughout this period. For example, an agreement involving tens of millions of dollars to establish a Libyan-Pakistani joint stock company was signed in October 1978, as was another with Saudi Arabia for $100 million in January. This aid was of special interest because of persistent news reports that Libya and Saudi Arabia were paying for Pakistan's development of nuclear weapons, in exchange for a share of whatever weapons were produced. In August 1978 France had canceled a contract to build a nuclear reprocessing plant in Pakistan, for fear that the plant would be used in the production of atomic weapons. The following April the United States canceled its military and development assistance programs in Pakistan for the same reason.(33)

7

REPRESSION AND TERROR AT HOME, DEATH SQUADS ABROAD

Qaddafi started 1980 with a hijacking and a military attack on Gafsa, Tunisia. It was to be a most violent year for the Libyan leader. Before 1980 was over, Qaddafi would begin a campaign of assassination and intimidation of Libyans living abroad and would send his troops into battle again in Chad.

For several years past there had been a hijacking to mark the anniversary of the failed merger between Libya and Tunisia and 1980 was no exception. On January 12, a Tunisian hijacked a Rome-Tunis Alitalia flight and ordered the pilot to fly to Libya. The pilot was able to convince the hijacker to allow a landing in Palermo, Italy, where the incident ended.(1) Two weeks later, Qaddafi initiated a military assault by Tunisian dissidents against Gafsa, a small Tunisian mining town 300 kilometers southeast of Tunis. The attack took place on January 27 and was timed to coincide with the anniversary of a general strike in Tunisia two years earlier, during which the Tunisian army had fired on the strikers, killing dozens of them. In well-planned moves a large force of Tunisians attacked the military barracks, militia headquarters, and a police station at Gafsa. After some days of fighting the raiders were defeated and either killed or captured by units of the Tunisian army which were flown to Gafsa in French military transports.

According to the official Tunisian version of the attack about 50 raiders crossed into Tunisia from Libya; they actually entered from Algerian soil in an effort to disguise their starting point. The Tunisian minister of interior, Othman Kechrid, said that 30 of the attackers were Tunisian and 20 were Libyan. According to Tunisian sources 41 people died in the fighting at Gafsa: 22 Tunisian soldiers,

15 civilians, and 4 raiders; 120 were said to have been wounded.(2) The raiding party may have been much larger and the casualties much heavier than this. Eyewitness accounts of the raid given to the press by Europeans in Gafsa said that casualties were at least five times higher than the number given by the Tunisian government. A number of witnesses also spoke of summary executions of groups of young men by Tunisian soldiers. A report published in Le Monde on January 31 said there were still sounds of gunfire in Gafsa, several days after the Tunisian government had claimed the raiders had been killed or captured.(3)

There was little doubt of Libya's responsibility for the raid. A number of the prisoners taken at Gafsa said their plan was to establish a "revolutionary government" in Gafsa and then to appeal for Libyan assistance. Tunisian military officers were convinced that Libya would have intervened if the raid had touched off a rebellion in Gafsa. The leader of the assault, Ezzadine Cherif, described his unit's training at camps in Libya. He and other prisoners also reported seeing large numbers of Moroccans, Algerians, Egyptians, Sudanese, and Syrians in the camps, along with many more Tunisians. One of the prisoners said there were Cuban and Soviet military instructors in the camps.(4)

The appearance of a large raiding party at Gafsa composed of Tunisians raised the question of who they were and how they had come to be under Libyan direction. There were undoubtedly a number of political dissidents who had chosen to seek Libyan aid. But what of the ordinary soldiers and the bulk of the Tunisians still in Libya in the camps? There is no shortage of Tunisians in Libya; they number around 50,000. Many have entered the country illegally. They are drawn to Libya in much the same way and for the same reasons that thousands of Mexicans illegally cross into the United States every year. Most are seeking work and higher wages. Some are criminals fleeing arrest and prosecution. Simply by making periodic sweeps through the immigrant population the Libyan authorities could easily have found large numbers of young men fearful of having broken the law in Libya or Tunisia or both. These men could then be confronted with the choice of going to jail or to a military camp to train for the "struggle against Israel." As an article in Le Monde observed, only in the second phase of training would the recruits be subjected to anti-Tunisian propaganda and told they would have to fight against the Tunisian government.(5)

Tunisia reacted to the assault by appealing to France and the United States for military aid. France intervened immediately and directly and flew Tunisian reinforcements to Gafsa in French transports. A French naval force of three surface ships and two submarines also sailed from Toulon to patrol along the Tunisian coast.(6) The United States announced on January 31 that it was considering an expansion of its military aid program to Tunisia "on an urgent basis."(7) The Tunisian chief of staff of the armed forces,

General Boubaker Balma, came to Washington to seek more military aid for his country.(8) In addition, according to a high U.S. official, vessels from the Sixth Fleet were sent to cruise in the Gulf of Gabes in support of Tunisia.(9) The consideration of expanded U.S. military aid resulted in the dispatch of ten armored personnel carriers to Tunisia by air. At the end of February the State Department announced a decision to send a total of thirty armored personnel carriers and six helicopters to Tunisia worth $23 million. France supplied six military transports, and Italy provided an unspecified number of helicopters. The United States also stressed that it would "view with concern" any outside interference in Tunisian affairs. Tunisia recalled its ambassador in Tripoli, expelled the Libyan ambassador in Tunis, and closed Libyan cultural centers in Tunisia. At Tunisia's request the Arab League met in Tunis in late February to discuss the dispute between Libya and Tunisia. Tunisia sought a strong condemnation of Libya, but the other League members counseled that bilateral negotiations should be used to resolve the quarrel.

Libya's reaction was to denounce the Tunisian government and to attack and burn the French embassy in Tripoli and ransack the French consulate in Benghazi. A French diplomat, Hubert Isnard, described the attack on his offices for the press. His account made clear that the assault had been an official act by the Libyan government: "There were five or six policemen outside," Isnard said, "while there had been none during the day. Then buses arrived, demonstrators got off, Libyan television cameras appeared, and the consulate was ransacked."(10) "Radio Free Gafsa" beamed grossly abusive antigovernment propaganda into Tunisia from Libya for a time after the raid. The official Tripoli media extended themselves in condemnation and invective. For example, on February 4 JANA reported that "the masses" held a demonstration in Tripoli to condemn France for acting according to a "middle ages colonialist mentality, as if peoples could be herded like cattle and sold in the marketplace like slaves." The demonstrators' statement also referred to the "fading fascist regime in Tunisia," which had murdered thousands of people and driven hundreds of thousands into exile.(11) They were answered in kind. In a broadcast on the same day Tunisia radio spoke of a "grotesque phantasmagoria" of lies issuing from Libya about the raid. Qaddafi, the broadcast said, was "the Libyan moron," trying desperately to export Libya's revolutionary experience and failing again and again.(12)

Qaddafi never admitted responsibility for the Gafsa raid. Instead, he maintained that an uprising had occurred because of the oppressiveness of the Tunisian regime. Contrary to what Tunisia claimed, he asserted, the uprising had actually succeeded; the police, the army, the entire Tunisian government had been defeated. "Nothing remained but to ask for help from the French army." In other words France invaded Tunisia to put down an indigenous revolt. Reality was not a <u>Putsch</u> by Tunisian dissidents who had been trained, armed, and launched at Gafsa from military training camps in Libya. Reality was a spontaneous revolutionary uprising that defeated the old regime and was denied victory only by a counter-revolutionary foreign intervention. This was Qaddafi's ploy: to shift the blame to France when the Gafsa raiders were captured and began to tell their story of Libyan complicity, of the military camps, of Soviet, Cuban, and North Korean instructors, of hundreds of Tunisians and thousands of Egyptians, Sudanese, Syrians, Algerians in the camps. France could not be "Africa's policeman," he told Agence France-Presse on February 11. Libya would oppose France in Africa by "every means, including war," he warned. The government of Valery Giscard d'Estaing had turned France into "the claw in America's paw." France fought Tunisians at Gafsa, he claimed, not foreigners. Qaddafi scoffed at the stories of military camps; one had been named by the Tunisian authorities. It was a Boy Scouts' camp, he said; he would let anyone who wished come and inspect it.(13) A few days earlier Tripoli radio had claimed that "people's resistance forces" at Gafsa were fighting "French invasion forces," land and naval units sent by France "within the framework of its invasion of Tunisia and its transformation into a French protectorate."(14) Qaddafi added to the image of a French coloni-alist counterrevolution by allowing the broadcast of a report, allegedly from the Tunisian Popular Army (Union of Popular Forces) that units from the U.S. Sixth Fleet had occupied Tunis to prevent demonstrations there.(15)

In keeping with this interpretation, the Libyan government requested urgent meetings of the Arab League Council, the OAU, and the Islamic Conference to discuss the French invasion of Tunisia. The attack on the French embassy was portrayed by Libya as a protest against the French invasion of Tunisia. JANA, the official Libyan news agency, gave prominence to frequent announce-ments by a shadowy "General Revolutionary Committee for the Liberation of Tunisia," which claimed victory at Gafsa and denounced French intervention. The Libyan government also appeared to have been behind a barrage of news releases received in Paris by the international news services.

While portraying the raid he had initiated as a spontaneous revolution crushed by the forces of colonialism and imperialism, Qaddafi also stepped up his hostility toward Tunisia. Since the Tunisian people had tried to free themselves by armed resistance to the Bourguiba regime, he declared, Libya would stand by their side. Qaddafi's explanation of this also appeared in the Agence France-Presse interview on February 11:

We believe that contradictions [can] only be solved through conflicts in which one side is eliminated. Accordingly, we consider that the Tunisian regime contradicts the people's revolution in Libya. The healthy situation . . . is to prolong this contradiction [until the Tunisian government], which failed to follow the course of history and lost its "raison d'etre" is eliminated. . . . And this will happen this time . . . we will not accept any mediation, reconciliation, and truce in this conflict which was created by the Tunisian government.(16)

The Tunisian prime minister, Hedi Nouira, reacted to this by declaring "Tunisia is in danger," and pledging to bring Qaddafi's threats before the UN Security Council as a menace to world peace. However, Tunisia's main defense and its principal reaction to Libya's attempted subversion was to draw closer to France and the United States. This was evident in the quick help obtained from France in transporting reinforcements to Gafsa, and in two symbolic gestures by the United States: the shipment of some heavy weapons to Tunisia in a very few days after the raid, mentioned earlier, and the visit to Tunis on February 20 of the United States UN ambassador, Donald McHenry, and his expressions of U.S. interest in Tunisian security. The Tunisian approach was to stress the common interests between Tunisia and the West and to emphasize that Tunisia was worth saving. "There is an 'interdependence of interests' between the West and Islam," Prime Minister Nouira told Le Figaro on February 9. The countries of the Mediterranean are linked by instinct and geopolitics. Moreover, with or without the "Islamic bomb," Nouira said, Qaddafi was reckless enough to plunge the world into nuclear conflict. "This is why I say to the free world, the West, Europe, and France: 'You have loyal partners. Listen to them and help them while showing respect for them. You won't be let down.' "(17)

In addition to securing this help from "its friends" Tunisia also sought to mobilize the opinion of the Arab and African nations against Libya. While the concrete results were slight — Libya was not censured or punished in any way — Tunisia had not expected another result. The occasions nonetheless focused attention on an intra-Arab conflict and this may have served to strengthen Tunisia's position and to justify the more effective measures it had already taken for its self-defense. Tunisia also brought its case against Libya before the Board of Ministers of the Organization of African Unity in Addis Ababa on February 14. After hearing Libya's rebuttal, the African ministers decided to receive a report on the situation at the board's next session and to invite the OAU president, William Tubman of Liberia, to use his good offices to resolve the dispute.

After several postponements the Arab League Council met in an extraordinary session in Tunis on February 27. All twenty-one members of the League sent delegations. The meeting was called to discuss the dispute between Tunisia and Libya, but on Syria's motion two other matters were added to the agenda: Egyptian-Israeli normalization and a concentration of Israeli forces on the Syrian frontier. Predictably, Tunisia blamed Libya, and Libya claimed it was not involved in what had been an internal uprising. First, the council established an interim committee to start discussions on the dispute. In its final resolution the council invited Tunisia and Libya to stop all their campaigns against each other and seek to normalize their relations. The committee, composed of Iraq, Syria, Kuwait, Jordan, and a member of the League Secretariat, was asked to contact the two governments and invite them to carry out the council's recommendations. The committee was also authorized to convene the council at any time in the event this recommendation was not followed.(18)

Just as the council was taking up the dispute a tragic coincidence occurred. On February 26 Prime Minister Hedi Nouira of Tunisia, Bourguiba's chosen successor and Qaddafi's nemesis, apparently suffered a stroke, was flown to Paris, and admitted to the hospital for neurosurgical tests. The stroke removed him from political life and left him partly paralyzed. The scurrilousness of Qaddafi's policy emerged in Libya's treatment of Nouira's crippling. Citing a report by "Gafsa Radio" which it had allegedly monitored in "southern Italy," the Tripoli station, Voice of the Arab Homeland, described Nouira's stroke as an injury resulting from an attempted assassination by Tunisian revolutionaries. Qaddafi then used Nouira's misfortune to distort the outcome of the Arab League Council meeting. Because Nouira was no longer in power, and because contacts between Libya and France had allegedly resulted in French withdrawal from Tunisia, Qaddafi concluded that there was actually only one item on the League Council's agenda: the normalization of relations between Egypt and Israel.(19) Qaddafi took advantage of Nouira's departure to stop the most slanderous attacks on Tunisia, and he made friendly gestures to Nouira's successor, Mohammed Mazli.

As the uproar caused by the attack settled down, there were many attempts to explain Qaddafi's motives. The most obvious and undoubtedly his fundamental object was to destroy the Tunisian government, which Qaddafi regarded as a vestige of French colonialism, and criticized as anti-Islamic. Before he was stricken, Hedi Nouira recalled that for at least two years Qaddafi had been following a path of subversion and violence against many states, not just Tunisia. On Libya's revolutionary anniversary in 1978, Nouira said, Qaddafi had announced that people's committees would be made active throughout the Arab world. "These committees," Qaddafi had said, "are to work, openly or clandestinely, for the seizure of power and the realization of unity."

Other motives cited were envy of Tunisia's stability and progress, frustration over Libya's recent failures in Africa and the Middle East, subservience to the Soviet Union, and a desire to revive the fundamentalist spirit of Islam. Another view, favored by French experts on Tunisia was: "Libya is an armed camp, and Qaddafi needs outlets for that pent-up aggression."(20) A high Tunisian official in the presidential palace speculated that Qaddafi had been after a "mini-Kabul," comparing Gafsa, somewhat implausibly, to the Soviet invasion of Afghanistan.(21)

Clearly, no single explanation will suffice, and there are undoubtedly elements of truth in all of these. The very existence of Tunisia – moderate, Francophile, resilient – is undoubtedly an affront to Qaddafi, a constant reproach. What, after all, does the Jamahiriyah's power amount to if after all the words, all the oil money, all the Soviet weapons, Libya can't even alter the government of small, weak Tunisia? Therefore, a more helpful way of grasping the reasons behind Qaddafi's action may be to postulate his enormous hostility to Tunisia and seek not motives for the assault which are ever-present, but a conjunction of factors that might have led him to decide to attack in late January 1980 instead of three months earlier or six months later.

Exactly what triggered the Gafsa raid is unknown. It was well rehearsed, which argues for a long period of preparation and advance. In what may have been a mere coincidence but is certainly intriguing, Qaddafi and Jalloud watched a military exercise on January 24 described as the use of "border-crossing missiles" to defeat a hypothetical attack on Libya. On the other hand the Tunisian commandos were in the camps, and a number of them were apparently veterans of combat in Lebanon and Uganda. It would not have taken an excessively long time to ready them for the attack on Gafsa. It is guesswork, of course, but there was something unique about January 26-27, and that uniqueness may have convinced Qaddafi to attack Tunisia then rather than at some other time. These days did not simply include the anniversary of the Tunisian general strike and the prophet Mohammed's birthday. They marked the opening of the Islamic conference in Islamabad, which was called to discuss and, as it proved, to condemn the Soviet invasion of Afghanistan. Libya opposed this and had requested a postponement. They also marked the time when Israel and Egypt began the normalization of their relations, as provided for in their peace treaty.

In an interview with the Jordanian publication Ar-ra'y a few days before the raid, the Libyan foreign minister complained that the very nature of the Islamic conference was being perverted. The conference was born, he said, after the fire in the Al-Aqsa Mosque, as a way to defend Jerusalem and the Palestinians. How could this be done when "the world and Islamic public will be preoccupied with the normalization of Egyptian-Israeli relations?"(22) At the first closed session of the conference Libya made a violent attack on the United States. Its delegate (Libya had declined to send its foreign minister) charged that all the "fuss" about the invasion of Afghanistan was a ploy by the United States "to divert attention from its aims on other regions."(23) Despite this Libyan demarche and the refusal of the PLO to oppose the Soviet invasion in public the conference unanimously condemned the invasion and demanded the immediate and unconditional withdrawal of all Soviet troops from Afghanistan. The Islamic states were invited not to recognize the new Afghan regime, to sever ties with Afghanistan, and to boycott the Olympic Games. The resolution had been drafted by Saudi Arabia. Its overwhelming approval was not only a victory for the desert kingdom but brought the Islamic Conference closely in line with U.S. policy on the invasion, as well. The conference also condemned the exchange of ambassadors between Egypt and Israel, and agreed to call on all Muslim countries to boycott Egypt politically, economically, and culturally because of the normalization.

By attacking Tunisia during the meeting at Islamabad and in the first days of the Egyptian-Israeli normalization Qaddafi may have planned to wrench the international initiative out of the hands of those who supported − or tolerated − Camp David and were anti-Soviet. If he could snatch the headlines away from Sadat and the anti-Soviet coalition at Islamabad perhaps he could force the world to turn back to militancy against Israel. At a minimum, the Gafsa raid, coming so close on the heels of the capture of the Grand Mosque at Mecca, would serve as a warning to moderate Arab regimes of the dangers of friendship with the West. Qaddafi may also have hoped to benefit from the preoccupation of the West with the Soviet invasion, which would diminish as time passed. It was not necessary for Qaddafi to win at Gafsa to achieve any of these objectives, and one assumes he was not unrealistically optimistic about the likelihood that the raid would cause the fall of Tunisia.

Any opinion on the results of the raid is even more speculative than the assessment of motives behind it. The chief gain for Libya appears to have been rhetorical and not real. Once again Libya wished to appear as the uncompromising champion of revolution, liberation, and Arab unity. The stand Qaddafi wished to take would have been: It is not Libya but the Tunisian government which divides the Arab world, oppresses the Tunisian Arab people, and degrades Islam. Libya will always stand for freedom of the masses, Arab unity, and Islam. But the Tunisian government did not fall. If anything the attack rallied the public to the government and stifled unrest, as one after another of the main opposition leaders spoke out against foreign intervention; some even offered their services to the government. The raid also came as the Carter administration sought congressional approval for a major expansion in military aid to Morocco. Not only did the Gafsa assault greatly simplify this task, but it also added momentum to the policy of giving U.S. arms and support to friendly governments near Libya. Tunisia had been pushed into an even stronger pro-Western stance, and now joined Morocco, Egypt, and Sudan. Somalia and Oman would soon be added, though their concerns lay more with Ethiopia and South Yemen (Peoples Democratic Republic of Yemen, or PDRY) than with Libya.

Whether by accident or design news about Libya flooded the media in the United States in 1980 and 1981: torrents of scandal, dirty tricks, and assassinations; a cast of conmen, mercenaries, and terrorists. Over it all loomed the stiffly grinning face of Muammar Qaddafi, a being divorced from reality, a gaudily dressed, leering spider at the center of a web of intrigue, money, and death. The Billy Carter affair dragged on, fed by partisan politics, revenge-seeking Republicans, and yellow journalism. A full-blown Senate inquiry finally quieted the controversy, but not before an attempt had been made to wrench control of the Democratic National Convention out of the president's hands. Above all, there were constant revelations and near obsession in the industrial democracies with two aspects of Libyan terrorism: the Libyan assassination teams or "hit-squads" operating in foreign countries, and the U.S. mercenaries training and arming Libyan terrorists in Libya.

In 1980 Qaddafi sent assassins to kill Libyans living abroad, a practice he had started at least five years earlier. A dozen Libyans died in Western Europe and the United States. This set the stage for the U.S. accusation in late 1981 that Qaddafi had sent a hit-squad into the United States to assassinate President Reagan and other high American officials. Also in 1980 the first accounts became known of the extraordinary terrorist entrepreneurship of Edwin Wilson and Frank Terpil. These two Americans undertook — for huge fees — to conduct a "technology transfer" from the United States to Libya. This time it was not automated steel mills or microcomputer chips that changed hands but terrorist know-how. In exchange for millions of dollars, Wilson and Terpil are said: "to have helped Libya set up a manufacturing plant for the production of assassination weapons; to have themselves helped Qaddafi plan political assassinations; to have recruited dozens of former Green Berets [U.S. Special Forces] to teach Libyan soldiers and Arab terrorists how to handle volatile explosives — how, for example, to turn ashtrays into weapons of terror; to have illegally shipped arms explosives to Libya with the aid of forged and fraudulent State Department export certificates; and to have involved other former CIA employees in their projects."(24)

While terrorism and the exploits of adventurers like Wilson and Terpil sell newspapers the U.S. fascination with Libyan terrorism in 1980 and 1981 surpasses the normal interest in a good news story. There are several reasons for this. The most obvious is the United States' repeated losses and vulnerability to assassination and violence: John and Robert Kennedy, Martin Luther King, Jr., George Wallace, Gerald Ford, Ronald Reagan, all victims of assassination attempts. It is a dreadful record, without parallel anywhere in the contemporary world, and perhaps at no time in history since the days of the likes of Caligula and the Praetorian Guard. These repeated numbing experiences of political decapitation, whether consummated or not, have left American society more sensitive to this kind of violence than the counsels of history and realism would recommend. Their extreme sensitivity blinds Americans to both the likelihood of assassination as a common weapon in societies undergoing rapid political, social, and economic change, and to the frustrations and ambitions that might lead nations and movements to resort to political terrorism. At the same time, the frequency of political assassination in the United States creates a ready audience for stories about Libyan or Palestinian or Soviet hit-squads. Not only are media consumers attentive and accepting, but seeing others in the act gives them a vicarious shudder of fright and, in a sense, some reassurance of the "normality" of the United States; since other nations are killing their own, the frequency of political violence in the United States appears to be more or less ordinary and not uniquely barbaric and distressing.

Stereotyping may be the second cause for the excessive stir caused by Qaddafi's terrorism. This is true in both senses. By resorting to terrorism Qaddafi appears to fit a familiar mold: he is "just another Arab": violent, erratic, untrustworthy, a zealot, perhaps even a psychotic. At the same time, because he can be seen as a general stereotype, and thus not a specific, human, political leader, public opinion grows accustomed to thinking of Qaddafi as inhuman or dehumanized, and an important bridge has been crossed toward the use of force against Libya and, by extension, against other Arabs, as well. Why not? They are really less than human. Look at the way they are behaving!

One could also observe that Americans are fascinated with Qaddafi's violence because their own society is so violent, unable even to ban the sale of handguns in a country where the murder rate is five to ten times higher than it is in any other industrial society. Qaddafi, as the saying goes, is as American as the Saturday-night special. In addition, Qaddafi's trail of murder and terror has been uncovered while the memory is still fresh of the CIA's exploding sea shells and other frightful devices for killing enemies of the United States. Many of the same reporters who in the 1970s covered the Church committee's astonishing revelations about CIA excesses were covering the "Qaddafi connection" in the 1980s. Here is another way in which the audience is ready to learn the worst.

Whatever the exact reasons for the American fixation on Qaddafi's terrorism, there is no doubt that this obsession became an important political force in its own right. It thus became subject to manipulation by Qaddafi and others abroad and, above all, required the president and his advisors to exercise great care in order to control the public backlash, rather than be controlled by it. As will be seen, this appears to have been one of the principal reasons for publicizing the story about the hit-squad targeted on President Reagan. The fantasylike, nightmarish quality of it all could in this way be broken, because the U.S. government could be seen to be taking limited, real, and effective measures to combat the threat. It was also a way for the administration to seize the initiative away from the terrorists, who draw most of their results – the terror in terrorism – precisely from the shock of surprise and the profanation of what are ordinarily sacred or immune parts of daily life.

There is no doubt of Qaddafi's responsibility for the attacks on Libyan exiles. The attacks had been going on at least since the failed attempts to kill Omar Meheishi in 1975 and 1976. The decision to escalate the attacks became publicly known in January and February 1980, and coincided with a drastic resort to purges and repression in Libya and greater militancy abroad. The connection between internal political developments and Libya's foreign policy is particularly strong during this period. The Fifth General People's Congress, which ended on January 6, 1980, confirmed the replacement of six cabinet ministers and the severance of ties with Fatah, Yasir Arafat's branch of the PLO. These decisions indicated dissatisfaction with the past and a turn toward greater militancy at home and abroad. Foreign Minister Turayki confirmed the link between foreign and domestic policy or, as he put it: "Socialist People's Libyan Arab Jamahiriyah foreign policy is a reflection of the great achievements and revolution which has been and continues to be witnessed in the Jamahiriyah."(25) Relations were also broken with China. However, it remained for Qaddafi to give a hint of what lay ahead. In his message to the congress pariticipants "the commander of the revoltuion" observed that "the people's authority" had been established in Libya. "People can now do without governments, presidents, and parliaments," he added. The Libyan people were already "deciding their future, drawing their internal and foreign policies, and dispensing their country's wealth freely" without the aid of government. The people's revolutionary committees now have nothing to do but "agitate the masses and guard them." Despite this happy news, Qaddafi struck an ominous note toward the end of his telegram: "We are only left," he said, "with the task of a final onslaught on the exploitative society and the experiment of a totally armed people."

The words are vague, but their meaning soon became all too clear. At home they meant the murder of some and the dismissal and arrest of as many as 2,000 people as Qaddafi tightened his control of Libyan society and systematically completed the destruction of the wealth and power of the middle class. News of these convulsions reached the outside world throughout the first half of 1980. Their foreign counterpart was the break with Fatah, a drawing closer to the Soviet Union, and Qaddafi's decision to send his agents abroad to murder Libyans living in Europe and the United States.(26) In early May, for example, a senior U.S. official told newsmen that 2,000 and possibly as many as 4,000 people had been arrested in a massive purge in Libya.

The explanation of the mass arrests and violence that was generally accepted in the West was given by Youssef Ibrahim in an article published in the New York Times on May 15. According to British and American diplomats and at least one scholarly expert the extraordinary repression and violence perpetrated by Qaddafi in Libya and abroad was his response to growing opposition at home aroused by an attempt "to change the structure of the state by abolishing the traditional tools of government and turning power over to the masses." This appeared to have resulted in "political and economic chaos." The opposition had not developed overnight but had been building since 1978 when Qaddafi had begun to put the principles of the Green Book into practice. For example, one of the precepts of the Green Book was that everyone should own the house they lived in. When renters learned this and saw that the government encouraged them, they simply stopped paying rent. In other words, there was a nationwide expropriation of property. But in Libya, as elsewhere in the developing world, one of the few legal ways for members of the middle class to increase their income had been to build houses and charge rent. At a stroke they lost a traditional means of amassing wealth. Other edicts followed that nationalized wholesale trade, hitting directly at the large merchants. It is understandable that these kinds of policies would alienate the merchants, the middle class, the educated, many of whom had benefited from and supported the revolution in its early phases. They were soon joined by middle and senior level government officials and army officers who opposed the apparent decentralization of authority into the hands of people's committees and revolutionary committees, whose interventions in the daily operations of business and government often ended in the "political and economic chaos" mentioned by Western diplomats.(27)

It is possible to take another view. The repression and assassinations may have been logical and ought to have been expected. They may have been the planned culmination of a series of policies designed not merely to restructure Libyan society but, through the use of class warfare, to destroy the wealth and power of the one segment of Libyan society capable of posing a challenge to Qaddafi. The same was true of the Libyans living abroad. There are nearly 40,000 of them. Enough recruits could be found in such a large group to form the nucleus of an educated effective opposition movement. Indeed, a number of opposition groups had already been formed and had begun to operate. Idi Amin had been overthrown by just such an exile coalition, with foreign assistance. To survive, Qaddafi would have to intimidate or kill the most daring of the expatriates and to fashion ways to control the rest. In other words, the internal repression and the campaign of foreign assassination were not an ad hoc response to emergency but part of a calculated plan to change Libyan society and solidify Qaddafi's control of power.

From all reports the plan was a striking success, and Qaddafi was able to moderate it in his remarks at the revolutionary anniversary ceremonies the following September 1. "The process of agitation should be reasonable," he said. "No one is allowed to take individual or unlimited initiatives except in extreme situations where defense of the revolution and the people's authority is called for." By that time Qaddafi had ample reason to be extremely pleased with what had been accomplished. The expatriates were cowed. At least ten had been murdered in Europe and the United States, and if anyone had failed to get the message the hullabaloo in the Western and particularly U.S. press would have frightened into apathy all but the hardiest souls. At home, the revolutionary committees had cast "a pall of fear" over Libyan society. According to one report the committees were under Jalloud's personal supervision. According to another they were supervised out of Qaddafi's personal office. They had become the regime's political police, in the words of a foreign diplomat. Until August there had been nightly telecasts of trials by revolutionary tribunals. The revolutionary committees had spread "a crippling fear of denunciation and arrest" into every factory, office, and military unit. Much of the economy, except the oil industry, was paralyzed. Everyone feared that an order or a contact would be turned against them. Libyans were too frightened to meet foreigners who were old friends and refused even to return their phone calls. Professors at Al Fatah University in Tripoli said education had stopped because of the extreme political agitation of the students. In some cases the revolutionary committees had assumed the power to hire and fire, and to determine who, for example, was assigned to the people's bureaus (embassies) abroad.(28) Whether Libya's terror was planned or resulted from an excess of zeal need not be decided at this time. It is enough to describe its main features and to note the possibility that it was turned on, and turned off, by Qaddafi to accomplish specific political and economic ends.

The campaign to intimidate and control the exile community appears to have been launched in early February. It was first publicized at the conclusion of a nationwide meeting of revolutionary committees held at Qaryunis University in Benghazi. The deliberations of the revolutionary committees touched domestic as well as foreign concerns. Meeting under the slogan "for the preparation for the final storming of the society of exploitation and dictatorship" the revolutionary committees issued a frightening declaration: "Physical elimination becomes the end stage in the conflict of the revolutionary struggle for a final solution when removing economic, political and social weapons from the counter-revolutionaries [by establishing Jamahiriyah, people's committees?] fails to put an end to their activities." This terrible warning would be used by Qaddafi's agents both at home and to frighten Libyan expatriates in Europe and the United States. In case anyone missed the point the revolutionary committees made it unmistakable. Their task included, they declared: "The physical elimination of the enemies of the revolution abroad."(29)

The revolutionary committees moved quickly. Before the month was out, a Libyan expatriate was murdered in Malta, where thousands of Libyans had moved. By early March, Western antiterrorist services had begun to warn their governments that Qaddafi had launched an assassination campaign against Libyans abroad. Acting on this warning on April 5 the State Department quietly ordered two Libyan diplomats to leave the country within 48 hours. According to a department spokesman the two were expelled for distributing leaflets calling for the assassination of opponents of Qaddafi (the leaflets repeated the "physical elimination" line from the revolutionary committees' declaration) and for using "coercive methods" to control the 3,000 to 4,000 Libyan students in the United States. The two diplomats, Moftah S. Ibrahim, a third Secretary, and Mohammed Tarhuni, cultural attaché, were also said to have been trying to prevent the students from expressing opposition to Qaddafi. The Libyan leader had openly called for the assassination of dissidents two weeks earlier, according to the spokesman. The situation was unusual. The Libyan embassy had been taken over by "students" in the fall of 1979 and turned into a "people's bureau" on Qaddafi's orders. Ostensibly, there were no Libyan diplomats in the country, only members of a five-man committee in charge of the people's bureau. This committee supervised about twenty employees.

The release of information about the expulsions was delayed partly to protect the two remaining U.S. diplomats in Libya, who had been sent on an "extended shopping trip" to Tunisia at the time the expulsion order was issued. But the silent deportation was also meant to convey a strong signal to Qaddafi not to bring his strong-arm tactics and death squads into the United States. That may have been the intention, but Qaddafi wasn't willing to respond to such deferential gestures.(30) He reiterated his death threat in early April. With the news of the Washington expulsions suppressed, the world was even less prepared than it might have been for the string of gruesome murders that followed as the Libyan death squads went into action. On April 11 two gunmen shot a Libyan journalist several times in the stomach as he distributed an Arabic publication to worshippers leaving the Islamic Center mosque in London. The victim, Mohammed Mostafa Ramadan, died in a nearby hospital. His murderers were caught. Scotland Yard described them as of Middle Eastern origin, "believed to be Libyan." Ramadan was said by a friend to have been "a bitter opponent of Colonel Qaddafi," someone who regarded himself as a political exile from Libya. He worked free-lance for Al Arab, an Arabic newspaper published in London, and contributed to the Arabic service of the BBC. The report of Ramadan's murder also carried another disturbing bit of information. Western officials thought that the murder campaign would focus on Italy and England, but they feared that the visa files seized in the December attack on the U.S. embassy in Tripoli would be used to track down Libyan dissidents living in the United States. A companion article reported even more startling news. The flight plan of Anwar Sadat's trip to the United States that week had been changed to forestall a Libyan terrorist attack. The plan apparently was to attack Sadat's plane with a surface-to-air missile as it landed to refuel in the Azores. The evidence of the plot was not conclusive, but the Egyptian authorities had taken it seriously enough to order the plane to fly instead to England to refuel.(31)

On April 24 the U.S. raid into Iran ended in failure followed by an aircraft collision and fire in the eastern Iranian desert that left eight dead. On the next day two developments took place, one in London with immediately tragic consequences and the other, in Washington, repulsive but without any apparent direct connection with the assassination campaign. In London two Arab gunmen walked into a legal office in West Kensington and asked for a Libyan expatriate, Mohmoud Noufa, who worked at the agency as a legal consultant. When he was pointed out they approached him and opened fire. Noufa was hit several times and died as his fellow employees looked on.(32)

In Washington two former CIA agents, Edwin P. Wilson and Frank Terpil, were indicted by a federal grand jury for illegally shipping explosives abroad, conspiring to commit murder, and training terrorists in Libya. A third American, Jerome S. Brower, president of an explosives firm in Pomona, California, was indicted on the explosives charge – technically, for conspiring to ship a variety of high-powered explosives, explosive boosters, explosive blasting caps, and other hazardous materials to Libya for a terrorist training project. Although the suspects claimed that the explosives had been shipped for use in clearing mines, the indictment charged that they had been used to make exploding ashtrays, lamps, alarm clocks, flower vases, refrigerators, television sets, and radios, and that Libyans had been trained to make the devices. Brower was also a consultant to the joint House-Senate Office of Technical Assistance, which was working on antiterrorist legislation, according to federal sources. He was convicted in December, fined $5,000, and sentenced to prison for a term of which all but four months was suspended. A warrant was issued for Wilson's arrest because he was outside the country in North Africa or Europe. Terpil was arrested at the U.S. Secret Service Academy in Beltsville, Maryland while attending a law enforcement trade show and, inexplicably, freed on bail. His release is inexplicable because he was an associate of Wilson, who had already fled, and because he had been arrested and charged in December in Manhattan for trying to sell 10,000 machine guns to undercover detectives. He had also been released on bail at that time.(33) The district attorney in Manhattan, Robert Morgenthau, said that Terpil boasted of selling $3.2 million in arms and other goods to Idi Amin. In an interview in March Terpil had admitted he was an arms dealer, but he denied breaking the law.(34) Wilson and Terpil were also indicted for conspiring to murder a former member of Libya's Revolutionary Council, Omar Meheishi, in 1976. Terpil was said to have used his association with the CIA to find an assassin, who was to be paid $1 million for the killing, and Wilson allegedly provided $30,000 in expenses. The plot was never carried out.

Of the three, Wilson was the most important to Libya for he was the brains behind the transfer of terrorist technology and know-how. Wilson was described in the indictment at the president of Consultants International, a "marketing" firm. He has boasted of controlling more than 100 companies in Europe and America.(35) Wilson, a large, outgoing, former Marine, served in the CIA for twenty years in a variety of assignments, from infiltrating the Seafarer's International Union to the Bay of Pigs operation, and other jobs in Southeast Asia and Latin America. In 1971 he retired from the CIA and joined Task Force 157, a highly secret organization whose clandestine responsibilities included the collection of information on Soviet military and commercial shipping for the Navy, and the infiltration of spies from Taiwan to mainland China.(36) Over the years Wilson became friends with a remarkable number of influential and powerful members of government, especially in the Congress, men like Senators Strom Thurmond of South Carolina and John McClellan of Arkansas, and Congressman Silvio Conte of Massachusetts.(37) He also had friends who would do him favors in the Internal Revenue Service and the headquarters of the District of Columbia police department. His long service in the CIA had made him known to senior officials at the Agency, such as Theodore Shackley, the assistant to the deputy director of clandestine operations. While he was still in government service Wilson lived very well. He bought a 1,500-acre estate in Upperville, Virginia and began to raise horses and cattle. His next-door neighbors were Senator John Warner and Elizabeth Taylor, and Wilson entertained lavishly. When questioned at the CIA about his growing fortune, Wilson said he had made the money in real estate.(38) After he left government service Wilson's wealth and enterprises multiplied wondrously.

The indictments against Wilson, Terpil, and Brower explained Wilson's remarkable business achievements. He was selling terrorism to Qaddafi for princely sums. The indictments were the result of a two-year investigation by the U.S. Attorney's office in Washington, agents of the FBI, and the Treasury Department's Bureau of Alchol, Tobacco, and Firearms (BATF). Among those named as active in the Washington investigation were FBI agent William Hart and special agents Richard Pedersen and Richard Wadsworth of BATF. The indictments contained deeply troubling revelations of amorality and indifference to national interest inside the CIA, one of the nation's most trusted and secret organizations. There was much worse to come. Wilson's and Terpil's betrayal of trust was much more extensive and damaging than was at first apparent. And Wilson was directly involved with the assassination campaign. Finally, it would become apparent that the CIA was either protecting its own, at the expense of innocent lives and the national interest, or was exploiting Wilson's ties to Qaddafi in order to infiltrate agents into Libya to spy on the Libyan leader's terrorist projects and massive arsenal of Soviet arms. All of this would become known in the year ahead. In 1980 there were the indictments and the mounting toll of murder as the Libyan revolutionary committees set about their work in deadly earnest.

On May 2, four Libyan diplomats were ordered to leave the United States within 72 hours. They were expelled for attempting to intimidate Libyans in the United States who were opposed to Qaddafi. Although the State Department announced that the United States still maintained diplomatic relations with Libya, it ordered the last two U.S. diplomats in Tripoli to come home. The four Libyans ordered to leave were members of the five-man committee in charge of the Libyan People's Bureau in Washington. They were Nuri Swedan, Ali Ramram, Muhammed Gamudi, and Abdulla Zbedgi. They claimed to be students but three had not been taking classes for some time. In explaining the deportation the State Department said that Qaddafi had publicly warned on April 27 that unless all Libyan dissidents returned home within ten days they would be killed, wherever they were.(39) According to the department, the four to be deported were "linked to an international campaign of terror that has resulted in the murders of four Libyan dissidents in London and Rome in the last two months." A U.S. official told reporters that "scores" of Libyans in the United States had been threatened with violence unless they returned to Libya. The Carter administration was trying to use the expulsions to deter the violence that had happened in Europe from happening in the United States.

The four Libyans surprised everyone by taking refuge in the people's bureau and refusing to leave the country. This produced an interesting legal tangle. If the four were not diplomats, because the embassy had been converted to a people's bureau, then they couldn't be deported without a judicial hearing. If they were diplomats, and the bureau was still an embassy, then the men and the building were protected by the customs of diplomatic immunity against seizure by U.S. police. The puzzle was only of theoretical interest. Police and FBI agents surrounded the building, and it was made clear to the Libyan spokesman, Dr. Ali Houderi, and his Arab-American attorney, Richard Shadyac, that unless the four agreed to leave voluntarily they would be denied water, food, and electricity. Finally, on May 9 the Libyan govenment agreed to withdraw the four diplomats. Hours later Qaddafi threatened to cut off the shipment of Libyan oil to the United States and Britain and withdraw Libyan assets from those countries.(40)

The day before the original expulsion order expired the Washington-ton Post reported that in London an Arabic language newspaper, Al Shark al-Jadid, had published a "death list" obtained from Libyan intelligence sources. The list included twenty names of Libyans living in the United States. One of the names was Faisal Zagallai, a graduate student in sociology at Colorado State University in Fort Collins. Other evidence of official Libyan sanction for murder appeared in the spring issue of Jamahiriya, an Arabic publication of the government-controlled student union, which repeated Qaddafi's threat of "physical liquidation" of the enemies of the revolution abroad.(41)

In Rome on May 10 a Libyan opponent of Qaddafi was killed by another Libyan in a cafe. Abdullah Mohammed el-Kazmi was the sixth Libyan to be assassinated in two months in Rome, Beirut, and London. He was the third Libyan killed in Rome in less than two months. Kazmi had gone to the cafe of the Hotel Turin near the Termini train station half an hour before noon to meet his cousin, who had brought someone else along. They talked for a few minutes. Then the third man pulled a gun and shot Kazmi twice in the face. The murderer and Kazmi's cousin fled. On the same day in Bonn, West Germany, a former Libyan diplomat, Omran M. el-Mehdawi, 43, was killed by another Libyan who approached Mehdawi on a crowded street and fired at him four times. He then threw down his gun and ran away. Captured by passers-by, he claimed he had shot Mehdawi because of a bad debt. The murderer was an employee of the Libyan information bureau. Police doubted his story.(42) The day after Mehdawi and Kazmi died, the four expelled Libyan diplomats boarded a plane in Washington for Rome, where police had just arrested Kazmi's cousin, Mohammed Fadi Kazmi, and accused him of arranging the fatal meeting at the Hotel Turin.

The British government then took action against the London people's bureau. Saying that "London should not be a battleground for Middle East factions," Britain expelled four Libyan diplomats for taking part in a campaign to harass Libyans living in Britain. Two weeks earlier a senior British official had gone to Libya and told Qaddafi of the government's determination to stop the harassment. Gradually the authorities were able to restrain the threats and murders in Britain but not before more Libyans and other Arab nationals had been killed and the Iranian embassy had been seized by terrorists. In acting against Libya the British government had to bear in mind that there were some 6,000 British citizens living in that country, and that British exports to Libya amounted to more than $600 million annually. After the calculated violation of dip-lomatic immunity in Iran, no Western government would dare ignore the consequences of its political actions for its nationals living within the reach of a revolutionary government in the Middle East or elsewhere in Africa and Asia. In what may have been an unrelated development on May 12, the Red Brigades ambushed and killed

Alfredo Albanese, the head of the antiterrorist police force in the Venice region. The same day more Libyan embassies were converted to people's bureaus in Austria, Bangladesh, Czechoslovakia, Greece, East Germany, West Germany, Rumania, Switzerland, Turkey, and Yugoslavia.

As tragic as the foreign assassinations were, they were surpassed by the ferocity of events inside Libya. According to the <u>Neue Zuricher Zeitung</u> hundreds of Libyans had been executed in the purge that was underway there. The Swiss paper added that there had been a rebellion against the people's committees in Jobuck, in which 11 died and 32 were wounded. Qaddafi chose this moment to expel 25 Americans and arrest two others, Michael Price and Roger Frey, who were later freed. The two were employees of an oil company and had been arrested for taking pictures of port facilities.(43)

Two more Libyans were killed, one in Rome, one in Athens, on Wednesday, May 21. They were the seventh and eighth to die in the assassination campaign. In Rome, Mohammed Fouad Buohjar, 55, the Libyan-born head of a lumber trading company, was strangled with a nylon cord and stabbed repeatedly in the chest and stomach. Calling themselves the "Libyan Revolutionary Committees," his murderers left a note saying "enemies of the people will be reached wherever they are." In Athens a former Libyan army officer, Abdel Rahman Abu Bakr, a well-known critic of Qaddafi, was slashed to death, virtually decapitated with a sharp instrument. On the walls of his room in the working-class suburb of Haidari his murderers had painted slogans such as "Revolution will live forever."(44) The dead man worked in a furniture factory for $13 a day. On ABC-TV's "Issues and Answers" the previous Sunday Qaddafi had denied ordering any killings. He wanted the exiles to come home, he said, in order to protect them from the revolutionary committees.

The assaults and deaths continued. Rome police arrested a Libyan, Monsur Mezaroni Belgazem, 25, after he fired three shots at the owner of a restaurant on May 22. "I was sent by the people to kill him," he told police. "He is a traitor and an enemy of the people." The intended victim was Salem Mohammed Fezzani, a naturalized Italian of Libyan origin. Fezzani said there had been two other men with Belgazem.(45) Still another Libyan was shot and killed on June 11. Dead was Azedin Lahderi of Tripoli, who had resided in Bolzano. He was killed in Milan's central railroad station, the ninth Libyan to die in Europe, the fifth in Italy in two months. Earlier the same day a Libyan had been wounded in a Rome suburb after lunching with his assailant. Qaddafi had announced the week before Lahderi's death that he could not guarantee the safety of any Libyans living abroad after June 11.

Immediately after the murder of Lahderi, Britain expelled Musa Kusa, the head of the people's bureau in London. The day after Lahderi was shot Kusa had stood on the steps of the bureau and told a reporter from the London Times that on June 11 the revolutionary committees had decided "to kill two more people" in the United Kingdom. "I approve of this," he added. Next day, after receiving his expulsion order, Kusa told reporters that Qaddafi's enemies abroad would continue to be killed whether the bureau was closed or not. Who is to be killed in Britain, he was asked, and how will it be done? I don't know their names or the means that will be used, he answered, but they were "former government employees who now presented themselves as spokesmen for the anti-revolution."

Regardless of Kusa's bravado, the killings slowed. An article in the Washington Post stated that around June 10 Qaddafi had ordered the killings stopped.(46) They did not stop, but there was a pause in the killing, at least outside Libya. It ended on October 15 in a bizarre case that ultimately connected the terrorist entrepreneur, Ed Wilson, to the assassination campaign. Faisal Zagallai, 35, a Ph.D. student in sociology at Colorado State University, was shot twice in the head by a Caucasian man, who then vanished. But Zagallai survived, blinded in one eye, with a bullet lodged near his palate, and his attacker was caught and brought to trial. The government's fuddled handling of this case, together with the peculiarly slow-moving investigation of Wilson's "technology transfers," again suggests a larger U.S. interest in Wilson's Libyan enterprises than has generally been recognized. Here is what is publicly known about Zagallai's brush with death and its relation to Ed Wilson's merchandising of terror.

In the early evening of October 14, 1980 a Libyan graduate student, Faisal Zagallai, 35, was shot twice in the head by a gunman in Fort Collins, Colorado. Hundreds of shootings must have occurred that day all over the United States. But this was not just another felony. Zagallai's name had been on the "death list" of the Libyan government. In May the FBI had warned him that he had been marked for death. In response Zagallai had obtained a permit to carry a gun. Nor was Zagallai simply a Ph.D. candidate in sociology at Colorado State University. Faisal Zagallai and his wife, Farida, were from prominent Libyan business families. Faisal's father had been critical of the monarchy, but Farida's had been a minister of education during King Idris's reign. Both children had welcomed the revolution. In 1973 they came to study in the United States on government scholarships to learn English and obtain professional training.(47) In the 1970s Faisal Zagallai was chosen by the Libyan students in the United States to represent them at several conferences in Libya. At the conferences he spoke persuasively in favor of a free student union, a free press, and the return of an orderly legal system to Libya.(48)

In 1976 Faisal and Farida were ordered home, where they were warned by Libyan authorities and told not to participate in opposition activities. Faisal disregarded the warning. On his return he played a part in the establishment of a Free Libyan Student Union.

It was supposed to be a clandestine organization of 2,000 members, a number Western officials suggest is exaggerated. One of its chief activities was apparently to smuggle antiregime propaganda into Libya. When Qaddafi hanged six dissidents in 1977, Faisal helped organize public demonstrations of opposition in the United States; the demonstrators wore masks to conceal their faces from informers. In 1979 both Zagallais lost their scholarships and were ordered home. They declined to go and had to rely on odd jobs and help from their families in order to live and complete their degrees.

Their lack of capital made them all the more receptive to the phone call on October 13 from a "well-spoken woman" who said she was looking for people who could translate technical manuals into Arabic for IBM. The job paid $2,000 a month. A recruitment interview was arranged for the following evening at the Zagallais' apartment at 7 P.M. Shortly before 7 the next night Farida asked her husband if he thought the "recruiter" was a Libyan hitman. Faisal admitted having had the same thought, but he needed the job. When the "recruiter" arrived, the Zagallais noticed that he was nervous and asked the wrong kinds of questions. They realized he had been drinking. After a few minutes Farida went to the kitchen to prepare refreshments for the guest. She heard the sounds of a scuffle and ran back to the living room. The "recruiter" was struggling with Faisal, trying to force him down on the couch. "It's him, Farida!" her husband shouted. She ran to the bedroom, tried to jump out the ground floor window, screamed for help. Neighbors appeared but no one intervened. She heard three shots. Faisal lay on the floor near death with wounds from two .22-caliber bullets. The "recruiter" had fled. Four days later JANA, the official Libyan news agency, accused Faisal Zagallai of being "an agent and spy for American intelligence" and said he had been dealt with by the revolutionary committees.(49)

November, December, January went by. There were no clues, no leads. The trail was cold. There was no doubt of Libya's responsibility for the shooting, but the murderer had vanished. Then in February two boys playing in a ditch a mile from the Zagallais' home found a .22-caliber pistol. The police were able to trace the gun to a pawnshop in Fayetteville, North Carolina, where Fort Bragg is located, home of the U.S. Special Forces (Green Berets). Here was the first hint of a connection with Ed Wilson, who had recruited Green Berets to train terrorists in Libya. Records at the pawn shop showed the pistol had been sold to Tully Frances Strong, who was found in Osmond Beach, Florida. Strong said he had sold it to an acquaintance, Eugene Tafoya, in 1976. Here was no "Phi Beta Kappa killer" in the words of an FBI agent. Not only had Tafoya thrown the gun in a ditch near the Zagallais' home, but he had rented a Dollar-Rent-A-Car in his own name at the Denver airport on October 14. The police had their man.

Tafoya, who was living in Truth or Consequences, New Mexico, was arrested on April 22, 1981 and charged with the attempted murder of Faisal Zagallai. Two weeks after Tafoya's arrest the State Department ordered the closure of the Libyan people's bureau in Washington. There was a good chance, a Department spokesman said, that the attack on Zagallai had been arranged and paid for through the bureau. Tafoya admitted nothing when first questioned. However a search of his house yielded an abundance of evidence that not only incriminated Tafoya in the Zagallai shooting but tied him directly to Ed Wilson, the terrorist entrepreneur. Among the items found in Tafoya's house: a hand-drawn map of an apartment resembling the Zagallais', a copy of Qaddafi's Green Book, some .22-caliber ammunition, a Libyan newspaper, and a Kuwaiti driver's license. Items that linked Tafoya directly to Wilson included: the telephone numbers for Wilson in Libya, London, and Geneva; the number and name of a woman close to Wilson; a code name Wilson used in international Telex communications; phone numbers of associates of Wilson in the United States; four U.S. passports with entry stamps showing that Tafoya had traveled to Libya and Malta in the summer of 1980 at the same time Wilson was there, and again in January 1981, three months after the shooting; banking records showing that after his return from Libya in January Tafoya received $8,623, by wire deposit directly into his checking account from Union Bank of Switzerland (this squared with statements by Tafoya's neighbors who said he left town frequently and returned with large sums of cash); incorporation papers for a company called Operational Systems International: Tafoya was apparently planning to file them in Virginia (in the mid-1970s Wilson had owned a company of the same name, and investigators believed Wilson may have intended to set Tafoya up in business); explosives primers; a tape recording of a telephone conversation in 1979 between Tafoya and, apparently, an associate of Wilson's, during which Tafoya discussed the bombing of a car that belonged to an enemy of Wilson's and Tafoya asked: "Do you know somebody that should quit breathing? Permanently?" Among these signs of Tafoya's liaison with Wilson were seventeen pages of handwritten notes taken by Tafoya about the behavior patterns of seven of Wilson's business associates, how and when they traveled to work, and how and where they spent their leisure time: the sort of information a hired murderer would need.(50)

As spring became summer Ed Wilson's "Qaddafi Connection" attracted more and more public attention, and this heightened interest in the links between Wilson and the shooting of Faisal Zagallai. But it was like running in molasses. Great efforts were made by law enforcement officers at the state and federal levels but they encountered foot-dragging, indifference, and a stunning lack of cooperation and coordination between the various government agencies with an interest in the case. There always seemed to be something holding back the investigation of anything having to do with Ed Wilson.

By mid-July 1981 frustrated investigators were telling reporters that the links between Tafoya and Wilson were so strong that they believed Wilson may have ordered the attack on Faisal Zagallai. But there was more. Other evidence found in Tafoya's house linked him to Douglas Haden, an employee at the Naval Weapons Center at China Lake, California. Tafoya had Haden's phone number and phone records showed Tafoya had called Haden several times at his home near China Lake. Haden said the connection was purely a social one. He had dated Tafoya's half-sister for a while. Four employees at the Naval Weapons Center were already under investigation for criminal activity and links to Libya. Two of these men, Robert Swallow and Dennis Wilson, had taken unpaid leaves from their jobs in late 1976 and early 1977 to go to Libya to work in terrorist training camps. They had been recruited by Jerome Brower, the Pomona explosives company executive. According to federal investigators Swallow and Wilson (no relation) apparently violated no laws. This was not so for the other two men, James Nichols and Ralph Calrani. They had been indicted along with three other men for stealing ten Starlight nightscopes, a low-light television camera, and a small remote-control helicopter. Then came the twist. When first arrested, Nichols said he believed they had been acting for the CIA when they took the equipment. The idea was to exchange the U.S. weapons for an advanced Soviet radar. The defense was a familiar one. Eugene Tafoya also claimed to have been working for the CIA. As Kevin Mulcahy, another of Ed Wilson's people, put it: "I thought he was agency . . . I had no question in my mind."(51) The CIA denied having any role in Ed Wilson's overseas activities and denied that Tafoya ever worked for the agency.

In short, the links between Wilson and Tafoya were numerous and strong, and a serious national security problem – the illegal transfer to Libya of sophisticated knowledge and equipment – had arisen. But federal prosecutors and investigators had begun to complain to reporters that nothing was being done in a systematic and coordinated way. The links between Tafoya and Wilson were not being pursued. No interagency group had been formed to investigate the three apparently linked cases: Wilson's terrorist entrepreneurism, the China Lake weapons theft, and the shooting of Faisal Zagallai. Several federal investigators said there was enough evidence to justify the indictment of Wilson as a coconspirator in the attempt to murder Zagallai. Some officials believed the investigations were being hampered because of "a general concern that if Mr. Wilson stands trial he could produce documents and other materials that could compromise national security and prove embarrassing to Federal authorities." The government was unwilling to move aggressively against Wilson in areas where criminal wrongdoing was suspected.(52) It was exactly what Kevin Mulcahy had been forced to endure for five years after coming to the government with proof of Wilson's illegal actions for Libya.

Just as these complaints surfaced, as if to remind everyone of the costs of delay and muddle, another Libyan student died in curious circumstances. On July 17 Nabil Abuzed Mansour, 32, was found dead in the trunk of a parked car in Ogden, Utah. He had been shot in the face five times with a .22-caliber pistol. Mansour had been dead about seven days. A fellow student at Weber State College, Mohammed A. Shabata, 35, was arrested at Chicago's O'Hare Airport as he waited to board a flight to Tripoli. Mansour's roommate, Mohammed al-Otaiby of Saudi Arabia, said Shabata had returned to Libya the previous year "to train with the military," but that Mansour had refused to go. It was a reminder that the killings of expatriates hadn't stopped. In London three weeks earlier a Libyan airline worker had tried to poison a Libyan expatriate and his family because they refused to return home. After dining with Faraq Ghesouda, and his English-born wife at their home, Hosni Farhat, 33, left a package of poisoned peanuts on the table. Ghesouda's two children found them. The poison killed the family dog and made the two children dangerously ill. Farhat was sentenced to life imprisonment.(53)

Although the investigation of the shooting of Faisal Zagallai uncovered some of Ed Wilson's activities, there was much more to be learned. In the summer of 1981 a New York <u>Times</u> reporter, Seymour Hersh, published the most thorough inventory of Wilson's enterprises that had so far come to light. In a two-part article published in mid-June Hersh told Wilson's story as seen by Kevin Mulcahy, someone who had worked for Wilson for six months. When he realized how dangerously illegal Wilson's activities were Mulcahy quit his job and went to the CIA and FBI. That was in the fall of 1976.(1)

Wilson and Terpil were not indicted for exporting terrorism, it will be recalled, until April 25, 1980. The Hersh articles raised and attempted to answer two questions about the Wilson affair: exactly what had Wilson done for Qaddafi's Libya, and why was he able to get away with it for so long? Hersh's third contribution was to force his readers to realize that Ed Wilson's doings in Libya, as repugnant as they are, constituted only a part of a much broader problem. At present, as Hersh showed through an interview with Philip Heymann, assistant attorney general for the Criminal Division in the Carter administration: "There is no control over an American intelligence official taking his know-how and selling it to the highest bidder. . . ."

After taking office the Reagan administration launched a major drive to combat international terrorism. But, as Heymann observed, "If terrorism is to be taken as a major national problem, we'll have to start at home and draft statutes that would bar the sale of fancy American equipment and fancy American expertise for terrorist purposes."(2) While this clearly is the most significant problem raised by Ed Wilson's apparent abuse of the knowledge and contacts he gained in his work for the CIA, Hersh's two questions about Wilson and Libya are intriguing and of immediate concern.

When Ed Wilson hired Kevin Mulcahy to run an office for him in Washington, Mulcahy, a former communications expert in the CIA, had weathered a broken marriage and a bout with alcoholism. He was starting over as a counselor of young people with drug and drinking problems. Wilson persuaded him to accept a job by promising to pay him $50,000 a year and, if he stayed a year, to give him a small farmhouse to use as a halfway house for youngsters with drug problems. When Mulcahy went to work for Wilson he discovered that much of what Wilson was doing was legal, such as the sale of large quantities of military items from canned food to aircraft. Mulcahy worked hard and, apparently convinced Wilson he could be trusted.

However, Wilson had other plans for his new employee. Early in 1976 Wilson invited Mulcahy to join a new firm, Inter-Technology Company, as equal partners with him and a third man, Frank Terpil. Inter-Technology, Wilson said, was formed to export communications and computer equipment; all perfectly legal. Mulcahy had a few doubts when he came across a sales order for the shipment of machine-gun silencers to an arms dealer in Zambia. He was concerned enough to check with the FBI and the Bureau of Alcohol, Tobacco, and Firearms (BATF). Both agencies told Mulcahy that the sale was legal and that they had no evidence of criminal activity by Wison and Terpil.

Wilson had in mind more ways to use Mulcahy. As part of a larger plan he took Mulcahy to a meeting in late May 1976 at the home of a senior CIA official, Theodore Shackley, then assistant to the deputy director for clandestine operations. The meeting persuaded Mulcahy that Wilson was working for the CIA. "I thought Ed was in bed with the CIA," he told Hersh.(3) Shackley maintains that he met Wilson simply because Wilson cultivated many sources of information and was well informed: Wilson was preparing to visit Qaddafi when this meeting occurred, and had brought along another man, Harry Rasfatter, with information for Shackley from SAVAK, the Iranian secret police. Shackley insists that Wilson's activities were never given official sanction of any kind.

After Mulcahy had been to Shackley's house, Wilson took him to a meeting directly concerned wtih Libya. Wilson's story to Mulcahy and officials at the American Electronics Laboratory in Falls Church, Virginia, was that the Libyans wanted electronic timers for use in clearing mines sown in Libyan waters during the 1973 war. Once again Wilson gave the impression that official CIA business was being transacted. Prototypes would be needed for a demonstration in Libya in June. Also present at the meeting with Mulcahy, Wilson, and the American Electronics people was Patry Loomis, an active CIA officer, who was working for Wilson illegally. Eventually several people at American Electronics, including another active CIA officer who had been assigned to work there, agreed to make some prototype timers after regular working hours. The unit price to the Libyans was set at $1,500; each cost $150 to make. So far the work was dubious, perhaps unethical, but Mulcahy (and his father) had worked for the CIA, and he was not naive.

At a security show in Brighton, England, Mulcahy came still closer to the line separating legal and illegal. A Syrian company, Abdallah Engineering, wanted to buy communications equipment that would encode, intercept, track, and decode messages. Mulcahy told Terpil the State Department would never issue an export license. Terpil replied: "Don't worry about it. We don't need licenses. Just get the order."(4) There were also buyers from the IRA interested in M-16 rifles. There were plenty of these on the market, since North Vietnam had sold much of its huge captured arsenal to Interarmco after the fall of South Vietnam.

Terpil then invited Mulcahy to step over the line. Did he want to make $5,000 for dropping off a gun without a serial number in Cairo? Mulcahy refused, but on other occasions he closed his eyes and acquiesced in illegality. It became routine for Mulcahy to falsify the end-user certificate that gave the destination of a shipment. A U.S. military vehicle with night-viewing equipment was shipped to Libya through Canada without clearances of any kind. The profit on the transaction was a cool $930,000, according to federal prosecutors. There were the infrared scopes for M-16 rifles mentioned earlier. And there was illegal ammunition for South Africa. On one occasion Terpil and Mulcahy went to Defense Apparel, a firm in Hartford, Connecticut, in search of 100,000 suits that were safe against radioactivity.(5) It was deep water. Suddenly it got deeper.

In July 1976 after the demonstration of the prototype timers in Libya by John Harper, another ex-CIA man who now worked for American Electronics, Mulcahy learned that the Libyans wanted 100,000 of the devices immediately. Terpil was eventually able to increase the order to 300,000. According to Seymour Hersh, the final contract called for 500,000 timers at $7,000 each, or $35 million for equipment that cost $2.5 million to manufacture. A new contractor had to be found, since American Electronics would not agree to build 300,000 timers without first making sure the offer had the official approval of the CIA. Mulcahy met an agent of Scientific Communications, Inc., a Dallas firm and regular CIA supplier, in a bar in Virginia to arrange the delivery of 500 timers within 30 days. Ed Wilson was there, along with yet two more senior CIA officers: William Weisenburger, an official in the agency's Technical Services Division and Thomas G. Clines, of the Office of Training. Clines was a close friend of Shackley; the two men went into the consulting business together after Shackley retired from the

CIA in 1979. Scientific Communications honored its contract, and the timers were delivered on schedule.

The timers were useless without explosives. This was where Brower came in. At a meeting in early August 1976, Brower, with his knowledge of explosives, immediately recognized that what Wilson and Terpil wanted had little to do with mine-clearing. Improvising, Wilson said something about a laboratory in Tripoli and demonstrations. He emphasized that there would be a great deal more business to come. Brower demanded a large advance payment, $38,000 according to Mulcahy, and then picked up the phone and called his plant in Pomona, California, with instructions on how to pack the dangerous materials, which included RDX, or cyclotri-methyline trinatramine. They are so easily exploded that it is illegal to ship them on passenger airplanes. But Brower, Terpil, Wilson, and Mulcahy arranged to pack them in drums filled with a gelatinous substance and ship them to Dulles Airport, where they were joined with the timers and equipment needed for a laboratory in Tripoli, and sent to Libya — all on passenger planes. Despite the callous and flagrantly illegal character of this act, Mulcahy still couldn't bring himself to break with Wilson and Terpil. "I was impressed by the money and the possibility of making a fortune," he told Hersh later.(6) However, Mulcahy was beginning to have second thoughts. These may have intensified when during another trip to England in August 1976, he was invited to a boating party near Oxford at which two of the guests were the terrorist "Carlos" and Sayad Qaddafi, a cousin of the Libyan leader and head of Libyan intelligence.

Mulcahy then went to Copenhagen for Inter-Technology. There he received a peremptory cable from Wilson and Terpil in Libya: Drop everything, fly to Washington, and order one Redeye missile from General Dynamics. The Redeye is a combat-tested shoulder-launched antiaircraft missile. The instructions upset Mulcahy. The Redeye could easily be transferred to Libya, whatever Wilson told him or ordered him to tell General Dynamics. Mulcahy began to dread the possibility that Qaddafi would use the missile against a fully loaded 747, or in some other hideous way. He walked the streets of Copenhagen filled with doubt and anxiety. If he left Wilson and Terpil he would lose all the money he'd been making, the good life, the travel, the parties. Even if he kept his mouth shut they might kill him to keep him from going to the FBI. He had broken the law in many small ways. Wouldn't he be as guilty in the eyes of a prosecutor as Wilson and Terpil? Hadn't he gone too far to turn back? Wasn't he damned if he went to the FBI and damned if he didn't? Finally decided to try to discover what Inter-Technology was really up to.

In Washington he went to his office and began to go over the files. What he found confirmed his worst fears. Documents which he had never seen but which carried his forged signature made all too clear that Inter-Technology was a fake, a front behind which Wilson and Terpil promised to train terrorists in Libya. Specifically, they had contracted with the Libyan government to provide a six-month course in "espionage, sabotage, and general psychological warfare." The training program would stress "the design, manufacture, implementation, and detonation of explosive devices."(7) So convoluted and strange is the world of espionage that even these stunning discoveries had not truly liberated Mulcahy. What if it was all in some way a CIA operation? If he went to the FBI or even a lower-level officer at the CIA he might destroy a carefully built screen of secrecy and endanger the lives of the agents involved. At the same time, to keep silent was to remain an accomplice in terror, and someone who might become the fall guy for all the crimes that had been perpetrated under Inter-Technology's cover. Mulcahy came to a decision late at night in September 1976. Typically he called the CIA: He talked to Theodore Shackley and, to cover himself, a friend in the agency's Office of Security. Agonizingly, Shackley wouldn't say whether or not Wilson and Terpil were involved in a CIA operation. Mulcahy's friend reviewed the documents at Inter-Technology and advised Mulcahy to take his story to the FBI. He did.

Such was Mulcahy's odyssey. He broke his partnership with Ed Wilson and Frank Terpil, left the presidency of Inter-Technology, and became an FBI informant. But his journey wasn't over. Incredibly, Wilson and Terpil were not indicted for another forty-three months! Mulcahy spent some of that time hiding for his life and much of the rest dealing with investigators and prosecutors who didn't seem to take him or Wilson and Terpil very seriously. One can't avoid asking why it took so long to bring criminal actions against these men. Another question intrudes: Why, after so long, were indictments brought? There are a multitude of other unanswered questions, as well.

The delay in prosecution and exposure is all the more puzzling, because not only had Mulcahy revealed the past activities of Wilson and Terpil, but they kept on servicing Qaddafi's appetite for terrorist and military know-how, and their services were either described to the government by others or became public knowledge! John Harper, the explosives expert who had conducted the first timer-prototype demonstration, had stayed in Libya to build assassination weapons under contract to Ed Wilson. Harper learned of Mulcahy's desertion, and in October 1976 he went to the CIA and described what he had been doing at the explosives laboratory in Libya. About this time three Cuban exiles told the CIA an extraordinary story. They had been hired by Ed Wilson to assassinate Carlos somewhere in Europe. Wilson paid them $30,000 in advance, but when they got to Europe they learned the target was actually the Libyan, Omar Meheishi, who had tried to overthrow Qaddafi. Indignant, they rejected the mission, and returned to the United States. The CIA passed the information to the FBI. One of the active-duty CIA officers, Pat Loomis, and others began to recruit Green Berets for service with

Wilson in Libya. A Green Beret contacted by Lomis told military intelligence about the approach. Another Green Beret who had gone to Libya took his story to military intelligence and the FBI. Still nothing happened. Then, astonishingly, in December 1977 the Foreign Agents Registration Office advised the Justice Department that Wilson and Terpil had broken no U.S. laws. Recommendation? Drop the case. How could this have happened?

In his excellent articles Seymour Hersh offers a number of plausible explanations for the delay. Hersh appears to be convinced that there was no institutional cover-up involved, at worst just the loyalty of a few CIA agents to their kind. Hersh doesn't evaluate except obliquely the most likely alternative explanation, that Wilson and Terpil were being used to penetrate Qaddafi's terrorist operations, not directly, perhaps, but through the recruits that went to Libya to work for Wilson, such as Pat Loomis, John Harper, and the pilots, mechanics, and Green Berets. If this view is correct, the delay in prosecuting Wilson and Terpil occurred because time was needed to get U.S. agents in place inside Libya. Any harm the terrorist support might cause could be ignored, for Qaddafi could have and in fact soon did obtain the same or better services from Bulgarians or East Germans. Since Qaddafi was determined to have a terrorist training program he might as well get it from Americans, since this would at least give the United States a slight chance to penetrate Libya's clandestine services. This was made all the more imperative by the severe restrictions clamped on covert CIA operations by Congress and the president.

Instead of this admittedly conspiratorial interpretation Hersh offers a muddy stew of reasons that is persuasive, because it smells like a standard American mess, but leaves many questions unanswered. By Hersh's account the four-year delay occurred because of (A) a legal loophole: no U.S. statutes explicitly forbid conducting terrorist activities abroad; the FBI could intervene only if the illegal acts were committed inside the United States; (B) Ed Wilson's intelligence, charm, and contacts: he had been extremely careful all along, and his links with high officials seemed to put him above suspicion. As Hersh described it: "By the mid-1970s, Wilson was regularly throwing parties and offering hunting excursions at [his] estate, where senior members of the Carter Administration mingled with influential politicians and members of the intelligence community. Ted Shackley was also one of the guests. 'The name of the game is legitimacy,' one Federal official said. 'Ed Wilson brings three guys from the C.I.A. and Carter's man brings two senators. Everybody's legitimizing everybody else.' " (8) (C) bureaucratic rivalry: the CIA was reluctant to share its information with the U.S. Attorney's Office; the FBI, Bureau of Alcohol, Tobacco, Firearms (BATF), and Customs Service weren't frank with each other either; (D) incompetence or misplaced loyalty: when Stansfield Turner replaced Shackley and his superior William Wells, Turner was apparently not told of Ed Wilson's extensive use of active-duty CIA officers in his operations, of his attempt to have Meheishi killed, or of John Harper's description of the explosives laboratory in Libya. Hersh's comment on this is intriguing: "The primary loyalty of the men in the clandestine service was to Ed Wilson, their former colleague and associate and not to the new Director of Central Intelligence, who was viewed as an outsider who could not understand the mentality of an operative in the field. Kevin Mulcahy had violated the code." Whose operative in which field? Or was Hersh suggesting that Wilson was still working for the CIA? (E) Mulcahy's lack of credibility as a witness: in the fall of 1976 Shackley was ordered to write an official memorandum about the decisive phone call from Mulcahy, a conversation which Shackley, strangely, had not reported on his own; in the memo Shackley described Mulcahy as "irrational, paranoid, alcoholic, and an unreliable informant," someone "not in full control of his faculties."(9) Such an emphatic, purely negative view of Mulcahy's character from someone in Shackley's position understandably reduced the willingness of FBI agents to trust his information. In addition, Mulcahy's work as a drug counsellor and his constant association with addicts and near-criminals probably disgusted the agents and turned them away from the case. (F) the Letelier murder: the assassination of Orlando Letelier, former Chilean ambassador to the United States, in Washington in September 1976, preoccupied the U.S. attorney's office in the District of Columbia.

Is it enough to explain a delay of four years, while Wilson and Terpil continued their deadly work in the United States and Libya and, at least in Terpil's case, in Idi Amin's Uganda? It is a great deal, so much, in fact, that one wonders how the indictments were ever brought. The indictments started with the "legal epiphany" of Eugene Propper, an assistant U.S. attorney, who was in charge of the Letelier investigation. Convinced that Wilson was lying about his operations in Libya, Propper persuaded Mulcahy to work closely with his office and a grand jury in 1978. The problem was the lack of a statute on which to base prosecution: solicitation to commit murder, which Wilson had done with the Cuban exiles, was not a federal crime and could not ordinarily be prosecuted in Washington. Then Propper remembered that Maryland law applied in the district and, on that basis, he was able to investigate Wilson's part in the attempt to murder Omar Meheishi. Eventually this investigation resulted in one of the charges in the April 1980 indictment. But not for two more years. Propper and his principal assistant, E. Lawrence Barcella, were giving most of their time to the Letelier case.(10)

Another line of investigation conducted by agents of the BATF appeared to have run into a cul de sac. The two agents assigned to the case in mid-1978, Richard Wadsworth and Richard Pedersen, believed Mulcahy's story, but for a year they could not find the precise evidence they needed to justify prosecution. None of the witnesses would admit that any explosives had been shipped to Libya, legally or illegally. By late May 1979 the U.S. attorney's office was ready to let the case drop. Then, over the Memorial Day weekend Wadsworth decided to review all the evidence and testimony once more. In the files Mulcahy had given to the FBI when he broke with Wilson in 1976 Wadsworth found a worksheet in Brower's handwriting giving the kinds and amounts of explosives he had promised to send to Libya at the August 1976 meeting with Wilson, Terpil, and Mulcahy. These figures exactly matched a bill describing a shipment from Brower's factory the week of the meeting. Confronted with this, Brower refused for a year to admit he had done anything illegal. Ultimately he agreed to help investigators in exchange for a reduction in the charges he faced. In late 1980 Brower testified and confirmed Mulcahy's story. He was given a suspended sentence and made to serve four months in jail. His firm had made $1 million on the first shipment to Libya.

After Propper's resignation to go into private practice, Lawrence Barcella had supported Wadsworth and Pedersen in their pursuit of Brower. It remained for yet a third U.S. attorney, Carol Bruce, to bring the case home. A few months later in December 1979, Terpil was caught on the machine-gun charge in New York. Then in April 1980 came the federal indictments against Wilson, Brower, and Terpil. Incredibly, Terpil's bond was reduced from $500,000 to $75,000. Terpil had to pay only $15,000 of this in cash. It was an opportunity Terpil couldn't resist. On September 3, the day before his trial was to start in New York, Terpil escaped to Europe.(11)

Terpil's flight and Wilson's decision to stay abroad left many questions unanswered. To begin, there are the questions Mulcahy put to Hersh after having seen the pitiful results of nearly four years of cooperating with the U.S. government, of living in fear, while Wilson and Terpil continued to work for the Libyans and to live well abroad.

> Why didn't the CIA cooperate fully and aggressively with the United States Attorney's office? Why didn't the Government ask the agency for its assistance in locating and apprehending Wilson and Terpil? Why wasn't a combined Federal task force set up to coordinate the investigation? Why wasn't a special prosecutor used? Why did the FBI give the case such low priority? Where are we going to find Qaddafi's bombs in the future? What does it take − short of a big body count − to get the attention of the Congress and the White House to a potentially lethal situation? What is the responsibility of the United States to the world in a case like this?(12)

Hersh's answer is that Wilson and Terpil were allowed to continue their entrepreneurial terrorism for nearly four years and then to escape imprisonment because (a) Wilson was a slick operator; and (b) the U.S. government is nearly paralyzed by bureaucratic rivalry and sluggishness. It is a persuasive answer, and it is an image of the U.S. government that has been popularized to the point of stereotype. Can one make the other case: a conspiracy to quash the prosecution or at least drag out the investigation? Probably not on the evidence available, but here is a try. A conspiratorial motive is needed: let it be either that a number of CIA officials, including Shackley, had compromised themselves by working illegally for Wilson and, therefore, feared prosecution — Wilson repeatedly vowed to put the CIA on trial if he was ever brought to court; or, let it be that Shackley and his superiors at the CIA and in the National Security Council were prepared to tolerate Wilson's wrongdoing and moneymaking as the price for getting agents into Libya to find out firsthand what Qaddafi was up to. The two are not exclusive. Someone who feared blackmail by Ed Wilson might have argued in favor of impeding the investigation until there were U.S. agents well in place in Libya; one could always hope that the investigation would die out after a while, as it almost did on several occasions. That the CIA was forced to operate within newly restrictive guidelines during this period supports the idea of trying to exploit the activities of "free-lance" operators like Wilson.

What evidence is there in favor of a conspiracy, even the "benign" conspiracy on behalf of national intelligence? There is Shackley's memorandum, which wrongly shredded Mulcahy's reputation for trustworthiness. There is Shackley's failure to report the September 1976 phone conservation with Mulcahy. There is the very early conclusion by the Foreign Agents Registration Office that there was no case against Ed Wilson. There is the prolonged unwillingness of the Justice Department to assign a higher priority to the case, which would have put more FBI agents to work on it. The Wilson-Terpil case was never deemed "Special," which would have allowed the agents to work only on it and nothing else.(13) There is Ed Wilson's escape from Malta. Arrested and held in Malta for three days in August 1980, well after his April indictment, Wilson was nonetheless able to leave Malta unimpeded and fly to London on a revoked passport. Even if there was bribery in Malta, what about customs at Heathrow airport? Above all, there is the logic of the situation. Here was an American going freely into Libya, meeting often with Qaddafi, engaging in top secret clandestine work for the leader of the Libyan revolution. And Wilson was not just any American, but a skilled, intelligent, experienced, resourceful, charming, extremely well-connected CIA agent. Wilson may be a double agent, as one line of reasoning would suggest. But in a way, it makes more sense for the United States to have let him alone and to have tried to penetrate his operation around the edges, a Green Beret here, a mechanic there, a bomb-maker like John Harper, or even Mulcahy himself, who might have gone public not out of conscience but for reasons best known to readers of John Le Carre's spy novels.

Given the secrecy that surrounds intelligence operations it is quite possible that there will never be a full explanation of the coincidences and curious delays that blanket Ed Wilson's Libyan operations. However, the evidence against a simple bureaucratic rivalry/incompetence interpretation continues to mount. In August 1981 Douglas Schlachter was indicted by a federal grand jury for shipping explosives to Libya while employed by Ed Wilson. The indictment was made public in November. According to news stories Schlachter was a supervisor of one of Wilson's terrorist projects in Libya. In December 1981 Schlachter left Burundi, where he had been living, and returned to the United States. In return for his cooperation with federal prosecutors Schlachter was allowed to plead guilty to two lesser charges in early January 1982. Schlachter admitted his guilt; that was not an issue. But he claimed that he had been cooperating with the CIA from the start. His contacts at the CIA were familiar: Theodore G. Shackley and Thomas Clines, both high officials in the clandestine branch of the agency. Specifically, Schlachter claimed, in his attorney's words, "to have reported to and received instructions from Shackley and Clines in 1976 and 1977." The attorney, Alvin Askew, was emphatic: "The CIA knew what he was doing in Libya and approved it." Schlachter had concealed nothing: "My client met with Mr. Clines and Mr. Shackley several times," Askew said. "He told them he was shipping explosives to Libya, that he was involved in training Libyans how to make bombs, and that Ed Wilson had recruited former Green Berets to help train the Libyans." After Schlachter's reports Cline told him to gather intelligence in Libya and to try to get hold of a variety of Soviet military equipment, including radar components and a surface-to-air missile. There were lots of documents to confirm Schlachter's story, Askew said, and witnesses, too. Here it was again: Schlachter thought he was working for the CIA. Schlachter never took any money from the CIA, Askew said: "He was getting paid by Wilson, which was the same as the CIA, or so he thought." Schlachter's story was important because it tied a CIA intelligence operation to the delays in investigating and prosecuting Ed Wilson. The evidence was inconclusive and self-interested. Alone, Schlachter's story did not establish a CIA penetration. But it certainly made the theory more credible.(14)

Ed Wilson's name was in the papers again in October 1981. Reporters for the New York Times on the trial of Eugene Tafoya in the Zagallai shooting had discovered still another connection between Tafoya and Wilson. For three weeks in February 1981, four months after he shot Zagallai, Tafoya had lived in a bungalow at Broxmead Farm, about 35 miles south of London. The owner of the farm and another nearby retreat, Staplefield Grange, was Ed Wilson.(15) According to neighbors a business associate of Wilson's had brought Tafoya to the farm. Investigators familiar with the Wilson and Zagallai cases said they were unaware that Tafoya had visited the farm. They had not known about the farm until March, and since then the FBI and Scotland yard had been watching both Broxmead Farm and Staplefield Grange in hopes Wilson would go there. Tafoya's telephone records showed numerous calls to a number that proved to belong to the farm bungalow.

Tafoya was not the only "associate" of Ed Wilson to come to the farm and the grange. John Heath, a bomb expert recruited in 1976, had used the bungalow in early October. He was the "associate" of Wilson who brought Tafoya there in February. The two rural properties, worth about $1 million, had been bought by a Swiss corporation controlled by Wilson in 1978, the year Wilson began transferring his operations to Europe from the United States. Presumably he moved to protect his operations in case the investigations started by Mulcahy's revelations turned into a real threat to his freedom. Broxmead is a Tudor-style mansion built in the seventeenth century. Neighbors said large amounts of money had been spent to restore the main building: new wiring and plumbing, a new kitchen, a tenant farmer to keep the farm's more than 120 acres from growing wild. However, the mansion was left unfurnished and unoccupied. But, the bungalow, a small two-bedroom house near the entrance to the grounds, was used frequently. A Jeep Renegade, licensed in Virginia, was kept ready for the use of visitors.

Staplefield Grange is an old manor house, once owned by the Marquis of Reading. The grange now sits on two acres of ground and has a tennis court, swimming pool, and formal garden. The house has been divided, and Wilson owns the larger part, which was converted into a two-story apartment. The visitors at both retreats were mostly Americans. They often used the garden at the grange for barbecues and parties. There were Telex hookups at both the grange and Broxmead Farm.(16) Wilson also maintained an office in London, headquarters for at least five of his European and African companies.(17) According to the Times report, the London office supervised the recruitment of American and other Western mercenary pilots and aircraft mechanics, who, since at least 1980, had been flying and maintaining Libyan air force planes. A number of these men have told reporters that Qaddafi could not have invaded Chad without the technical support he received from these mercenaries.

Although Tafoya's connection to Wilson is clear, and through Wilson to the Libyan campaign of assassination and Wilson's entire terrorist empire, little of this mass of evidence was considered at Tafoya's trial. District Judge J. Robert Miller repeatedly ruled against a broadening of the trial's context. For example, the tape recording of Tafoya asking for an assignment to murder someone in 1979 was excluded.(18) These rulings weakened the efforts of District Attorney Stuart Van Meveren to portray Tafoya as Wilson's hired assassin. The judge forced the case into a narrow frame: what had happened when Tafoya and Faisal Zagallai were alone in the living room together? There were no witnesses. At the critical moments, Farida had either been in her kitchen preparing to serve orange juice or in the bedroom screaming for help. It was Tafoya's word against Zagallai's, and the judge refused to allow the prosecution to introduce the evidence of Tafoya's ties to Wilson that would have shaken the jury's willingness to believe Tafoya's story.

The case was tried as one man's word against another's. Faisal Zagallai stuck to his story. Tafoya had come to his apartment posing as an IBM recruiter. After a few minutes of unconvincing conversation and when Faisal's wife left the room, Tafoya had struck him and after a struggle, had shot him twice in the face.(19) Tafoya pleaded self-defense. He had never meant to shoot Zagallai and had certainly never been ordered to kill Zagallai by Ed Wilson. Tafoya's main line of defense had a familiar ring to it: he thought he was working for the CIA. According to Tafoya he was approached in London by a CIA agent who told him that Zagallai's propaganda was endangering the emerging peace process between Israel and Egypt. He was asked to visit Zagallai and scare him. The CIA would then follow up with an intimidating phone call. He shot Zagallai, Tafoya said, only in self-defense after the Libyan student pulled a gun.(20) At least some members of the jury found "a reasonable doubt" and refused to convict Tafoya of attempted murder. Instead, they found Tafoya guilty of two misdemeanors: third-degree assault and conspiracy to commit third-degree assault. On January 5, 1982, Judge Miller imposed the maximum sentences of two years and six months for both counts and ordered that they be served concurrently. Tafoya had been free on $5,000 bond since December 4 and would be set free on a $10,000 appeal bond as soon as he posted the money. Tafoya's attorney, Walter Gerash, told reporters that Tafoya would appeal the decision. Even if he lost the appeal, Tafoya would have to serve only sixteen and a half months in jail, because of time already served. He was also obliged to reimburse Larimer County for court costs. Meanwhile, he was a free man.

9
DETENTE TURNS TO DEBACLE: BILLYGATE

Qaddafi made a crude but concerted effort to improve relations with the United States in late 1978 and early 1979, and initially the Carter administration responded favorably. For example, in early March the State Department approved the sale to Libya of three Boeing 747s and two 727s. And in June Undersecretary of State David Newsom held several meetings with Libyan Foreign Minister Turayki to discuss ways to improve U.S.-Libyan relations. There apparently was even an attempt by the White House to use Libya as an intermediary in an effort to free the Americans who had been taken hostage in the embassy in Teheran. However, the possibility of improvement was ruined both by Libya's intervention in Uganda, which led the United States to cancel the 747 sale, and by the bad feelings and notoriety resulting from the entanglement of Billy Carter, the U.S. president's brother, in a variety of financial deals and lobbying schemes involving Libyan money and influence. What had looked so promising in the spring ended in winter-time disappointment and violence when, on December 2, a crowd of 2,000 Libyans occupied the U.S. embassy. The dozen Americans on the staff escaped without injury.

Since there are no indications that about this time Qaddafi had decided to change his views or policies to accommodate the interests of the United States in the Middle East and Africa, the abortive detente with the United States is probably best understood in the terms in which it presented itself. Qaddafi wanted the large aircraft, the 747s and 727s, and he wanted the C-130s even more. Perhaps the sale of the civilian aircraft would lead to the eventual release of the military transports, as well. The civilian planes could always be pressed into military service. The contacts with Billy Carter appear to have been an attempt to acquire a "friend at court" and at least a rudimentary lobbying capability. The Libyans were not to blame for Billy Carter's maladroitness or alcoholism, although they would surely have used both weaknesses, had the relationship continued for several years, as would most governments in a similar situation. The Libyans showed bad judgment in trying to do business with Billy Carter. A fat retainer paid to a prestigious Washington law firm would have shown better judgment ("playing by the rules of the game") and would have avoided the smell of conflict of interest that came with setting up Billy Carter in the nonprofit business of promoting cultural exchange and funneling Libyan "investments" into the United States.

To those with a more suspicious turn of mind the affair smacks of bribery, and possibly even espionage and subversion. A suspicious observer would say that anyone who spent five minutes with Billy Carter would know that he was unsuited as a lobbyist and inter-mediary for himself, let alone for a foreign revolutionary govern-ment. Either Billy Carter's Libyan contacts were naive and inept or they wanted to use him for other purposes. In the latter case his personal weaknesses would have been an advantage to Libya because they would have made him open to manipulation. For example, as long as the money kept coming Carter might not have paid much attention to where it went or for what purposes it was used. The Carter corporation could thus have become a conduit for funds to pay for the services of more effective and worldly lobbyists who would procure the 747s, or to support the actions of revolutionary and terrorist groups in the United States. Here again, Carter's weaknesses would have been an advantage. Who would suspect clumsy Billy, with his beer cans and occasional anti-Semitisms, of being involved in anything effective, let alone dangerous, even as a figurehead?

In 1979 little of this was visible. One saw only the surface disturbances. They were unusual. To begin with, there was already a scandal in the Carter administration. President Carter's budget director, Bert Lance, who had resigned in September 1977, was suspected of and eventually brought to trial for misusing the funds of two Georgia banks for his own benefit. At the same time a federal grand jury was investigating the manipulation of the assets of the Carter family peanut business to finance the president's 1976 election campaign. Some of the loans to the Carter business had come from one of Bert Lance's banks. Billy Carter had been running the family business at the time. The president and his brother were cleared of wrongdoing by the Department of Justice in October.

Then in early January Billy Carter welcomed a delegation of Libyans to Plains, Georgia. This quickly became the administration's third and most damaging scandal. The Libyan delegation was led by Ahmed el Shahati, head of Libya's Foreign Liaison Office. Shahati had also met with Undersecretary of State Newsom, and deputy assistant secretary for the Near East, Morris Draper. When the mayor of Atlanta refused to see the Libyan group Billy told reporters that "Jewish pressure" was behind the snub. His criticism of the "Jewish media" treatment of Arabs brought immediate protests from the Anti-Defamation League of B'nai B'rith and the chairman of the Republican Party. The story made the front page of the New York Times on January 12, and the president issued a statement disassociating himself from his brother's remarks. A spokesman for the State Department told reporters that if Billy were receiving money from Libya he would have to register under the Foreign Agents Registration Act, as an employee of a foreign government. Billy had visited Libya for eight days in the fall of 1978, the Times article indicated. He denied receiving payment to act as a host to the Libyan delegation. The Justice Department sent Billy a letter asking him to explain the nature of his ties to the Libyan group. Characteristically, Billy's response to the outcry in the Jewish community was obscene.(1)

In an article prompted by Billy's gaffes William Safire wrote that Billy Carter was not the only American contacted by Libya. There had been a determined effort to influence politicians and farmers in Idaho, the home of Senator Frank Church, chairman of the Senate Foreign Relations Committee. According to Safire, the Libyans worked through an Iraqi-born faculty member at the University of Idaho to arrange for the purchase of Idaho wheat for export to Libya. A number of farmers, businessmen, and politicians from Idaho traveled to Libya, including Senator James McClure and Congressman Steve Simms who would challenge and defeat Church a year later. According to Simms the Libyans wanted airplanes. "The first question they ask everybody is how they're going to get their jets delivered."(2) Shahati went to lunch with McClure when Billy took him to Washington and McClure arranged an off-the-record luncheon with the Agriculture Committee, some of whose members declined to attend when news of the meeting made the papers. Senator Church was visited by Idaho farmers and businessmen seeking his help to expand trade with Libya. Church was not impressed and issued a statement categorically rejecting the release of the C-130s. Ironically, the Libyans' continued interest in the transports made clear that the Soviet government had also refused to include aircraft of this type in the huge deliveries then underway to Libya.

Against this background there were two seemingly contradictory developments in late February and early March. On February 26 the senior vice-president of a company that controlled the arms manufacturer, Smith & Wesson, told the New York Times that he felt "encouraged" by the decision of the Justice Department to negotiate a civil settlement with the parent firm rather than to bring criminal charges against it for the illegal sale of night surveillance devices, called Startrons, to Libya. Dudley C. Phillips of Bangor Punta Corporation acknowledged that the Startrons had been shipped to Germany and then transshipped to a French agent for the illegal delivery to Libya. Federal investigators had concluded, according to the Times article, that when the Munitions Control Board denied Smith & Wesson's request in 1974 to sell 3,000 Startrons to Libya at $2,600 each, the company then received orders from a German company in Stuttgart and a French company, Regie Monceau, for the devices. These companies made false declarations to Smith & Wesson about the ultimate destination of the Startrons. Not only were the devices then illegally transshipped to Libya but the German firm apparently also displayed them to Soviet intelligence agents in Budapest, according to a memo from the Swiss branch of the arms maker to Smith & Wesson headquarters in Springfield, Massachusetts. At issue was whether or not Smith & Wesson officials knew of the false declarations before the deal was closed. Federal officers had found documents proving that at least some Smith & Wesson employees knew about the falsifications; Phillips did not deny it. There was ample evidence to support a criminal prosecution, according to federal officials involved in the case. "When the case got to Washington," one of them told the Times, "it was treated differently." Bangor Punta had hired one of Washington's most prestigious law firms to negotiate on its behalf with the Justice Department. Phillips said his company was discussing the payment of a $120,000 fine to avoid criminal prosecution. There was a great deal at stake. If an arms manufacturer is convicted of a felony, the Secretary of the Treasury may revoke its license to sell weapons in the United States. While internally the lesson of the Startron Affair was that wealthy corporations often escape the legal consequences of their wrongdoing, in Libyan eyes the lesson would have been that money talks in the United States and that with friends in the right places it was possible to circumvent the law. This view, confirmed by other similar deeds where the letter or spirit of the U.S. arms embargo against Libya were disregarded surely encouraged the Libyans to keep trying, particularly for something they wanted as badly as the C-130 airplanes.(3)

A week later during hearings before the Senate Foreign Relations Committee, the deputy assistant secretary of state for the Near East, Morris Draper, who had seen Shahati at the start of his tour with Billy Carter, said that the State Department had approved the sale of three 747s and two 727s to Libya. The United States had received assurances from Libya, Draper said, that the aircraft would only be used by Libya's national airlines. A Libyan request to buy two Lockheed L-100s, the civilian model of the C-130, had been refused.(4) Toward the end of March Egypt reinforced its troops along the border with Libya. The move, which was called routine at armed forces headquarters in Cairo, was apparently intended to warn Libya not to go too far in its opposition to the Egypt-Israel peace treaty. The move, which involved elements of the Second and Third Armies, continued the transfer of forces out of the Sinai into the western desert. The Fourth Armored Division with 600 tanks had already been moved along with major air and air defense units.(5)

Billy Carter's liaison with his Libyan "friends," as he called them, had rubbed several raw spots in American life. One was the wounded feelings of Nixon loyalists and Republicans in general over the Watergate scandal. They thirsted for revenge against the Democrats and used every opportunity over the next fifteen months to fan speculation about "Billygate," to promote investigations in the press and the Congress, and to embarrass a sitting president and his party. Billy's Libyan fling also outraged sensibilities of U.S. Jews on at least two counts. He shared a number of fairly widespread beliefs about Jews — for example, that they enjoy more political influence in the United States and the world than their numbers might have suggested they would — and he was perfectly willing to say this to reporters. Because he was a close relative of the president his comments made the front pages, and Jewish leaders demanded that the president repudiate the remarks. Libya is also one of Israel's most determined if not most dangerous oponents. Qaddafi's support for terrorist acts against Jews was particularly galling. Billy's deals with Libya thus awakened the fiercest loyalties of U.S. Jews to Israel, as well as their anger at his ethnic slurs. Once this double dynamo of political and ethnic revenge-seeking started spinning it could not easily be stopped.

In early April the New York Times published a background article on Billy's trip to Libya in September 1978 and the details of a business arrangement with Libya involving Billy and other Georgia businessmen. Billy was not contacted directly about the article; he was in a Navy hospital in California undergoing treatment for alcoholism. The Libyan contact had been originated by an Italian businessman, Michele Papa, in Italy. Papa represented an organization of Italian and Arab businessmen. He approached an Atlanta real estate broker, Mario Lianza, during a visit by Lianza to his birthplace in Catania, Sicily, in early 1978. Could Lianza arrange for Billy to visit Tripoli, Papa asked? If he did there was a lot of money in it for Lianza, in the form of large commissions on Libyan property investments in Atlanta. Lianza declined, saying he did not know Billy. But Papa wasn't easily discouraged and kept after Lianza during the six weeks he spent in Catania. Toward the end of April 1978 Papa sent Lianza a letter with an invitation in it for Billy to come to Tripoli, all expenses to be paid by the Libyan government.

At this point Lianza brought in another real estate broker, Tom Jordan, who contacted state Senator Floyd Hudgins of Columbus, Georgia. Hudgins knew Billy and set up a larger meeting at Plains, Georgia. Present were the Libyan ambassador to Italy, Gibrill Shalouf, Billy Carter, Lianza, and Jordan. At the meeting Billy accepted the invitation to visit Tripoli and it was agreed that a delegation would be put together to accompany him. In addition to Billy there would be two state senators, Hudgins and Henry Russel of Boston, Georgia; Jordan; Lianza and two friends of his from Atlanta; and a companion of Billy's named Randy Coleman.

The Libyans spared no expense. The party stayed at one of the best hotels in Rome and had two chauffeured cars available for their use. A week in Tripoli followed. Billy was treated as if he held high office, and was driven about with a motorcycle escort in a car flying the U.S. flag. A return visit to the United States by a Libyan delegation was planned during the group's stay in Tripoli. It was also decided to creat a nonprofit corporation in Georgia for the investment of Libyan funds in the United States. The partners according to Lianza were to be Billy Carter, a 40 percent share; Lianza, 12.5 percent; Senator Hudgins, 12.5 percent; Randy Coleman, 12.5 percent; Tom Jordan, 12.5 percent; and 10 percent unassigned. Billy told Lianza that David Gambrell, a well-known attorney in Atlanta, would handle the legal arrangements. Gambrell denied acting as attorney for the group, although he said he had spoken with Billy about the reception of the Libyan delegation during its visit to Georgia. During their visit, the Times learned, most of the U.S. group that had traveled to Libya and a number of other people signed a friendship agreement with the Libyan government. This was to be the basis of the corporation, according to Tom Jordan, who said he had understood the nonprofit corporation's purpose was to have been to establish a center for information about Libyan trade and culture and not to make money for the participants. Contacted by the Times, at an alcoholism treatment center in Long Beach, California in mid-April Billy confirmed that the cost of his trip to Tripoli had been paid by the Libyan government. But he denied doing business with Libya and denied Lianza's story about the nonprofit corporation. He had agree to take part in the 1978 trip and had invited the Libyan delegation to visit Atlanta simply in order to increase U.S.-Libyan trade, which would be a good thing for both countries. However, he was not opposed to doing business with Libya, he said.(6)

William Safire, once a speechwriter for Richard Nixon, kept the pot boiling with a muckraking attack on the Carter Justice Department. Safire criticized Justice for having its policy set in Atlanta by Charles Kirbo, an attorney and close advisor of the president, and for overlooking or stalling its investigation of six alleged coverups or scandals, including Billy's failure to register as a lobbyist for Libya.(7) Two weeks later reporters were told that the FBI had been ordered to investigate Billy's connection with the Libyan government.(8)

The first certain evidence that an improvement in Libyan-U.S. relations would be difficult to achieve came on May 25 when Secretary of State Cyrus Vance asked the Commerce Department not to approve the sale of the 747s and 727s and other aircraft, including the Lockheed L-100 cargo transports. A number of senators, including Richard Stone of Florida, a state with a large Jewish population, had been vehemently opposed to the sale.(9) Shortly after the suspension of the aircraft sale, Undersecretary Newsom made a three-day visit to Libya for talks with Foreign Minister Turayki on improving relations between the two countries.(10) Neither side would give ground on their differences over the Camp David process, terrorism, and Libyan intervention in Africa. The talks were inconclusive and left relations between the two governments unchanged. Given the ripening Billy Carter affair and the partisan and ethnic pressures it had brought to bear on the White House and Congress, Libyan-U.S. relations were to get much worse.

It should already have been obvious that Billy Carter had a knack for saying and doing the wrong thing at the wrong time. Any doubts on that score vanished when he turned up in Tripoli on September 1 for the festivities marking the tenth anniversary of Qaddafi's seizure of power.(11) In an eighty-minute speech prior to a military review Qaddafi attacked Israel and the "treachery" of Anwar Sadat in signing a peace treaty with Israel. A number of guerrilla organizations marched in the parade, including units from the PLO, the Zimbabwe (Rhodesia) Patriotic Front, and the Southwest Africa People's Organization (SWAPO), fighting for control of Namibia. The next day the Libyan embassies in Washington, Rome, Athens, Bonn, Madrid, and Malta were taken over by Libyans living abroad who acted on orders from Tripoli and renamed the embassies "people's bureaus." The move came after two years of similar changes in Libya, starting with the formation in 1977 of people's committees from the local to national level, and the order in 1978 for workers' committees to take over businesses.

A startling development two weeks later indicated that Qaddafi's campaign for influence in the United States went beyond contacts with businessmen and quasi-celebrities like Billy Carter. On September 16 Reuters news agency, quoting the official Libyan JANA news agency, reported that a group of black Americans had arrived in Tripoli and had conferred "the decoration of Martin Luther King" on Qaddafi, who had promised Libya would help blacks in the United States "to end racial discrimination and achieve freedom and equality."(12)

Additional evidence on the scope of the Libyan effort to obtain the aircraft became public at the end of September. For the previous eight months, the Justice Department had conducted a major, covert investigation of the possibility that Libya had bribed high U.S. officials with huge sums of money in order to win the release of the transports. An informer, whose identity was being kept secret, had triggered the investigation by telling the Justice Department that a bribery plot had been undertaken by Libya and Robert L. Vesco, a financier who had fled the United States a decade earlier when charged with a million dollar international stock swindle. Vesco was to receive $5 million for his services, according to the informer, who also said that Libya was willing to spend $30 million to obtain the airplanes.

In the spring of 1979, about the same time that the Justice Department learned of the alleged Vesco connection, the Libyan ambassador to the United Nations, Mansur Rashid Kikhia, contacted John C. White, chairman of the Democratic National Committee, through a mutual acquaintance, James C. Day, a former Texas state representative. Kikhia wanted White to arrange a meeting for him with President Carter to discuss Libyan-U.S. relations and airplane sales to Libya. White agreed to meet with Kikhia but declined to make the appointment with President Carter and advised the Libyan diplomat to contact the State Department. White denied that he had been offered any Libyan money. Kikhia did go to the State Department and had several secret conversations with Undersecretary Newsom, with whom he was acquainted.(13)

The informer also said that Day was involved in the plot. Day had pleaded guilty in April to federal charges that he had made false statements to obtain bank loans. White's recollection was that Day asked him to arrange an appointment for Kikhia with President Carter. According to his recollection he refused and told Day it would be improper for him to act in that way, but that he had met Kikhia later the same day for five or ten minutes. Day remembered things differently. There had been no request for a presidential appointment and the sale of aircraft had never been mentioned at either meeting.

In trying to make sense of what they had learned Justice Department officials had begun to suspect they were dealing not with a bribery scheme but a confidence game run by Vesco to defraud the Libyan government of the bribery money. The plan apparently was for Day to arrange numerous contacts and meetings for Libyans with administration officials. This would then be used as evidence to persuade the Libyans to put up money for bribes, and the plotters would then keep the money.(14) Reporters learned of the investigation when its covert phase ended. Federal investigators were virtually certain that no U.S. officials had taken bribes. From the Bahamas, Vesco told a Times reporter that he had not conspired with Day to bribe anybody. Day was just as emphatic. He knew Vesco and had met with him recently, but not about Libya. He had asked White to meet Kikhia, he said, for strictly social reasons, just because they'd never had a chance to meet each other before. Day also said he was in the process of negotiating an arrangement to open a Washington office for the Libyan government. When the deal became final, he said, he would register as a foreign lobbyist.

Predictably, William Safire pounced on the story and in his column alleged that a coverup was underway of corruption so vast as to constitute "a modern Teapot Dome" scandal. According to Safire, a witness seeking immunity from prosecution had claimed that Hamilton Jordan, Vesco, White, and "possibly" Billy Carter had "an agreement" with one another. Vesco himself was the subject of a grand jury investigation and this figured in another of Safire's bits of information. A friend of Hamilton Jordan, Spencer Lee, was paid $10,000 by an associate of Vesco, allegedly to have the president urge the attorney general to see Vesco's man. The note was never delivered and because of this, according to Safire, the foreman of the grand jury investigating Vesco had charged the Justice Department with a year-long coverup. Moreover, the photographs taken during the covert investigation by the FBI of the meetings between White and Kikhia had not been given to the Vesco grand jury. "No wonder the jury foreman suspects a coverup," Safire gloated.(15)

Why all the separate investigations? The FBI was investigating the Libyan plot, what Vesco called "Sandbox"; other FBI agents were looking into Billy Carter's failure to register as a foreign agent. Why weren't the two being looked at together? Safire wanted to know. There was also evidence that Vesco had sought a 50 cent-a-barrel commission for the sale of Libyan crude to an oil dealer "with Democratic connections." This money was allegedly to have been paid to Billy Carter and a high White House aide. "Is there any connection between Vesco and Libya, and Billy and Libya?" Safire wanted to know. "This obvious question is studiously not being looked into by the Vesco grand jury, or by special counsel Paul Curran's grand jury investigating Bert Lance's bank manipulations, some of which involved Billy Carter, or by the F.B.I. agents wearing blinders on their separate assignments." Safire speculated that Vesco may have hoped to use the Libyan money to ensnare and compromise high administration officials who could then be manipulated to quash an investigation into his stock-swindle.

Finally, Safire asked, what about White? He was a protégé of Robert Strauss, and Strauss's successor chairman of the Democratic Committee. Strauss was now the Carter administration's special Middle East negotiator. This made White "a logical target" of a Libyan bribery scheme. At the least White ought to be made to testify before a grand jury. To Safire, there was enough evidence of influence-peddling and wrongdoing to justify bringing all the little probes into the hands of a single special prosecutor. That this wasn't being done, Safire implied none too subtly, was in itself evidence of a coverup. In mid-October a federal grand jury was convened in New York to investigate the "Sandbox" affair. White was one of the first to testify.(16)

With this legal and political mess on its hands, the Carter administration was in no position to improve relations with Libya, even if Newsom's meetings with Kikhia and Turayki had yielded positive results, which they had not. Moreover, U.S. relations with Muslim countries were subjected to additional strain in the fall of 1979 by the seizure of the hostages in Iran on November 4, by the attacks on Medina and the Grand Mosque in Mecca, Saudi Arabia on November 21, and by the sacking of the U.S. embassies in Pakistan and Libya. The attack in Karachi on November 21 may have been precipitated by false rumors about U.S. responsibility for the attack on the Grand Mosque. The Libyan assault appears to have been premeditated, an act of government policy, intended to embarrass the United States, which already found itself in a very awkward situation in the Middle East and Gulf, and to put Libya forward as militantly anti-U.S.

Like the pain of an old injury "Billygate" kept returning to torment the Carter administration in the final months of what was the president's first and, as it turned out, only term. There was a rhythm to the publicity about the case. It burst out in late 1979 and early 1980 then subsided as Billy entered the hospital for alcoholism and a grand jury took up the question of high-level bribery to obtain the C-130s for Libya. The lowest ebb in notoriety came when Billy entered into a consent agreement with the Justice Department on July 14, 1980. This was, in essence, a court injunction which bound Billy to fully disclose his past activities on behalf of the Libyan government and, in future, to comply with all relevant statutes, and particularly the Foreign Agents Registration Act. If he failed to comply Billy would be exposed to criminal penalties. There was not a little irony in the settlement. It had been arranged by the president's counsel, Lloyd Cutler, and negotiated by two influential Washington attorneys, Stephen Pollak and Henry Ruth. All three, and especially Cutler, were Washington insiders. But President Carter had campaigned against Washington and had clung to his "outsider" image.

With the help of the president's high-powered insiders Billy escaped criminal and civil punishment for what he had already done for the Libyan government. This included, according to the Justice Department, the conduct of a "propaganda campaign" on behalf of Libyan foreign policy objectives. The Libyan government had paid Billy $20,000 in January, and $200,000 in April 1980 as part of a $500,000 loan, and given him two all-expense paid trips to Libya in October 1978 and September 1979, four gold bracelets, and expensive saddle, a serving platter, and a ceremonial sword.(17) Although the consent agreement was meant to conclude an eighteen-month Justice Department investigation it did not end public interest in Billy's ties to Libya. The timing couldn't have been worse for the president and his brother or better for the Republican Party, which was holding its national convention in Detroit. The White House, trying to let the matter drop, refused to comment. Billy maintained that his only crime was to show friendship for an unpopular government, and asserted that he had never influenced the president in regard to Libya.(18)

Opponents of the Carter administration thought otherwise. Republican Senator William Roth announced in Detroit that when he returned to Washington he would demand a Senate investigation into whether or not Billy had improperly influenced U.S. foreign policy. "It's absolutely outrageous," he said. William Safire continued to work on the guilty-until-proven-innocent line he had taken from the first. From the editorial page of the New York Times, Safire demanded that Billy be punished and, when he was not, imputed the most corrupt motives to the Carter Justice Department and White House. On June 26, for example, Safire compared the swift and harsh treatment givern by the Kennedy administration to Igor Cassini, an unannounced lobbyist for Trujillo, with the dilatory and fuddled handling of Billy Carter's failure to register as a foreign agent by his brother's appointees at Justice. Safire left no doubt of his belief that the difference between Kennedy and Carter was a corrupt incompetency in the Carter White House. According to Safire, Billy even traded on the plight of the Iranian hostages to enrich himself.(19) Under this kind of fire interest quickened in the affair. First came the disclosure statement negotiated with the Justice Department. Then came the newspaper stories, as reporters followed the leads in the statement. Their probes fostered leaks, and their stories kept the controversy alive and raised disturbing questions about illegality and, above all, about the possibility of a presidential coverup. The stories and Safire's savage columns fed the growing public belief in Carter's incompetence. It was tailor-made for the media and for Republican campaign managers – scandal, corruption, Qaddafi, oil, coverup. Both the reporters and the politicians already smelled blood.

There were embarrassing disclosures about White House contacts and an oil deal with Libya in Billy's statement to Justice. When reporters questioned the White House about Billy's declaration, they found that he had been telling the truth. In 1978, for example, Billy and Henry Coleman, one of his partners in the Libyan deals, met with two members of the staff of the National Security Council for a briefing on the nature of relations between Libya and the United States. The two staff men were William Quandt and Karl Inderfurth. There were four meetings, according to the Washington Star.(20) Inderfurth was a special assistant to Zbigniew Brzezinski, President Carter's national security advisor. The briefing was arranged by Phillip J. Wise, the president's appointments secretary and hometown friend from Plains, Georgia. The briefing Billy and Henry Coleman received included some advice: Don't make the trip to Libya. Characteristically, Billy ignored the warning and told Quandt: "I don't need anybody up in Washington telling me about Libya. I've met more Libyans than all of you put together."(21) A leader of Republican conservatives, Senator Bob Dole of Kansas, promptly called for an investigation by the Senate Judiciary Committee.(22)

It was enough to persuade editors to turn loose their investigative reporters, and what they found fed the scandal. One of these reporters, Philip Taubman, wrote in the New York Times on July 20

that Billy's consent agreement had actually resulted from a discovery in May 1980 that the Libyan government was trying to use
Billy to "penetrate the innermost circles of the United States
Government."(23) An informant, whose identity the Justice Department refused to disclose, had provided the tip about a Libyan effort
to "gain political influence inside the White House by paying off the
President's brother."(24) Spurred on by this realization, officials told
Taubman, investigators learned on June 2 of the $220,000 Libyan
payments to Billy. Then a peculiar thing happened. About a week
after Justice learned of the payments Billy Carter showed up at the
department in Washington to inquire about the investigation into his
ties to Libya. At this point Cutler intervened and helped Billy get
the powerful legal aid of Ruth and Pollak. All this raised the
question of an improper White House role in the investigation, or an
attempted coverup, or both.

In regard to an improper White House role, the question was had
someone at Justice tipped the White House about the evidence
against Billy, which included the $220,000, causing the president and
Cutler to act instantaneously to choke off the investigation by a
consent agreement. Everyone in the administration claimed dis-
interest and ignorance. The attorney general, Benjamin Civiletti,
declared that no one at Justice had said anything to the White House
about the developing case against Billy. Cutler said he and the
president didn't learn about the money until July 11. The president
said that on July 17 he had advised Billy to make a complete
confession, adding: "I did not know about the activities before
that."(25) The emphasis in the media on the $220,000 was beside the
point. Civiletti need only have said something brief and vague to
Cutler, or have answered a question from the president with a nod
and a certain expression on his face to have galvanized everyone
into action to defend the administration. Then followed a story
confirming Billy's Libyan oil deal. The Washington _Star_ had sent a
list of questions to the chairman of Charter Oil Company, Raymond
Mason, at Ballynahinch Castle, Ireland. The answers came from
Lewis Nasife, Charter Crude Oil president and were conveyed to the
Star by William Coleman, the Charter official who had met twice
with Billy. An agreement had been negotiated, Coleman said, to give
Billy from 4 to 50 cents for every barrel of Libyan crude he brought
to Charter. So far, Coleman added, no oil had been delivered.
Charter had not been contacted by the Libyan government or the
Libyan National Oil Company. The company's allotment of Libyan
crude had fallen from 125,000 barrels a day in early 1979 to 60,000 a
day.

This double corroboration of Billy's statement to Justice caused
an ever greater outcry in Washington. In a column entitled "None
Dare Call It Billygate," William Safire bitterly denounced the
"favoritism" that had been shown to Billy and raised disturbing
questions about the involvement of the National Security Council in

Billy's dealings. Safire charged that Billy would not be prosecuted for breaking the registration law. If Billy was apparently warned about the new leads against him, had clandestine intelligence sources been compromised when he was warned? Such clandestine materials fall in the province of Security Advisor Brzezinski, but he denied having received information about Billy's Libyan deals and even denied knowing that two members of his staff had briefed Billy on four different occasions. And yet, on June 11 when he realized he needed help, Billy's first telephone call from the Justice Department went to Brzezinski. Taubman then reported the U.S. government had known about the Libyan bribery plot and Billy Carter's involvement in it for months but that neither the Justice Department nor the New York grand jury had pursued the leads. The information about the plot had come from participants in it and "an informant considered to be reliable" by senior officials in the U.S. attorney's office in southern New York. Taubman based his article about the lack of aggressiveness in the investigations on information from "sources close to the matter" and "government officials." Republican senators, led by Bob Dole, repeated their call for a formal investigation, and Senator Kennedy, still a presidential candidate, had no choice but to allow his Judiciary Committee to make its own decision about how to proceed.

These developments were so embarrassing that President Carter directed Cutler, Ray Jenkins, and Jody Powell to draft a White House statement on Billy's contacts with administration officials. Far from smothering the clamor it added new reasons for doubt. According to the statement Billy had arranged a meeting between Brzezinski and Ali Houderi, the chief of the Libyan people's bureau, on November 27, 1979, three weeks after the seizure of the American hostages in Teheran. Brzezinski asked the help of Libya in obtaining the release of the hostages. Two points about the meeting deserve mention. First, it would obviously have led the Libyans to believe that Billy was an extremely influential figure in the Carter administration. And second, Qaddafi may have been referring, in however garbled a way, to what was said in these meetings when he spoke in late 1979 of having learned of an impending change in the U.S. position on the Arab-Israeli conflict. The statement repeated the general position taken by the White House earlier, that neither the president nor Brzezinski had any prior knowledge of Libyan payments to Billy, and stuck to the earlier claim that the White House had not played any part in the investigation of Billy's Libyan deals: "at no time ... has there been any contact in either direction between the White House and the Justice Department concerning the conduct of this investigation."(26)

As the White House statement acknowledged, there had been another kind of contact between Brzezinski and Billy. In March 1980 intelligence reports were circulated throughout the intelligence community and higher levels of the executive branch. These reports described an elaborate Libyan plan, in Taubman's words, "to gain political influence in the United States through labor unions, black organizations, oil companies and politically important individuals."(27) The plan was for Libya to establish friendly relations with these individuals and organizations and, in some cases, to make secret payments to them. The goal was to obtain the C-130s and to improve relations between Libya and the United States. "They are looking for help anywhere they can get it or buy it," one intelligence official said. "Billy Carter is just part of a major campaign to win friends and influence people." The intelligence officials Taubman interviewed said that the Libyan plan was covert and included payoffs. In their eyes this made it radically different from other foreign efforts to gain political support in the United States. It was potentially illegal, they added, and "unusually brazen." Charter Oil Company, Operation PUSH headed by the Reverend Jesse Jackson, and other independent oil companies were mentioned as Libyan targets in the report. Recalling the operations of other foreign agents from the China lobby to Trujillo, one wonders about the uniqueness and exceptionally brazen character of the Libyan plot. However, the reports were apparently read with great seriousness. One of the reports did not mention Billy Carter by name but the description was unmistakable: "an individual with important political ties who was in financial difficulty and in touch with Charter Oil." When Brzezinski read this in March he called Billy and urged him not to go ahead, or in the words of the White House statement: not to "engage in any activity that could cause embarrassment to the administration." The White House had been connected once before indirectly to Arab money. Carter's campaign chairman, Raymond Mason, had established himself as a friend of the Arab point of view. In 1974, he suggested that Saudi Arabia finance a publicity campaign in the United States. News reports about this proposal apparently caused Mason's plans to fall through.(28)

Discussing the July 22 White House statement with reporters, Jody Powell defended the use of Billy's Libyan contacts. "At that time we were engaged in exploring every possible avenue to obtain assistance in getting our people held hostage in Teheran released." Ali Houderi was thought to be a close personal friend of Qaddafi, Powell said. Qaddafi did send a message urging the release of the hostages, Powell added. On the other major contact with the White House, Powell insisted that the March intelligence reports which had prompted Brzezinski's telephone call to Billy contained no reference to the Libyan payments. In other words, according to Powell, no one at the White House knew of the payments either in March or before July 11, when Billy began to talk, and therefore, no one could have warned Billy that the Justice Department had found out about them. Conceivably Phillip Wise, presidential appointments secretary, could have told Billy. He was interviewed on March 14 and June 4 by the

FBI. But Powell said that neither Wise nor anyone in his office had told Billy the FBI knew about the money.(29)

Interviews with Democratic party leaders made clear that Billy's Libyan affair had hurt President Carter politically. The chairman of the Carter campaign in New York, Lt. Governor Mario Cuomo, said: "It hurts bad. It hurts with Jewish people." A Carter ally in the south, Donald Fowler, party chairman in South Carolina, described the president's political problem in a different way: "It's another element that fits into the Bert Lance, Hamilton Jordan pattern of personalized complications that have troubled President Carter before." Officials in the White House were telling reporters that because the president lacked the allies in the Senate he needed to prevent or control a congressional investigation, the president would be subjected to damaging publicity for weeks to come.(30)

On July 23 there were a number of new developments in the growing scandal. First, the White House announced that President Carter had met Ali Houderi a second time on December 6. The sole purpose of the meeting, according to Jody Powell, was to allow the president a chance to convey his displeasure over the attack on the U.S. embassy in Tripoli on December 2. It was not a serious admission and Billy had not been involved in the meeting in any way, but it undeniably added to the growing impression that the Carter White House was not telling the whole truth.

Senate leaders of both parties agreed to hold a bipartisan investigation of the entire matter. They intended to examine Billy's conduct as a paid agent of the Libyan government and the Carter administration's handling of the affair. The preferred forum, according to Republican Senator Roger Jepsen (Iowa) would be a nine-member select committee, seven of whom would come from the Judiciary Committee. In a typical congressional maneuver the Senate Judiciary Committee also pressed its claim to jurisdiction over any inquiry. Although Senator Edward Kennedy could not serve as the committee's chairman because of his political contest with the president, he had turned his duties over to Senator Birch Bayh of Indiana. Senator Bayh favored a strong investigation by the Judiciary Committee, but one free of witchhunting and demagoguery. As Bayh recognized, "That's pretty hard in an election year." Bayh and three other members of the Judiciary Committee were appointed to consult with the Senate leadership and to decide who would conduct the investigation. Meanwhile, Senator Dole was indulging his sharp wit and just plain enjoying himself: "I'm not here to push anybody into the buzzsaw," he told reporters. "That will be coming fast enough . . . I'm not here to embarrass anyone – unless they deserve it." A Senate Judiciary subcommittee was given permission to investigate Robert Vesco's role in the Libyan scheme to obtain the C-130s. Democratic Senator Dennis DeConcini of Arizona, subcommittee chairman, and Republican Orrin Hatch had already interviewed Vesco at length in the Bahamas. Hatch thought that the Vesco and Billy Carter cases might be related. And in the House, Robert Bauman of Maryland introduced a "resolution of inquiry" signed by 75 other Republican congressmen calling for the president to give the Congress documents and answer questions about what his brother had done.(31)

William Safire capped what had been a truly horrible day in the press for the Carter administration. In his most savage column yet, Safire attacked the president's concealment of his "dirtiest little secret" — that he had used "his besotted bigoted brother" in a diplomatic effort to free the hostages and that Billy had promptly betrayed that trust placed in him by trying to make money out of his apparent importance. Reduced to its essentials Safire's contention was this: after impressing the Libyans by his access to Brzezinski, a meeting in which Brzezinski may have conveyed some hint of a change in future U.S. Mideast policy as a sweetener for Qaddafi's intervention on behalf of the hostages, Billy then sought to strike an incredibly lucrative oil deal and obtain a loan of hundreds of thousands of dollars from Libya. Safire argued that Houderi probably agreed to make the $500,000 loan to Billy and encouraged him to go ahead with the oil deal after Billy promised to turn Brzezinski's hints into a real policy change and to open a "pipeline into the Oval office." Using his considerable rhetorical skills in the worst way, Safire then managed to suggest that the president was manipulating the hostage crisis for political gain while his brother was busily trying to "make a bundle out of a tragedy."(32)

While July 23 had been a bad day for the administration the days ahead were even worse, as the White House had foreseen. On July 24 the Senate established a nine-member bipartisan special committee to investigate Billy's work for Libya. Seven of the members would come from the Judiciary Committee and two from the Foreign Relations Committee. Senator Bayh was named chairman. The special committee was directed to submit at least an interim report by October 4, the day Congress would adjourn for the election campaign. The names of three of the Republican members of the investigating panel were known immediately. They were Strom Thurmond of South Carolina as vice-chairman (he was ranking minority member on Judiciary), Charles Mathias of Maryland, and Bob Dole of Kansas. Senator Bayh pledged to conduct a quick, thorough, fair investigation and to "let the chips fall where they may."(33) Getting into the act, the House Foreign Affairs Committee scheduled a hearing at the first of the week on the Republican resolution of inquiry. The White House pledged its full cooperation with the inquiry and suggested that executive privilege would not be involved. Other political flak came from Carter supporters. Mayor Koch of New York City weighed in with a call for a grand jury to investigate Billy's deals with Libya. Governor Ella F. Grasso of Connecticut asked the president to give a full public explanation of the entire matter.(34) Perhaps the most damaging admission on a damaging day again came from the White House. The president's wife, Rosalynn, had not only suggested that Billy be used to arrange a meeting with Houderi, but she had telephoned Billy to ask him to do it. Here was not only further evidence of an ill-advised reliance on family to conduct official business, but another small contradiction as well. The White House had earlier said that Brzezinski had contacted Billy to arrange the Libyan meeting.

There was worse to come. On July 25 Attorney General Civiletti was obliged to go back and correct his previous statements that he had not spoken to anyone at the White House about the Billy Carter investigation. For two weeks, he said, I have been telling reporters that there were no discussions at the White House about the case. On July 18, for example, he told the New York Times: "No, it was never discussed with anyone over there."(35) Then Civiletti made a startling admission. "I have said no, and that is so. . . . However, I had one informal, brief exchange with the President during which I raised the topic, but expressly said that I would not discuss the investigation."(36) On June 17, after a talk about judicial appointments Civiletti said he told the president he couldn't discuss Billy's case but that Billy had been foolish not to register as a Libyan agent. When the president asked what would happen if Billy came forward and registered, Civiletti replied that if "the person tells the truth and registers" it was department practice not to prosecute him for his previous failure to register."(37)

With Civiletti's admission the outline of the Carter administration's defense strategy became clear. Certain they would eventually be cleared of any wrongdoing the administration was systematically making public all the most damaging evidence before the start of the Senate investigation and the opening of the Democratic National Convention. In this way as much as possible of the harm would be neutralized and the case would not wreck the president's delegate strength on the floor of the convention. Also, after his renomination, the worst would not come out in a series of dramatic appearances before the special panel with its vengeful Republican members eager to stage a reverse Watergate production. In other words, the damage to the president's reelection campaign would occur all at once in July instead of in a crescendo toward October. Civiletti confirmed this to reporters. Lloyd Cutler had told him he said that the president had found a memorandum in his files describing the June 17 talk with Civiletti. If that is first disclosed in a congressional investigation, Cutler told Civiletti, it would be given "great significance."(38)

The attorney general's statement delighted the administration's opponents. Senator Dole found it to be "a startling disclosure that totally alters the complexion of this already bizarre case" and negates the administration's position that there had been no contact between the White House and Justice Department about the case.(39)

William Safire could not control his pleasure or conceal that it was really the ruin of the Nixon administration in Watergate that was still eating at him. "Let's not go for blood," he suggested ironically:

If the "informal brief exchange" in the Oval office leading to a tip-off and a no-penalty deal for a law breaker is not seen as an obstruction of justice; and if the week-long lying by the I'll-never-lie-to-you White House and Attorney General is not seen as a cover-up — then the Congress, the courts and the press will have ratified the pardon of Nixon.(40)

In other related developments, Randy Coleman registered as a foreign agent for Libya, declaring that he had expected to share in the commissions from Charter Oil. Senator Bayh apointed three Democrats to the special committee: Dennis DeConcini, Max Baucus of Montana, and Patrick Leahy of Vermont. Bayh also told reporters he thought the president and his wife should testify before his committee in person.

The political damage to the president continued to grow. On the same day Civiletti admitted talking with President Carter about Billy's case, forty Democratic members of Congress began to consider ways to throw open the Democratic National Convention. President Carter was already far behind Ronald Reagan in the polls, they argued, and if he and Senator Kennedy released their delegates the party would be able to choose a third nominee, such as Walter Mondale or Edmund Muskie. Senator Kennedy endorsed the idea; losing to Carter in delegate count he had already broached the idea of an open convention. A leader of the move, Congressman Jerome Ambro of Long Island, insisted it was not a pro-Kennedy ploy.(41) As the discussions continued on opening the convention, Senate Majority Leader Robert Byrd of West Virginia called Billy's case "an embarrassment of the Democratic Party."(42) Leaders of Americans for Democratic Action, a liberal Democratic group, called for Civiletti's resignation, and the Justice Department began an internal investigation to determine whether or not the attorney general had acted improperly in his discussion of the case with President Carter. The key, of course, was that Civiletti's talk with the president came after the June 2 discovery of the Libyan payments to Billy. According to the White House the president spoke to Billy on June 28 and July 1. The two discussed the case, and during the second call the president urged Billy to register as a foreign agent. Not until July 14, according to the White House, did the president learn of the Libyan payments to Billy.

On July 29 President Carter made his first public statement about the case. He expressed his assurance that the investigation would show that his brother had at no time influenced U.S. policy or his actions toward Libya. He promised to give the special committee a full report within the next week and said he was willing "to respond in person" in an appropriate way to any questions the committee members might have. The report would be made public, he said, and he would answer questions from the press about it.(43) At the Senate, the Bayh committee had decided to hire a special counsel to conduct the investigation. The committee released the text of a letter to the president saying it would investigate "Libya's alleged efforts to influence American policy, Billy Carter's connections with the Libyans, the Department of Justice's investigation of that relationship and all contacts by White House officials with the Justice Department, Billy Carter, or Libyan officials."(44) Requests for documents were also sent to the Departments of State, Energy, Commerce, Justice, the CIA, the FBI, and the National Security Agency. A subpoena was issued to Charter Oil for documents about Billy and the Libyan oil deal.

The Billy Carter affair had become so controversial that it had given birth or impetus to several independent but related altercations. One of these was the open convention idea; without Billy, it would have been even less plausible than its brief flurry suggested. There were also the curious accusations of Robert Vesco from the Bahamas. Senators DeConcini and Hatch had taken their Judiciary subcommittee's investigation of the Justice Department's handling of public corruption cases to the fugitive financier himself in the Bahamas. On their return the two legislators told reporters a remarkable story: Vesco claimed credit for the Libyan payments to Billy, "for orchestrating the entire matter," as DeConcini put it. Vesco wanted "vengeance" against the Carter administration, DeConcini said, because it had tried to bring him back to the United States for trial on embezzlement charges. Vesco then turned the whole thing into a farce by telling the Times during a telephone interview that DeConcini and Hatch had it all wrong. There had been no attempt to set up Billy, and he, Vesco, had not been paid any money by the Libyans. Senator Bayh's reaction was appropriate. Vesco, Bayh said, had "as much credibility as an empty glass."(45)

Once the executive branch documents on the Billy affair began to reach the Congress the leaks were bound to start. The first big leak came on July 30, and it became front-page news. Several congressmen who had read FBI documents promptly told reporters that the president had given State Department cables to his brother concerning his visit to Libya in September 1978. The White House was then obliged to issue a statement confirming that the cables, which carried the lowest secrecy classification, had been shown to Billy. The president could remember discussing the messages with Billy, but could not recall if he had given copies to his brother. It was a perfect bit of scandal, for it carried hints of the misuse of secret documents as well as once again the suggestion of a coverup. Why hadn't the documents been mentioned before? Moreover, the new display of bad judgment increased the uneasiness of Democratic politicians about the president's candidacy. Majority Leader Byrd was told that most of the Democrats in the Senate, especially those from the Northeast and Midwest, wanted an open convention. However, no one wanted to bell the cat, and all agreed that there was no feasible way to stop Carter's renomination. A Louis Harris/ABC poll showed Carter received approval for his performance from only 22 percent of likely voters. A Mervyn Field poll in California showed the president behind Ronald Reagan by 53 to 20.(46)

Alongside stories about the cables appeared the news that Billy had lied to the Justice Department about the payments from Libya, and thus called into question "the veracity of his entire registration statements," according to Joel Lisker, chief of the foreign registration unit. In his registration statement in July Billy had declared that he was paid $20,000 in January. But on January 16 Billy had told Lisker he had received no Libyan money. Bank records showed that the check was dated December 27, 1979, and deposited December 31. The $200,000 payment occurred in April. There was also the matter of the cables. If Billy had them, Lisker said, this raised new questions about his contacts with the administration. As a result the Justice Department had decided to begin another investigation of Billy's activities. A State Department official added another piece of information. Morris Draper, deputy assistant secretary of state for the Near East, told reporters that at the request of William Quandt of the National Security Council he had spoken to Randy Coleman about the C-130s in late January 1979. The House Judiciary Committee joined the investigation by resolving to obtain documents from the White House and answers to a list of questions about Billy's activities. Terence Smith wrote in the Times that the new disclosures, which came the same day the Justice Department sent the documents to Capitol Hill, had "contributed to a tense and uncertain atmosphere in official Washington over the Billy Carter affair." There was anguish among White House aides, Smith reported, about the piecemeal disclosures, which "makes it seem worse than it is."(47)

In all the furor, little attention was given to what the cables actually said. There were seven messages from the charge in Tripoli. They indicated that in a small way Billy's 1978 visit had helped U.S. policy by making it possible for the U.S. charge in Tripoli, William L. Eagleton, to meet high-ranking Libyans he would not normally have been able to meet.(48) In an attempt to blunt the impact of the cables story the White House released the text of the messages on July 31, just in time for Billy to deny that he had copies of them.(49) Jody Powell was exultant because, in his words, the cables "didn't amount to a hill of beans." Technically Powell was right. But he was, no doubt intentionally, off the point. The problem came not from what was in the cables but that the cables story undermined the president's whole approach to the affair. His position had been throughout that he had had nothing to do with Billy's Libyan deals.

But here was evidence that in 1978 he and his brother had discussed State Department reports about Billy's visit to Libya. Now, with the Democratic National Convention ten days away, there was a mood of "frustration and exasperation" at the White House.

More leaks came from the Congress. This time members of Congress said the documents showed Billy to have been inconsistent in his statements about a machine gun deal for Libya. Two documents spoke of Billy's contacts with — who else? — Frank Terpil. They had met in Libya in 1979. According to one of the documents Billy stated that Terpil later contacted him in Americus, Georgia about a machine gun deal, "but nothing came of it." Subsequently Billy told Joel Lisker that he had never discussed an arms deal with Terpil. The link between the two men had not been pursued, according to a senior Justice official, because Billy was not in the arms business, and it was not certain that he had talked with Terpil about arms.(50) In this context the White House must have welcomed news that the Bayh committee would try to finish its investigation in three weeks.

By the end of July the media and partisan politics — two of the most powerful forces in U.S. society — had turned the Billy Carter affair into a major national scandal. At their best the journalists were determined to get to the bottom of an unsavory mess; at worst they knew their stories, based on leaks and speculation, would sell papers and puff ratings. The politicians who opposed President Carter, from the camp of Edward Kennedy to that of Ronald Reagan, found the scandal a perfect opportunity to damage and defeat the incumbent, or even to strip him of the nomination of his own party. The start of the Senate investigation was thus a blessing and a curse. Even as the hearings promised an end to the scandal, the lengthy, intimate testimony of all the principals, including Billy, the president's personal counsel, and his national security advisor, kept the affair in the news and gave the president's political enemies a wonderful forum. At the same time the nation's foreign policy and its relations with Libya continued to unfold.

In short, the investigation of Billy Carter's dealings with Libya touched four different parts of U.S. public life. The print and broadcast media conducted their own investigations and reported to a waiting public in a fragmentary and episodic manner. The Senate and House each conducted an investigation into different aspects of the case, and these inquiries had their own pattern and logic to them. Third, there was President Carter's need to assure his renomination and election and to minimize the domestic political damage caused to both by the scandal and investigations. And finally, the investigations revealed much about Libyan-U.S. relations in the recent past and, undoubtedly worsened those relations for the present and immediate future. The discussion that follows concentrates on two of these four areas: the congressional investigations and what they revealed about Libyan-U.S. relations. Before turning to these, however, several things should be said about the media investigations and reporting and about the effect of the scandal on presidential politics in an election year.

The media displayed no new virtues or faults in their handling of the Billy Carter affair. Once the editors of the New York Times and Washington Post turned loose their investigative reporters a familiar pattern emerged. If there is an absolute good in journalism it is to be the first to tell a news story. This value displaces all others. The bigger the story the more important it is to be first. Although they seldom wish to falsify or misrepresent the facts, journalists usually decide to print what they have learned — even if it is fragmentary or one-sided — in order to be first, to beat their competition to the story. Their reasoning is the rest of the story will eventually come out, and any omissions or misimpressions can be corrected in later articles. Thus, one's overall impression of the media and particularly newspaper coverage of "Billygate" is of a desperate haste to print the latest leak or investigative interview and as a result, the creation of a partial and, ultimately, misleading public impression of what Billy Carter had actually managed to do on behalf of Libya. For example, in an article published in the New York Times on August 3, the day before the Senate committee started its hearings, Jack McGregor, an oil entrepreneur and friend of Billy's, was quoted as saying that Billy's oil deal with Libya was entirely political. Billy never talked to the officials of the Libyan National Oil Company, according to McGregor, but instead dealt only with people like Ahmed Shahati, who was responsible for Libyan-U.S. relations in the Libyan government. McGregor's statement was true. It was accurately reported: McGregor would tell the Bayh committee the same thing two weeks later. But, one must add, the article leaves a disturbing impression of things not done properly, of political oil deals, perhaps of influence peddling. The point here is not to contest or challenge the right of the media to operate in this way. That right enjoys constitutional protection in the United States. The point is to observe the effect of the media coverage on the developing scandal. It made everybody think the worst. That compounded President Carter's already difficult political problems.

Given this inevitable media effect, there were two remedies available to the White House. The first was to prevent Billy from even trying to deal with Libya. The president never really tried seriously to stop Billy. He asked him to stop several times in 1979, but he never actually used any of the ample resources of the White House to demonstrate publicly that Billy was without any influence on the foreign policy of the Carter administration and, therefore, of no use to the Libyans. A flat public denial of Billy's influence by the president, repeated whenever necessary, would have gone far toward this end. A private communication from the president to the Libyan government stating that any further attempt to use his brother for any purpose would be offensive to the administration and would be opposed by every possible legal means, would also have helped. The Carter White House apparently did neither. Having failed to stop Billy from compromising himself and the administration the White House was left at the mercy of the inevitable effects of the investigations launched by the media. To stop the political losses that followed became the principal concern of the White House.

President Carter adopted an imaginative and forthright approach to save his nomination and improve his chances in November. First, he worked to hold his convention delegates firmly on his side. "It's almost incomprehensible," he told 400 cheering Carter delegates at the White House on August 1, "how a brokered, horse-trading, smoke-filled convention can be labeled open, and a decision made by 20 million Democrats in the open primaries and open caucuses be called closed."(51) The same day, at White House urging, 75 Democrats in Congress released a statement supporting the president. Hopeful officials in the White House told reporters that for the first time in days they thought it might be possible to contain the Billy Carter scandal and focus on the uphill battle for the presidency.(52) But the political losses continued. On August 2 Senate Majority Leader Robert Byrd endorsed an open convention. The Billy Carter affair showed "bad judgment and a rather amateurish" conduct of foreign policy, Byrd said. "I don't believe in family diplomacy."

In addition to holding his delegates, the president chose to make the fullest possible disclosure of his administration's knowledge of and dealings with Billy Carter and Libya. Carter did this both in his news conference and statement of August 4 and in his directives to the executive branch to give complete cooperation to the Bayh committee and to the Justice Department. The strength of the full-disclosure approach is that it short-circuits the media's fragmentary method. If it is truly complete disclosure, and there has been no wrongdoing, then the assumption behind the media and congressional inquiries is transformed. Gradually, journalists, senators, and citizens stop thinking of impropriety and begin to focus on incompetence. In the long-run this is exactly what the August 4 statement and the full-disclosure/full-cooperation approach accomplished. The political gains were immediate. At the time of the news conference on August 4, President Carter had fallen to a tie with Edward Kennedy in the support of Democrats, 43 percent to 43 percent. On August 3 Tom Wicker wrote in the New York Times that President Carter's approval rating had fallen lower than Richard Nixon's during the worst days of the Watergate crisis: Carter was disapproved 77 percent to 22 percent, while Nixon's worst rating had been 75 percent to 25 percent disapproval. The president's handling of the Iranian revolution was rejected by 79 percent, of unemployment by 87 percent, and 85 percent thought he didn't know how to get the job done.(53) A New York Times/CBS News poll published on August 10 showed Carter ahead of Kennedy 49-38, and with an overall positive rating 57 to 32. The poll also showed a 25 percent gain in those who believed the president was telling the truth about Billy and Libya, from 47 to 59 percent.(54) However, even a change as dramatic and favorable as this in the Billy Carter affair could not remedy the president's other popular weaknesses. In the August 10 poll, for example, Carter still trailed Reagan 47-27 (13 percent for Anderson) among all voters. Even so, the positive effect of the administration's handling of the scandal after Billy finally registered was apparent.

The congressional hearings ultimately found the president and his administration innocent of any wrongdoing in the Billy Carter affair. Billy and the Libyans had not influenced U.S. policy in any way, and there had been no influence peddling or obstruction of justice by the administration. The Bayh committee did this by painstakingly reconstructing what Billy and his cronies had been trying to do with Libya during the previous two years. In the process the committee uncovered a number of important developments in Libyan-U.S. relations that might otherwise have remained unknown.

The Bayh committee held hearings on Billy Carter and Libya off and on for three months. The members of the Bayh committee were Democrats Birch Bayh of Indiana (chairman), Claiborne Pell of Rhode Island, Dennis DeConcini of Arizona, Patrick Leahy of Vermont, Max Baucus of Montana; and Republicans Strom Thurmond of South Carolina (vice-chairman), Charles Mathias of Maryland, Robert Dole of Kansas, and Richard Lugar of Indiana. All but Pell, Dole, and Lugar were members of the Judiciary Committee. Officially the Bayh committee was a subcommittee of Judiciary with the formal title: "Subcommittee to Investigate the Activities of Individuals Representing the Interests of Foreign Governments." The Bayh committee's special counsel was Philip W. Tone, formerly a federal judge from the Chicago area. Taken together, the testimony and interim and final reports fill more than 2,000 pages.(55) The House Intelligence Committee also examined classified material on Billy Carter's relations with Libya.(56) The story the congressional documents reveal is one of the personal weakness and greed of Billy Carter and of serious political miscalculation by the Libyan government. They show President Carter to have failed to anticipate, even to have been oblivious to the pitfalls of allowing his family to become involved in international diplomacy.

Relying on the testimony of a number of foreign policy officials, notably Undersecretary of State for Political Affairs David Newsom, the Bayh committee was able to reconstruct the tenor of Libyan-U.S. relations at the time Billy Carter began his escapade. Relations were bad. For years there had been virtually no high-level contacts between Libya and the United States. In 1972 the United States had withdrawn its ambassador, Joseph Palmer, at his request. No one of consequence in the Libyan government would talk to him or respond to his overtures. He was wasting his time and had the good sense to say so and come home. That left U.S. interests in

Libya in the hands of a charge d'affaires. Also in 1973 the State Department forbade the sale to Libya of equipment that could add to Libya's military capacity. This action blocked the export to Libya of eight C-130s as a way of showing U.S. opposition to Qaddafi's support for terrorism and Libya's intervention in other countries. (The government of King Idris had bought and paid for the eight C-130s before the September 1 revolution.) The nationalization of Libyan oil started in 1973 but did not cause serious damage to U.S.-Libyan relations. Most of the oil companies' claims were settled by the late 1970s and stable working relationships had grown up between the government, the companies, and other oil purchasers.

Although the sale of military equipment was blocked, other trade flourished. The export of Libyan oil to the United States expanded steadily, growing from 4 percent of U.S. imports in September 1973 (153,000 barrels/day) to 9 percent in December and to 10.8 percent in August 1980 (700,000 barrels/day). In return, the United States sold food and industrial products to Libya, including nine Boeing 727 aircraft and one 707. In the State Department's view there were solid economic arguments in favor of trying to maintain unrestricted trade between the two countries. Libyan oil was bought by U.S. companies and sold in the U.S. market, profiting U.S. businesses and consumers. The decisive argument clearly was that this mutually advantageous relationship should be among the last, not the first, areas of Libyan-U.S. relations to be subjected to stringent political control. The U.S. oil companies doing business in Libya also quietly made the argument to the State Department that a loss or disruption of their access to Libyan oil would hurt them severely: their refineries had been built to handle Libya's low-sulphur crude and could not be converted to accept lesser grades without great expense and loss of revenue.(57) But the oil and aircraft deals were clearly running against the current of deteriorating political relations. Qaddafi's support for terrorism and his intense opposition to Sadat and the Camp David process fostered antagonism in the White House and State Department. Moreover, U.S. officials had to respond to a growing popular demand in the United States for a more assertive and demonstrably successful foreign policy.

With these considerations in mind, in January and February 1978 the State Department recommended that the sale of two more Boeing 727s be prevented. In March the Department blocked the sale of 400 heavy trucks to Libya, because they were suitable for use as tank transporters. This was unwelcome news to Oshkosh Truck Corporation of Oshkosh, Wisconsin. Not only did they stand to lose the revenue from the sale, but they would have to honor an expensive performance bond and this, according to company officials, would bankrupt the firm. Although the company is small, with only 850 employees, it is the largest employer in Oshkosh, a city of 49,000. In an attempt to overturn the State Department's decision, Oshkosh Truck hired a lobbyist, attorney James N. Bierman, and enlisted the aid of Wisconsin's Senator William Proxmire and the congressman representing Oshkosh, Representative William A. Steiger. What followed offers on a small scale a text-book case of the circumvention of public policy by a special interest group with good connections.(58)

At the time, Oshkosh Truck sold its vehicles abroad through Rioca, a separate company based in Switzerland and operated by Canadians. Oshkosh's first step in overturning the ban on its sale to Libya was to arrange with Libya and Rioca for the sale of a smaller truck, which allegedly could not economically be converted to use as a tank transporter. Next, the Libyan government was asked to promise that the trucks would be used for farming and would not be diverted to military use. The company then informed State of the proposed change in the sale. The trucks could not carry tanks, the Oshkosh lobbyist wrote Secretary Vance in August: "Even a cursory review of engineering drawings ... will confirm that fact."(59) Senator Proxmire and Congressman Steiger then played their part. Proxmire arranged a meeting between Secretary Vance and Oshkosh Truck executives. He and Steiger also attended. According to a senior executive of the truck company, Proxmire "championed our cause." Proxmire's recollection is that he did nothing but champion Oshkosh's right "to get a fair hearing at the State Department."(60) It was a distinction that may have escaped Secretary Vance and his advisors, who had to bear in mind Proxmire's great influence on budgetary decisions in the Senate. In any case, the State Department reversed its earlier decision in September 1978. The sale could proceed, provided the smaller trucks were built and the Libyan government gave its assurances that they would not be used for military purposes. In October 1978 the Libyan Ministry of Agriculture obligingly gave the U.S. embassy the necessary written guarantee. The trucks were then built and shipped to Libya by April 1980, arriving well in advance of the invasion of Chad.

Four years later, officials of Oshkosh Truck showed journalists copies of company documents that turned the elaborate and responsible procedures required by U.S. law into a meaningless charade. From the outset Libya and Rioca had planned that the trucks would be used for military purposes. One of the main arguments offered by Oshkosh executives in favor of the deal was that it would have been uneconomical for Libya to modify the smaller trucks for use as tank transporters. "It wouldn't make sense for a prudent business-man," said Oshkosh President Robert J. Sill. The Libyans would be better advised simply to purchase tank transporters as such from a European supplier. According to the Oshkosh documents, however, Rioca thought otherwise. In June 1980, two months after the last trucks arrived in Libya, Rioca proposed to the technical committee of the Libyan Armed Forces that they be converted to tank transporters at a cost of $15 million. Canadian mechanics using Austrian parts completed the transformation at Libyan military bases. Later, other Canadian mechanics who went to Libya to service the vehicles would report that they were being used to haul Soviet tanks.(61)

What is most apparent in this sorry story is the greed of the executives at Rioca and Oshkosh. Rioca managed a very attractive double-dip, profiting as middleman between Oshkosh and Libya on the original sale, and then again as prime contractor to Libya for the "uneconomical" modifications. Their role was cynical and devious throughout the affair but perhaps not hypocritical. The Oshkosh executives appear to have allowed themselves to be persuaded by the preposterous idea that Libya could be trusted not to use the trucks to haul tanks. In any case they needed to act as if they believed this in order to overturn the State Department ban. But it was greed that had led them into the deal without first clearing it with the State Department. They must have reasoned either that they could squeeze through what they mistakenly saw as a loophole in export regulations or that if the worst happened and State tried to stop the sale, they could overturn the ban by political pressure.

After the modification of the trucks became publicly known in early 1982 the reaction of the principals involved was characteristic. Reached in Toronto, Canada, by the New York Times, the president of Rioca, Mrs. Jackie Pass, dismissed her questioner coldly: "All I do is work for a living like anyone else. . . . If you have any questions about the use of the trucks, you should address them to the Libyans." Senator Proxmire was rueful: "We were double-crossed. If I knew then what I know now, I would not have taken the position that I did." Oshkosh President Sill was plaintive: "We were not a party to the modifications. We were trying to be a good citizen company. I'd like to have the whole thing go away." In the end every interest was served except the national interest of the United States. Rioca got its double-dip profit. Oshkosh sold the trucks and escaped paying 10 percent of the purchase price as a performance bond. Libya got 400 tank transporters. And Proxmire and Steiger held some important political support. Only the interest of the United States and its allies in restraining Libya's military adventures was harmed. Although it could not transform Billy Carter's almost perversely willful bad judgment into wisdom, the Oshkosh Truck deal revealed how often and how readily the public interest is subordinated to private gain in the making of U.S. foreign policy. Moreover, looked at from the standpoint of the Libyan government the whole affair was a lesson in how to get around the State Department and manipulate the U.S. political and legal system. It was, in short, a lesson in lobbying and bureaucratic politics.

Qaddafi and the Libyan officials in charge of relations with the United States appeared to have learned the lesson well. In March 1978, a month after the initial disapproval of the Oshkosh Truck deal, the State Department disapproved the sale of two Boeing 727s to Libya. The procedures for the licensing of exports are complex and are well explained in Undersecretary Newsom's testimony to the Bayh committee of August 4 and September 16.(62) In essence, there are three kinds of exports: (1) munitions, which are subject to regulation under the Arms Export Control Act; (2) items that may be shipped abroad under a general license, without review; and (3) those items on a review list that require a validated license for shipment. State controls the export of munitions in consultation with the Department of Defense, and approves validated licenses under various Export Administration Acts in consultation with the Commerce Department.(63) In May, the Commerce Department asked State to reconsider, and State agreed to review its decision. In late October the department reversed itself and allowed the sale of the 727s. This action together with the Oshkosh Truck decision, suggest a pattern in U.S. policy, and Undersecretary Newsom's testimony to the Bayh committee revealed that, in the fall of 1978 the United States began a concerted effort to explore the possibility of a significant improvement in Libyan-U.S. relations. The truck and aircraft deals were meant to signal a strong U.S. interest in improved relations. Libya was sending similar messages to the United States. Moreover, Libya signed the Hague Convention on air piracy in October 1978 and agreed, as it had on the truck deal, to guarantee in writing that the 727s would not be used for military purposes. Then came what Newsom termed "candid talks" in Tripoli in late 1978 and discussions between Foreign Secretary Turayki and Newsom in Washington in October. With these developments in mind, and after making certain that there would be enough civilian passengers to fill the planes and consulting with the interested congressional committees, State approved the 727 sale in late October and formally notified Commerce on November 2.

The hopes for an improvement in Libyan-U.S. relations continued. Early in 1979 the State Department approved the sale of three 747s to Libya. In January 1979 the head of the State Department Office for Combating Terrorism went to Tripoli for talks with Turayki and other Libyan officials. He stressed that Libyan-U.S. relations could improve only if Libya stopped its support of terrorism. Within a month, however, the movement toward a Libyan-U.S. detente received a sharp check. In February, Qaddafi intervened in Uganda in his futile effort to save the regime of Idi Amin. It soon became obvious that the Libyan leader was using the C-130s and some of the older 727s to move Libyan troops and supplies into Uganda. There was an outcry in Congress, and in May the State Department stopped the export of the 747s.

In April 1980 Boeing applied for a new license to sell the 747s and also three 737s, probably in order to be able to invoke a force majeure clause in their contract. Libya had already made partial payment for the aircraft. On June 11, 1980, the Commerce Department denied the license.(64) Libya, nonetheless, continued to tell Washington it wanted better relations. During a state visit in the spring of 1979, for example, President Tito of Yugoslavia secretly told President Carter that Qaddafi wished to improve relations.(65) Impressed by the continued signals and in hopes of softening Qaddafi's opposition to Camp David, Newsom went to Tripoli in mid-June 1979 and met with Jalloud. "The frankness of this meeting," Newsom said, "despite the absence of tangible results, encouraged further contacts in October."(66) There were meetings between Vance and Turayki at the UN in October and between Kikhia and Newsom in New York on November 8. But it proved impossible to sustain the movement toward detente. Inside Libya Qaddafi had already embarked on his "people's revolution" and the country's embassies abroad were being transformed into people's bureaus. But it was Libya's reaction to the seizure of the American hostages in Iran that ended progress. Newsom cited in particular Turayki's call on November 15 at the Arab Foreign Ministers Conference in Tripoli for a boycott of the United States. On November 16 Newsom met with Kikhia again and condemned Turayki's statements. He told Kikhia that the bilateral talks on improving relations would have to be delayed because of Libya's position on the hostages. Charge Eagleton delivered the same messages to Libyan officials in Tripoli on November 17, 18, and 19. The Libyans then issued a more supportive statement on November 22, and, following Houderi's meeting with Brzezinski in the White House on November 26 (arranged by Billy Carter), Qaddafi promised to try to help secure the release of the hostages. Any remaining hopes for detente were lost with the sacking of the U.S. embassy on December 2. The murder campaign against Libyan exiles followed, and relations worsened steadily until broken off completely by the Reagan administration.

Newsom had several reasons for going into the abortive detente in such detail. The first was to establish the independence and integrity of the deliberations concerning the sale of the Oshkosh trucks and Boeing aircraft. This was necessary because of the nagging coincidences between Billy Carter's clumsy interventions and the various actions of administration as it tried to improve Libyan-U.S. relations. For example, at about the time Billy made his first inquiries about the C-130s, State was deciding to allow the sale of the 747s. Was there a connection, some of the members of the Bayh committee wanted to know? In his questioning of Newsom and Roy, Senator Lugar gave an extreme example of the degree of suspicion that prevailed, at least among conservative Republicans. First, Lugar wanted to know if there was a connection between the $200,000 payment to Billy Carter by Libya in April 1980 and Boeing's reapplication for an export license for the 747s on April 23. Assured that there was not, Lugar then asked for an explanation of the coincidence between the decision by Commerce (on June 11) to stop the 747 sale and Billy Carter's showdown with the Justice Department on virtually the same day over his activities as a Libyan agent. "Now is it conceivable," Lugar asked Newsom and Roy, "that the administration, for various reasons, didn't want to leave anything to chance, that in conjunction with problems that were occurring in the Department of Justice, not too far away, Commerce decided to reject the application formally?"(67) Patiently, Roy explained that the first license had indeed been allowed to expire, but this had been done as a way of blocking the export of the aircraft. By January 1980, when the first license expired, the planes wouldn't have been finished and thus could not have been shipped. The new application needed a formal denial because there was no existing license and a yes or no answer was required.(68)

Newsom's other reason for answering so carefully was to make clear that although they seemed to coincide with various actions by Billy Carter, Houderi, Vesco, and others, the numerous U.S. government contacts with Libyan officials — in late 1978, and in January, June, October, and November 1979 — came from an official decision taken independently to try to improve Libyan-U.S. relations and not as a result of the intervention of some influence-peddler or another. Newsom also took care to show that the disruption of these efforts to bring about a detente occurred not because of the disclosures associated with the Billy Carter affair but because of developments outside the control of the administration, principally the Libyan intervention in Uganda, and the sacking of the U.S. embassy in Tripoli.

Newsom's testimony also revealed that the Libyan approach to Billy Carter was not an isolated event but part of a sustained campaign by the Libyan government to try to modify U.S. foreign policy by working directly with a variety of grass-roots organizations, universities, and prominent individuals in the United States. The idea was that eventually Libya's good relations with these groups and individuals would somehow allow Libya to gain access to U.S. weapons, technical systems, and other goods, including the C-130s. The head of Libya's Foreign Liaison Office, Ahmed Shahati, was in charge of the campaign.

The effort got under way in 1977 with the visits of two U.S. groups to Libya and the arrival of the first Libyan delegations to the United States in April. Libya appears to have made four kinds of contacts in the United States as part of this effort. There were contacts with a number of universities, including Georgetown, the University of Michigan, the University of Idaho, and the University of Georgia. To Georgetown, Libya donated $600,000 for the establishment of a chair in Arabic and Islamic studies. Several years later Georgetown returned the money because of fundamental disagreements with Libyan policies. A second set of contacts was developed between Libya and various minority organizations, such as the Black Muslims, the National Council of American Indians, and the National

Association of Arab Americans. The third Libyan method was organized by the "Arab-American Dialogue Committtee," an organization registered in Washington under the Foreign Agents Registration Act as representing the Libyan government.(69) Of particular note, the Dialogue Committee arranged a people-to-people conference in Libya from October 8-15, 1978, with better relations between Libya and the United States as the theme. More than 100 prominent Americans attended, according to the Libyan government, including former Senators J. William Fulbright, Vance Hartke, Najib Halabi, and the former U.S. ambassador to Jordan, Gene Brown. Billy Carter's first visit to Libya took place September 27-October 1, 1978, just before the people-to-people conference. The fourth Libyan contact method was to send delegations of Libyan officials to the United States for visits to various parts of the country. During their stay, the Libyans would circulate a petition calling for the establishment of a Libyan-U.S. friendship society, and the Libyan government claimed that such societies had been established in Idaho, Louisiana, Wyoming, Georgia, and Michigan. In a sense Billy Carter's national troubles began with his decision to act as host to a visiting Libyan delegation in January 1979.

When the Billy Carter affair became a national scandal in the summer of 1980, the Libyan government gave a detailed public description of some of its people-to-people activities in the United States.(70) The Libyan government's purpose was to show that the Foreign Liaison Office's contacts with Billy Carter were nothing out of the ordinary and, indeed, were only a small part of a much larger effort to promote better understanding between Libyans and Americans. Libya laid the blame for the outcry against Billy on a "biased Zionist campaign, the aim of which is to damage the name of the Socialist People's Libyan Arab Jamahiriyah and its friends."(71) In a sense, the Libyans were correct. There was a major effort underway, and Billy Carter was only one of a number of Americans who were involved. But the Libyans protested too much when they asserted that "Relations between the Office of Foreign Contacts and Billy Carter are purely natural and a relationship which could have existed with any other person." This is simply not so. Billy was the brother of the president of the United States, and as such any of his contacts with a foreign government were unique and, to the extent they went beyond the barest formalities, improper. Moreover, the Libyans insisted that "Billy Carter's relations with certain Libyan economic establishments are similar to those of other Americans having similar ties with such establishments." Again, because of Billy's kinship with the president, this can not be so. But leaving this aside, Billy's economic dealings with Libya were highly unusual, as will be seen, and if other Americans had struck similar deals that was a cause for alarm rather than the complacency the Libyan govenment suggested was appropriate.

A Libyan web began to be spun about Billy Carter in March 1978 when Mario Lianza, an Atlanta real estate developer, returned to his native town of Catania, Italy for a vacation.(72) There Lianza met Michele Papa, a Sicilian corporate lawyer. Papa had founded a Sicilian-Arab Association in the early 1970s dedicated to the promotion of trade and cultural exchange between Libya and Italy. Papa told Lianza that if he could get Billy Carter to visit Libya there was a lot of money to be made from Libyan investments in the Atlanta area. Lianza had not met Billy, so after returning home, he arranged for Thomas Jordan and himself to meet the Libyan ambassador, Gibril Shalouf, in Atlanta in late June. Through Jordan and several others, including Randy Coleman, Lianza set up a meeting between Shalouf and Billy at Billy's service station in Plains in early 1978. Shalouf used the occasion to invite everyone present to come to Libya at the Libyan government's expense. Although he did not accept immediately, before long Billy decided to go, and he received a more formal invitation in September. He then invited an old friend, Donald Carter (no relation), a realtor in Gainesville, Georgia. Donald Carter was more cautious than Billy, and he asked a specialist at the Southern Center for International Studies in Atlanta for a briefing on Libya. Carter was told that Libya was hostile to Camp David and would try to use Billy's trip against the Carter administration. This persuaded Donald Carter not to accept Billy's invitation, and he tried and failed to dissuade Billy. Here was the first of numerous well-informed and well-meaning attempts to keep Billy from hurting himself, his brother, and his country. Billy ignored his friend's advice, as he would ignore the repeated official counsel he received advising against the trip. Billy's alcoholism made clear that there was a self-destructive side to his personality, but his refusal to heed the repeated warnings that his dealings with Libya would hurt his brother has an element of sibling rivalry to it. Billy persisted until his Libyan deals had inflicted serious political losses on the president; he certainly contributed to, although he was not responsible for, the president's defeat in the 1980 election. Short of violence, it is hard to imagine how Billy could have hurt his brother – an intensely political person – more than he did.

President Carter's appointments secretary, Phillip Wise, learned of Billy's Libya trip in August or September and asked Karl Inderfurth, special assistant to the advisor on national security affairs, Zbigniew Brzezinski, to telephone Randy Coleman to discuss the visit. Coleman told Inderfurth that a trip to Libya was planned and asked for information about the North African country. Inderfurth then asked William Quandt, a staff member of the National Security Council responsible for Middle Eastern affairs, to speak to Coleman about the general state of Libyan-U.S. relations. Quandt remembered first speaking to Randy Coleman sometime in August. He stressed Qaddafi's hostility to Camp David and warned that the Libyans would try to use Billy Carter's visit to embarrass Presidents

Carter and Sadat. Quandt particularly hoped the Georgians would not go to Libya until after the negotiations at Camp David, scheduled for early September, had concluded. Coleman called Quandt back a day or two later and during that conversation Billy Carter came on the phone and told Quandt to mind his own business. He knew more about Libya than all the bureaucrats at the State Department put together, Billy said.(73) Once again, Billy ignored expert and well-intentioned advice.

The Georgia delegation went to Libya by way of Rome. In addition to Billy Carter and Randy Coleman there were Lianza and Jordan, Georgia State Senators Floyd Hudgins and Henry Russell, Leonard Long, J. C. Long, and Ambassador Shalouf. Their itinerary in Libya was a standard tourist schedule, with the expectation of a meeting with Jalloud. Charge Eagleton wrote the State Department that the visit had been uneventful, that Billy had scrupulously refrained from making political comments, and that all the excitement had raised the morale of the U.S. community. Lianza told investigators later that when Libyan officials mentioned the C-130s at a dinner party, Billy, who had been drinking, said he'd "try to do something about it."(74) Billy denied having said this, but whether he did or not, the visit passed with far less bad publicity than the White House might have feared would result from it.

After the group returned to Georgia several of them got together to discuss the establishment of a trade group to do business with Libya. Present were Billy, Randy Coleman, Billy's accountant Donny Roland, Lianza, Jordan, Hudgins, and Jimmy Murray, part owner of the Best Western Motel in Americus, Georgia and a friend of Billy's. They decided to go ahead. On November 2 Billy sent Ahmed Shahati a written invitation to visit Georgia. The Libyan accepted, and Ambassador Shalouf came down with Mohammed al-Burki, head of the Department of Parties and Popular Organizations in the Libyan offices of the General People's Congress, to meet with the Georgians and plan the visit. Shalouf discussed possible business deals with Murray, Coleman, and Hudgins and encouraged the Americans to think about trade in farm commodities produced in Georgia. Later, Coleman recalled that one of the Libyans had mentioned the C-130s.

As part of the preparations for the visit of the Libyan delegation Coleman telephoned the State Department on December 6 to make sure the U.S. government did not object. There was no objection, but the country officer for Libya, Leonard Scensny, gave Coleman a stern and accurate warning about Libyan intentions. Although Shahati would discuss business and even cultural and educational exchanges, Scensny wrote Coleman on December 12, Shahati was in charge of Libyan efforts to influence U.S. policy toward Libya and the Arab world by building and using contacts in the United States outside the official U.S. government in Washington. Shahati's motives, Scensny warned, were "basically political." Again, Billy ignored expert advice. Far from breaking off his contacts with the Libyans, Billy intensified them. He instructed Randy to contact Phil Wise and ask for a briefing on the status of the C-130s. Wise referred Coleman to Quandt again, but Quandt managed to pass the chore to Morris Draper, deputy assistant secretary of state for the Near East. Draper told Coleman that the sale of the C-130s had been blocked since 1973, and that this policy was unlikely to change.

Meanwhile, some of the Georgians pursued the commodities deal. During the visit of the Libyans to Georgia Coleman called Bert Lance for the name of someone knowledgeable about commodities. Lance gave him the name of Robert L. Schwind, an attorney in Atlanta and friend of Lance. Schwind talked with Coleman, Shahati, and Burki. The Georgians then formed a group to sell commodities: Billy Carter, Coleman, Arthur Cheokas, an Americus, Georgia businessman, Murray, and Roland. They met Schwind in Macon, Georgia in February and agreed that Schwind would send some samples of commodities for sale from the Gold-Kist Corporation to Burki at the Libyan embassy. The group would split their profits, and Coleman and Schwind would share their commissions with Billy and Bert Lance, respectively.

About this time, according to the Bayh committee, Billy received another warning about his Libyan activities. Clint Murchison, a wealthy businessman, ran into Billy at the Super Bowl football game in Miami. Murchison had built a $200 million military facility for Libya and was having trouble collecting payment. He offered Billy 1 percent of anything he recovered. Billy declined. During their conversation Murchison advised Billy to register as a foreign agent, and Billy said he intended to. Later Billy denied ever having the conversation, but Murchison had no reason to mis-represent what was said, and it seems likely that Billy once again chose to ignore some good advice about his dealings with Libya.

As mentioned earlier Billy traveled for a time with Shahati and the Libyan delegation. He attended a reception at the Libyan embassy in early February and saw W. Alan Roy, the desk officer for Libya. What about "those Boeing airplanes?" Billy asked. Thinking he must mean the sale of the two 727s that had been approved in November, Roy said that they'd been sent to Libya. "Good," Billy replied. The Bayh committee found no evidence that Billy was involved in any way in the decisions on the Oshkosh trucks or the Boeing 727s and 747s; the overlap in Billy's association with Libya and the reversal of the ban on these sales was coincidental and a result of an overlapping decision by the State Department to try to open a "more constructive dialogue on the issues dividing the United States and Libya."(75) Billy also appeared with Shahati on the national television program "Good Morning, America" in New York City. Whether he thought it did or not the television appearance made Billy a foreign agent, because by appearing with Shahati, Billy lent his own name and, in some sense, his brother's to the Libyans' effort to change their popular image in the United States.

It is not clear that he could have been successfully prosecuted at this point, because the Foreign Agents Registration Act requires firm proof of "agency," which means that someone is not merely speaking up for a foreign government — which is protected by the First Amendment — but is acting under the direction and control of that government. One proof of such control is payment for services, and there were no indications as yet that Billy had taken any Libyan money.(76) It is certain, however, that the publicity generated by Billy's trip to Libya, the Libyan delegation's visit, and the formation of the trade group had attracted the attention of the Foreign Registration Unit in the Justice Department and in particular the notice of Joel Lisker, the head of the unit. On January 12, 1979, Lisker sent Billy Carter a letter asking him to say whether the Libyan-Arab-Georgia Friendship Society, which had been "established" by a petition circulated at a reception for the Libyans in Georgia, was under the direction or control of the Libyan government. Lisker also asked Billy if he was acting as an agent for Libya. Billy simply ignored Lisker's letter and two other attempts to get an answer on January 30 and April 10. This persuaded Lisker that something was wrong, and in late April he called in the FBI and asked them to find out how and why Billy had been invited to Libya, what evidence there was of Billy having acted under the direction and control of the Libyan government, and whether or not Billy was taking Libyan money.

Before this second phase of the Justice Department investigation began, Billy had entered the hospital for treatment for alcoholism. His personal life had become so disordered that, according to his agent, he no longer was receiving invitations to make paid appearances and endorsements. Billy claimed that it was the unfair press he received after hosting the Libyan delegation that cut off his appearances and endorsements. And he turned this into a claim on Libyan generosity, a claim the Libyans were willing to accept, for their own reasons.

From his hospital bed Billy continued to dream of making big money from his Libyan connections. On March 6 he sent Randy Coleman to Rome with Cheokas to meet Shahati and Shalouf. Oil had come up briefly during the delegation's visit.(77) Now, the Libyan ambassador said to forget about farm commodities and deal in oil. It was easier to manage, and there was more money in it. Shahati said that although he would have to obtain final clearance in Libya, he believed there would be no problem in obtaining an oil concession for Billy. Coleman and Cheokas had prepared for the Rome meeting by asking the ubiquitous Bert Lance to recommend someone to discuss the international oil business with. Lance remembered mentioning a firm, rather than an individual, the Bank of Commerce and Credit International in London. Coleman recalled that Lance had given them someone's name.(78) On the return from Rome, Coleman and Cheokas stopped in London to see the banker Lance had recommended, and were given a brief introduction to some of the intricacies of the international oil market.

In addition to sending Coleman and Cheokas to Rome to discuss an oil deal with the Libyans Billy also asked President Carter directly about the possible repercussions of his contacts with Libya. According to the documents in his report to the Judiciary Committee, President Carter had been trying since the previous February to discourage Billy from having anything else to do with Libya. He said this to Billy's wife, Sybil, and Randy Coleman on February 23, while Billy was in the Americus, Georgia hospital undergoing treatment for alcoholism. He asked Bert Lance to visit Billy and repeat the message. Then in early April, when Billy was in the Navy Alcohol Rehabilitation Unit in Long Beach, California, he and the president discussed Libya on the telephone. President Carter told his brother it would be "a mistake and embarrassment" for him to go. Just before reaching Billy, the president had written him a short letter saying that if Billy went to Libya "it would create severe problems for us because of their threats against Sadat and because they are fighting in Uganda for Idi Amin."(79)

By the time of this conversation with President Carter, Billy already knew he might obtain an oil allocation from Libya. In fact he had probably already discussed the oil deal with an old friend from the Marines, Jack McGregor, who had become an oil company executive.(80) McGregor had been a lieutenant in the same artillery battery in which Billy had served as a non-commissioned officer in the 1950s. McGregor described the motive for his contacts with Billy in mid-February 1979 as deriving from a personal concern aroused by the newspaper articles on Billy's Libyan connections. When he telephoned him about this, McGregor immediately realized that Billy had a drinking problem, and he advised Billy to seek medical treatment, which he did. Billy stayed in touch with McGregor while he was in the hospital and mentioned the possibility of an oil deal. Grateful for the help with his brother, President Carter invited McGregor to the White House to thank him. The president had his picture taken with McGregor, and said kind things to him. Worried that the president might not be aware of the full extent of Billy's problems McGregor advised him that Billy might need financial help to pay the costs of his defense in the Carter warehouse investigation and suggested the establishment of a legal defense fund.

But there was something more than friendship in Jack McGregor's interest in Billy Carter in the spring of 1979. In January McGregor was executive vice-president and chief operating officer of an oil company, Carey Energy Corporation, that was in serious financial trouble. Carey Energy had been founded by Edward Carey in the 1950s as an oil products marketing firm on the east coast of the United States.(81) In 1967 Carey teamed with Standard Oil of California (Socal) to build a refinery in the Bahamas to produce residual fuel oil, chiefly for consumption by northeastern utilities companies. The refinery was designed to process low-sulphur crude, which suited both partners: Socal supplied Carey with "sweet" Libyan crude from its new holdings in that country. But in 1973 Qaddafi started nationalizing the Libyan oil industry, and Socal, pleading force majeure, couldn't supply Carey any longer. To maintain his crude supply Carey contracted directly with the Libyan National Oil Corporation. That was easy enough. But to move it he had to accept three- to five-year contracts for tankers in late 1973 at rates as high as $2.20/barrel. Then the Libyans joined the oil price escalation after the October War, and before long tanker rates plummeted as low as 16 cents/barrel. Because Carey had to buy the expensive Libyan oil and pay extremely high transportation rates, his costs were not competitive. After earning $38 million in the first quarter of 1974, Carey finished the year with a $20 million loss.(82)

Locked into the high tanker rates until 1978 and forced to pay Libya's premium crude prices, Carey still might have remained afloat because it had a well-run distribution system and, with its Bahamian refinery 1,400 miles closer to the United States than other Caribbean refineries, was able to gain back some of its lost cost advantage. But then in late 1974 the U.S. government lowered the costs of domestic refiners by, in effect, subsidizing some of their crude costs as a way of delivering them from some of the effects of sky-rocketing prices. It was good interest-group politics, and Carey had no problem with the idea of relief for refiners. The trouble was that Carey's refinery was in the Bahamas and, therefore, was ineligible for the assistance. Carey lost $40 million in 1975. He was now having trouble paying for his Libyan crude. When his debt to the Libyans reached $100 million in 1975 they stopped Carey's oil. Desperate for low-sulphur crude he turned to Socal and exchanged liens on his company's assets for supplies of petroleum.

A momentary respite came in 1977 when the Shah of Iran offered oil on easy credit terms. He needed the money to pay for a massive military buildup. Even though he was losing $8 million a month Carey took more Iranian crude than he could pay for, as much as 100,000 barrels a day. In effect he was making a colossal wager that the U.S. government would rescind its relief program for domestic refiners before Carey Energy went broke. Carey was right about the end of the relief program. To increase residual fuel supplies on the East Coast, the U.S. Energy Department in September 1978 reduced the advantages enjoyed by domestic refiners. Carey Energy began to make money again a month later.

But it was too late. Carey had contracted huge debts along the way: to the Libyan National Oil Company (NOC), $191 million; to the National Iranian Oil Company (NIOC), $166 million; to Socal, $108 million; and to others $20 million. No longer willing to put up with Carey, the Libyans and Iranians went to court in the Bahamas and, in August 1978, won a judgment for the liquidation of Carey's assets in payment for Carey's purchases of crude oil from NOC and NIOC. The main assets affected by the judgment were the Grand Bahama Petroleum Company, Ltd. (Petco), owner of most of the Borco refinery in Freeport, Bahamas.(83) In August, the Bahamian Court appointed a liquidator, Peter Evans, to supervise the sale of Carey's assets. An oil consultant, Robert McGrath, president of Oil Agents, Incorporated, put Evans in touch with Charter Oil Company in September. That contact led to the purchase of Carey Energy by Charter on May 15, 1979, and to the assumption by Charter of Petco's debts to NOC and NIOC.

But before all this happened Carey apparently continued to try to resolve his crude supply problems with the Libyans. If nothing else, Libyan agreement to supply crude as part of an overall debt settlement was necessary to make Carey Energy viable as a candidate for takeover by Charter or any other company.(84) In searching for a way to get a renewal of Libyan crude supplies in January 1979 Carey pointed out to Jack McGregor that Billy Carter was host to a Libyan delegation. Carey suggested to McGregor that one of the Libyan officials in the delegation might be able to help Carey Energy in its dealings with the Libyan National Oil Co. It sounded like an excellent idea to McGregor, and he checked the idea with Carey's outside consultant on Libyan affairs. A few days later the consultant reported that the Libyan in question was "more of a foreign liaison, foreign trade type" and had no connection with NOC. The consultant advised against contacting Billy Carter. On the advice of another consultant, Edward Carey then directed McGregor to contact former Senator James Abourezk, an Arab-American, which he did. Abourezk tried and failed to help Carey Energy with NOC. Although McGregor did not ask Billy Carter to help in the negotiations with NOC he did contact him several weeks after Edward Carey mentioned his name and his association with the Libyan delegation. Moreover a few weeks after McGregor called, Billy spoke to him about getting an allocation of Libyan oil. At the time McGregor was chief operating officer of Carey Energy. After Charter Oil acquired Carey Energy McGregor would go into business for himself and become a consultant to Charter.

The next development occurred in late May 1979 when Ahmed Shahati invited Billy to come to Rome to discuss the oil deal Randy Coleman had discussed in March. In mid-June Billy and Randy Coleman flew to Rome for a weekend. There they met Shahati, Shalouf, and Ali Houderi, who was then Shahati's deputy in the Foreign Liaison Office. Not only did Billy ask for an oil allocation, but he also requested a $500,000 loan. The Libyans said both were possible. They did set three conditions on the oil allocation: Libya would only deal with an oil company, which meant Billy would have to be paid by the oil company; Libya would approve the oil company named by Billy; and the oil company would have to meet whatever other conditions Libya set. Billy and the Libyans also discussed a possible visit by Billy during the tenth anniversary celebration of the September revolution.(85)

In mid-June, immediately after his return Billy contacted Jack McGregor again, this time to talk seriously about a Libyan oil allocation. McGregor's account of what happened next is in the published hearings of the Bayh committee. They met at the May-flower Hotel in Washington on June 26 and 27. At this point McGregor was a consultant for Charter Oil, which had acquired Carey Energy. As part of the arrangement by which Charter assumed Carey Energy's debts to Libya's National Oil company, Libya had agreed to allow Charter to buy 100,000 barrels/day of Libya's low sulphur, waxy crude for the Bahamian refinery. Billy told McGregor the Libyans had offered him an allocation of 100,000 barrels/day, that is, enough to double Charter's crude oil supply. Moreover, the Libyans had told Billy that his allocation would never be embargoed should Libya decide to embargo oil shipments to the United States.(86) The other reason for Charter's interest was that in August 1979 there was a worldwide shortage of crude oil. Prices were up, and so were profits on all products refined and sold. A year later, when the Bayh committee was holding its hearings, there was an oil glut and Nasife told the committee he probably wouldn't have wanted Billy's oil.

At the Mayflower McGregor advised Billy to register as a foreign agent. Billy said he had done nothing to justify registration. Well, at least have your attorney answer the Justice Department's letters, McGregor advised. Billy told McGregor repeatedly that the Libyans wanted nothing from him in exchange for the oil allocation. They might be doing it, he said, because of the financial losses Billy had suffered after his contacts with Libya became known. Billy then asked McGregor if he should deal with a foreign oil company, because of all the bad publicity that had resulted from his contacts with the Libyans. McGregor understandably turned Billy toward his client, Charter Oil. There's nothing wrong with brokering oil, he told Billy, and it might as well go to a U.S. company for the use of American consumers. Charter's headquarters were in Jacksonville, Florida, he said, not far from southern Georgia. Charter got on well with the Libyans, and its refinery had been designed especially to handle Libyan oil. Billy agreed that his allocation should go to Charter, and McGregor said he would approach the oil company.(87)

Although there was obviously much to interest Charter in Billy's oil allocation, when McGregor discussed bringing it to Charter, the company's president, Jack Donnell, worried that any connection with Billy could harm Charter's existing good relations with the Libyan National Oil Company. Billy had not dealt with officials of NOC but with men like Shahati and Houderi, representing the political side of the Libyan government, the Foreign Liaison Office. Donnell told

McGregor he would think about the deal. Several weeks later Donnell told McGregor to take it up with Lewis Nasife, president of Charter Crude Oil, a subsidiary company. Nasife, too, was anxious to protect the existing allocation, but he was interested enough to agree to try to find out what the Libyans thought of Billy Carter. Apparently, they thought well of him, well enough, at least to persuade Nasife to meet with Billy, McGregor, and Randy Coleman in Columbus, Georgia, on August 17.(88) At this meeting Charter and Billy agreed that Billy's allocation would go to Charter, and that Charter would pay Billy a broker's commission of from 5 cents to 55 cents a barrel (on 100,000 barrels), with the fees lower when crude prices fell and higher when they rose.(89) Although this arrangement promised Billy more money for less work than he could ever have imagined obtaining – from $5,000 to $55,000 every day – Charter had played Scrooge and offered Billy from one-sixth to one-tenth the $3 to $5 a barrel they would have paid an experienced oil broker.(90)

This lucrative deal was the first result of Billy's trip to Rome in June. It was not a contract with Charter, but an agreement on the terms of a contract to be signed when the oil was delivered. The other development to result from the June meeting was Billy's first negotiation with the Libyans on the $500,000 he had asked Ahmed Shahati to loan him. In August Billy sent Randy Coleman and his accountant, Donnie Roland, to Washington. They, and an Atlanta attorney, Helen Medlin, met a Libyan banker and discussed the terms of the $500,000 loan. Essentially, Billy offered a first mortgage on all his property as collateral for a $500,000 loan to be repaid at 10 percent in five years. At first glance the deal seems preposterous. On his own Billy could never have found the money to repay the loan. But the entire half-million could have been repaid with just nine days' income from the oil commission deal with Charter Oil. To the end Billy insisted that the Libyans expected nothing from him. According to Billy the loan was just that, a loan that both parties expected to be repaid; the stunning oil commission arrangement was an effort by Libya to make amends to a good friend for the losses he had suffered because of his friendship for Libya. Nothing else was involved, Billy maintained. Nothing. A more accurate assessment would be that by the time Billy, his family, and friends attended the tenth anniversary celebration of the Libyan revolution in September Libya had two "hooks" deep in Billy's hide (the term is Jack McGregor's): the $500,000 loan, and the oil broker's fees. Not surprisingly, the Libyans decided to play their quarry. When Billy and Randy Coleman raised the loan and the oil allocation with Shahati in Tripoli they got the runaround and went home empty-handed.(91)

On November 4 Iranian militants seized the Americans remaining in the U.S. embassy in Teheran. President Carter's reaction was to make the release of the hostages the most important foreign goal of his administration. He became obsessed with the hostages and, in an effort to leave nothing untried, invited Billy to arrange a meeting between Houderi, now head of the People's Bureau in Washington, and Brzezinski. This essay in family diplomacy raises four questions. The first concerns the idea itself: the use of an informal presidential envoy, someone in this case who was also related to the president, to make a "back-channel" approach to a foreign government. The second is State vs. NSC, or the problem of the fragmentation of the control of U.S. foreign policy within the executive branch. Third, to what use did Billy put his new status as high-level diplomatic emissary? And last, what was the result of this effort in family diplomacy?

U.S. presidents seem unable to resist the use of personal envoys. The approach to the Libyans through Billy was suggested to the president by his wife, Rosalynn, during a visit to Camp David. Rosalynn called Billy about it, and Billy told her he thought he could help. President Carter then called Brzezinski on November 20 and told him to ask Billy to contact the Libyans and arrange a meeting. When Brzezinski met Houderi at the White House on Novemer 27 he stressed the importance to the United States of a universal condemnation of the Iranian action. One of the main efforts of the Carter administration was to show the Iranian revolutionaries that the seizure of the hostages had isolated their country internationally. Accordingly Brzezinski suggested to Houderi that Libya condemn the seizure, and he asked him to tell Qaddafi of President Carter's hope that the Libyan leader would use all his influence to obtain the release of the hostages. As with all such efforts, there was a rationale for going outside normal diplomatic channels. The use of a relative of the president's might dramatize the administration's concern for the hostages. A direct approach of this kind might have more impact on the unconventional Qaddafi. The Arabs valued family ties, and so on.(92) When compared to the use of other personal envoys by other presidents, particularly Franklin Roosevelt, President Carter's use of his brother to arrange a brief meeting as part of a larger formal diplomatic effort to isolate Iran appears limited and precise.

It is a curse of the U.S. system that the control of foreign policy is fragmented. Lately the chief contestants for control have been the secretary of state and the national security advisor. But in the last analysis, as Dean Acheson argued, the president alone decides how foreign policy is to be conducted. If he is deeply interested in international affairs much of the action will take place in the White House, and the State Department will have to occupy itself with what falls off the president's agenda. The president can control foreign policy from the White House and accomplish a great deal, as Nixon and Kissinger showed. Control can also be given to the secretary of state, as Presidents Truman and Eisenhower did. The greatest danger is to fail to choose one or the other of these approaches. The willingness of Brzezinski to use Billy to contact Houderi and the ease with which he did it show that the Carter administration tilted toward the White House system for the control of U.S. foreign policy.

Tapped without warning as a diplomatic emissary Billy success-fully arranged the Brzezinski-Houderi meeting with several phone calls and a quick visit to the Libyan embassy. However, once Brzezinski and Houderi had met on November 27, Billy began trying frantically to clinch the oil deal. In other words Billy sought immediately to exploit the impression of his usefulness and influ-ence that the meeting at the White House would inevitably have given the Libyans. Clear evidence of this appears in Billy's phone records, subpoenaed and published by the Bayh committee.(93) During the seven weeks before the Brzezinski-Houderi meeting of November 27, Billy telephoned Jack McGregor only once, on October 1. During the thirty days after the meeting, Billy tele-phoned McGregor twenty-five times. Billy's last call to Charter Oil had been more than three months before Houderi went to the White House. In the month after the Libyan diplomat's visit Billy called Charter Oil seven times and New England Petroleum, a subsidiary of Charter, twice. A similar pattern marked his contacts with the Libyan people's bureau. Before Brzezinski and Houderi met, Billy called the embassy about once a week. In the month after the meeting Billy telephoned the people's bureau nineteen times. Clearly, Billy sensed that his involvement in the efforts of the administration to free the hostages had enhanced his image as an influential person – it was, after all, the first trip of any Libyan to the White House since the revolution – and he wanted to take advantage of the improvement before it was dissipated. Billy must have been keenly disappointed when the Libyans continued to stall the oil deal. In fact, there never would be a Libyan oil allocation to Billy Carter. There appear to have been two reasons for this. The Libyans probably concluded that the $500,000 loan offered a better means of controlling Billy, particularly if it were not diluted by the rich oil commissions, which had been promised. Second, as Billy's notoriety grew, Charter Oil executives undoubtedly grew less and less willing to form any kind of liaison with Billy, both because of the notoriety and unwelcome legal entanglements it was almost certain to draw to the company, and because they feared there would be damage to their ties with NOC. They were surely right about both. Although Billy never was able to close an oil deal with the Libyans, the visit at the White House convinced the Libyans they had received something of value. The day after Christmas Houderi paid Billy $20,000, and in April 1980 Billy was paid $200,000, both sums ostensibly given as advances on the half-million dollar loan.

The use of personal envoys in diplomacy seldom yields good results, and this was true of President Carter's engagement of Billy to arrange the Brzezinski-Houderi meeting. In his statement in the president's report to the Judiciary Committee Brzezinski tried to establish that the contact had contributed to Libya's decision to join in the international isolation of Iran for the seizure of the hostages. But the evidence is thin and unconvincing. On November 22 Libya publicly condemned the taking of hostages, but as has been seen earlier, that initiative seems almost certainly to have resulted from the State Department breaking off the move toward detente, which had occurred a week earlier, because of Libya's refusal to condemn the hostage taking. On November 29, possibly in response to the Brzezinski-Houderi meeting, Qaddafi sent a message to President Carter in which he repeated his opposition to the taking of hostages and said he had sent a Libyan delegation to Teheran to try to obtain the release of the hostages. Qaddafi also expressed a wish for better relations with the United States. Four days later demonstrators in Tripoli, chanting support for Iran, sacked and burned the U.S. embassy. President Carter discussed the attack with Secretary of State Vance and then told Brzezinski to invite Houderi to the White House. The president met with Houderi for ten minutes. After saying he appreciated Libya's help with the hostages, Carter told Houderi he expected the Libyan government to apologize for the attack and pay for repairs to the embassy. If those things were done, the president added, the United States would be interested in improved relations with Libya. It was after this meeting that Qaddafi said in the December 10 interview with the New York Times that he opposed taking hostages and had told Khomeini that nothing in the Koran justified this action. Qaddafi also went further to say that he had been led to believe by the U.S. government that after Carter's re-election the United States would adopt a policy more favorable to the Palestinians. The White House promptly denied this. Two days after the interview Qaddafi sent a private message to President Carter through Houderi. In it Qaddafi accepted responsibility for the embassy attack, reiterated his opposition to the seizure of the hostages, welcomed closer communication with the United States, and said he hoped the United States would change its policy toward Libya.(94) These developments are the most that can be connected in any way, however distant, with Billy Carter's brief role as a personal emissary for the president of the United States.

For months Billy Carter had been living on the edge of a dream built of the promise of great wealth and the recovery of his reputation by his own wits and dogged perseverance. Along the way he had tried alternately to exploit his relation to the president and to live his life as if he were not Jimmy Carter's brother. Ironically, it was kinship that brought him down, because that alone caused federal investigators to mount and prolong a much larger and costlier investigation than they would otherwise have done. In his testimony to the Bayh committee Assistant Attorney General Heymann listed ten irregularities about the Justice Department's investigation of Billy Carter's ties to Libya. They ranged from the utilization of extremely sensitive foreign and U.S. intelligence information in the investigation to the threat to bring a criminal prosecution against Billy, which would have been the first such action in seventeen years. All these actions were far in excess of the steps normally taken in investigations under the Foreign Agents Registration Act. Heymann gave two reasons for this. Because of Billy's kinship to the president the Justice Department was determined to avoid even the appearance of a lack of vigilance and thoroughness. Also, Billy's ready access to the White House put him in a position to meet and, therefore, to influence high officials of the U.S. government. But the real reason was because Billy was the president's brother. In Heymann's words: "A case that would ordinarily have been closed long before the summer of 1980 was kept open month after month for further inquiries because of lingering suspicions that we might be missing an agency relationship unusually important because it involved the President's brother."(95)

What this meant in practice became obvious during Heymann's testimony to the Bayh committee. By August 1979, Heymann reported, although the FBI had learned of Billy's all-expense-paid trip to Libya, the gifts he had received there, and the Libyan-Arab-Georgian Friendship Society, the Justice Department had found no evidence of the critical agency relationship with Libya. However, instead of discontinuing the investigation the Foreign Registration Unit began to explore the coincidence between the decision of October 6, 1978 to reverse an earlier veto and to allow the sale of the 727s and Billy's return from his first Libyan visit only five days earlier. The inquiry into the plane sales required access to State and Commerce Department files. But the Commerce Department withheld access to its files for months. When they were finally examined they confirmed that the most important decisions had been taken independently of any possible influence by Billy. It looked like another dead end.

To close this third phase of the investigation Lisker and an FBI agent, Richard Fugatt, interviewed Billy Carter at the Best Western Motel on January 16, 1980. There are two interesting things about the interview. First, Billy said he had met Frank Terpil in Tripoli, that Terpil had contacted him in Americus about selling large numbers of machine guns to Libya, and that nothing had come of the deal. Billy later denied ever having said this. Second, Billy said nothing at all to Lisker or Fugatt about the pending oil deal or the $500,000 loan, although he had deposited the Libyan check for $20,000 only two weeks earlier. He did not deny having asked for oil and money, he simply kept silent about them. There is no doubt that this misled federal investigators, because by late March 1980 Lisker and his immediate superior had concluded that the investigation should be closed for lack of evidence.(96)

Then two remarkable developments occurred which touched the White House and Justice Department and worked to prolong the investigation of Billy's ties to Libya. The White House learned of Billy Carter's pending oil deal on March 31, 1980, when Stansfield Turner, director of the CIA, handed a brief intelligence report to Brzezinski in the latter's office at the White House. The report described Billy's contacts with Charter Oil and Libya's efforts to exploit them.(97) This disclosure was obviously of momentous importance to the president and the entire administration, particularly in an election year. Brzezinski ate lunch alone at his desk that day and thought about how he might best serve the president. He decided to talk to Billy about the oil deal, taking care to protect the source of the intelligence, before he told the president about the report from Stansfield Turner. After he had acted, Brzezinski would inform the president of the contents of the report, of what he had done about it, and of Billy's reaction. Brzezinski's purpose in calling Billy was to try to scare him off, in polite terms, to try to deter him from closing the oil deal. Billy's phone records show that he and Brzezinski probably talked on April 1. Brzezinski remembered telling Billy that the Libyans could try to exploit his oil deal for political purposes, which would embarrass the United States and the president personally. The national security advisor repeatedly asked Billy not to do anything inappropriate or embarrassing. Billy reacted predictably. I am entitled to my privacy, he told Brzezinski. You have no right to meddle in my personal affairs. I have a right to make a living, Billy added. Brzezinski then reported to the president on the intelligence report, his action, and Billy's response, and that was the last that the national security advisor had to do with Billy until Billy called him in June. The president told Brzezinski he had done the right thing.

Curiously, no other action was taken by the White House. The president didn't try to stop the oil deal: a phone call to Charter from an appropriate presidential advisor would have scotched the deal. Nor did Brzezinski order any kind of intelligence follow-up, although the oil deal clearly could harm the interests of the United States. Brzezinski explained his omission of any follow-up in two ways. First, the existence of the intelligence report suggested that the appropriate intelligence agencies were "monitoring the Libyans," in Brzezinski's words.(98) Brzezinski's choice of terms suggests that the U.S. government learned of the oil through electronic surveillance of the Libyan people's bureau in Washington, but there are many other possible sources, ranging from Charter executives to Libyan agents in Tripoli or the United States, to Israeli or Egyptian intelligence. The other explanation Brzezinski gave was that the contact with Billy coincided with a crisis in the hostage negotiations with Iran and preceded by just a few days the decision to stage the ill-fated rescue mission into Iran. Everybody's thoughts and virtually all their time were concentrated on the hostages and the use of force.(99)

By coincidence, Billy had sent Randy Coleman and another accountant, Ronald Sprague, back to Tripoli in mid-March to press the Libyans for the rest of the loan. Sprague was the son-in-law of a California rancher and businessman, George Belluomini, who offered his services to Billy, with the understanding that Billy would pay him out of the oil commission money. Coleman and Sprague were talking with a Libyan banker, Mohammed Layas, of the Libyan Arab Foreign Bank, at virtually the same time Brzezinski called Billy to try to stop the oil deal. Coleman and Sprague also had several meetings with Shahati about the oil allocation. Sprague assured the Libyans that Billy had sufficient assets to cover the loan and negotiated a 10 percent interest rate on $500,000 for five years. Randy Coleman handled the oil negotiations and insisted that Billy urgently needed the money. Finally Shahati told Coleman but not Sprague that Billy could have a sizable advance on the loan. Go home and wait a week, Shahati told Coleman, and then go to Houderi and he will give you the advance. On April 7 Coleman picked up a check for $200,000 at the Libyan People's Bureau in Washington. Not only did Billy fail to report this income to the Foreign Agent Registration Unit, but he didn't even tell Ronald Sprague about it. As a result, Sprague continued to pester the Libyan bank for the full $500,000 loan.

Although he didn't know it, Billy's freewheeling was about to catch up with him. In April, apparently before Billy received the $200,000, Attorney General Benjamin Civiletti was shown two highly sensitive intelligence documents that indicated Billy might be about to receive money from the Libyan government.(100) According to his testimony before the Bayh committee Civiletti felt that this confronted him with a double dilemma. If he told anyone, or even asked to be given the documents he might compromise the source of the intelligence if there were a leak. A leak might also prevent the passing of the money to Billy, which could be the evidence needed to force Billy to register as a foreign agent. Moreover, the information could not be used as evidence in a trial unless there was another source from which it had come. With these considerations in mind Civiletti decided to tell no one, not even the president, and he declined to ask for the intelligence documents. At the same time, Civiletti knew the Foreign Agents Registration Unit was about to close the investigation into Billy's ties to Libya. To prevent that from happening he told the head of the Criminal Division, Heymann, that he had been given highly sensitive intelligence information regarding Billy Carter and instructed him not to close the investigation of Billy's ties to Libya until he had received that information. (It was not given to Heymann until May 30.) Civiletti insisted in his testimony that he was motivated solely by a concern for the security of the intelligence sources. Republican senators on the Bayh committee reminded him that this period was the height of the presidential primary season, and that Civiletti's action put the whole matter on ice for forty-five extremely important days. In response, Civiletti reiterated the need to protect intelligence sources. To a question from Democratic Senator Patrick Leahy of Vermont, Civiletti added that he hadn't told the president anything in April because there was a strong risk that this might have ended up prejudicing the investigation. The president might have forced or persuaded Billy to register. But what if the president had felt too personally involved to act objectively and had turned the matter over to his staff? Civiletti described what might have happened next:

> Then you have three or four or more staff people involved in determining what to do. They start wanting to know all of the facts. They get Billy in. What have you done or not done? They call people in the Department of Justice, the line attorneys begin to think perhaps that they are being intimidated in one fasion of another, and it becomes or deteriorates into a mess or a greater mess than otherwise. . . . It looks as if . . . in that kind of an instance, somehow there is an attempt to give favoritism or special treatment or to interfere with a legitimate investigation of the Department of Justice by agents of the White House because it is the President's brother.(101)

Heymann remembered that the attorney general told him about the intelligence information on about April 15. He kept the investigation open and about two weeks later, presumably through the FBI, the Criminal Division had a lead on another scheme to transfer money indirectly from Libya to Billy Carter, not involving Charter Oil. "The investigation," as Heymann said, "was once again in full tilt."(102) The new lead didn't produce any immediate results. On May 30 Heymann learned that there was independent confirmation of the $220,000 payment and the Charter Oil deal from "separate highly sensitive" intelligence sources. Heymann informed the attorney general and on June 4 (the day after some extremely important primaries, as Republican Senator Dole pointed out) Civiletti showed him the April documents. They were also shown to Heymann's colleagues in the Criminal Division, including Joel Lisker.

Five days after seeing the documents Heymann met with these men to consider their possible courses of action. They were angry because they felt Billy had made fools of them. They had been investigating him for a year without result, and it now appeared that he might have secretly been on the payroll of the Libyan government the whole time. They decided their options were: to open a civil prosecution and use court orders to disclose what they had learned from the intelligence reports; to convene a grand jury; to confront Billy and ask him if he didn't have more to tell; to interview Charter Oil executives. None of them were very promising. The grand jury was worst of all, because it is a secret procedure itself and would have tied up information for six to eighteen months that the law was meant to disclose. A civil suit would allow the use of disclosure but it would also allow Billy to raise some embarrassing "gray mail" questions.

On June 10, in a coincidence that seemed strange to nearly everyone, Billy called the Justice Department and arranged an interview with Joel Lisker for the next day. "After a little prodding," as Heymann put it, Billy admitted taking the $220,000 and trying to conclude an oil deal with Charter and Libya. "He gave us in usable form the information that we had no very brilliant ideas about how to quickly obtain in usable form."(103)

After meeting alone with Lisker on June 11 for about an hour Billy broke off the meeting, saying he had to go to the White House to ask Brzezinski for guidance on whether or not he could reveal information about his involvement in a matter touching national security. He was referring to his brief role as a diplomatic emissary the previous November. Billy saw Brzezinski alone at the White House for about ten minutes and asked if his role in arranging the meeting with Houderi could be disclosed. Brzezinski said he saw no reason why not. Because the Justice Department was involved Brzezinski invited the president's legal counsel, Lloyd Cutler, to join them. Cutler agreed about disclosing the November activities, but this concerned him much less than Billy's admission that he had talked to Lisker without the aid of an attorney. Cutler took charge of the meeting and soon led Billy back to his office where he telephoned a prestigious Washington law firm and arranged for Billy to be represented by two highly qualified lawyers, Henry Ruth and Stephen Pollak of the firm of Shea & Gardner. Under their guidance Billy did not return to the Justice Department that afternoon, as he had told Lisker he would.

A delay followed, while Ruth and Pollak familiarized themselves with Billy's activities and tried to discover their negotiating room with the Justice Department. They soon realized that Heymann was determined to force the disclosure of the Libyan payments to Billy, as indeed he was obliged to do by the Foreign Agents Registration Act, by whatever legal means were necessary to do this. Heymann and his colleagues had also resolved to declare publicly and formally that the Justice Department believed Billy was a foreign agent. They doubted that criminal prosecution of Billy would succeed: "The evidence of agency was weak and circumstantial; evidence of willfulness or criminal intent was non-existent; and the case did not share the characteristics of past criminal prosecutions under the statute."(104)

This line of reasoning led the federal prosecutors to choose to bring a civil suit for an injunction against Billy. The advantages of this for the government were that it would (1) cause the immediate public disclosure of the payments by Billy; (2) provide federal prosecutors a means to compel Billy to disclose his activities if he refused the judgment against him; (3) bring Billy under the powerful and instantaneous contempt powers of the court if he violated the law or the judgment again, assuming Billy lost the case; and (4) oblige Billy to register as a foreign agent. Billy's attorneys quickly realized that this was the best course for Billy to follow since, in effect, the only penalty would be registration as a foreign agent. By consenting to the injunction, to the disclosure of the payments and oil deal, and to registration, Billy would admit nothing and could technically maintain his claim that he was not a foreign agent. But it took Ruth and Pollak nearly a month to convince Billy to consent to this arrangement. He finally agreed in early July. When he did, the Billy Carter affair was over in a legal and practical sense. The Justice Department had caused the disclosure of the payments and had wrapped Billy in an injunction and registration. If he broke or even stretched the law he would be subject to sudden and stern penalties. Billy's cloak of secrecy was gone, his posture of wounded innocence was no longer credible. The publicity ended any chance of an oil deal with a reputable oil company, and demolished Libya's hopes of controlling a friend with access to the highest foreign policy officials in the U.S. government.(105)

If the private and practical side of Billygate had ended, the public and political side had really only just begun. All of this – the Senate investigation, the partisan accusations, the popular indignation – went on for another three months, until just a few weeks before the 1980 presidential election. In the end only one important blunder was discovered in the public political phase of the affair that had not been uncovered by the Justice Department prosecutors. This was a serious lapse in judgment by Attorney General Benjamin Civiletti. On June 17, a week after Billy had told Lisker of the $220,000 and the oil deal, Civiletti saw the president at the White House about the appointment of federal judges and other Justice Department business. Lloyd Cutler was present, but left after the discussion of the judicial appointments. Alone with the president, the attorney general said that he could not discuss the Billy Carter case. Civiletti added that Billy had acted foolishly and ought to have registered long before. What will happen to Billy, the president asked. Civiletti answered that if Billy was honest and cooperated with the Justice Department he probably would not be prosecuted. Five weeks later, under the glare of national publicity and the cackle of political attack, Lloyd Cutler called Civiletti and asked if the White House could safely release a statement saying there had been no contacts of any kind between the Justice Department and the White House about the investigation of Billy Carter's ties to Libya. Choosing to construe "contact" as interference and discussion of the substance of the investigation Civiletti told Cutler the proposed statement was an accurate one and could safely be given to the press. In fact, the statement read quite differently than Civiletti's interpretation of it, for it denied "contact in either direction between the White House and the Department of Justice concerning the conduct of this investigation."(106) Three days later, on July 24, Civiletti held a regularly scheduled press conference. A reporter asked: "Did you or your colleagues, Mr. Renfrew and Mr. Heymann, ever talk to the President or any other White House aides about the Billy Carter case?" Civiletti answered flatly: "No." In doing so he followed the same fine legal definition of contact meaning interference or substantive discussion that he had used in his response to Cutler's question concerning the White House statement. But the question made no such fine distinctions, and Civiletti's answer was, therefore, a misleading one. That same day the president found a note about the June 17 conversation with Civiletti. When Cutler told him of this, Civiletti decided to admit his error publicly, and he did so at a news conference the next day. His blunder made him and the administration an easy target for Watergate-sore Republicans. It did not change the final judgment of the Bayh committee that there had been no wrongdoing in the handling of the Billy Carter investigation, and that Billy and Libya had never influenced U.S. foreign policy.

The last word in this story belonged to the Bayh committee. There was criticism of all the principals: of Billy for disgracing and harming his country, of the president for failing to state clearly in public that Billy could never influence U.S. policy, of the president again for using Billy as a diplomatic emissary despite the obvious negative consequences of this, and of the national security advisor and the attorney general for acting on intelligence information in such a way as to prevent the president "from taking personal responsibility for the proper course of conduct in a situation which involved both foreign policy and law enforcement aspects."(107)

A number of senators attached additional views to the Bayh committee's report. Among these, those of Senators Claiborne Pell and Richard Lugar stand out. Pell was deeply disturbed by the evidence of Libya's increasing efforts to manipulate U.S. policy and opinion, particularly by involving itself in the internal working of the U.S. political process. Libya's vast financial resources made it likely that these efforts would intensify. They were extremely dangerous and should be dealt with by increasing the efforts of the Justice Department to apply the Foreign Agents Registration Act and by a systematic use by Justice of all relevant intelligence information.(108)

Senator Lugar's remarks were bitingly partisan, but cogent and provocative as well. "The Carter Administration," he argued, "has failed from the beginning to understand the depth and consistency of Colonel Qaddafi's hatred for the United States and his single-minded devotion to frustrating our policies in the Middle East." Lugar then added the following:

The Carter Administration's policies have been characterized by starts and stops, reversals, and misplaced hopes. On the whole, Libyan policies toward the United States have been far less "eccentric" than United States policies toward Libya. For example, Libya had tried through a number of means, including terrorist activity and assassination attempts to unravel the Camp David accords. Libyan training of terrorists has contributed substantially to the undermining of European governments. In addition, more recently, Libya has exercised economic pressures to frustrate all United States policies to free the American hostages through proposed joint allied economic sanctions against Iran.(109)

Despite the repeated efforts of Libya to harm the interests of the United States, Lugar was saying, the Carter administration actually tried to move toward detente with Libya. Then, in a nice phrase, Lugar summed up President Carter's strange silences about Billy's activities: "The Administration's ambivalence toward Libya characterized the Administration's attitude toward Billy Carter's involvement with Libya."(110) Lugar was one of the Republicans still smarting from the beating given his party because of Watergate, and he wrongly tried to equate the Billy Carter affair with Watergate. But he had cut to the heart of the main policy problem in U.S.-Libyan relations: How does one deal with a little enemy?

The Bayh committee's report concluded that Libya's efforts to use Billy could have originated in its campaign to change U.S. opinion. By February 1979, certainly no later, the Libyans must have known that Billy was useless for this end, even counterproductive. Yet high Libyan officials continued to court him, and large amounts of Libyan money were given to him. Libya's ends in trying to gain a hold over Billy can only be speculated about, the committee concluded. Perhaps they were to gain a means of communicating directly to the president, to be used when they needed it; perhaps they were preparing to embarrass the president; perhaps they sought insight into the president's personality. It is clear, nonetheless, that "the Libyan purpose, in creating and maintaining the relationship was to benefit the Libyan government and Libyan policy."(111) With the appearance of the Bayh committee's report both the private legal and public political phases of the Billy Carter affair ended. Although the controversy was over, its effects were not. The Billy Carter affair contributed to the growing suspicion and resentment of Libya in Washington, feelings and attitudes that outlived the Carter administration and were taken up and intensified by the newly elected Reagan administration.

10

THE ANNEXATION OF CHAD

As might have been foreseen the agreements reached at the fourth Lagos conference in August 1979 did not lead to an end to the fighting or the struggle for power in Chad. War had been going on in Chad for sixteen of the twenty years of the country's independence, and could not so easily be stopped. Peace and order were once again the victims of too many ambitious leaders in control of armed bands and too many outside supporters happy to send money and weapons. As many as 40,000 people had died in the fighting in 1978 and 1979. The French minister of cooperation, Robert Galley, observed that there were more than 30,000 armed men in Chad, "a country whose economy at best could support a few thousand gendarmes."(1) The Lagos accords had required the establishment of a transitional national government, the demilitarization of Ndjamena by February 5, 1980, and the introduction into the country of an African peace-keeping force. A Congolese detachment of 500 men arrived in Chad in January 1980, but the units promised by Benin and Guinea were nowhere to be seen. According to the Chadian minister of higher education, Abba Siddick, Ndjamena was filled with undisciplined soldiers, and government officials had not been paid in months.

Not surprisingly, in late March fighting broke out in Ndjamena between the forces of President Goukouni Oueddei and Prime Minister Hissene Habre. Although there were still 1,200 French troops in Chad, neither they nor the Congolese detachment intervened in the fighting. With the soldiers firing cannon, mortars, rocket launchers, and machine guns at each other and at the buildings in the capital, the estimate offered newsmen by diplomats of 700 dead in the first four days of fighting seemed all too likely.(2) The city was soon split, with Oueddei's troops in control of the diplomatic quarter of Ndjamena, and Habre's of the rest. On March 24, the French military commander evacuated 400 of the 900 whites living in Ndjamena, including the U.S. ambassador, Donald Norland.

A lull in the fighting on March 25 was broken by renewed firing the next day. With the help of the representatives of Egypt, France, and Saudi Arabia a cease-fire was arranged on March 30 between Oueddei and Habre, who spoke to one another on the telephone to confirm it. It lasted a day, and then the forces of Acyl Ahmat, foreign minister in the interim government, joined with units loyal to President Oueddei against Habre. This decision by Ahmat, who had Libyan support, meant that all the principal factions in Chad had sided with Oueddei against Habre. This included the Forces armees tchadiennes (FAT) of Wadel Abdelkader Kamougue, and the Front d'action commune (FAC) of Acyl Ahmat; the latter also headed the Conseil democratique revolutionnaire or "New Volcano."(3) Libya supported the Forces armées populaires (FAP) of President Oueddei as well as FAT and FAC. Some news reports indicated that Hissene Habre's Forces armées du nord (FAN) were receiving supplies and money from Egypt and Sudan.(4) Both sides continued to shoot their mortars and heavy machine guns at each other with no obvious result save the loss of innocent lives.

The president of Togo, Gnassingbe Eyadema, went to Ndjamena on April 5 to try to arrange a cease-fire. Both Oueddei and Habre cooperated with Eyadema and signed a cease-fire on April 6. Eyadema announced that the truce would be supervised by an eight-man observer team, comprised of two senior officers from Cameroon, Nigeria, Liberia, and Togo. The Togolese president indicated that these eight were merely the first of a much larger peacekeeping force to be sent by the Organization of African Unity. But there were a number of reasons to doubt that it would all work this way. First, the 500-man Congolese peacekeeping unit had simply gone home a week earlier. And even as he signed the cease-fire President Oueddei doubted the agreement would end the fighting. It did not. The shooting started again on April 9.

A new lull in the violence occurred in late April. The French government took advantage of it to announce its intention to withdraw its military forces from Chad. The French troops, who had left Chad in 1975 after the overthrow and murder of Tombalbaye had returned in 1978 to support President Malloum. But Malloum's regime collapsed and he fled Chad in 1979. The French stayed, but took no part in the fighting. They were able to help evacuate foreigners. Under the terms of the Lagos agreement France had recalled 1,400 of this detachment, leaving 1,100, who had remained with the consent of Oueddei and Habre. At this point observers in Ndjamena put the death toll at 1,500 in five weeks of fighting. It was estimated that between 5,000 and 6,000 people were killed in the first part of 1980.(5) The French withdrawal began on April 28 and was completed May 16.

From April 28-30, as the French prepared to withdraw, an OAU economic conference of heads of state was convened in Lagos during which a number of agreements were reached concerning Chad. An ad hoc committee of the OAU was directed to arrange a cease-fire in Chad. The heads of state of Guinea, Nigeria, and Togo were members of the committee, with President Leopold Senghor of Senegal as chairman. President Oueddei accepted the dispatch to Chad of 2,000 troops from Congo, Benin, and Guinea as an OAU peacekeeping force. This had, of course, been provided in the August 1979 Lagos agreements. (A budget of $60 million for peacekeeping was approved by the OAU Council of Ministers meeting at Freeport, Sierra Leone, June 23-29.)

But no peacekeeping force was sent, and none of this stopped the fighting, which soon spread outside Ndjamena. On June 6 Hissene Habre's forces captured Faya Largeau, the most important settlement in the northern quarter of the country. Oueddei's position had become precarious. The French were gone. The OAU could do nothing. And Habre was on the march. On June 15 Libya and the transitional government of Chad (FAP/FAT/FAC) signed a treaty of alliance in Tripoli, whose precise terms were kept secret by Qaddafi until September 28. The treaty committed Libya and Chad to defend one another in case either faced "direct or indirect external aggression." The two countries agreed to exchange military and internal security plans. Libya pledged to aid Chad's reconstruction, and Chad bound itself not to permit the establishment of foreign bases or the stationing of foreign troops on its soil. The two countries also proclaimed that Libya and Chad were united by "spiritual, economic and human ties," as well as "by geography and centuries of history between the two peoples."(6) Some news reports stated that Libyan troops began entering Chad in June.(7)

Two days after the signature of the alliance between Libya and Chad, a macabre incident happened in Moscow that was full of double meanings, if one cared to find them. Baba Hassan, Chad's ambassador in Moscow, had died of a cerebral hemorrhage on June 7. The ambassador's funeral delegation left for home by plane on June 17. But during a stop in Nigeria the delegation established that the ambassador's body was not on the plane! A member of the Chad embassy in Moscow looked and found the coffin still on the runway at the Moscow airport. Embarrassed, Soviet officials promised to send the body home immediately.

The ad hoc OAU committee on Chad made an effort in mid-October to stop the war in Chad. The group met in Togo, and although they persuaded Habre and Oueddei to attend, the conference was unsuccessful. During the conference Libyan aircraft and troops reportedly attacked FAN around Faya Largeau, and Libyan aircraft struck at FAN areas in Ndjamena in mid-October and early

November. These attacks marked a dramatic escalation of Libyan military intervention in Chad. Libyan forces attacked Faya Largeau and established a supply center and landing strip at Donguia, in preparation for an attack on Ndjamena.

The first reports of the movement of large numbers of Libyan troops into Chad reached the press in early November. Libya was said to have sent two infantry divisions supported by armored units and aircraft more than 100 miles into northern Chad.(8) On November 6, Qaddafi flew to Faya Largeau for a meeting with Oueddei, according to a Libyan news release.(9) Meanwhile, the Libyan government simply denied intervening in Chad. As the construction of the staging area at Donguia proceded and Libyan troops were sent south in preparation for the attack on Ndjamena, Qaddafi announced that he had sent "a few military advisers" and some soldiers "to guard the presidential palace."(10)

In addition FAP/FAT/FAC units struck at FAN in eastern Chad, in an effort to break FAN's supply lines to Abeche, 70 miles from the Sudanese frontier. Initial estimates on November 7 and 8 by the governments of France and the United States put the number of Libya troops at 3,000 to 4,000. A month later the French government said there were 6,500 Libyan troops in Chad, of which 2,500 were in Ndjamena. The Libyan force was composed of regular Libyan units and an Islamic Legion, which had soldiers from Libya and various Arab and African states, including Benin, a member of the OAU committee on Chad. President Kerekou of Benin had converted to Islam and had signed a cooperation agreement with Libya during a vist to Tripoli the previous September.(11)

Ultimately, the Libyan intervention would provoke a strong negative reaction from a large number of African states. However, they moved slowly. The first reaction came from the OAU committee, now said to be Benin, Togo, Congo, and Guinea. The committee met November 27-28 in Lome, the capital of Togo, with Presidents Eyadema of Togo and Siaka Stevens of Sierra Leone acting as chairmen. They issued a communique, which was, in essence, the same message they had sent in mid-October from Lome. The committee called for a cease-fire, the dispatch of a neutral African peacekeeping force, and the demilitarization of Ndjamena. President Oueddei accepted it, but Habre refused on the grounds that the OAU had not condemned the Libyan intervention and that there were "Libyan agents" (Benin) taking part in the peace process. On November 28 the ad hoc committee did issue a demand for "the immediate withdrawal of all foreign forces present in Chad" and requested Nigeria to reconvene the group of nations present at the Lagos conference of August 1979. Deeply concerned by the Libyan moves and embarrassed at the failure of its policies the French government issued a veiled warning to Libya in late November and moved to strengthen the defenses of Gabon.

Undeterred, Qaddafi pressed forward. On December 6 some 2,500 Libyan troops using French <u>Mirage</u> aircraft and Soviet T-54 and T-55 tanks (transported, perhaps, by the Oshkosh trucks) joined FAP/FAT/FAC in a major assault on the positions of Hissene Habre's FAN troops in Ndjamena. For a few days FAN withstood repeated Libyan air, armor, and artillery strikes, although there were heavy civilian casualties. French officials estimated that 2,000 Libyan troops and 50 Soviet-made tanks took part in the battle 600 miles south of the Libyan border. News reports from the scene spoke of 20 tanks and at least a dozen jets — Tupolev-22 bombers according to the French — on Oueddei's side.(12) After dark on December 14-15 FAN troops and some 10,000 civilians fled to Cameroon. Others left for Abeche, which fell on December 17. Before the capture of Abeche thousands of refugees fled into the Sudan.

In Yaounde, capital of Cameroon, Habre yielded to the request of that country's president, Ahidjo, and signed the OAU committee's cease-fire of November 28. But he denounced Oueddei's government as illegal and pledged to renew the war against it. Habre was not the only victim of the Libyan invasion. Humiliated by the Libyan's success and angered at Qaddafi's disregard of its earlier warnings, the French government issued an unmistakable threat on December 13. Although Libya was not named, France expressed grave concern about the new turn of events in Central Africa and promised to support any collective African effort to restore peace to Chad and protect its independence. On December 19 the French foreign minister told Ahmed Shahati that France was adamantly opposed to foreign intervention in Chad. Reports in <u>Le Monde</u> indicated that France was willing to provide transportation, food, and other necessities for an African peacekeeping force and would, if necessary, intervene more directly to force Libya to comply with the Lome cease-fire agreement. One of France's main reasons for concern was the fear of Libyan expansionism in its former colonies in West Africa. Libya's actions had already caused adverse reactions in a number of African capitals. Senegal had broken relations with Libya in July, and Gabon had done the same in late October. Gabon, Ghana, Mauritania, and Niger had expelled Libyan diplomats, and Mauritania had expelled diplomats and closed a Libyan cultural center in Nouakchott in December. Nigeria would expel Libyan diplomats in early 1981.

The OAU committee in Chad went into action again after the fall of Ndjamena and organized a conference in Lagos, December 23-24. Eleven heads of state attended, including Oueddei, and Libyan Foreign Minister Turayki and Sudanese Interior Minister Izzeldin Hamid. There was no invitation for Habre. The president of the OAU, Siaka Stevens, described the purpose of the conference. His headings were sensible, humane, and impossible: an interim government of national unity; national elections; national reconstruction; and the return of all refugees. However, the conference split over the issue of Libyan withdrawal and was unable even to reach agreement on a final communique. Opposition to the Libyan intervention came from Sudan and the former French colonies of Cameroon, Central African Republic, Guinea, Niger, Senegal, and Togo. Their proposals specifically called not only for Libyan withdrawal from Chad but for a halt to Libyan intervention in West Africa. The chief of state of Nigeria, Shagari, refused to support any specific condemnation of Libya and was joined by President Stevens of Sierra Leone in this. Both had earlier publicly urged the withdrawal of Libyan troops from Chad. The others who refused to accept a condemnation of Libya were Benin, Chad, Congo, and of course, Libya. The group of nations which had demanded Libyan withdrawal responded by quitting the conference. This left Benin, Chad, Congo, Libya, Nigeria, and Sierra Leone to issue a lame communique that didn't mention Libya at all, called for the creation of an OAU peacekeeping force for Chad, and authorized the presence in Chad of only those foreign troops allowed by the Lagos accords of August 1979.(13)

Nigeria's reluctance to join in the immediate condemnation of Libya is understandable. Libya clearly had intervened with the blessing and cooperation of one of the principal factions in Chad, and in this sense had not invaded or acted illegitimately. Moreover, by giving Oueddei's FAP/FAT/FAC coalition a decisive military edge Qaddafi's action promised to end the deadly stalemate in Chad and to bring an end to the violence and senseless loss of life. Seen in this light the Libyan invasion held the promise of a constructive result. If, for example, Libya agreed to an early withdrawal and could be persuaded to act under the supervision of the OAU, thereby recognizing and accommodating itself to the interests of the African nations close to Chad, then Nigeria and other African states had every reason to play down the intervention and try to work with Qaddafi in Chad. Only the passage of time would reveal Qaddafi's precise motives. From this point of view, clearly shared by Nigeria and Sierra Leone, the inconclusive outcome of the conference was just what was needed. However, time did reveal Libyan motives. They were not constructive and cooperative but expansionist and disruptive, and the anti-Libyan position of Senegal, Cameroon, Sudan and the others proved to be a better indication of the direction of African opinion than did the rump communique. Nigeria gave an early indication of its misgivings by expelling Libyan diplomats in January 1981.

Recognizing chaos in Chad and the weakness of its many competing factions, Nigeria and a number of other African countries reacted cautiously to the Libyan intervention. The overt Libyan intervention had upset the balance of power in Central Africa. This was all the more disturbing to Chad's neighbors, and to France and the United States because there apparently had been explicit agreements about Libya's sphere of influence in Chad. <u>Jeune Afrique</u>, for example, reported that in 1978 France and Libya had divided control of Chad, with Libya to be dominant in the Muslim north and France dominant in the Christian south.(14) Qaddafi may have given pledges of restraint in Chad to African governments as well, to Nigeria, for example. Despite this, had Qaddafi proceeded carefully, he might have drawn an endorsement or at least tolerance of Libya's presence in Chad from many African governments, as, for example, Syria had won the backing of the Arab League for its occupation of Lebanon. Instead, barely two weeks after the defeat of Habre at Ndjamena, Qaddafi made a grab for Chad and attempted to drive it into a merger with Libya. The merger was announced on January 6, 1981, at the end of a five-day visit to Tripoli by Goukouni Oueddei. It immediately provoked a storm of criticism and protest around the world: in Africa, Sudan, Egypt, the Middle East, Europe, and the United States. And it led Libya's African neighbors, as well as Sudan, Egypt, France, and the United States to take extremely strong countermeasures. On the part of Egypt, France, and the United States these steps included substantial covert aid for Habre, and plans for demonstrations of force against Libya and the actual use of military force against Libyan forces in Chad. Sudan allowed Habre to conduct military operations across its western frontier against Oueddei's Interim Government of National Unity (GUNT). Even though the reaction against the Libyan-inspired merger was so strong little has been said or written about the terms of the merger agreement itself and, particularly, about the great reluctance of the Chadians to accept unity with Libya.

Chadian President Goukouni Oueddei arrived in Tripoli on the evening of January 2, 1981. Jalloud and a high-ranking Libyan delegation met him at the airport, which showed the importance the Libyans attributed to the visit. In his arrival statement Oueddei thanked Libya for its aid in winning the war, condemned Egypt and Sudan for supporting Habre, and asked Libya to continue to help his government in the reconstruction and development of Chad.(15) The speech was totally predictable, as were all the others Oueddei would give during his stay in Libya. Ordinarily, one would pay little attention to any of them. But it is clear that although Oueddei said many nice things about Libya, he never mentioned unity, not once in any statement that may be attributed directly to him. This is extraordinary, since the joint communique published at the end of the visit by the official Libyan news agency states that Chad and Libya had agreed "to work for the realization of complete unity between the two countries."(16) Oueddei's repeated refusal even to mention unity let alone having agreed to unite with Libya must be regarded as his way of dissenting from Libya's plans. At the very least Oueddei's peculiar silences appear to have been an attempt by the Chadian leaders in Tripoli to signal their dissent from some aspects of the Libyan plans. It may mean that they never agreed to a merger with Libya or agreed only under duress. First a review of Oueddei's public statements. He spoke at least three times: at the airport on arrival, as mentioned; before the opening session of the Libyan People's Congress on January 3; and at the airport before his departure. At the People's Congress, Oueddei's remarks followed the general tone of his earlier statement: he had defiance for Habre and any state supporting him; and he was appreciative of past Libyan aid and confident of receiving Libyan help in the future.(17) There was no mention of unity, no anticipation of unity, not even a foreshadowing of a major development in relations between Libya and Chad.

Talks began on January 4 with Jalloud on the Libyan side and, for Chad, Oueddei, Mahamat Abba Said, minister for interior and security; the ministers of agriculture and animal husbandry; and Mahamat Bour Adam Barka, the secretary-general of the Chadian government. On January 5 the People's Congress ratified the mutual security treaty signed between Libya and Chad the previous June. The next day, the visit was over. It had lasted only three working days, officially only two, for talks were said to have begun on January 4. At the airport on January 6 Oueddei again made no mention of unity. He again thanked Libya for its support and declared that he would not allow French troops to return to Chad or to use Chad "as a launching base." Then Oueddei took another tack. He praised the Lagos agreements and saluted the stance of the people of Nigeria.(18) These were strange comments, because at the same time the Nigerian Foreign Ministry was telling reporters that Libya was "a transparent proxy for Soviet influence in the West African region" and had moved one of its four army divisions, an air force squadron, and a large part of its artillery to Maiduguki, capital of the region bordering Chad.(19) And on January 8, the Nigerian foreign minister condemned the merger of Libya and Chad as "most unfortunate and indeed premature" and noted that only "a new and freely elected government" in Chad could do such a thing.(20) In its commentary accompanying Oueddei's departure statement Tripoli Domestic Service did add, not quoting Oueddei directly, that the Chadian president had stressed that Chad and Libya "are linked by firm relations." It was a far cry from unity.

All the references to unity came in what the official Libyan news service called a joint communique. According to the preamble to the communique there was much to justify the merger, including: "historic, cultural, human, racial, geographical, and spiritual ties" between the two peoples; their belief in unity as their "common fate"; the struggle of both against colonialism; and the mixing together of the two peoples over a long period of history: "tens of thousands" of Chadians had become Libyans and vice versa. For these reasons the two countries had agreed to work for "complete unity" in a state built clearly along Libyan lines: "a jamahiri [masses] unity in which authority, arms, and resources are in the hands of the people; its [foundation] is the people's congresses and committees."(21) The rest of the communiqué outlined three kinds of measures: those devoted to defending Chad, and those intended to advance the merger of the two countries, and those which appeared to be designed to strengthen the position of GUNT.

It wasn't always easy to separate merger activities from defense activities. To promote the merger, for example, the two governments would open their borders in order to allow the citizens of Libya and Chad "to move with full freedom and without any restrictions . . . to realize cohesion and interaction." In defense of Chad, Libya would continue its military and economic aid and, at Chad's request, would send "a number of military men" to assist in peacekeeping and the rebuilding of Chad's army and "security forces." Libya thus portrayed its intervention as the natural result of an invitation from the recognized government of Chad, with which, in any case, it intended to merge. However, the publication of the merger agreement, which was not publicly opposed by Oueddei, and the presence of 8,000 to 10,000 of its troops in the country, as well as its role as the only supplier of foreign aid, put Libya in a position to try to annex Chad or at the very least to control its territory and use it as a base for operations against Sudan to the east in cooperation with Ethiopia and South Yemen, and against Cameroon, Central African Republic, Nigeria, and Mali to the west. The future of this Libyan gamble depended very little on the support or opposition of Oueddei and the other leaders in GUNT. They were cowed and, in any case, could not defeat Hissene Habre without strong outside assistance. At the moment, Libya offered the only effective outside help, and Oueddei had no choice but to take it if he wished to escape defeat by Habre. But a question remained unanswered: why would Oueddei agree to the merger, thus exchanging French foreign occupation for Libyan?

New light was shed on this puzzle by a story out of Lagos that appeared in the London Times about ten days after the announcement of the merger by the Libyan government. The Times' correspondent in Lagos, Karan Thapar, had filed an astonishing story. Sources close to Nigerian President Shagari had told him that Oueddei had been forced to agree to the merger and had signed a merger agreement only because he believed his life was in danger. Libya's coercion of Chad had actually begun a month earlier, Thapar's sources had said. After an OAU conference on Chad in Lagos in December two senior Chadian army officers were invited to Tripoli. When Oueddei arrived in Tripoli on January 2 he found that the two men had been murdered by Libyan authorities. The Libyans then presented Oueddei with the merger agreement and said he must accept it. They also ordered him to appoint three or four Libyans to his cabinet. Oueddei tried but failed to resist the pressure. He delayed accepting the merger agreement, as his public statements made clear, but he signed at the airport because he feared he might be killed too.(22)

It is impossible to verify this account of Libyan coercion and Chadian surprise at the merger and resistance to it. It is clear why the Nigerians would leak such a tale, for by January 15 they had become the leader of African opposition to Libya's merger with Chad. Because of Nigeria's leadership against the merger Oueddei might have told the Nigerians such a story in order to enlist their support against other Libyan protégés in GUNT. There is no doubt that such a story from Oueddei would have stiffened Nigeria's determination to oust Qaddafi from Chad. Was it true? It was consistent with Oueddei's silences in Tripoli and the opposition to the merger by other Chadian leaders, such as Kamougue, who called the merger "an impossible marriage."(23) Unfortunately, it may be years before we know whether or not the story was true: However the political significance of its release a day after Oueddei paid a surprise visit to Lagos was immediately apparent. On the Chadian side, the political meaning of the story was that Oueddei didn't like the merger and wanted political support from Nigeria against Qaddafi inside and outside GUNT. Certainly, Nigeria's willingness to air such a tale, which could only discredit Qaddafi and the merger plan, gave dramatic evidence of its support for Oueddei and its opposition to Libya's annexation of Chad.

In what may have been a coincidence, Libya announced the establishment of a full-scale nuclear energy program the day after the publication of the plan to merge with Chad. An atomic energy secretariat was to be created, together with a nuclear research center. The Soviet Union had already promised to build a 300-megawatt nuclear power plant for Libya, although construction had not yet begun, and in 1981 had also undertaken to build a 10-megawatt research reactor for Libya. The Soviets began construction of a reactor, which appeared to be of 40-megawatt capacity, in October-November 1981. It passed the safeguard inspection of the International Atomic Energy Agency in July. Libya had also signed the nuclear Non-Proliferation Treaty apparently at the insistence of the Soviets. Libya had been unable to obtain this kind of assistance from France, Canada, Sweden, or West Germany. Although it had sent technicians to Argentina to learn the techniques of extracting uranium from ore, Libya lacked its own uranium deposits. There had been persistent reports that there were large deposits of uranium in northern Chad, in areas geologically similar to those in nearby Niger, which held important reserves, although some experts doubted the importance of the Chadian deposits.(24)

Whether a coincidence or not, the reports of Libyan nuclear activities could only add to the mounting concern of other nations over the merger with Chad. Nigeria was not alone in its dislike of the merger. First, there was more evidence that Oueddei's curious omissions while in Tripoli indicated serious Chadian reservations about unity with Libya. As mentioned earlier the vice-president of GUNT, Lt. Colonel Wadal Abdel Kader Kamougue, a Christian and head of Chad's armed forces (FAT) called the merger "an impossible marriage" in an interview with Agence France Presse on January 8 in Ndjamena. Teh French news agency also reported all GUNT ministers had returned to Ndjamena except Foreign Minister Acyl Ahmat, who was believed to be in Tripoli: Ahmet's presence in Tripoli showed that Qaddafi intended to continue playing off the Chadian factions against each other. On January 11 Tripoli radio reported that Ahmat had "received" the French and Sudanese ambassadors and warned them not to support Habre. The official Chadian news agency (ATP) had published the Tripoli communique, but had added two important reservations. According to ATP: (1) Oueddei had made no formal commitment to Qaddafi on unity with Libya; and (2) the Tripoli accord was to be regarded as a "declaration of intention" to unite the two countries sometime in the future.(25) The rift between Oueddei and Ahmat would grow wider in the months ahead as Oueddei tried to reduce his dependence on Libya and worked with other African nations seeking the withdrawal of Libyan forces from Chad. Although Oueddei's approach made sense from the standpoint of Chadian nationalism it undoubtedly weakened the military capabilities of GUNT against Habre's FAN. Ultimately Oueddei and his African allies were able to force Qaddafi out, but only at the price of the destruction of GUNT. Habre's forces continued fighting throughout 1981 and early 1982 and, despite the presence of an African peacekeeping force in the country, captured Ndjamena in June 1982.

The leaders of GUNT made clear the political outline of their opposition to the Libyan intervention in a communique published on January 15 after a cabinet meeting convened to discuss Oueddei's visit to Libya. The proposed merger was "not enforceable," the Chadian leaders announced; presumably Ahmat did not agree. The merger agreement was a declaration of intent, nothing more. The cabinet thanked Libya for its help in ending the rebellion but emphasized its intention to cooperate with Libya only on the basis of "national sovereignty, mutual respect, and the interests of two brotherly peoples." GUNT reaffirmed its commitment to the Lagos agreements, particularly to those parts that prohibited the maintenance of foreign bases in Chad and provided for the establishment of a national army. All friendly countries were asked to assist in the creation of a national army. Chad would never serve as a "springboard for the destabilization of the countries in the region," they added, and invited the secretary-general of the OAU to take up once more the problems of peace and reconstruction in Chad. The cabinet called on all countries to refrain from supporting the rebellion or interfering in Chad's affairs. At the same time the leaders of GUNT stated their wish to have normal relations with all countries that had signed cooperation agreements with Chad, "particularly France."(26)

Other declarations of opposition followed. A week after the cabinet meeting the Chadian ambassador to Egypt, Homala Ouangmotching, declared that Qaddafi was trying to annex Chad by fait accompli. The Libyan intervention, he added, threatened Chad and its neighbors. The people of Chad must rise against "Libyan treachery," and they must be helped by friendly nations before it was too late.(27) Vice-President Kamougue was equally outspoken in an interview for Le Monde that was published on January 25. "What merger?" he asked his questioner. The unification of Libya and Chad is "impossible," he declared. "What sort of union can there be between Arabian Berbers and Negro Africans?" Libyan troops would be withdrawn, he said, and Chad would welcome military aid from France.(28)

The positions of the African states interested in Chad varied, but they can be grouped into three categories for the purposes of analysis: strong opposition to the Libyan intervention; support for a negotiated settlement that would end the war in Chad and bring about Libyan withdrawal; and solidarity with Libya (there were few if any outright endorsements of the intervention). Egypt and Sudan took the strongest measures against Libya in Chad. Immediately after the merger was announced the Egyptian government broke diplomatic relations with Chad and condemned the merger as part of a Libyan plot to control the "independent African state" next to Libya. Taking a position that was widely shared in Africa and beyond, Egypt declared that GUNT had no legitimate authority to agree to a merger because it was only a transitional government.(29) In an interview after Friday prayers at Al-Khazzan mosque in Aswan, President Sadat described the merger as "harmful to all Africa" and said it violated the Lagos accords. The Egyptian leader added that Goukouni Oueddei had overstepped his legitimate authority. The next day the Egyptian foreign minister, Kamal Hassan Ali, described the basis of Egyptian policy and a number of the steps Egypt had taken to oppose the Libyan-Chad merger. Urgent "African and world contacts" had been initiated, he said, about the merger. Egypt was alarmed because the enhancement of Libya's position in Chad menaced Uganda and the sources of the Nile. "Egypt would absolutely not permit such a thing to happen." The Soviet Union, with its immense presence in Libya, was the cause of Libya's expansionism and its attempt to "encircle" Egypt and Sudan. The Libyan intervention in Chad was part of "this Soviet plan."(30) Other Egyptian comments were less diplomatic. Al-Akhbar, for example, called Libya a base for the Soviet Union in Africa and a tool of the Soviet Union which, it alleged, had planned and carried out the invasion of Chad with Cuban, East German and other "Soviet-trained mercenaries" from Libyan camps.(31)

Sadat didn't confine his response to words. On January 17 the Sunday edition of the Egyptian magazine <u>October</u> reported that the Egyptian president had met Hissene Habre for two hours in Aswan.(32) In mid-March Foreign Minister Ali corroborated reports that Egypt was giving military assistance to Habre.(33) A week after his meeting with Habre at Aswan Sadat announced that Egypt would provide military aid to any African country that made a stand against Libya's occupation of Chad. Egypt was prepared, he added, to send troops to help defend Sudan against Libyan attack. Removing all doubts of Egypt's intentions, an Egyptian deputy foreign secretary, Samir Ahmed, taking Egypt's message to Dakar, Senegal, told AFP that Egypt would support "any Chadian nationalist front" that would safeguard Chad's independence. Moreover, Egypt was resolved to thwart any new Libyan aggression and would regard an attack on Sudan as an attack on Egypt. His government, Ahmed said, would back diplomatic action through the OAU to obtain Libyan compliance with the Lome accords and would provide logistical help for an African peacekeeping force in Chad.

Like Egypt, Sudan vehemently opposed the merger and an expanded Libyan role in Chad with both diplomatic and military means. In mid-January Sudanese President Nimeiry repeatedly asked OAU President Siaka Stevens to convene an urgent meeting of the organization in Khartoum to discuss the situation in Chad.(34) The public Sudanese position was that the Libyan presence in Chad would lead to "direct Soviet intervention in the whole region." Sudan closed its western border and began moving troops toward its frontier with Chad.(35) With Egypt giving military aid to Habre, Sudan's major contribution to FAN appears to have been to allow Habre's forces to use Sudanese territory as a sanctuary from which to launch attacks against Libyan and GUNT units around the town of Abeche in eastern Chad near the border.

In addition to these measures, Sudan conducted a sustained campaign of political warfare against Libya. In mid-January a leader of one of the factions within Frolinat, Hagrou Sanosi, was allowed to say in Khartoum that Oueddei had broken faith with the other Chadian groups which were party to the Lagos agreements and, therefore, should no longer be regarded as the president of Chad. On March 24 Sudan petitioned the Arab League to expel Libya from that organization because it had granted military bases to the Soviet Union.(36) On the last day of March Nimeiry called on Libya's neighbors to join together to "overthrow or kill" Qaddafi. Sudan also picked up the charges of Soviet participation in Libyan military operations in Chad, alleging that Soviet advisors had helped in the construction of a Libyan base at Qarat Bishi, a few score miles from the Sudanese border. French and American officials made similar accusations to newsmen in late February and early March. Both charged that Soviet technicians were helping to repair and service military equipment for Libyan forces in Chad. The French added that the Soviets were helping to supply Acyl Ahmat's troops in eastern Chad. The Americans claimed that "less than 50" Soviets and some East Germans were in Chad to perform maintenance services.(37) All concerned, Libyans, Soviets, and East Germans, denied the accusations. The provision of sanctuary for Habre's forces and the public attacks by Sudan provoked a Libyan response in kind. Tripoli radio publicized the activities of two groups hostile to the Nimeiry regime, the Sudanese Socialist People's Front, and the Organization of Officers and People's Armed Forces for the Salvation of the Homeland. The latter was said to have been established on June 18.(38)

However natural they might have been, Sudan took two more steps in response to the invasion and merger that could only have alienated and alarmed Libya even further. The first was to draw closer to Egypt. Nimeiry invited Sadat to visit Sudan. He came on May 24-25, and then Nimeiry returned the visit July 20-27. Nimeiry's reception of Sadat in Khartoum marked the first time since the signature of the Egypt-Israel peace treaty two years before that the Egyptian president had been able to visit another Arab state. During this period, as mentioned earlier, Egypt extended military protection to Sudan, and the two governments also began to coordinate their opposition to the Libyan presence in Chad. This played a part in the other Sudanese action certain to offend Qaddafi: the decision to turn to the United States for military and economic assistance. After Nimeiry's visit to Cairo in July the Egyptian and Sudanese leaders announced in a communique that they agreed that Sudan and Egypt should both provide military facilities to the United States. Earlier, the Sudanese government had reported that the Reagan administration had promised to provide Sudan $100 million in military assistance for 1981 and to make a major increase in economic aid as well.

France also reacted strongly against the merger and drew a number of West African states in its path. On January 8 the French Foreign Ministry condemned the merger on three grounds: as a violation of the Lagos agreements, as a derogation of the rights of the people of Chad, and as a threat to the security of Africa.(39) For a short while the economic and diplomatic strands of French policy crossed and embarrassed Giscard's government in Africa. Two days before the Foreign Ministry condemned the Libyan-Chad merger news of a major oil deal between Libya and Elf Aquitaine, an oil company controlled by the French government, was released in Tripoli. France was also honoring a lucrative contract signed in 1977, and worth over $500 million, to supply Libya with ten fast patrol boats. Embarrassed, French officials paused, backed up, and hurried to straighten out the mess. On January 14, Elf Aquitaine was told that the government had not yet approved the oil deal, and on February 28 delivery of the patrol boats was stopped. To relieve the fears of its eighteen African allies France strengthened its military forces in the Central African Republic, Ivory Coast, Senegal, and Gabon. News reports indicated that France had asked Cameroon and Niger (supplier of 20 percent of France's uranium) if they wished to receive French troops. Following a threat by Qaddafi to boycott France economically and use all its weapons against France, including the "revolutionary weapon" France put its Mediterranean fleet on alert and ordered the armed forces to be prepared to evacuate French nationals from Chad and Libya. According to news reports, French troops in the Central African Republic were prepared to go into southern Chad to evacuate French citizens, if that became necessary.(40) The French foreign minister, Jean Francois-Poncet, was then sent on a tour of West Africa. In the Ivory Coast at the start of the tour he held a conference for French ambassadors and told them that France would extend military protection to any African country that requested it out of a concern for their security.

The leaders of a number of West African states, formerly French colonies, joined France in opposition to the Libyan merger and intervention. The president of Gabon, Omar Bongo, called the merger an "attempt to annex Chad." The existing economic structure of central Africa would be disrupted by the merger, he added, which in any case violated the Lagos accords and exceeded the authority of Chad's transitional government.(41) In Senegal, the newspaper Le Soleil, which was close to the government of President Abdou Diouf, called for African opposition to the merger. Under a facade of legitimacy a dictatorship was being built in Chad. The paper also warned that the attempted merger with Chad was more evidence of Qaddafi's plan to create a united states of the Sahel (north central Africa) and must now be taken seriously. In an interview with French government radio on January 18 President Diouf made clear his opposition to Libyan policy and left no doubts that he depended greatly on French help, both in ending the Libyan intervention in Chad and in protecting Senegal against external pressure. All states linked to France must be assured, he said, that if they were threatened from the outside France would protect them.(42) The timing of the closure of the Libyan People's Bureau, consulate, and culture center in Niger on January 13 was clearly linked to the merger agreement, although the government of Niger spoke only of a Libyan failure to consult in advance of the conversion and of certain "undiplomatic dealings" by Libyan officials.(43) The foreign minister of Upper Volta "deplored and condemned" the merger of Libya and Chad as a denial of self-determination. Referring directly to Mali and Niger, the foreign minister added: "The threats of destabilization which are weighing down the countries that have common borders with the Libyan Arab Jamahiriyah – some of whom are our direct neighbors – concern us in many ways."(44)

By far the strongest African criticism came from the Central African Republic (CAR), where the Emperor Bokassa had recently been overthrown with French help and the new regime of President David Dacko held power so tenuously it too would fall within the year. On January 12, President Dacko told his countrymen that the danger posed by the Chad-Libya merger was "really great." French troops were in the CAR, he acknowledged, but they had been asked in to protect the country and to rebuild the national army, which Bokassa had destroyed. France had no "annexationist intention." As Dacko put it, Libya's intervention in Chad violated the Lagos accords. The December 1980 OAU meeting in Lagos ought to have told Libya and Chad "to respect the rules of the game." Now the merger had also violated the Lagos accords. The union of Chad and Libya had been decided without reference to the people of Chad and before the establishment of a permanent government for the country, contrary to the provisions of the Lagos accords. The economic consequences of the merger would be disastrous. It would not solve the problems created by the large number of refugees from Chad. The merger was actually "a show of force by Libya." If it were allowed to succeed Libya would have advanced far toward the realization of its plans of "creating a vast community subject to Islam," and this would create difficulties for all states which were not Muslim.(45)

While not as directly involved as France in opposing the Libyan intervention in Chad the United States took a strong stand against the merger. U.S. opposition was expressed in part through the decision of the Reagan administration to boost military aid to the countries in northern Africa opposed to Libya, Morocco, Tunisia, and Sudan.(46) The huge U.S. commitment to Egypt was to be continued. But opposition was also revealed in, for example, U.S. criticism of the decision at Nairobi to give the presidency of the OAU to Libya and by U.S. willingness to back French efforts to obtain Libyan withdrawal from Chad, most evident in Mitterand's demarche at the Cancun economic summit in October.

Nigeria and Sierra Leone played a leading part in the African effort to bring an end to the fighting and arrange Libyan withdrawal by means of negotiations. Sierra Leone's interest derived from the tenure of its president, Siaka Stevens, at the head of the OAU. President Stevens repeatedly sought a diplomatic resolution of the difficult problems between the parties, although success eluded him and his term ran out. Nigeria's concern was at once more ambitious and more direct. The direct concern arises because Chad and Nigeria share a common border in Lake Chad, a huge body of water in north-central Africa. The ambition resides in Nigerian aspirations to play the leading international role in black African affairs. Taken together the two explain the repeated Nigerian efforts to obtain a settlement in Chad and their continuation throughout 1981 and 1982. Signs of Nigerian leadership were apparent, for example, at the

Lome conference on Chad. Alarmed by the Libya-Chad merger and the growing African and Arab opposition to it, OAU President Stevens convened the OAU ad hoc committee on Chad in Lome, on January 12, 1981. Taking advantage of the existing plans of many African heads of state to attend ceremonies in Lome honoring President Eyadema on the fourteenth anniversary of his term in office, President Stevens also invited a number of other countries to send representatives, including Libya, Chad, Egypt, and Sudan. According to news reports out of Lagos, Nigeria a Chadian delegation did not attend because the Libyans would not allow it. Sudan declined, and gave the ticklish conditions along its frontiers with Libya and Chad as the reason. When the negotiations opened, the Libyan delegate, Foreign Minister Turayki, immediately objected to the presence of an Egyptian delegate and walked out. The Egyptian, Deputy Foreign Secretary Samir Ahmed, then withdrew in order, as he put it, to deny the Libyans a pretext to boycott a meeting which was going to condemn them.(47) After the departure of the Egyptian, Turayki returned, and some difficult negotiations began.

Continuing its leadership of the effort to find a negotiated settlement in Chad, Nigeria put forward a draft resolution that was adopted virtually word-for-word by twelve of the nations at the Lome conference.(48) In essence the signatories acted as if the Libyan intervention in Chad was meaningless. They handed Qaddafi a stunning diplomatic defeat. First the twelve reaffirmed the validity of the Lagos accords "as the basis for the establishment of real and lasting peace and security in a sovereign independent and stable Chad." This meant that all foreign troops would have to be withdrawn from Chad (Libyan troops were explicitly named), that an African peacekeeping force would be introduced into Chad, and that elections would be held. An overly optimistic date of April 1981 was set for the elections. Second, the Lome communique specifically declared the Libya-Chad merger to be contrary to the Lagos agreements and called on Libya and Chad to set it aside as "null and void." Only a freely elected government was qualified to conclude such a "fundamental and significant" accord.

Qaddafi brushed off the communique as "nothing but a piece of paper." Everyone at Lome knew that the declarations by themselves, however unequivocal, would never solve anything in Chad or bring about Libyan withdrawal. But it was unclear what course might lead to these outcomes. Nigerian President Shagari followed up the Lome conference with a proposal that Libya, Chad, and Nigeria negotiate a solution. The Nigerians' insistence on the withdrawal of Libyan troops defeated the approach in mid-February, but the Lagos government persisted. Before long the Nigerians suggested another approach: After France withdrew its troops from the Central African Republic, Libya would withdraw from Chad. Although Giscard's government rejected such an arrangement in February the government of Francois Mitterand, elected in May, would be much more receptive to the idea which would, after being modified, provide a rationale for Libyan withdrawal. At this time there were also talks at the UN about Chad and at a meeting of the OAU Council of Ministers in Addis Ababa, February 23-March 2. Sudan and Egypt sharply attacked Libya, which answered in kind.

On May 22 another effort was made to reach a settlement by the heads of state of Libya, Sierra Leone, Nigeria, and Chad. The meeting was held in Ndjamena and ended without agreement on Libyan withdrawal or the introduction of an African peacekeeping force. Nigerian officials let it be known that the conference had failed because Libya refused to withdraw. President Shagari had accepted an invitation to Ndjamena, they said, only because he had understood that Qaddafi had agreed to withdraw his troops from Chad. News reports in Tripoli maintained that Libya was not opposed to a withdrawal from Chad but that Quaddafi had concluded during the Ndjamena talks that a withdrawal would lead to a resumption of the fighting in Chad.(49)

The situation in Chad was raised at the OAU summit in Nairobi, June 24-26. Once again Sudan and Libya attacked each other bitterly. Sudanese President Nimeiry insisted on the terms of Lome: total Libyan withdrawal, the introduction of a peackeeping force, and free elections. Libyan expansionism, he said, threatened all of Africa, and especially Sudan, Niger, Cameroon, Nigeria, and the CAR. Turayki replied that Nimeiry was a tool of imperialists who was himself intervening in Chad and disregarding the Lagos agreements. The resolution on Chad adopted at Nairobi was bland and limited to the noncontroversial. The OAU supported GUNT, it said, favored economic assistance for Chad, and reaffirmed the need to send an African peacekeeping force to that country. There was no mention at all of Libyan troops in Chad or of the possible participation of military units from Benin, Congo, and Guinea in a peace force, which had been prescribed at Lagos in August 1979.(50) Judged by past OAU actions on controversial issues, the blandness of the resolution meant that new diplomatic overtures were underway, which Nigeria and other parties to the dispute wanted to push forward without the political backlash that might result from a highly critical OAU resolution.

Another part of the package solution for Chad became apparent when Nigeria's foreign minister, Ishaya Audu, supported the holding of the 1982 OAU summit in Tripoli, which would give Qaddafi the presidency of the organization for a year. Sudan, Egypt, Gabon, Ghana and other "moderates" opposed Qaddafi's bid for the presidency, which was nonetheless approved by acclamation at Nairobi. The third piece of the puzzle fell into place when Francois Mitterand took office in May. The new Socialist government in Paris promptly expressed its willingness to give aid to Chad and felt free to show an openness to negotiation with Libya that its predecessor – embarrased by the Libyan invasion – had regarded as inappropriate.

All of these developments were promising, but much diplomatic and military effort would be required before the problems caused by civil war in Chad and the Libyan invasion and merger attempt could be resolved.

Qaddafi had undoubtedly anticipated an international outcry as he planned the move into southern Chad and the merger. He may have been surprised at the ferocity of the opposition and the speed with which most black African states led by Nigeria would formulate and announce a demand for Libya's total withdrawal from Chad. He may also have overlooked the political leverage his bold steps would create for Sudan and Egypt, and for France and the United States as well. Libya's invasion of Chad and the merger attempt moved the political fulcrum significantly in favor of Qaddafi's opponents, especially Egypt and Sudan, and the advantage they gained in this way multiplied the effectiveness of their efforts to force Libya out of Chad. In addition, the fears stirred by Qaddafi's actions enabled the United States and France to justify taking other steps in areas only tangentially related to Chad but with considerable effect on Libya's freedom of action in northern, central, and eastern Africa. The dramatic increases in U.S. aid to Morocco and Sudan, for example, were principally directed toward securing the use of territory and facilities necessary to the projection of U.S. military power into the oil-rich Gulf. Arguably, the Sudan is important primarily because of its strategic value to Egypt, but this merely shifts the purpose of the Sudanese aid northward to the preservation of Egypt's alignment with the United States. U.S. policy remained firmly oriented toward the Gulf. Provided he could be forced out of Chad, Qaddafi had actually made the task of building military and diplomatic stability that much easier. In a similar way the invasion and merger fostered a context in central and western Africa very favorable to French policy, after the initial embarrassment passed. The regimes there were reminded of their military vulnerabilities, and many of them turned to France, which found itself able to move several thousand troops into Africa with general approval.

Whatever his calculations, Qaddafi's initial reaction to all this was defiance. He sent Turayki on a tour of "progressive" African countries with the assignment of coordinating opposition to the activities of the imperialists in Africa led by France. In Benin on January 12 Turayki declared: "Chad has forever left the circle of those who strangled the Chadian people's freedom. . . . "(51) Turayki also asked why the opponents of Libya's presence in Chad didn't criticize the imperialist military bases that existed in many places in Africa. Qaddafi posed the same question to an audience of students in Benghazi two days later. Libya would not be bound, he said, by any decision taken at Lome. It would be no more than "ink on paper." It could not affect Frolinat, which was an African liberation movement "just like" those of Algeria, Angola,

Mozambique, and Guinea-Bissau. Goukouni Oueddei was the legitimate leader of Chad. He alone could ask Libya to withdraw, and he alone would be obeyed. Libyan forces went into Chad in accord with an agreement with the government there, and at the call of President Goukouni Oueddei. The arrival of French forces in Africa had caused Libya to reinforce its troops in Chad. "Libyan forces will not leave Chad until French forces leave Central Africa," Qaddafi said. First, Libya would defeat the "imperialist and reactionary" effort to turn Chad into an "aggressive base." Why don't those people in Lome condemn the movement of French troops into the Central African Republic? Or the coup against Bokassa that was organized by France? Or the French troops in Cameroon, Gabon, and Senegal? Or Egyptian troops in Sudan? Tanzanian troops in Uganda?

Qaddafi then issued a series of threats. If Chad is important to the security of France and the United States, he asserted: "How could Libya not regard Chad's security as related to its own?" France must not expect good relations with Libya at the expense of Libyan security. If France interfered with Libyan security, Libya would respond with all its wepons: the oil weapon, the political and economic weapon, and the "revolutionary weapon"; Libya would boycott France economically and in all fields. Libya would fight against any intervention in Chad, Qaddafi vowed, because "we are the allies of the African peoples and revolutionary movements." Moreover, let the conferees at Lome be warned, Libya would seriously consider stopping all economic aid to any country that supported a decision against Libya and Chad.(52) The Libyan news agency (JANA) attacked France as a "harlot," and a junior partner of U.S. imperialism, using its "lackeys" in Central Africa to create a base from which to invade Chad.(53)

However, after his initial outburst of defiance and after he had time to weigh the mounting international opposition, particularly the extremely negative Lome declaration, Qaddafi began to soft-pedal the merger. The first sign of this may have been a statement by Turayki on January 16 that elections would be held in Chad within a year.(54) This was an ambiguous statement, however, because elections held while Libyan troops were still occupying Chad could hardly be expected to reveal the true sentiments of the Chadians. Three days later during a radio interview in Upper Volta, Turayki removed all doubts about a change in Libyan policy. "In all communiques issued at the end of visits by heads of state," he told his interviewer, "one always talks about unity between two peoples. That was what he did." Libya and Chad have not merged. Libya is simply being attacked because of its anti-imperialist policy. There will be elections in Chad and a permanent government will be formed. If the Chadian people then want to merge with Libya, it will be possible. But the interviewer was persistent. At what stage are the merger talks? Back came Turayki's answer: "I have already told you that there is no merger. There is not even a plan. We did not hold such a discussion. There is no plan to merge Libya and Chad."(55)

Qaddafi was less frank in an address to the final session of the Arab People's Congress in Tripoli on January 20, but his remarks also seemed to signal that he had decided to downplay the importance of the merger with Chad. At this point it was unclear whether this meant the merger had been abandoned or the Libyan government merely wanted to reduce international opposition temporarily. Even so, Qaddafi's speech and the statements by other Libyan officials suggested a backing away from the merger. "The main and most pressing issue," Qaddafi told the delegates, "is to achieve Arab unity from the Atlantic to the Gulf, or at least unity between several Arab countries such as Algeria, Libya, Egypt, and Sudan, then work can be done to achieve unity with Chad." Although they seem to be clear enough, such statements are difficult to interpret, and can not be taken at face value. Elsewhere in the speech, for example, Qaddafi spoke of the people of Chad as if they were Arab. A large proportion of Chadians are Arab, he assured the audience, "by origin and race." Most are Muslim, he added, and the "prevailing" culture is Arab. In Qaddafi's eyes the people of Chad were very different from all other black African peoples and resembled the people of the Sudan. For these reasons, Qaddafi said, the "complete mass unity" sought between Libya and Chad was unlike the "familiar constitutional political unity" attempted by other nations.(56)

Qaddafi's statements were unclear, probably intentionally so. He appeared to be backing away from the merger with Chad. But when one looks closely at his statements they do not actually say that. On the one hand, he said that unity with Chad should follow unity with countries such as Egypt and Sudan. On the other hand, by virtually making Chad an Arab nation, he did not exclude it from an Arab union stretching from the Atlantic to the Gulf. Moreover, unlike Turayki, Qaddafi did not deny that a merger had taken place but sought instead to suggest that it was not the familiar kind of political unity. In short Qaddafi was dealing with appearances. He was hinting at a retreat over Chad but had in fact left himself completely free to do as he wished. Spreading the word, Qaddafi's nephew, Lt. Colonel Ahmad Al-Qaddafi, told French journalists that Libya had no intention of taking Chad. "Libya is rich," Ahmad said disingenuously. "Why would it wish to annex Chad? This is ridiculous." Libya advocates liberation and rapprochement between Muslims, he added. "What is wrong with that?"(57) Meanwhile, in Chad, the factions in GUNT continued to disagree with one another and to lose ground to Hissene Habre's forces in a series of small fights around Adre, Iriba, and Guerada in the east near the border with Sudan during the months of the summer and early fall.

11
QADDAFI RUNS OUT OF ROOM

For four years after the congressional veto of U.S. covert intervention in Angola, the United States avoided any dramatic displays of its military power in Africa or the Middle East. The last years of the Ford administration passed in stalemate and step-by-step diplomacy and the Carter administration initially sought to treat Middle Eastern and African issues as local conflicts rather than to emphasize their strategic implications for Soviet-U.S. relations. However, the scope of Soviet interventions in Angola and Ethiopia and the fall of the Shah of Iran made it impossible for the U.S. to stick to this noninterventionist approach. These developments inevitably worsened U.S. relations with Libya, particularly after Qaddafi's decision to invade and annex Chad.

In February and March 1979 the United States made a strong demonstration of military support on behalf of North Yemen, which was threatened with invasion from South Yemen. The U.S. initiatives included speeded up and increased arms deliveries, the dispatch of the aircraft carrier Constellation, and the authorization of Saudi use of U.S. equipment to defend North Yemen, if necessary. The North Yemenis also took Soviet arms, for a time, until dissuaded by Saudi Arabia from continuing. On October 25 in Moscow, Presidents Brezhnev and Ismail of South Yemen signed a twenty-year treaty of friendship and cooperation, in essence a military and political alliance, as well as economic aid agreements: South Yemen and Ethiopia signed a similar military and political agreement of 15 years' duration on December 2.(1) These actions and the various other steps taken by the United States to strengthen its military capabilities in the Gulf and Indian Ocean were soon of importance in Libyan-U.S. relations, for Qaddafi would enter into security agreements with South Yemen and Ethiopia. These two states, together with Syria and Algeria, were virtually the only nations in the Middle East and North and Central Africa with whom Qaddafi could establish normal relations, let alone close cooperation. The overlap with Soviet policy is again clear.

Starting in early November 1979, after the seizure of U.S. hostages in Teheran, the United States began a major increase of its military strength in the Indian Ocean. The occupation of the Grand Mosque in Mecca, Saudi Arabia on November 20 and the Soviet invasion of Afghanistan on December 25-26 heightened the desire of the Carter administration to augment U.S. capabilities near the Gulf and triggered a number of concrete and far-reaching military and political actions by the United States. The United States and Britain held joint naval maneuvers in the area in November. In January 1980 the nuclear aircraft carrier Nimitz was sent to the Indian Ocean to join the carriers Midway and Kitty Hawk, which were already on station there with British and Australian vessels. A team of U.S. defense and diplomatic specialists visited Gulf states in December 1979. In early January the United States announced that it would maintain a naval force in the Indian Ocean indefinitely and would seek the use of military facilities in Oman, Kenya, and Somalia. As part of this plan the United States informed Britain of a decision to strengthen the base on Diego Garcia. The build-up of a rapid deployment force of 100,000 men had been announced by the United States in June 1979. The force had been described as of primary importance for the Middle East, but had obvious utility elsewhere in the Third World.(2) Impetus for its creation was added by the popular and congressional outcry over the series of adverse developments in the Gulf and Southwest Asia.

The United States also made vigorous if not immediately successful efforts to strengthen Pakistan by coordinating policy with China and Japan during visits to those two countries by Secretary of Defense Harold Brown in January, and by offering to renew military aid to Pakistan at the level of hundreds of millions of dollars. Pakistan, which had hoped for billions, initially rejected the U.S. overtures, although a mutually satisfactory arrangement was later worked out for aid at much higher levels than the original U.S. offer. President Carter struck an even more determined note in his State of the Union message to Congress on January 23, 1980. Citing the embargo of U.S. grain shipments, the withdrawal of the SALT II treaty, and other economic and political sanctions against the Soviet Union, the president called for a collective effort to deal with the new Soviet threat to security in the Persian Gulf and Southwest Asia. He supplied a new doctrine in the speech, the Carter Doctrine: "An attempt by any outside force to gain control of the Persian Gulf region will be regarded as an assault on the vital interests of the United States. It will be repelled by use of any means necessary, including military force." Carter also confirmed a U.S. commitment to defend Pakistan's independence and integrity and promised more military and economic aid to that country.(3)

The build-up of U.S. forces in the region continued into the spring and, in retrospect, was obviously connected with secret planning to rescue the American hostages in Iran. In March 1980 Secretary of Defense Harold Brown said that airborne warning and control (AWACS) missions and B-52 sea reconnaissance flights had been carried out in the Indian Ocean. News reports indicated that these flights were launched from Egypt and Saudi Arabia. In mid-March a naval task force carrying 1,800 Marines and heavy combat equipment, such as tanks and helicopters, was deployed in the Indian Ocean.(4)

In testimony before the House Foreign Affairs Committee in early April, Undersecretary of Defense Robert Komer described the build-up. U.S. forces in the Gulf and Indian Ocean had been strengthened, he said. Two carrier task forces had been assembled in several weeks in the Arabian Sea. The United States could send air units to the Middle East even more quickly than this, Komer reported. Although the deployment of land forces was much more difficult, the United States could transfer a light brigade in a week, and a light division and various Marine amphibious units in about two weeks. However, these plans would succeed only if the United States were able to use staging and port facilities around the Gulf and Indian Ocean. The administration proposed to deal with this by a "network concept" of acquiring permission from a number of countries to use their facilities, thus assuring access even if several countries revoked their consent. Centered around an expanded base at Diego Garcia, this "regional network" comprised the use in Oman of air bases at Seeb, Thumrait, and Masirah, and the ports of Mutrah and Salalah (Mina Qaboos and Mina Raysut respectively); increased use in Kenya of air and naval facilities in Mombasa, Embakasi, and Nanyuki; and use in Somalia of airfields and ports at Berbera and Mogadishu.

On June 4, 1980, in an exchange of diplomatic notes the United States and Oman agreed to cooperate in security, trade, and economic matters. The agreement was plainly meant to extend explicit U.S. protection to Oman and the crucial Straits of Hormuz through which most Gulf oil moved to Europe, Japan, and the rest of the world.(5) A few days earlier the British government announced its agreement to the stationing at Diego Garcia of six or seven cargo ships loaded with U.S. military equipment for use in case U.S. troops were sent to the region on short notice. On June 26 Kenya and the United States reached agreement to expand their cooperation in mutual security assistance and increase U.S. economic aid for Kenyan development. A longer negotiation with Somalia was concluded on August 21 with an agreement allowing the United States to use air and naval facilities at Berbera and Mogadishu. In return the United States offered Somalia $40 million in military sales credits over two years and $5 million in budgetary support.(6) While Libya was only indirectly involved in these developments because of its alliances with Yemen and Ethiopia, it participated in a number of other conflicts that touched U.S. interests in Asia as well as Africa. The effect of the U.S. build-up in the Gulf was to engage the United States much more intimately in regional conflicts and to make much more likely a collision with Libya in Africa.

There was no end to the Muslim rebellion in the Philippines in 1979. The Philippine government pressed on with its plans to establish regional governments, but the main Muslim factions refused to cooperate with the Marcos regime. The elections of 1979 were boycotted by the Moro National Liberation Front, whose different factions were supported by Libya and Saudi Arabia. The Muslim Democratic Party put forward only six candidates for 42 seats, 21 in each of two regional assemblies of which 10 were reserved for Muslims in each house. In September 1979, the Libyan ambassador in Manila, Moustafa Dreiza, said that his government supported peace talks between the MNLF and the Philippine government, but that other factions of MNLF supported by Egypt and Saudi Arabia could not agree on who was to represent the Muslim side.(7) In the absence of negotiations the fighting continued in the southern provinces and the number of refugees fleeing to Sabah, Malaysia increased to at least 90,000.

The conflict over the Western Sahara also went unresolved in 1980, although Polisario continued to make diplomatic gains. On November 21 the United Nations General Assembly passed a resolution recognizing Polisario as "the representative of the people of Western Sahara." The resolution also deplored Morocco's occupation of the Western Sahara. It passed 85-6 and was opposed by Central African Republic, Equatorial Guinea, Gabon, Guatemala, Morocco, and Saudi Arabia. There were 41 abstentions including the United States, most of the nations of Western Europe, Cameroon, Egypt, and Tunisia.(8)

The Saharan Arab Democratic Republic (SADR) had been recognized by some forty countries by mid-1980, including Cuba and Iran. The Steadfastness and Resistance Front of Algeria, Libya, the PLO, Syria, and South Yemen gave its recognition on April 15. At a summit conference of Saharan states in early March — boycotted by Tunisia and Morocco — Algeria, Chad, Libya, Mali, Mauritania, and Niger agreed on their support of the right of the Sahrawi people to self-determination.(9) However, despite winning the support of a majority (26 states) of the OAU, Polisario was not granted membership in the African organization. The issue was hotly debated at the annual OAU summit conference held in Freetown, Sierra Leone, July 1-4. Samora Machel, president of Mozambique, and Robert Mugabe, prime minister of Zimbabwe, led the attack, accusing Morocco of committing aggression, colonialism, and genocide in the Western

Sahara. Morocco's prime minister, Maati Bouabid, replied that the Western Sahara was Moroccan territory, and that no state could legitimately intervene in the internal affairs of another. The supporters of Polisario sought the admission of SADR as a member of the OAU. President Senghor of Senegal proposed that a decision on membership be deferred and a new effort be made to reach a negotiated settlement under the leadership of President Stevens of Sierra Leone. Senghor proposed to bring all the parties together: Mauritania, Polisario, Morocco, the Saharan organizations supporting Morocco, and Algeria. If agreement were reached on a cease-fire and referendum a special OAU summit could be convened to consider SADR's membership in the OAU. Knowing that a majority of the OAU supported Polisario's admission, its supporters pressed for a decision by majority vote. Morocco countered that since Polisario was clearly not a sovereign state, a two-thirds majority was necessary. When Morocco and seven other states — Egypt, Gabon, Gambia, Ivory Coast, Senegal, Somalia, Sudan, Tunisia — threatened to quit the OAU if Polisario were admitted, the conference reached agreement on a compromise: a decision on SADR's membership was postponed, and the "committee of wise men" which had been established in 1978 to help solve the Saharan conflict was instructed to hold a meeting of all the parties in Freetown within three months. The "wise men" were not neutral: in December 1979, at a conference attended by Polisario and Algeria, but not Morocco, they had already called on Morocco to accept a cease-fire and to permit a referendum in the Western Sahara.

Given this diplomatic stalemate, it is not surprising that the fighting between Morocco and Polisario intensified throughout 1980. Strengthened by aid from Algeria, Polisario carried the war deeper and deeper into southern Morocco. In response, Morocco pursued Polisario's forces across the borders of Algeria and Mauritania and appealed for U.S. help. The Carter administration was keenly aware of Morocco's critical geographic position as a staging area for the projection of U.S. power into the Middle East and North Africa. Intent on strengthening its military capabilities in these regions, it responded promptly. On October 20, 1979, President Carter announced that the United States would sell helicopters and aircraft worth $235 million to Morocco. The sale, to be paid for by Saudi Arabia, represented a departure from a twenty-year-old secret agreement with Morocco under which the United States supplied arms intended only for use inside Morocco. The aircraft were especially well suited for antiguerrilla warfare and included six OV-10 Bronco armed reconnaissance planes, 24 Cobra helicopter gunships, and 20 F5-E fighters, to be armed with Maverick air-to-surface missiles. The intention of the sale, the president said, was to strengthen Morocco's negotiating position. In early 1980 Congress approved the sale, but attached a binding condition which prohibited delivery of the aircraft until there was progress on the initiation of negotiations between Morocco and Polisario. By the end of 1980 no aircraft had been delivered to Morocco.(10)

Libya's increasingly aggressive and militant international actions in 1980 produced an astonishing series of foreign policy setbacks for the North African country. No less than thirteen nations in Africa and the Middle East as well as the United States either broke diplomatic relations with Libya or expelled Libyan diplomatic personnel. In addition there were tensions or a serious deterioration of relations between Libyan and eight other governments, from Uganda to France. During the months from July 1980-January 1981 Libyan diplomats were expelled from four West African countries: Gabon in July, Ghana in November, and Niger and Nigeria in January. Much more serious were the tensions between Libya and Gambia, Senegal, the Central African Republic, Iraq, and Saudi Arabia. On July 1 Senegal broke diplomatic relations with Libya. President Senghor accused Libya of training Senegalese in military camps in Libya to fight for the exiled Senegalese Islamic leader, Ahmet Khalifa Niasse, who had gone to Libya in February 1980. According to the Senegalese president, the pattern was for Libyan diplomats or other agents to offer young Senegalese civilian employment in Libya. Once they reached Libya they were taken instead to military camps. On July 14 Senghor accused Qaddafi of training a mercenary army and trying to overthrow Chad, Mali, Niger, and Senegal in order to be able to dominate the region.

Then Gambia, a crooked little finger of a country surrounded by Senegal on three sides, had a similar grievance. Because Gambia is so small, Libya's false recruitment of Gambians and their subjection to military training was an even more serious problem for it than for Senegal. On October 29 Gambia severed relations with Libya and permitted several hundred Senegalese troops to enter the capital, Banjul. The Senegalese withdrew after a week. On October 31 Gambia accused Libya of recruiting Gambians for civilian work and then forcing them into military camps. Forty Gambians had been recruited in this way and had refused military training, the government said. Then 200 more Gambians had been taken in the same fraudulent manner. In September 1980 the Libyan embassy in Banjul had been involved in the recruitment of 14 more. Gambian officials also charged that Libya was using its "money and power" to subvert Gambia. Senegalese officials told Le Monde of a Libyan plot to overthrow Gambia, which had been forestalled by Senegal's intervention.

On September 10, 1980, in response to an invitation by Qaddafi issued during a speech celebrating the September 1 revolution, Syrian President Hafez Assad and the Libyan leader signed an agreement in Tripoli to merge Libya and Syria into one country. The name of the new country was to be the "Arab Masses State." The Tripoli agreement provided for a unitary state with one "revolutionary command," a "general national congress," and a "single executive power." The union was to be open to all Arab states, and was to form a base for the "Arab revolutionary movement" and "for confronting the Zionist presence in the Arab homeland and for liberating Palestine." Qaddafi and Assad pledged that the new state would promote Arab opposition to the Camp David agreements. A few days later a news report indicated that as part of the merger Libya would pay Syria's $1 billion debt to the Soviet Union for arms purchased in October 1979.(11)

The Libyan-Syrian merger agreement was signed only eleven days before the outbreak of full-scale war between Iran and Iraq. Both Assad and Qaddafi promptly sided with Iran. On October 10 Qaddafi informed the leaders of Saudi Arabia and the Arab states on the Gulf that it was their "Islamic duty" to side with Iran. Moreover, he warned, if Saudi Arabia didn't expel the American AWACS (four more were sent in early October and two jet tankers for airborne refuelling) then Libya would attack the "U.S. military presence." In letters to President Carter and Republican presidential nominee Ronald Reagan, Qaddafi demanded the withdrawal of the United States from Oman and Somalia. Otherwise, he said, there would be a military confrontation, even war. Far from withdrawing, the United States, alarmed by the Iraq-Iran war, had taken additional steps to strengthen U.S. military capabilities in the Gulf. In addition to the four more AWACS the United States transferred three ships from the Sixth Fleet to the Gulf, including the helicopter carrier Saipan with 8,000 Marines, 30 helicopters, and 50 landing craft. Before their arrival there were already 60 Australian, British, French, and United States warships in the Indian Ocean to guard the Straits of Hormuz and friendly states. Thiry of the ships were American and included the carriers Midway and Eisenhower. The Soviet Union had 29 of its warships in the area, as well.

Syria, meanwhile, poured out anti-Iraqi propaganda – at one point describing Saddam Hussein as "a crazy fascist" and an "imperialist agent" making war at the request of the United States. Syria also sent antitank missiles and SAM-7 aircraft missiles to Iran, allowing Iranian transports to land in Damascus. In response Iraq withdrew its diplomatic staffs from Syria and Libya on October 10. Two weeks later Saudi Arabia, which along with Jordan had strongly taken Iraq's side in the war, broke diplomatic relations with Libya. Morocco had broken relations with Libya the previous April after Libya recognized SADR.

In addition to these severances of relations and expulsions, Libya suffered severe strains in its relations with a number of other states. These included the United States, Egypt, France, Italy, Malta, Morocco, Uganda, and Upper Volta. Against this steady loss of friends and influence, Libya could set only its merger in principle with Syria and the alliance with South Yemen and Ethiopia. In May 1980, as mentioned earlier, the United States had expelled all but one of the diplomats in the Libyan people's bureau in Washington because of the campaign of intimidation being waged against Libyan nationals in the United States. In retaliation Libya expelled twenty-five Americans on May 12 and arrested two oil company employees on charges of spying. They were subsequently released. On June 17, 1980, Egypt ended martial law in the Sinai but maintained military control of the area near the border with Libya because of poor relations between the two countries. Before the Carter administration expired there were a series of military clashes between Libyan and U.S. aircraft over the Mediterranean, which contributed to a further worsening of Libyan-U.S. relations. On September 1 the Washington Post reported that two Libyan fighters appeared to have tried to shoot down a U.S. Air Force EC-135 electronic espionage plane as it flew close to Libyan airspace. The administration had not protested the attack because the evidence was somewhat ambiguous. Neither of the pilots of the EC-135 had seen the Libyan fighters or the missiles they fired. But the electronic gear on the plane had caught a conversation between the two Libyan pilots and their ground control in which they were ordered to fire. They each fired one missile and missed their U.S. target.(12)

A second clash occurred less than a week later. On September 21, another EC-135 flew some 200 miles off the Libyan coast in what U.S. officials asserted was international airspace. It was accompanied by three Navy F-14s from the carrier John F. Kennedy. However only one of the U.S. fighters was close to the military 707; the other two were far enough away to ambush any Libyan attackers. Seeing what they believed to be a transport accompanied by only one fighter, the Libyans sent eight fighters up – four Mirages and four MIGs – perhaps to attempt to shoot down the U.S. planes or to force one or both of them to land in Libya. As they approached, the Libyan pilots realized there were three U.S. fighters instead of one. When they reported this to their ground control, they were ordered to return to base without attacking, according to U.S. reports of their intercepted messages. The Arabic used in these exchanges indicated that the pilots and their controllers were from Syria.(13)

On October 22 the Libyan people's bureau published a full-page advertisement in the Washington Post which reproduced the text of Qaddafi's message of October 16 to presidential candidates Carter and Reagan. In his message Qaddafi issued a number of warnings. There would be war with the Arabs unless the United States ended its military presence in Egypt, Oman, and Somalia, withdrew its AWACs from Saudi Arabia, and stopped sending its reconnaissance planes to spy across Libyan borders. There was much more, of course, all based on the assumption that U.S. actions alone were the cause of the difficulties and the possibility of war, from the manipulation of Arab lands as pawns in the U.S. struggle with the Soviet Union to U.S. support for Israel. But in light of the ongoing air skirmishes over the Mediterranean and the serious clash to come during the Reagan administration's first year in office, Qaddafi's comments about U.S. spying deserve special attention.(14) Under Qaddafi, Libya has claimed what in international law is known as "point-to-point" sovereignty over the Gulf of Sidra, a large body of water formed by a deep southern scoop in the Libyan coastline separating Tripoli and Benghazi. Although this principle is a legitimate basis in international law for a claim of sovereignty, other powers must accept and honor the claim for it to be valid. Recognition of the claim may be won through an international convention, bilateral treaties, and through the practice of nations. The United States refuses to acknowledge that the Gulf of Sidra lies wholly within Libya's territorial waters and regularly sails its warships and sends its warplanes into the Gulf to give effect to its view of the Gulf as an international waterway. No doubt Libya makes the claim for several reasons. With sovereignty goes control of all natural resources in the Gulf, such as oil and fishing. In addition, if it were won, the Libyan claim would, in peacetime, force the vessels and aircraft of the United States and any other nation away from virtually the entire length of the Libyan coast; they could legally approach only with the consent of the Libyan government. The buffer zone thus created would add considerably to Libyan security.

The skirmishes between Libyan and U.S. aircraft in September 1980 were not the first of these kinds of encounters to take place between the two countries. In 1972 the United States had begun flying reconnaissance missions off the Libyan coast because of the huge amounts of Soviet military equipment that had begun pouring into the North African country. In March 1973 two Libyan Mirage fighters had fired at a U.S. Hercules C-130, which escaped undamaged. For the next six years Libya occasionally sent fighters to inspect the reconnaissance flights, but they stayed a good distance away. In September 1980 there was an interception at close range and one apparent attack. One possible reason for the heightening of tension in the summer and fall of 1980 was to further embarrass President Carter, architect of Camp David, so detested by Qaddafi, particularly if a U.S. plane could have been shot down or captured. U.S. officials told reporters that there were several additional explanations. The Libyan air force had improved: 150 of its 200 pilots had now qualified as jet pilots. Also, it seemed likely that the more frequent intercepts were used to provide realistic training exercises. More and more missions were being flown by experienced Syrian and North Korean pilots.(15)

By the fall of 1979, the sources of tension between the United States and Libya were numerous. They included Libya's attempt to assassinate the U.S. ambassador in Cairo, Herman Eilts;(16) Libya's violent opposition to Camp David; the air skirmishes; the campaign of intimidation and assassination against Libyan nationals living in the United States; Libyan intervention in central and west Africa;

and the Billy Carter affair and Libyan efforts to influence U.S. officials. These disagreements had led to a complete diplomatic rupture in everything but name, with the U.S. embassy in Tripoli closed and a single Libyan diplomat in the people's bureau in Washington.

The events in Iran, Pakistan, and Saudi Arabia were sufficiently alarming to persuade the Carter administration to advise Americans not to travel in Muslim countries unless it couldn't be avoided. On November 27 the State Department told reporters that it was conducting a voluntary evacuation in eleven Muslim countries to reduce the size of embassy staffs and numbers of dependents there. Its spokesman also urged against travel to Bangladesh, United Arab Emirates, Bahrain, Kuwait, Qatar, Oman, Yemen, Iraq, Libya, Syria, and Lebanon.

The travel warning and quiet evacuation were timely moves. On the morning of December 2 a crowd of Libyans began a demonstration in front of the U.S. embassy in Tripoli. Many of the demonstrators shouted pro-Khomeini slogans. The crowd grew to about 2,000. One policeman stood guard in front of the embassy. There were no other efforts by the Libyan government to control the crowd or protect the embassy. In months past right down to the very week of the attack, the State Department had repeatedly asked Libya to provide additional protection for the embassy, and had been rebuffed. Libya had even prohibited the small contingent of lightly armed U.S. Marines from being stationed at the mission, as is standard U.S. practice around the world. At about 10:15 the Libyan mob charged the embassy. The dozen Americans inside, two wives of embassy personnel, and seven other employees escaped through a side exit. A dozen of the 26 dependents of embassy personnel had already been evacuated, following the November 27 evacuation order. The U.S. charge d'affaires, William Eagleton – there had been no ambassador since Joseph Palmer's recall in 1972 – made a strong protest in Tripoli, and a similar protest was made to the head of the Libyan people's bureau in Washington.

Libyan Foreign Minister Turayki responded with an expression of regret for the attack on the building. The State Department rejected the gesture as inadequate, holding that the Libyan government was obliged to admit responsibility for the damage because it had refused to give adequate protection to the embassy despite repeated requests for it. Moreover Libya must offer compensation for the loss. The department spokesman, Hodding Carter, added that U.S. relations with Libya were under review, and he would not rule out a severance of ties. A further cutback in the staff of the embassy was likely, officials told reporters, unless Libya accepted responsibility for the attack and paid for the damage. Ironically, the assault had occurred at a time when, according to Libyan officials at the UN, a Libyan delegation had gone to Teheran to ask for the release of the American hostages. Indirect confirmation came in an interview given by Qaddafi to the Italian journalist, Oriana Fallaci, on December 2, 1979. He had advised Khomeini to release the Americans, he told Fallaci.(17)

When Libya continued to refuse to accept responsibility and pay damages, the Carter administration suspended the operation of the mission in Tripoli. Ten people would remain at the embassy but during the suspension they would be allowed to conduct only limited consular duties and no diplomatic work of any kind. On December 5 Undersecretary Newsom advised the Libyan charge Ali el-Houderi of the unacceptability of his government's position, advised him of the suspension, and demanded, in addition, "firm assurances about the future safety of our embassy and its personnel."(18) A few days later the Libyan government agreed to pay for the damages.

The attacks on U.S. diplomatic posts in three Muslim countries within a month, and the siege of the Grand Mosque in Saudi Arabia during the same period understandably invited second thoughts in the Carter administration. Was an inevitable conflict emerging between a "resurgent Islam" and the United States? When interviewed by reporters the administration experts insisted that they could detect no consistent anti-U.S. theme, and that the evident Islamic revival did not imply an anti-U.S. "Muslim world."(19) Qaddafi would not have agreed. In his mind Libya and he have a special, prophetic role to play in hastening the downfall of the United States and transforming the world. He believes that the era of world revolution has arrived and that this means the end for the United States.

Qaddafi finished 1979 in a flurry of words, in hours of interviews with at least two Western journalists, once just before the attack on the embassy in Tripoli and once shortly after. The interviews are revealing. They expose some of Qaddafi's basic conceptions of politics and world affairs. They show him – his own words show him – to be intelligent, even brilliant, ruthless, and calculating. There is rashness, but it is a rashness of concept not of practice, a rashness in strategy not in tactics. In fact, Qaddafi's daring words, like his cautious actions over the past decade, recall one of Mao's dicta on guerrilla war: Despise the enemy strategically but respect him tactically.

It is clear from the interviews that Qaddafi's conflicts with the West, and with the United States and Israel in particular, are fundamental and bitter, and that he is prepared to oppose the West with every promising weapon; nothing foolhardy is implied for a moment. In these fundamental conflicts of concept and strategy lies the source of the disputes between Libya and the United States. In 1979 Qaddafi's determination to act on his beliefs was matched by the Carter administration's commitment to achieve its goals, epitomized by Camp David, and the Egypt-Israel treaty. In these profound differences, and all they symbolized for the Palestinians, and Western influence in the Middle East lay the reasons for the cancellation of the aircraft sales, for the Libyan bribery plot, for the Libyan interventions in Chad and Uganda, for the Libyan support of terrorism, for U.S. opposition to Libyan intervention and terrorism, and for U.S. support of Libya's neighbors, especially Morocco, Sudan, Egypt, and Tunisia. It was this fundamental conflict that doomed Libya's quest for outside assistance from the United States in 1979.

On November 23 Qaddafi spent part of two days talking with the Italian journalist, Oriana Fallaci. The "news" in the interview, published by the New York Times Magazine two weeks later, was that Qaddafi was seeking the release of the American hostages held in Teheran. "I am trying to persuade the Iranians to release the hostages," he told Fallaci. An Iranian delegation had just arrived in Tripoli and included men close to Khomeini. "I will give them a personal message for the Imam, asking him to free the hostages," he added.(20) Qaddafi denied that the recent attacks on Americans in Muslim countries had been planned in advance. This was simply "international revolution against America," he said. They happened because "everybody hates America, everybody." Showing keen political insight, Qaddafi then very effectively criticized the U.S. reaction to the taking of the hostages. "If I were in the place of the Americans," he told the Italian woman who was making little effort to conceal her dislike of the Libyan leader, "I would not react as they are. I would take into account the revolutionary circumstances under which the incident took place and is taking place. And I would remember what American policy in Iran was like before the whole thing began."(21) It was sound advice, and was based on the quintessential political attribute, the ability to put oneself in another's place, in this case both that of the Iranian revolutionaries and U.S. policymakers. Revolutions are chaotic, Qaddafi added. Iran doesn't even appear to have a government. Even so, what had happened in Iran — kicking out the shah and kicking out the United States — made Qaddafi happy and, in his eyes, strengthened his "revolutionary role."

The remainder of the interview as published by the Times fell into two parts. The first was political. Fallaci confronted Qaddafi with the apparent inconsistencies and inhumanities of his foreign policy. The Libyan leader claimed to be profoundly bored by it all. The second part, which Qaddafi urged on his interrogator, and which he clearly relished, concerned his Green Book and his basic conceptions of politics, domestic and foreign. Beginning with political controversy, Fallaci challenged Qaddafi: If Libya is non-aligned, she asked, why does it always take the Soviet side internationally? Why did Qaddafi say that the Soviet Union was a country without ulterior motives? This was easy stuff for Qaddafi. I judge things by my own experience, and that's my own experience of the Soviets, he said. Besides, they are on the Arab side against Israel. Are you saying the United States is the only imperialist power in the world? Qaddafi answered by feigning ignorance: I just know that there are two superpowers in the world. They are competing. One of them, the Soviet Union, is Libya's friend. What about the 2,500 Soviet tanks in Libya? Simple, Qaddafi answered. They are here because of Egypt's aggressiveness toward Libya. So far, Fallaci had not laid a glove on Qaddafi, who obviously could field questions such as this forever without breathing hard. However, she managed to goad him into anger and a remarkable frankness by opening the questions of Qaddafi's unpopularity in the world, his support for terrorism, and his African interventions.

Do you know you are nearly universally hated, she asked? Only by those who are "opposed to the masses," and are "against freedom," he answered. If that is so, she persisted, why did you support Idi Amin? You take the side of the oppressed only when it suits you and intervene too much in other nations, such as Chad. Libya is in Chad by right, Qaddafi replied, in order to help the people of Chad drive out the French. We had the same right to intervene in Uganda because Nyerere had invaded that country. But you were in Uganda before Nyerere invaded, Fallaci insisted. Why? Qaddafi exploded: "Because Amin was and is against Israel." He was the first African ruler to kick the Jews out. They had taken over high administrative and military posts in Uganda in order "to seek an alliance with African nations in opposition to Arab nations." Then, in a breathtaking display of political amorality, reminiscent of European diplomacy of the sixteenth and seventeenth centuries, and, one could add, of contemporary Israeli diplomacy, Qaddafi told the basis of his Ugandan policy:

> Amin's internal policies do not interest me; what I am interested in is Amin's position in the field of international relations. . . . That is, the private personality of Bokassa and Amin might not be to my liking. I might even disagree with their internal policies; but I dislike even more the interference of France and Tanzania, and worst of all I dislike the support provided by the Westerners to Israel.(22)

Israel has nothing to do with Bokassa, who roasts children and eats them, Fallaci insisted. But it has, Qaddafi replied, saying in essence that he supported monstrous rulers such as Amin and Bokassa because they opposed Israel, and opposition to Israel aided the Palestinians.

> It is your attitude that drives the fedayeen to die and to kill the Israelis in Palestine. Your giving of arms to Israel! Your unwillingness to understand the Palestinians, your refusal to

help them! You Westerners are the ones who make war the only possible solution.(23)

Fallaci then took the discussion to the subject of Qaddafi's support for international terrorism in Europe. Qaddafi insisted on answering as if she had accused the Palestinians of terrorism. He pretended to have forgotten the massacre at Fiumicino airport. Palestinians are not terrorists, he asserted. If you won't speak about Libyan involvement in terrorism in Italy, the journalist continued, then what about the murders at the Munich games. Was that terrorism? Acts of violence between Palestinians and Israelis are reciprocal, Qaddafi answered. Doesn't that mean that when the terrorism is Palestinian you accept it? No. I say that it's a reaction to Israeli terrorism. Fallaci tried again to turn the discussion to Italy. You are aiding those who make war in a country that is not at war with you, she said. What about the Red Brigades? Qaddafi replied as if she had spoken of the Palestinians. "What you are saying won't stop me from helping the Palestinians. . . . I consider your words to be an attempt to persuade me from helping the Palestinians." But what if they give their Soviet weapons to Italian terrorists? Qaddafi's answer: "We are not responsible for the use that is made for the arms we give to the Palestinians. We give them to the Palestinians because we believe in their cause and because we feel it is our duty to help them. Whatever happens afterward is not my responsibility. . . . Frankly, these are matters which bore me profoundly."(24)

This facile, callous answer is shocking and morally repugnant. In international relations, moral opportunity is severly constrained. The willingness of national leaders to accept accountability for the eventual consequences of their actions regardless of motive is a crucial element in the restraint of violence and loss of value. To ignore the consequences of the provision of arms to the Palestinians, as Qaddafi claimed to do, was to act without moral restraint. At the same time, Qaddafi clearly intended his answer and his actions to throw the questions back at the Western world: What are the consequences of your support for Israel? In his words: "You Westerners are the ones who make war the only possible solution." To the West's support of Israel his counter was his support of the Palestinians. To the West's indifference to the consequences for the Palestinians of their support for Israel he replied with his indifference to the consequences of his support for the Palestinians. In Fallaci's case it was terrorism in Italy by the Red Brigade with Libyan weapons supplied by the Palestinians. Qaddafi shrugged. "Frankly, these matters bore me profoundly."

Fallaci then made a curious shift in the argument. Rather than ask Qaddafi to give the reasons why he opposed Israel, she equated Qaddafi's support for the Palestinians with hatred of the United States, the Jews, and the entire West. In short she equated a very specific, politically directed position with a very general undiscriminating, irrational position. Doesn't this set the world back a thousand years, she asked, to the era of Saladin and the Crusades? At a stroke she had wiped out time, specificity, and rationality. She was saying that under all the seeming complexity there really was just the age-old confrontation between "Islam and the West." Badgered by a hostile interviewer, Qaddafi was perfectly ready to answer in kind. Was he setting the world back to the time of Saladin? "Yes, and the fault is yours: the Americans, the West. Even a thousand years ago the blame was yours, the West. You have always been the ones who have massacred us. Yesterday as today."

Fallaci also questioned Qaddafi about his Green Book, a slim volume that, in the manner of the last two centuries of revolutionary leaders around the world, offered to generalize the meaning of his country's particular revolutionary experience. A revolution occurs, the Libyan leader averred, when the masses make the revolution or when "others" achieve a revolution that is an "expression of what the masses want." That's what Hitler and Mussolini claimed, Fallaci said. She had also compared Khomeini to the German and Italian dictators in an earlier interview. Qaddafi rejected both comparisons. They exploited the people in order to govern, he said. "Khomeini and I, instead, profit from the support of the masses to help the people to become capable of governing themselves. I say to my people: 'If you love me, listen to me and govern yourselves.' ... They love me because I tell them, 'Do it yourselves'." Well, if you don't consider yourself a dictator, and not even a president, not even a minister, what are you? "I am the leader of the revolution," Qaddafi answered, meaning the world revolution as well as Libya's.(25)

Qaddafi then laid out his political philosophy. It is embarrassingly thin, a sham, a facade. When Qaddafi speaks about the Green Book, he resembles the Wizard of Oz. It is all appearance. There is no substance. Behind the facade ropes and levers are pulled just as they are to move every government in the world. But Qaddafi wishes to speak as if only the facade were real. According to Qaddafi, Jamahiriyah (people's command or people's congress) is the final stage in the evolution of government throughout the ages. The entire people participates in governing the country. There is no opposition and no need for opposition. "When everyone participates in the congress of the people, what need is there for an opposition? ... If the government disappears and the people govern themselves, what does one oppose? ... Jamahiriyah is the destiny of the world. ... This is freedom. The only true, real freedom. ...."

About the significance of the Green Book, Qaddafi made this grandiose claim:

The Green Book is the product of the struggle of mankind.
The Green Book is the guide to the emancipation of man. The

Green Book is the gospel. The new gospel. The gospel of the
new era, the era of the masses. . . .

In your gospel it's written: "In the beginning there was the
word." The Green Book is the word. One of its words can
destroy the world. Or save it. [The United States] can wage
any war against us: to defend itself, the third world only
needs my Green Book. My word. One word and the whole
world could blow up. The value of things could change. And
their weight. And their volume. Everywhere and forever.(26)

Fallaci's interview with Qaddafi is an example of what Edward
Said has named "the covering and covering up" of Islam. "It is only a
slight overstatement to say that Muslims and Arabs are essentially
covered, discussed, apprehended, either as oil suppliers or as potential terrorists."(27) Fallaci had decided before she began her
questioning of Qaddafi that he was a terrorist. As a committed
leftist Fallaci found Qaddafi's support of the Palestinians particularly distressing, because it tainted the moral and political
legitimacy of the Palestinian cause. By reducing Qaddafi to a
modern-day, simple-minded Saladin she could disregard the mental
dissonance created by his appearance alongside the otherwise
admirable, if indistinct, Palestinians. What is odd is that Fallaci's
hatred of Qaddafi is matched by observers and politicians on the
political right who probably share few if any other viewpoints with
her. "There is a consensus on 'Islam'," Said wrote, "as a kind of
scapegoat for everything we do not happen to like about the world's
new political, social, and economic patterns. For the right Islam
represents barbarism; for the left, medieval theocracy; for the
center a kind of distasteful exoticism. In all camps, however, there
is agreement that even though little enough is known about the
Islamic world there is not much to be approved of there."(28)

Fallaci chose not to probe Qaddafi's grounds for his support of
certain Palestinian factions. This would have meant raising the
question of Israel's legitimacy. Instead, she accused him of belonging
in the Middle Ages, and disposed of him as a medieval theocrat. She
also belittled his pretentious and shallow Green Book with a child's
ruse. "Do you believe in God?" she asked toward the end of the
interview. When Qaddafi said that he did, she joyfully sprang the
trap: "I thought you were God."

Given Fallaci's prejudice and ideological revulsion toward him, it
is not surprising that Qaddafi largely took up her categories and
tried to surpass her in vehement denunciations. In Said's terms
Qaddafi answered Fallaci's reductionism by a counterreductionism
of his own: "'Islam' can now have only two possible general
meanings," Said warned, "both of them unacceptable and misleading."

To Westerners and Americans, "Islam" represents a resurgent atavism, which suggests not only the threat of a return to the Middle Ages but the destruction of what is regularly referred to as the democratic order in the Western world. For a great many Muslims, on the other hand, "Islam" stands for a reactive counterresponse to the first image of Islam as a threat. Anything said about "Islam" gets more or less forced into the apologetic form of a statement about Islam's humanism, its contribution to civilization, development, and moral righteousness.(29)

Qaddafi gave a shorter and less grandiose interview to a reporter for the New York Times a week after the sacking of the U.S. embassy in Tripoli. The setting was different. He had welcomed Fallaci at an army camp protected by machine gunners and tanks. He took the Times reporter with him on a visit to Libyan land reclamation projects nearly 400 miles east of Tripoli. His entourage was limited to his wife and six children, and his father, traveling in a big bus. A dozen guards and staff followed in several land rovers. Late on December 10 they stopped at a small settlement on the Mediterranean. After midnight, alone in a tent on the shore of the sea, Qaddafi received the reporter and talked for three hours. "We wish to intensify our dialogue with the United States," he said. He had been told unofficially but authoritatively that after the 1980 elections, if Carter were elected, the United States would assume a "more neutral position" in the Middle East. He would watch for the changes, but meanwhile he had decided not to stop the export of Libyan oil to the United States or reduce production of some 2 million barrels per day, of which the United States took one-third, 10 percent of its imports, 5 percent of its oil consumption.

Qaddafi repeated the analysis he had made for Fallaci, that the attacks on the United States of the past weeks were only the beginning of an international revolution against the United States. But in the aftermath of the Libyan attack on the embassy in Tripoli he was less interested in philosophizing than in stressing his determination to prevent another attack on the U.S. mission. Libya would see to it that foreign embassies were protected and that such an attack never happened again. Implying that he had known about plans for a demonstration but was surprised by the violence, Qaddafi said: "We have demonstrations here because people get angry. We have had demonstations before in front of the American Embassy. But we were surely surprised by this attack."(30) Though the seizure of the hostages in Iran was understandable, this was not in accord with the Islamic faith and hurt Islam's reputation. Personally, Qaddafi said he opposed the taking of hostages. He had tried to get the hostages in Iran released and would continue to do so. If the Carter administration caused the shah to leave the United States and took some action to recover the money he had taken out of Iran,

Qaddafi believed a way could be found to end the siege of the Teheran embassy and free the hostages.

It is impossible to know what Qaddafi was up to in this interview. His words might have been meant to signal a desire for better relations with the United States. It seems more likely that he simply took advantage of the forum offered by an appearance in the Times to put the best face on his policies and to present himself as a reasonable and responsible leader. The interview boils down to his desire for more discussions with the United States; his decision not to embargo oil or cut oil production; his promise to see that foreign embassies in his country were safe from mob attack; his disavowal of any intention to manufacture nuclear weapons; his promise that Soviet ships had never used Libyan ports and would never be allowed to; his personal opposition to the seizing of hostages of any kind; and his willingness to work for the release of the American hostages held in Teheran. True, he did announce that an international revolution against the United States was underway; and he was cutting ties with the PLO for preparing to sell out the Palestinian cause, that is, presumably, for considering some form of compromise with Israel. The overall impression one takes away from the interview is that here is a statesman, not an outlaw, someone with whom it is possible to deal in a constructive and effective way. He has his principles — anti-Western, pro-Palestinian — but then all revolutionary leaders must have principles, mustn't they? However, with the exception of Libyan-PLO relations none of these disclosures touched a major policy of Qaddafi's or amounted to much more than the minimum standards of conduct and prudence that might be thought to apply to any national leader. Given verbally in this manner they signified nothing.

Libyan relations had deteriorated with a number of other states as well: with Malta, Mauritania, Uganda, and Upper Volta, and had not improved with Egypt and Tunisia. Following the Libyan intervention in Chad in December 1980, Libya's relations with Sudan and France grew worse as well. The strain between Libya and Malta derived from two causes: Malta's adoption of a West-leaning status of international neutrality (guaranteed by Italy acting with the consent of the EEC and NATO); and a quarrel between Libya and Malta over oil rights to the Medina Bank reserves in the Mediterranean floor some 70 miles south of Malta. Malta claimed control over an area of the Mediterranean to a point halfway between Libya and Malta, about 100 miles to the south. Libya claimed about two-thirds of the same area, including the Medina Bank. The announcement of Maltese neutrality came with the exchange of notes between the governments of Malta and Italy in September 1980. Malta agreed to refrain from joining any alliance, to prohibit the establishment of foreign bases and the stationing of foreign troops on its soil, and to deny the United States and Soviet Union the use of docking facilities on the island. For its part Italy promised to guarantee Maltese neutrality, to consult with Malta about the provision of military support if it felt threatened by outside forces, and to extend diplomatic backing to Malta. The two countries also agreed to seek similar agreements with other European nations.

Before the conclusion of the neutrality agreement Libyan-Maltese relations had been deteriorating for several months over the offshore oil question. In 1976 Malta and Libya had agreed to submit the oil dispute to the International Court of Justice in The Hague by the end of June 1980. Although Malta suspended the search for oil in the area, Libya apparently was stalling, and the dispute was not submitted to the World Court by June 30. Accordingly, in July the Maltese prime minister, Dom Mintoff, ordered the concessionaire, Texaco, to start drilling. The next month the captain of a Texaco drilling rig was ordered by a Libyan submarine to stop his operations. Malta contacted the Italian government, which advised compliance with the order and sent a warship which, along with a Libyan vessel, supervised the closing down of the rig. Malta then appealed to the UN Security Council for help in dealing with what it charged were Libya's "illegal actions." After discussing the dispute briefly, the Security Council adjourned to allow Libya and Malta to deal with the dispute themselves. But no agreement was reached, and the conflict dragged on throughout 1981. It appeared for a time that the Libyan General People's Congress which met from January 3-7, 1981, had agreed to the submission of the matter to the World Court. But the Libyan government added a requirement — that no drilling occur until the court had given its decision — which was promptly rejected by Malta. The two countries traded accusations during the spring and summer of 1981, and Malta then asked the Security Council to urge Libya to allow the court to consider the dispute.(31)

Relations between Uganda and Libya improved somewhat in late 1979 and early 1980. But the overthrow of Idi Amin and the expulsion of the Libyan troops sent to aid him did not bring peace and well-being to Uganda. By the time the last Tanzanian units left the country on June 30, 1981, thousands of Ugandans had perished from famine and steadily worsening repression and sporadic guerrilla war. The principal opponents of President Obote's government and party, the Uganda People's Congress, were: the Democratic Party (DP) led by Paul Semogerere, which cooperated with the government despite the arrest and intimidation of its members — the DP held 51 of 126 seats in the legislature; and several groups which claimed responsibility for numerous guerrilla attacks on the government, including the Uganda Freedom Movement, led from exile by Lukatome Andrew Kayiira; the Uganda Patriotic Movement, led by Yoweri Musereni; and the Movement for the Struggle for Political Rights.(32) In late June 1981 the Ugandan minister of internal affairs declared in the National Assembly that two members of the Libyan people's bureau in Kampala had covertly attempted to obtain landing rights for a Libyan airplane. He also alleged that Libyan planes had been flying across Uganda without permission and landing in neighboring countries. The implication was, of course, that Libya was supporting the rebellion against Obote. These kinds of charges would continue into 1982.(33) The two Libyans, Salim Khaliefa and Abdel-Monem Said, had been sent to Kampala two weeks earlier to transform the embassy into a people's bureau. The two were arrested, but Khaliefa, who called himself charge d'affaires, denied the allegations. They were released on June 28.

There were also strains in Libya's relations with Tunisia and Upper Volta. After a series of incidents on the border between Tunisia and Libya the Tunisian government in November 1980 declared an alert, a state of "heightened vigilance," and claimed that Libyan troops had crossed into Tunisia.(34) After successfully overthrowing the government of Aboubakr Sangoule Lamizana in Upper Volta in late November 1980 the country's new regime, led by Colonel Saye Zerba, rejected the transformation of the Libyan embassy into a people's bureau. On January 16 the foreign minister, Lt. Colonel Felix Tiemtarboum, announced in Ouagadougou that only those members of the people's bureau who were formally accredited as diplomats would be allowed to remain in the country. A similar grievance also led to the expulsion of Libyan diplomats from Nigeria in January. Upper Volta condemned the Libyan merger with Chad and established friendly relations with France. Both steps were certain to be resented in Tripoli.

Even the merger with Syria ran into difficulties before the year was out. In October 1980, a month after consenting to the merger agreement with Libya, President Assad went to Moscow and entered a twenty-year alliance with the Soviet Union. The Moscow treaty was a combination of non-aggression pact – neither country would join hostile coalitions or take other unfriendly actions toward the other – and military alliance – in the event of a threat to the peace or their security they would consult and cooperate to remove the threat. Assad was thought to have asked for the treaty as a way of increasing the flow of Soviet weapons and advisors to Syria, which was already very great. Presumably the additional weapons were to be paid for with Libyan money. Press reports stated that Libya had not only offered $1 billion for the arms but $600 million for economic development as well. However, the path to Syrian-Libyan unity was not to be a smooth one. At a conference in mid-December Syria and Libya were already disagreeing about how to proceed to unification. The communique issued on December 17 at the end of Assad's visit to Tripoli sounded all too familiar to those who remembered the fate of Qaddafi's past attempts to try and cajole his way to union with other Arab states. A joint committee would be established to plan the structure of the new state, the communique said. Talks on cooperation would continue. A joint "revolutionary leadership" had been formed to supervise progress toward unity.

There were other negative press reports as well: that Assad had sought and failed to obtain Libyan support against the Muslim Brotherhood, which had been waging a campaign of assassination against government officials and Soviet advisors in Syria; and, in the London Financial Times of January 5, 1981, that Kuwaiti sources believed that Libya and Syria had given up on unity altogether because they couldn't agree on how the new state would be governed.(35)

At the special OAU economic summit in Lagos, April 28-30, 1980, it was clear that the Western Sahara dispute had been "Africanized." Most African states had chosen sides, for Morocco or for Polisario, and as the months went by after the Lagos summit their differences not only divided them against one another but paralyzed and threatened to destroy the OAU itself. As requested by the Lagos summit the OAU ad hoc committee on Western Sahara brought together all the parties to the conflict in Freetown, September 9-12. Sierra Leone's President Stevens served as chairman of the conference, which included the other "wise men," Presidents Sekou Toure of Guinea, Moussa Traore of Mali, and Shagari of Nigeria, and delegations from Sudan and Tanzania. Among the interested parties, Morocco was represented by Prime Minister Bouabid and Foreign Minister Mohammed Boucetta; and Polisario by its Secretary-General Mohammed Abdelazziz. Presidents Bendjedid Chadli of Algeria and Khouna Ould Kaydalla of Mauritania were present, as were representatives of ten groups supported by Morocco as truly representative of the people of Western Sahara. Among the ten were three that had been backed by Morocco against Spain before Spain gave up its colony: the Front de liberation et de l'unite, the Parti de l'unification nationale du Sahara, and the Mouvement de resistance des hommes bleus.

The "wise men" were able to agree among themselves on a plan for a cease-fire and referendum in Western Sahara. Their main idea was to combine UN and OAU involvement to bring about a final settlement. A UN peacekeeping force would supervise a "fair and general" cease-fire, to take effect in December 1980; all troops would return to bases and barracks; and the OAU would supervise the referendum. Polisario and Mauritania accepted the plan, and Morocco rejected it. There was nothing new in it, Foreign Minister Boucetta explained, and the OAU should not "flee from its responsibilities" by calling in the UN. In any case, Boucetta asserted, all OAU decisions of this kind had to be taken by a two-thirds majority at a summit conference. Boucetta's statement made clear Morocco's intention to postpone any decision on the dispute, for the next regularly scheduled meeting of heads of state and government would not take place until July 1981 in Nairobi, Kenya.

By surrendering its claim to part of the Western Sahara in 1979 Mauritania had hoped to escape the losses and possible internal upheavals that the struggle with Polisario and its supporters, Algeria and Libya, would bring. But it was not to prove so simple. There were strains between high-ranking officials in the Mauritanian government who were sympathetic to Libya and Polisario, and others who had adopted a pan-Arab pro-Iraq orientation and sought to maintain Mauritanian neutrality and block the use of Mauritanian territory for attacks on Morocco. The pro-Libyan group included the president of the ruling Military Committee for National Salvation (CMSN), Lt. Colonel Khouna Ould Kaydalla. The prime minister, Sid Ahmed Ould Bneijara, was regarded as pro-Iraq.

The immediate upshot of these conflicting pressures was an attempted military coup on March 16, 1981, led by two former members of CMSN, Lt. Colonels Mohammed Ould Ba Ould Abdel-kader and Asmed Salem Ould Sidi. Although the rebels denied receiving any outside help, the Mauritanian government charged Morocco with having fomented the coup and broke diplomatic relations. The leading conspirators, members of the Alliance for a Democratic Mauritania (AMD), were executed on March 26 and others given heavy prison sentences or sentenced to death in absentia. Algeria strongly supported Mauritania and reportedly sent several transport aircraft loaded with weapons to Nouakchott. The Libyan government declared it would consider any attack against Mauritania an attack against Libya.

But the maneuvering didn't stop with the defeat of the coup. About three weeks later Mauritanian Prime Minister Bneijara spent two days in Libya and a week later Qaddafi and Turayki spent two days in Nouakchott. The visits suggested improvement in Libyan-Mauritanian relations, which had been strained by the expulsion of three Libyan diplomats in late December 1980 for allegedly fomenting a student strike against Iraqi teachers and the arrest of a number of Mauritanians on suspicion of taking Libyan support to plot against the government. After a visit by Turayki, some of those arrested were released in January and Libyan cultural centers were reopened. But in addition to giving the appearance of good will, Qaddafi and Bneijara held quite remarkable discussions. In Tripoli, with Polisario's Mohammed Abdelazziz present, Qaddafi apparently proposed a merger between SADR and Mauritania. He also invited Mauritania to join the Steadfastness and Rejection Front of Libya, Syria, Algeria, South Yemen, and the PLO. And Qaddafi proposed an alliance of Libya, Algeria, SADR, and Mauritania, although the exact nature of the agreement was not made public. When he came to Nouakchott by way of Algeria Qaddafi announced that the SADR-Mauritanian merger had been approved in principle. He added that he had held discussions about mergers between Libya and Mauritania and Mauritania and Algeria. The communique published after the Tripoli meeting made no mention of the merger, and was confined to expressions of opposition to Morocco for instigating the coup and occupying Western Sahara and of support for "the legitimate government of Chad." Qaddafi may have been trying to build support for a major initiative on the Western Sahara at the July meeting of the OAU in Nairobi. A Libyan envoy also visited King Hassan in Rabat on June 19 to discuss the resumption of diplomatic relations. Subsequently, however, the political balance in Nouakchott swung toward Iraq and Mauritanian neutrality. A brief period of civilian rule was brought to an end with the appointment of a number of military officers to the cabinet, most of whom were pro-Iraq.

Meanwhile, heavy fighting continued between Morocco and Polisario. The Moroccan government had in August 1980 begun a line of fortifications to defend the southwestern areas of the Western Sahara, notably around the "useful triangle" for phosphate production: El Aioun-Smara-Bou Craa. Another line of fortifications further north protected Zag and a Moroccan expeditionary force based nearby. The Moroccan defensive plan was an ambitious one and called for the extensive use of earthworks, mines, ditches, barbed wire, observation posts, and sophisticated electronic surveillance devices. Polisario answered by attacking the units at work on the fortifications, at Ras-el-Khanfra, Kreybichet, Bou Craa, and Smara, for example. In the spring of 1981 Morocco also orchestrated a concentrated diplomatic and propaganda campaign against Libya.

In addition to strengthening its fortifications Morocco benefited from a welcome change in U.S. aid policy. One of the first official actions taken by the new U.S. secretary of state, Alexander Haig, in January 1981 was to approve the sale to Morocco of aircraft and helicopters, requested earlier by Morocco and delayed by the Carter administration, and to authorize the sale of 180 M-60 tanks. Two months later the Reagan administration confirmed the change. The United States intended to drop the conditions that had been imposed on arms sales to Morocco by the Carter administration. Henceforth the conditions would be the same as "for other friends." Testifying in Congress, the deputy assistant secretary of state for the Near East, Morris Draper, indicated that the United States would no longer explicitly require "unilateral Moroccan attempts to show progress toward a peaceful settlement" before selling U.S. weapons to the North African country. According to Draper, this decision merely recognized that there were other players in the Western Sahara "with a capacity to influence the outcome." But Draper's words were meant to disguise a much more far-reaching policy change. The new administration had a two-pronged plan: to knit Morocco into a design to contain Qaddafi by military force and to secure the use of Moroccan facilities for the Rapid Deployment Force. The price to be paid in both cases was the embrace of the Moroccan position on Libya, Algeria, and the Western Sahara.(36)

As the Nairobi summit of the OAU drew closer, the diplomatic maneuvering intensified. A number of African, Middle Eastern, and European states sought to persuade King Hassan to accept a referendum in Western Sahara as a means of settling the conflict there. In his speech to the OAU summit the king said he had been approached by the presidents of the Ivory Coast, Guinea, Cameroon, Gabon, and Senegal, through the kings of Saudi Arabia and Jordan and the presidents of Iraq and the United Arab Emirates, and also by the presidents of France and Italy, the prime minister of Britain, the chancellor of West Germany, and the king of Spain. Accordingly, Hassan said, Morocco was willing to consider (envisager) a "controlled referendum" in the Sahara which would simultaneously "respect" the objectives of the latest plan proposed by the "wise men" as well as Morocco's conviction of the legitimacy of its claim to the disputed territory. Hassan's initiative softened the criticism of his country at the meeting, kept Morocco's supporters comfortably on his side, and postponed a decision once again.

There had been a scuffle between Moroccan and Polisario representatives during the Council of Ministers meeting before the summit. More fireworks came after Hassan's address when President Kaydallah of Mauritania criticized Morocco's interference in his country's internal affairs. Hassan protested and then walked out of the meeting when Kaydallah continued his criticisms. Kaydallah then went on to spell out his, and presumably Algeria's, Libya's, and Polisario's view of the circumstances that would have to be established before a valid referendum could be held. These included: the agreement of the states bordering the Western Sahara and Polisario about the procedures to be followed for the referendum; their agreement to accept the results of the vote; the appointment by the OAU of a provisional administration of the Western Sahara to arrange a cease-fire and to oversee public services; and the withdrawal of Moroccan military units from parts of Western Sahara to be agreed on the substitution of neutral forces for them. This approach ran closer to the proposal of the "wise men" and to the views of Polisario's more vocal supporters at Nairobi, such as Angola, Benin, Congo, Madagascar, and Mozambique. Taking Morocco's side during the debate were Gabon, Guinea, Ivory Coast, Senegal, and Zaire.

The final resolution on Western Sahara adopted by the Nairobi conference was silent about Polisario's claim to membership in the OAU and also omitted any reference to a withdrawal of Moroccan troops from the contested territory. While this no doubt pleased Morocco, the resolution also gave Polisario and its allies good reason for satisfaction. First, it urged the parties to accept a general cease-fire. The resolution created an "implementation committee," composed of Guinea, Kenya, Mali, Nigeria, Sierra Leone, and Tanzania, which was charged with obtaining a cease-fire and holding a referendum on self-determination for the Western Sahara. The resolution also requested the UN and OAU to provide a peacekeeping force to maintain order during the vote.

The question of Libya's presence in Chad was extensively debated at Nairobi, and the debate and the Nairobi resolution on Chad are discussed later. At this point one should observe, nonetheless, the connection between the Libyan withdrawal from Chad and Qaddafi's desire to host the 1982 summit in Tripoli and become president of the OAU. The conference agreed by voice vote to hold the next summit in Tripoli, over the opposition of Egypt, Gabon, Ghana, Sudan, and a number of other states. But Nigeria's minister of external affairs, Ishaya Audu, spoke for many member governments when he observed that Libya would have to agree to withdraw from Chad or the summit meeting would not be held in Tripoli.(37) As unlikely as it might have seemed in July 1981 the dispute within the OAU over Western Sahara rather than over Chad would soon explode and threaten not only Qaddafi's Tripoli summit and presidency of the OAU but the very existence of the organization itself.

III
RESORT TO HOSTILITY:
U.S.-LIBYAN RELATIONS
SINCE 1980

12
U.S. PRESSURE ON QADDAFI

The U.S. elections of 1980 brought Ronald Reagan to the presidency. During his campaign Reagan had pledged to restore U.S. military power and prestige around the world. Once in office, Reagan lost little time in making good on his promises. Massive increases in defense spending were obtained, and the U.S. government took a stern view of the Soviet Union. The administration had also pledged to combat international terrorism, and it moved fast in this area, as well. This meant conflict with Lilbya.

While Nigeria and France searched for a compromise to bring about Libyan withdrawal and an end to the civil war in Chad, the Reagan administration began a systematic effort to increase the diplomatic, military, and economic pressure on Qaddafi. The shift in U.S. policy was dramatic. The Carter, Nixon, and Ford administrations had ignored Libya as an unimportant nuisance which could not be punished because U.S. allies in Europe would not support sanctions. Throwing out this approach the Reagan administration ordered State and Defense to treat Qaddafi as a menace and a Soviet puppet who should be stopped and, if possible, overthrown. This basic policy decision was made by the political appointees in the new administration and endorsed by the president. Furious battles then followed as the appointees fought with the career diplomats, soldiers, and bureaucrats over precisely what steps would be taken to implement the new policy. To oversimplify, the political appointees wanted to take immediate, drastic, and, if necessary, unilateral steps to "get Qaddafi," that is to contain and punish Libya, and to undermine the stability of Qaddafi's control of the country. When the diplomats objected, for example, that the U.S.

allies in Europe did not regard Qaddafi as a menace, or even as terribly important, they were told: "We'll get them (the Europeans) next!" In the end, the careerists won most of the battles about the concrete steps that would be taken against Qaddafi. Not only were they limited steps, with slight although tangible impact on Libya, and therefore on other Arab and European governments, but they were executed only after careful consultation with Egypt and the Europeans. Although they were forced to compromise on specifics, the political appointees nonetheless succeeded in realizing their chief objective. In a little over a year the Reagan administration fundamentally altered U.S. policy toward Libya. Henceforth, the United States regarded Qaddafi as an enemy, not a nuisance, and would treat him and his country as enemies.(1)

The change in U.S. policy did not come about overnight. It was not possible, first of all, to reach agreement so broadly and quickly within the U.S. government as to what should be done "about Libya." The drastic measures that were contemplated, such as the use of military force against Qaddafi, took time to prepare. Still others, such as the recall of U.S. citizens or the ban on the importation of Libyan oil, could only be done after extensive consultation with U.S. allies. To be most effective the more severe measures had to be properly timed, and waiting for the right moment also caused delays. Finally, the decision to go ahead with one or another of the sanctions was affected by Libya's international behavior and, indeed by other international developments, such as the assassination of Sadat, which greatly increased the sense of urgency in Washington about all things affecting Egypt, Sudan, and the Gulf.

Libya's continued presence in Chad undoubtedly convinced U.S. policymakers of the need to threaten Libya with military reprisal. The glee shown by the Libyan leadership at Sadat's assassination also caused a very negative reaction. And the public outcry caused by the administration's claim that Qaddafi had sent a hit-squad to kill President Reagan was used to justify the recall of all Americans from Libya and to prepare the way for the ban on oil imports. Thus, although the change in U.S. policy did not occur instantaneously it proceeded from a fundamental decision to treat Libya as an enemy. Considered together, the various steps taken to implement the new approach amounted to a coherent set of measures which were systematically applied. There were three goals: to isolate, embarrass, and weaken Libya. An opaque catchword – "destabilize" – is normally used to describe such actions. In other words, if the increase in external pressure led to Qaddafi's overthrow, so much the better.

There were seven specific elements to the Reagan administration's campaign to put an end to Libyan interference with U.S. interests. To isolate, embarrass, and weaken Libya, the Reagan administration took the following actions:

- A rupture of Libyan-U.S. "political" relations: this took the form of the closure of the Libyan people's bureau in Washington (all U.S. diplomats had been withdrawn from Libya by the Carter administration), and the recall of all Americans from Libya.
- The initiation of a major propaganda campaign intended to portray Qaddafi and the Libyan government as unstable and dangerous, as sponsors of terrorism, subversion, and foreign intervention; in short, as international outlaws deserving of harsh punishment.
- The strengthening of governments that opposed Libya: this was one of the reasons for the increased U.S. aid to, for example, Morocco, Tunisia, and Sudan, although by no means the only reason.
- The calculated use of the threat of U.S. military intervention against Libya: this was done in three ways: by the entry of the U.S. naval task force into the Gulf of Sidra prepared in advance to give battle to Libyan planes if they rose to challenge the U.S. presence, as they always had; by U.S. support for an Egyptian and Sudanese strike against Libyan forces in Chad, given during then Vice-President Mubarak's visit to Washington in early October 1981; and, after Sadat's death, by the ostentatious display of U.S. strategic air power during "Operation Brightstar," a joint military exercise involving U.S., Egyptian, Sudanese, and Omani forces.
- The imposition of economic sanctions against Libya by banning the importation of Libyan oil into the United States and by prohibiting the export of high technology equipment – principally oil drilling rigs and spare parts for them – to Libya.
- The consideration of the overthrow of Qaddafi by a covert U.S. intervention: the administration apparently rejected such an undertaking, but when the deliberations on it were "leaked," U.S. pressure on Qaddafi increased and in this way, even a noncoup became part of the campaign against Qaddafi.
- The coordination of U.S. policy with France and other governments willing to oppose Libya: this meant, for example, following the French lead in Chad and swallowing objections to the renewal of French arms shipments to Libya. It also meant working with Nigeria and other African governments to support the OAU peacekeeping force in Chad, and with Morocco and Tunisia, both of whom opposed Qaddafi, although for different reasons. After the withdrawal of Libyan troops from southern Chad, U.S. opposition to Qaddafi was expressed through significant support for Hissene Habre's campaign against Oueddei and GUNT. In 1982 Habre won control of Chad, and Oueddei fled to Libya for protection and revenge.

The first public signs of a change toward Libya came in late March 1981 with the publication of a story in the Washington Post that the Reagan administration was reviewing U.S. policy toward Libya. "What to do about Qaddafi . . ." Michael Getler reported, "is now the subject of intense review within the administration." He added that the administration's interest in Qaddafi grew out of its larger concern to contain the spread of Soviet influence and the activities of states and movements it regarded as Soviet surrogates. Most worrisome to the administration were Qaddafi's foreign intervention in Chad and the reported $12 billion in Soviet arms he had stockpiled in his country. Getler said that two points of view on what to do about Qaddafi were in contention inside the administration. The first, which Getler's sources attributed to the State Department's African specialists, held that Qaddafi's Libya was essentially a regional problem. The United States could best deal with it by supporting the many African countries who opposed Qaddafi, along with France, which had strong continuing ties to northern Africa. The stockpile of Soviet arms, according to this view, was merely the result of the coincidence of Qaddafi's appetite for weapons and the desire of the Soviet leadership to get their hands on as much hard currency as possible. Qaddafi, in this skeptical view, was not a surrogate. He was too independent for this, or, as Getler put it, "too unpredictable, disorganized, and unreliable for Moscow ever to count on in a crunch." The Soviets probably regarded him, some had told Getler, as "another religious fanatic not unlike Iran's Ayatollah Khomeini."

The opponents of this view, many of whom had been appointed by the Reagan White House to the State Department policy planning staff, saw Qaddafi in a very different way. Qaddafi is a Soviet surrogate, they told Getler, echoing a position taken publicly by President Reagan. He was doing Moscow's work by destabilizing the countries of western and northern Africa, including Morocco and Tunisia, and by fanning unrest in Egypt and Saudi Arabia. Whatever Qaddafi's present intentions might be the huge arsenal of Soviet arms in Libya gave the Soviet Union the capability to intervene with great force against Egypt or Africa with a minimum effort, should it decide to send the tank crews, pilots, and armored infantry that Libya lacked.(2)

The Reagan administration's evaluation of its Libyan policy came at a time of mounting concern in Washington over the growth of Libyan military capabilities and the warmth of its relations with the Soviet Union. On March 1, 1981, Drew Middleton, military affairs analyst for the New York Times, had reported a deepening concern among the commanders of NATO that during a crisis in the eastern Mediterranean, Qaddafi would grant the Soviet Union the use of air bases in Libya. If some of Libya's 19 hard-surface airfields were lengthened the Soviets could land its extremely effective Backfire bomber. According to the NATO officers Middleton interviewed, including U.S. Admiral William Crowe, Commander of Allied Forces South, if the Backfires were supported by Sukhoi and MIG fighters, together with the enlarged Soviet naval force of 40 to 50 ships already in the eastern Mediterranean, the United States would be compelled to move its one remaining carrier battle group west of

Sicily. The other carrier group had been sent to the Indian Ocean. If this happened Turkey and Greece, at each other's throats over Cyprus, and Italy would be left alone to deal with some 24 Soviet and 8 Bulgarian divisions, backed by 1,100 Soviet tactical aircraft and additional Backfire and Bulgarian planes. "Sure it's serious," an officer told Middleton, "But the resources just aren't there. We face that every day. The public has got to face it some day."(3)

Another military report about Libya a few days later raised the possibility of the acquisition of a nuclear delivery system by Qaddafi. The report described the activities in Libya of a West German rocket manufacturing company, Orbital Transport-und Raketen-Aktiengesellschaft (Otrag), which claimed to have success-fully tested a suborbital rocket at a base at Sebha, in the Libyan desert on March 1. Otrag had been expelled from a large secret test facility in Zaire in April 1979. One version of the expulsion, based on official West German sources, held that Leonid Brezhnev had asked Helmut Schmidt to bring about the closing of the testing ground. Schmidt, according to this account, prevailed on Giscard d'Estaing to intercede with President Mobutu, and the site was closed. A Western journalist, Tad Szulc, writing in Penthouse magazine, had accused Otrag of testing cruise and intermediate-range ballistic missiles in Zaire. Szulc claimed his charge was based on information from "highly reliable informants in Washington and Western Europe." Officials in Bonn and Washington denied the charge and called it absurd, and Otrag maintained that it conducted no military research of any kind. The arrangement with Libya, according to an Otrag official, provided for free use of the Libyan facilities and for the eventual payment to Libya of a 5 percent commission on sales of Otrag rockets.(4)

The activities of a rocket company in Libya gained new sig-nificance when considered together with three other steps: Libya's large purchases of uranium from Niger, some 1,200 tons in the first six months of 1981; the organization of the Libyan government to manage a full-fledged nuclear program, mentioned earlier; and the start of construction on a nuclear reactor in Libya by the Soviet Union. All these have undoubted peaceful applications. Otrag officials could be telling the complete truth, for example, when they said their company conducted no military research. Similarly, Libya has signed the Nuclear Non-Proliferation Treaty, and the plans for the Soviet reactor meet International Atomic Energy Agency safe-guard standards. Even so, how difficult would it be for a government as determined as Qaddafi's to apply Otrag's commercial designs to military purposes? Otrag intended to test an inertial guidance system during the summer of 1981. Moreover, the experience of India and Iraq suggests that safeguards may not prevent the use of functioning reactors to obtain enriched uranium for military pur-poses.(5) According to a former IAEA inspector, Roger Richter, Iraq was developing nuclear weapons. In testimony to the Senate Foreign

Relations Committee, Richter said: "The available information points to an aggressive, coordinated program by Iraq to develop nuclear weapons capability during the next five years." Richter added that the IAEA's inspections were ineffective. They could occur only after two weeks' notice, during which time Iraq would remove any suspicious evidence. As proof of his contention, Richter said Iraq had bought 100 tons of yellowcake uranium ore and a hot-cell laboratory for the removal of plutonium. The laboratory was not subject to IAEA inspection. When notified of an imminent inspection, Richter said, Iraqi technicians could remove the ore being transformed into plutonium from its reactor and store it in the hot-cell laboratory which could not be inspected.(6)

On March 12 Moroccan officials accused Otrag of having signed a contract to provide the Libyan government with a medium-range missile capable of carrying a nuclear warhead by 1986. The Moroccan officials said Libya was developing nuclear weapons in a separate project. The Libyan government made no comment. An Otrag official dismissed the accusation as "complete nonsense."(7) A later story about Otrag did not lessen either the mystery or the concern that the company's missiles might find their way into the military arsenals of Libya and other countries. On August 14, the Washington Post reported that Otrag was negotiating for an additional test site. The firm kept the new location a secret but one candidate, apparently, was an island off the coast of Argentina. The president of Otrag, Frank Werkasch, said his company wanted the additional site as insurance against being expelled from Libya and to dilute the hostility toward Otrag arising from the tie to Qaddafi. But it was more complicated than this. Libya has a long-standing nuclear cooperation agreement with Argentina, and the South American country has received nuclear assistance from the Soviet Union. Moreover, Argentina's relations with the Soviet Union seemed likely to improve significantly because of Soviet help given to the military junta during the war over the Falkland Islands with Great Britain. By moving to Argentina Otrag linked its operations to two would-be nuclear powers, Argentina and Libya, who were themselves increasingly closely linked to the Soviet Union. The West German government had failed to control Otrag's operations, despite the passage of several pieces of legislation with that purpose. Bonn's distrust of Otrag had been raised with Jalloud during his visit to Bonn in July 1981, but the Libyans refused to expel the rocket company. According to the Post, officials in the West German government doubted that Qaddafi would have allowed Otrag to test its rockets without obtaining military benefits from the research in return.

According to Professor Harry Ruppe, director of the Institute of Space Technology at the Munich Technical University, Otrag and its low-budget rockets were the brainchildren of Lutz Kayser, a forty-two-year-old aerospace engineer, who had offered his concepts to the West German government in the early 1970s. Bonn had turned down the offer, because its expert consultants, including Professor Ruppe, doubted the feasibility of Kayser's approach. Kayser had, in essence, proposed to make satellite launching cheap. He proposed to build rockets from readily available parts, including standardized steel pipes used in clusters for the boosters, and would use a simple, cheap fuel made of diesel oil and nitric acid. Despite Kayser's failure to obtain public funding and the test failure, Ruppe said he hoped Otrag would succeed in developing an inexpensive way to launch satellites. The rockets had undeniable military uses, Ruppe added, although its reliance on liquid fuels would make it less effective as a weapon than it would be as a commercial or research vehicle. Here, of course, was the potential payoff for Libya.

As it pondered its policy toward Libya, the Reagan administration was aware not only of the growth in Libyan military capabilities, but also of a strengthening of the ties between Libya and the Soviet Union. Qaddafi paid his first visit to the Soviet Union in five years in late April 1981. Brezhnev met him at the airport and greeted him as "a true comrade." According to news accounts Brezhnev ridiculed Western accusations of Libyan involvement in terrorism, saying that this was the term imperialists used to describe national liberation movements. The Soviet president also emphasized his government's support for Arab governments that opposed Camp David.(8) Western diplomats in Moscow were said to believe Qaddafi had come to ask for more Soviet weapons. There was something to this, for the commander of the Libyan armed forces, Abu Bakr Ynes Jabr, met with Soviet Defense Minister Dimitri Ustinov on April 28. The new Libyan minister for atomic energy, Abdul Majidal-Qad, also was a member of the Libyan delegation. A Libyan spokesman was careful to stress that the talks would "improve the military balance" in the Middle East.

Much more was involved than tanks and planes and nuclear research. Qaddafi apparently came seeking Soviet backing for the Steadfastness and Rejection Front of Algeria, Libya, the PLO, South Yemen, and Syria. All that resulted, apparently, was a Soviet acceptance of a statement in the communique that Moscow "highly assessed" the front's accomplishments. The Soviet government undoubtedly pressed Qaddafi to endorse its intervention in Afghanistan. But Qaddafi was determined not to support the invasion, although he had refused to join most other Islamic nations in condemning the Soviet action. At a ceremonial dinner on April 27 Qaddafi had knowingly departed from the Soviet line by asserting the necessity "to guarantee [Afghanistan's] independence and neutrality and to stop all forms of outside interference." The Soviet position is that their intervention was necessary to halt Western interference in Afghanistan. The Soviets were so anxious to show they had the support of a Muslim leader for their occupation of Afghanistan that they simply falsified Qaddafi's statements. The

Communist party newspaper Pravda the next day reported that Qaddafi had asked for information on Brezhnev's proposals about the independence and sovereignty of Afghanistan. A Libyan diplomat immediately gave Western newsmen the correct version and unequivocally said that Qaddafi's reference to the need to end all forms of outside interference applied to "everyone," including the Soviet Union. Pravda also omitted Qaddafi's calls for "decisive" support of the Arabs and "more energetic" efforts to aid the Steadfastness and Rejection Front. The report carried by the Soviet News Agency TASS omitted all this and carried only praise of the foreign policy of the Soviet Union.(9)

The joint communique published at the end of the visit adhered to the Soviet line by mentioning only the intervention of "imperialist and reactionary forces" in Afghanistan.(10) Embracing the Soviet view of the occupation of Afghanistan the communique also endorsed the Libyan interpretation of the intervention in Chad, referring to "the positive role" played by Libya in Chad, at the request of "the legitimate Chadian government," and calling for an end to "imperialist and reactionary" intrigues in and around Chad. Aside from a few positive statements — in favor of the general foreign policy line ratified by the twenty-sixth Soviet Party Congress, or in praise of the Steadfastness and Rejection Front — much of the communique was given over to condemnation of Israel and the United States, something about which Qaddafi and Brezhnev could strongly agree. However, at the end of the joint statement came a discussion of Soviet-Libyan relations that undoubtedly caused concern in the Reagan administration. Libya intended to draw closer to the Soviet Union. The communique began: "The most important questions of relations between the Soviet Union and Libya and prospects for the development of their further cooperation were discussed during the talks." In recent years, the text continued, bilateral relations had been successfully developing, and the two leaders wished to continue that growth. Trade and economic contracts would be expanded. A program for "cultural and scientific" cooperation in 1981-82 had been signed during Qaddafi's stay in Moscow. The Libyan leader had invited Brezhnev to visit Libya, and he had accepted; the date of the visit would be set later. Both sides, the communique stated, were deeply satisfied with the results of the visit and considered that it had strengthened the friendship between Libya and the Soviet Union.(11)

As the Reagan administration increased its pressure on Libya, Qaddafi moved even closer to the Soviet Union. A short time after the air clash over the Gulf of Sidra, for example, Shahati, speaking as secretary general of the "Libyan Mediterranean Progressive Socialist Organization," warned that the United States was forcing Libya to turn to the Soviet bloc for help. "What we expect is an Israeli-Egyptian attack with American help over Libyan land," Shahati said.(12) The Libyans repeated this line often in the weeks ahead. Plainly Qaddafi was determined to use the threat of a Libyan alliance with the Soviet Union to deter the United States from making or countenancing moves against Libya that were too direct or were dangerously strong. In the threat of alliance Qaddafi held an important hostage, and it was of some value. The Reagan administration wanted to raise the costs of Qaddafi's foreign interventions without driving him into a Soviet alliance. However, if Qaddafi actually entered the alliance (killed the hostage) the value of the threat would be lost and United States and Arab enmity intensified. Before taking such a dangerous step Qaddafi had to be sure that the benefits from an alliance with the Soviet Union would be at least as great as the deterrent value of the threat had been. Meanwhile, Qaddafi couldn't resist twitting the Reagan administration in its own backyard. Fully aware of U.S. opposition to the new government in Nicaragua, Qaddafi extended a balance-of-payments loan of $100 million to the revolutionary Sandinistas in May. The Reagan administration had frozen all aid to Nicaragua when it took office the previous January, and charged Nicaragua with helping guerrillas to overthrow the government of neighboring El Salvador. Mexico and the Soviet Union also increased their economic aid at the same time.(13)

The closure of the Libyan people's bureau in Washington was the first concrete public step taken by the Reagan administration against Libya. This reduction of relations between the two countries to the lowest level possible short of a formal rupture was not very significant in itself; diplomatic relations had virtually stopped months earlier. But it was meant to signal the beginning of a new phase in Libyan-U.S. relations and to warn Qaddafi that worse could follow. On March 6 the U.S. government ordered the closure of the Libyan people's bureau and the withdrawal of the Libyan nationals assigned to it within five days. To justify the expulsion, senior U.S. officials emphasized Libyan suport for terrorism. They mentioned the murder of Qaddafi's opponents in Western Europe, the threats against Libyan students in the United States, and the shooting of Faisal Zagallai in Colorado. Shortly before the announcement, President Reagan had publicly linked Qaddafi to the Communist nations that he said had been exporting terrorism to El Salvador. The administration also referred to Libya's invasion of Chad, to Qaddafi's ambition to build a pan-Islamic empire, to Libya's close relations with the Soviet Union, to its huge ("$12 billion") arsenal of Soviet arms, and to its fostering of instability in Africa and the Middle East. However, the expulsion of Libyan diplomats was not an immediate reaction to these developments. Rather, the administration wished to make "a loud public statement that there will be no business as usual until Libya decides to play by the rules of international conduct," as State Department officials put it.

The administration took two related steps at the same time. First it ordered that all Libyan visa applications for travel to the

United States be subjected to a "mandatory security advisory opinion." In other words all Libyan applicants would be scrutinized by the FBI and national intelligence agencies, in addition to the routine approval procedure. Second, the day after it issued the expulsion order the State Department advised U.S. oil companies operating in Libya to start an "orderly drawdown" of Americans working for them there. Thirty oil company representatives attended an hour-long meeting at State and were given advice not orders, but the message was clear: Get Out. If something bad happens the U.S. government is in no position to help your employees. None of the six companies in Libya – Amerada-Hess, Conoco, Exxon, Marathon, Mobil, Occidental – responded by withdrawing their American employees from Libya. At this point Libyan oil production had fallen drastically: from 1.8 million barrels a day in 1980 to 700,000 a day at the start of 1981. The U.S. share of Libyan exports was also falling rapidly, from 552,000 barrels a day in 1980, about 10 percent of U.S. oil imports, to a reported 150,000 a day by September 1981, or 2 percent of U.S. imports. There were at least two reasons for the fall in Libyan exports. The Libyans had kept a very high price for their oil, and other members of OPEC, notably Saudi Arabia and Nigeria, were willing to offer their oil for less, $28 a barrel instead of $37.50 in the case of Saudi Arabia. Poor economic conditions in the industrial nations had also cut demand for oil.

The oil "glut" and the expulsion order raised questions about the ultimate intentions of the Reagan administration. Qaddafi was certain there was more to come. In an interview broadcast from Tripoli by satellite for the "MacNeil-Lehrer Report" Qaddafi called the Reagan administration's actions childish and unjustified. He would not retaliate now, he said, but he might cut off oil shipments to the United States in the future. Nothing would happen to Americans in Libya "until the situation deteriorates." Qaddafi and other Libyan spokesmen denied supporting terrorism. Libya was prepared to confront U.S. policy, a JANA release stated on May 7, if further hostile steps were taken.

When a nation closes its embassy or breaks relations with another government, it normally arranges with a third government to represent its interests. But this had not happened in Tripoli and would not now happen in Washington. According to one news story, Qaddafi had been worried for some time about the deterioration of relations with the United States. He had asked the Carter administration to reopen the U.S. embassy in Tripoli. The U.S. response was to offer to let Belgium represent U.S. interests in Tripoli. The Libyans rejected the idea. After the expulsion of the people's bureau the Reagan administration offered to allow the establishment of a Libyan "interests section" in Washington, provided the United States was allowed to make a similar arrangement in Tripoli.

A few weeks later Ahmed Shahati spent several days in Washington in "talks" at the State Department. Any doubts about the permanency of the rupture between Tripoli and Washington vanished after these talks ended in stalemate. Shahati spoke with the deputy assistant secretary of state for the Near East, Peter Constable, on June 18. There were major disagreements on bilateral issues. Afterward Shahati spoke at an Arab League luncheon in his honor and tried to show a desire on the part of Libya for improved relations. "The way is open for dialogue," he told his listeners. But, there would be no dialogue, and Libyan-U.S. relations would grow much worse in the months ahead.(14)

In retrospect the closure of the people's bureau was merely the first of a number of actions by which the Reagan administration intended to isolate, embarrass, and weaken Qaddafi. A second measure was a propaganda campaign designed to discredit the Libyan leader and turn him into an international outlaw. To this end, the Reagan administration has waged unrelenting psychological warfare against Qaddafi. Governments are drawn to propaganda because it is cheap and not very risky. When cleverly done propaganda can aid foreign policy slightly, although it is undoubtedly more effective on a captive domestic audience than on foreign observers. Even so, persistence and imagination will be rewarded with some impact on the target government's reputation and, therefore, on its foreign capabilities and freedom of action. The Reagan administration's propaganda campaign against Qaddafi was intended to limit both and, possibly, to foster internal and external opposition to his government. Although the choice may seem a puzzling one initially, I have included as part of the propaganda campaign the accusations that Qaddafi had sent assassination teams into the United States to murder President Reagan and other high officials. This is not because I doubt the president believed Qaddafi had done this. He appeared to believe it all very sincerely. In any case good propaganda always has an element of truth in it. The "hit-squad" charges are discussed here because they — and the withdrawal of the U.S. ambassador from Italy — were handled in a way that maximized their propaganda impact and departed significantly from the customary way such problems are handled. Moreover, while the Reagan administration may have looked a little silly before the controversy ended, it may well have accomplished its propaganda goal of further denigrating Qaddafi — in this case by branding him as an assassin in people's minds — even though its own credibility suffered a bit in the process. While the White House may have looked foolish Qaddafi once again looked sinister, as a result of the manner in which the administration handled the "hit-squad scare." Sometimes, the administration needed to do very little. It was enough to give the right slant to facts supplied during an interview. The journalists and editors involved would do the rest as they sought to gain maximum notoriety for their investigative reporting. This was the case during the spring and summer of 1981. The revelations and articles kept appearing again and again.

Starting in July there were stories every week about some aspect of Libyan terrorism, usually on the involvement of American nationals in training and assisting the Libyans, people like Edwin Wilson and Frank Terpil, or noncommissioned Green Berets, or aircraft mechanics, or explosives experts. In part this serialized melodrama on the evils of Muammar Qaddafi was accidental. The arrest of Eugene Tafoya on April 22, for example, was obviously not timed for any special effect by the Reagan administration. One has to assume, as well, that the front-page exposés in the New York Times of the bizarre and deadly games played by Wilson and Terpil and others in Qaddafi's pay were the work of hard-working, hard-headed independent investigative journalists who had seen smoke and began to look for fire.

Before the assassination of Anwar Sadat the Reagan administration was content to try to influence opinion about Qaddafi at the margin, by slanting the information given reporters, or leaking information about the grand jury inquiry into the activities of Wilson and Terpil, or with great fanfare, by bringing together all the law enforcement agencies investigating the involvement of American nationals in illegal acts on behalf of Libya.(15) A good example of this approach during the first stage of the anti-Libya propaganda campaign may be found in two articles by Bernard Nossiter in May on the closure of the people's bureau and the growth of opposition to Qaddafi among Libyan exiles. A second example is the announcement in late September that the Justice Department had decided to coordinate the variety of investigations being conducted around the country into the actions of Americans who broke the law in Qaddafi's service.

On May 23 the New York Times published an article by Bernard Nossiter on U.S.-Libyan relations. State Department officials were now saying, Nossiter reported, that the arrest of Eugene Tafoya on April 22 for the attack on Faisal Zagallai had been the "catalytic incident" that led to the expulsion of the Libyan diplomats several weeks later. The officials added that the expulsion was part of an administration effort to expose the "official use of terror by the Libyan Government."(16) However, this was not what officials had told reporters on May 6 when the people's bureau was closed and the Libyan diplomats were ordered to leave the United States within five days. At that time the official explanation was that the closure and expulsion had been ordered in response to "a wide range of Libyan provocations and misconduct, including support for international terrorism." When asked to be specific about Libyan misconduct officials had mentioned the Libyan intervention in Chad, efforts to destabilize Egypt and Sudan, and Libyan efforts to murder Qaddafi's opponents abroad.(17) In other words, in late May the administration decided to emphasize the "Qaddafi-as-terrorist" theme. It also chose to portray Qaddafi as politically insecure, for Nossiter was also told by the, as usual, unnamed State Department officials that the attack on Zagallai was evidence of Qaddafi's internal weakness. Despite Qaddafi's elaborate internal security apparatus, set up by the East Germans, more and more Libyans were opposing Qaddafi and defecting from his regime all over the world.

Qaddafi's opposition was the subject of another article by Nossiter that appeared three days later. The article was clearly a follow-up story generated by the earlier comments on Qaddafi's political insecurity and recent reports about the existence of a secret administration plan to overthrow Qaddafi (to be discussed later). The headlines on the second Nossiter article show its drift. "Qaddafi Opposition Is Getting Stronger" was the title on page one. Inside, the heading proclaimed: "Libyan Opposition to Qaddafi is Both Prominent and Expanding." However, the actual content of the story gives a much more ambiguous impression than the titles ought to permit. Basing his article on interviews with State Department officials and an "Arab diplomat familiar with Libyan affairs" Nossiter listed a number of Libyan defectors. The list included Qaddafi's first prime minister, Mahmoud Maghreby; former members of the Revolutionary Council, Abdel Moneim el-Houni and Abdullah Meheishi; several ambassadors, Mohammed Mogaryef, Mansur Rashid Kikhia, and Ezzedin Ghadamsi; and a number of other prominent defectors: Yahia Omar, Fadel Massoudi, Amnad Hwas, and Ahmed Shetwey. In addition, Nossiter pointed out that the Libyan opposition in exile was badly split into groups of conservatives, leftists, Islamic fundamentalists, liberals. So far several opposition groups had formed. They had managed to smuggle leaflets into Libya attacking Qaddafi, but little else. Although Qaddafi feared the exiles and had struck at many of them, he had virtually eliminated any internal danger to his government. "The balance of force within Libya is in Qaddafi's favor," Nossiter quoted his Arab source, who added: "The country is not dead." Inexplicably, Nossiter took this to mean that a "domestic underground" exists inside Libya. There then followed a number of statements about Libyan society and politics culled from articles published previously. Qaddafi took extraordinary measures to protect himself and his government. Army officers were transferred every few months. They weren't allowed to enter the enlisted men's barracks after 3 P.M. Qaddafi had stopped his habit of making impromptu public appearances; he now lived in a heavily fortified barracks in Tripoli. Despite oil revenues of $25 billion a year Libya was chronically short of food and other necessities and lacked skilled administrators.

The cumulative impression of the article was that Qaddafi's regime was politically weak, foolish, oppressive, and ripe for overthrow. Looked at coldly, none of the facts in the article justified such a conclusion, but when taken as a whole along with the exaggerated headlines, the message was clear. At the same time, the article implicitly raised questions about the role of outside powers, such as Egypt or the United States, in the overthrow of Qaddafi. If the opposition to Qaddafi were growing, as the headlines put it, or were feared by Qaddafi as Nossiter reported, it was nonetheless clear from the article that help would be needed for any serious attempt to bring down the Libyan regime. It looked very much as if the primary purpose of Nossiter's informants was to raise the possibility of U.S. assistance to Qaddafi's enemies.(18) A much more skeptical article, published several weeks earlier in the Washington Post, had raised the question directly. Qaddafi had crushed dissent in Libya, the author wrote. He had thoroughly cowed his opponents, driven some into exile, murdered others. In order for a coup to succeed there would have to be both internal unrest and U.S. support of Qaddafi's opponents. This raised the question of the Reagan administration's attitude toward helping the nascent opposition movements.(19) Again, one is led toward the view that U.S. officials wished to talk about the relatively harmless Libyan opposition groups in order to use the threat of U.S. aid to them as a means of increasing U.S. pressure on Qaddafi.

In late September, after the furor over the air combat in the Gulf of Sidra had subsided, the administration contrived to keep the publicity on Qaddafi-as-terrorist by appointing a senior attorney in the Justice Department to coordinate all the federal elements of the investigation into Wilson and Terpil. The appointment was made at the instigation of Attorney General William French Smith and the director of the FBI, William Webster. The administration had begun a major review of Libyan policy in September and the decision to provide better coordination of the Wilson-Terpil cases may have been Justice's contribution to that review. The review may also have been undertaken in order to enable Justice to cope more effectively with a full-scale congressional investigation into the Wilson-Terpil affair. Earlier in September the House Select Committee on Intelligence had announced its intention not only to study the case thoroughly but to look into how well the government had conducted the investigation into the activities of the two former CIA agents turned mercenaries.(20)

Anwar Sadat was assassinated by Islamic zealots on October 6, 1981. Just a few days before his death Hosni Mubarak, then Sadat's vice-president, was in Washington. Publicly, Mubarak sought increased military aid for Egypt and Sudan. In private, his mission was to obtain U.S. support for an Egyptian-Sudanese strike against Libyan forces in Chad.(21) Although there was no evidence of Libyan complicity in the Egyptian leader's death, the Reagan administration exploited the assassination to take a number of flashy but low-risk steps meant to intimidate Qaddafi, such as the use of B-52s in Operation Brightstar and a closer embrace of Nimeiry's Sudan. These are discussed in detail in Chapter 13. However, the hottest angle on Libyan-U.S. relations in the fall of 1981 concerned Libyan plots to assassinate the president of the United States and other high U.S. officials. As had become routine in Libyan-U.S. relations the drama was played simultaneously in secret and in public with both parties publicizing secret "intelligence" information when it suited them. By this time Libyan-U.S. relations had deteriorated to the level of name-calling. Accusations of serious wrongdoing were traded, and to some U.S. observers the public clamor resembled the preparations of the U.S. government for the invasion of Castro's Cuba at the Bay of Pigs. Sadat's assassination does appear to have intensified the anti-Qaddafi propaganda efforts of the Reagan administration.

This round in the propaganda campaign against Libya opened with a Libyan salvo. Speaking to the General Assembly one day after Sadat's murder, the Libyan official Abdel-Ati Obeidi, who had been denied permission to visit Washington, accused the United States of conspiring to assassinate Qaddafi.(22) A week later the first U.S. "leak" appeared in Jack Anderson's gossip column. The leak soon became a trickle and then a roaring torrent of newspaper articles and television reports. On October 13 Jack Anderson published an inflammatory story leaked to one of his associates. Presumably the informant was American, although Anderson did not say so, which meant the initial source of the tip could have been Israeli or Egyptian. Anderson's informant said that after the aerial dogfight the previous August, Qaddafi had telephoned the Ethiopian leader Mengistu. During their conversation Qaddafi had vowed that he would revenge the loss of the two Libyan warplanes by having Reagan assassinated. The call had been intercepted and translated by the U.S. National Security Agency, and a transcript had been sent to the White House. This wasn't the first Libyan threat against Reagan, Anderson asserted. A week before the air combat took place, a Libyan group, the Free Unionist officers, had publicly threatened to attack U.S. interests and to murder Americans, beginning with Reagan, if any harm came to Qaddafi, according to Anderson. What the gossip columnist didn't say was that the Free Unionists' threat, which Anderson presumably had traced and verified, came at about the same time that stories were appearing in the U.S. media of planning in the Reagan administration to overthrow Qaddafi. Although he did not place the Libyan reaction in its proper context, Anderson admitted that Qaddafi might have been provoked into making threats against Reagan. Quoting unnamed "intelligence officials" Anderson repeated one of his earlier "revelations." In July, he alleged, Edwin Wilson had met secretly in Rome with U.S. officials ostensibly to discuss the charges against him in the United States. Those he met included a CIA station chief, who tried and failed to gain Wilson's cooperation in the assassination of Qaddafi by a poisoned dart made to look like a black fly.(23) The

CIA denied the assassination plot and denied that the Rome meeting took place.

The United States then chose to engage in a show of force to strengthen the friendly governments of Egypt and Sudan. As part of Operation Brightstar, B-52 bombers were sent to bomb targets in western Egypt, while AWACS planes patrolled and U.S. troops landed in Egypt, Sudan, Somalia, and Oman. Pointedly, reporters were told of "intensive planning" with Egypt just before Sadat's death "for a combined response to a Libyan attack on the Sudan or other Soviet-backed aggression in North Africa . . . including a possible Egyptian invasion of Libya." Other contingencies shared with reporters included the dispatch of the Sixth Fleet to the Gulf of Sidra to divide the Libyan air force and intimidate oil tanker owners whose ships might be carrying oil out of Libya, if Libya attacked Sudan or took other dangerous actions. "Those two jets were a sample," a U.S. official said. "We are prepared to go to the legal limits."(24) Into this tense, warlike aftermath of Sadat's murder came widely publicized reports of a Libyan plot to assassinate the U.S. ambassador to Italy, Maxwell Rabb, 71, a Jew, a Reagan supporter, and a long-time Republican (he had campaigned for Eisenhower).

In its October 19 issue Newsweek reported that Qaddafi was behind a plot uncovered and scotched by Italian police to kill Ambassador Rabb. Reporters and editors from other news organizations jumped on the story. Quoting State Department officials the New York Times a week later confirmed the plot against Rabb. Italian police had learned of the attempt to kill the ambassador on October 14 while he was on a visit in Milan. He was immediately given a heavy guard and flown out of Italy without even a change of clothes. A "diplomatic source with detailed knowledge of the incident" said the assassination was to have been an act of revenge for the two lost Libyan planes. Ten people were involved, according to the Times' informant, including "top Libyan intelligence officers." Appointed by Reagan on June 24 the elderly, Jewish, very Republican Rabb, had been chosen as a symbolic target. Some U.S. officials in Washington and at the U.S. embassy in Rome denied the ambassador had been evacuated as a precaution against assassination. Their story was that he had been called home to help in the administration-wide approval for the sale of AWACS to Saudi Arabia. This time "a government source in a position to have intimate knowledge of the events" said no: Rabb had been recalled because of a murder plot. Ambassador Rabb returned to Rome on October 31.(25)

Shortly after Rabb's return to his post, Newsweek again carried an ominous story about Libyan mayhem again based on information supplied by senior U.S. government insiders. "U.S. intelligence," said Newsweek, had concluded that Qaddafi would sent Libyan terrorists to attack the buildings and grounds that make up the U.S. embassies in London, Paris, Vienna, and Rome. "He's gone from individuals to institutions" was the way one official described it.(26) This report was followed within days by what was apparently an assassination attempt against the U.S. chargé in Paris, Christian Chapman. A lone attacker emptied his pistol at Chapman as he left his residence on the way to work on the morning of November 12. Chapman escaped injury. He told newsmen later that the embassy had no evidence to link the shooting to any specific group or country. Testifying before the House Foreign Affairs Committee, Secretary of State Alexander Haig indicated that the Reagan administration viewed the shooting differently. Although there was no definite information about the assassin, Haig said, he wished to "underline once again that we do have repeated reports that come from reliable sources that Mr. Qaddafi has been funding, sponsoring, training, harboring terrorist groups who conduct activities against the lives and well-being of American diplomats and facilities."(27) The Libyan agency JANA denied Haig's accusation the same day. The general Libyan response throughout this period was to deny all U.S. charges and to insist that the United States was preparing public opinion to accept a direct U.S. attack on Libya.(28) On November 15 Reuters news agency reported from Beirut that the Lebanese Revolutionary Armed Faction, Salgh el-Misri Group, claimed responsibility for the attack on Chapman.

About this time NBC television news reported that security precautions for the president and vice-president had been significantly augmented after U.S. intelligence learned Qaddafi had ordered the assassination of President Reagan.(29) A few days later the Washington _Post_ put the assassination story on its front page. Security had been tightened, the _Post_ reported, because of intelligence reports that Libyan assassination teams were trying to enter the United States. The secretaries of state and defense had also been given additional protection as would, before long, the president's chief advisors Edwin Meese, James Baker, and Michael Deaver.(30) A front-page story in the New York _Times_, quoting "top Federal law enforcement officers," stated that five terrorists trained in Libya entered the United States during the weekend of November 30-December 1 with orders to kill the president or other high officials. A "huge nationwide search" was underway for the killers and for Americans who might help them, such as veterans of the U.S. Special Forces, or others with mercenary experience.(31)

Much of the information about the assassination plot came from an informer — allegedly a Lebanese terrorist — who defected in Western Europe. He claimed to have helped plan the assassinations and to have participated in the training of the assassins at a secret terrorist camp in Sebha, Libya. The assassins planned to choose among a number of methods to kill their victims. According to the informant they could shoot down Air Force One with a surface-to-air missile, destroy the president's limousine with a rocket, or shoot him or others with small arms at close range. The informant had been questioned by the FBI, the CIA, and the Secret Service. He had taken and passed several lie detector tests. His evidence, in other words, was believable if not finally convincing. It was certainly credible enough for the U.S. government to react by increasing the protection given to the apparent targets. As one "intelligence source" told the Washington Post: "We frankly don't know whether it is fact or fiction. But we can't afford to think in terms of how well [the informant] is to be trusted . . . we have got to act."(32) No one could quarrel with a prudent response of this kind. The wonder was not in the extra protection afforded Ronald Reagan but in all the fuss made in public about the whole affair. There were so many "senior administration officials" and "intelligence sources" ready to talk to the press that one had to conclude, at a minimum, that the administration had not ordered U.S. officials to play down the plot and refuse to comment.

For nearly a month the information continued to spill out of the administration. In a highly unusual step, the president himself took strong public stands about the plot. Returning from a fund-raising dinner in Cincinnati, for example, on board Air Force One, the president told the Cleveland Plain Dealer that he believed the intelligence reports should not be dismissed out of hand. Two days later he said he was concerned about the plots and believed they had to be taken seriously. At the peak of the controversy Qaddafi was interviewed by satellite on David Brinkley's television program. He denied everything. In fact, he denied too much: "It is not our character, not our behavior, to assassinate any person." The United States, on the other hand, had tried to poison his food many times. He demanded evidence and called for an investigation. He called the president a "liar," "silly," "ignorant," and "not qualified to lead the United States." Reagan responded: "We have the evidence, and he knows it . . . I wouldn't believe a thing that man says."(33)

Still, the information poured out. ABC television news reported on December 4 that the United States had "partially identified" some of the members of the hit-teams, by name and composite drawing. On December 6 "authoritative sources" confirmed that a detailed but somewhat puzzling report existed which dealt with a ten-man Libyan assassination squad under orders to assassinate President Reagan and his top cabinet officers, including Haig and Weinberger. Their names and aliases were given, and also where they were trained. Some were said to have been trained in Eastern Europe. About this time the San Diego Union printed a story based on a handout given to an office of the Immigration and Naturalization Service at a Mexican border-crossing. In the handout were the names, aliases, and origins of the members of two Libyan assassination teams, along with pictures of them made from composite drawings. The first team was headed by the notorious Carlos and was said to have six other members, including three Syrians and two

Libyans. The second team had five men, two Iranians, and an East German, a Palestinian, and a Lebanese. The names of Team 1: Ilich Ramirez Sanchez (Carlos); Hasan Al-Khayer, Ali Ahmed, Walid Abdul Rahman (all Syrian); Omar Ayad and Ali Saghayer (Libyan); and Milad Mohammed el-Hadi; of Team 2: Ahmed Juma and Ibrahim el-Naya (Iranian); Luitz Schweseman (East German); Ahmat Abass (Palestinian). With outrage and excitement at a peak in the United States, the House of Representatives passed an amendment to the Foreign Aid Bill condemning Libya for "its support of international terrorism" and directing the president to report to the Congress within six months on economic sanctions or other steps taken against Libya.(34)

The Reagan administration chose this moment to recall all Americans from Libya. On December 10, with Secretary Haig in Brussels for a NATO conference, Deputy Secretary of State William Clark announced that the administration had ordered U.S. passports invalidated for travel to Libya. The president was prepared to use all legal means, if that were necessary, Clark said, to require Americans to leave Libya. The recall had been issued, according to Clark, because of Qaddafi's well-known efforts over the course of many years "to undermine U.S. interests and those of our friends, as well as Libya's support for international terrorism." Plainly, the recall was ordered both to protect American nationals and to warn Libya, in the administration's terms, "to cease its lawless actions." Other steps against Libya were still under consideration. An oil boycott had been under consideration since September. The same day he ordered the recall, the president warned Libya through a third country that the most severe consequences would result if any Americans were killed on Libyan orders. Administration officials told reporters that the president had at least three military actions in mind: a naval blockade, to stop food imports and oil exports; a strike by B-52s against Qaddafi's terrorist camps; and the bombing of Libyan oil fields.(35)

To the surprise of the administration its reports about the Libyan assassination squads were treated with a great deal of skepticism, both in the United States and abroad. In part this came from the administration's refusal to release evidence of any kind or to reveal anything about how it had learned about the Libyan plot, other than to mention an "informant" in the vaguest terms. The skepticism also came from a strong suspicion among some journalists that the administration was using the assassination plot to shock U.S. opinion into acceptance of some drastic and probably military action against Libya. This proved to be a false concern. Only a weak preliminary step – the recall of Americans – was actually ordered, but this came as a huge anticlimax after the remarkable and blood curdling build-up that had preceded it.

One of the most persuasive skeptics was Haynes Johnson. Writing in the Washington Post on December 8, Johnson argued that the administration was "setting a new standard of incredibility" with its various intelligence reports on the Libyan assassination squads. Johnson wasn't dubious about the notion that Qaddafi might try such a thing. Rather, it was "the public nature of the accusations" that troubled him. If the Libyan leader actually had laid plans to kill President Reagan and the United States found out about it, would it be handled so openly? And wouldn't there be a stronger response against Libya? The administration had for days been building a "concerted case" that Qaddafi had sent assassins into the United States to kill the president. The television news programs and the newspapers were full of stories of terrorists infiltrating into the country, of the FBI mobilizing to capture them, of heavily armed SWAT teams on the roof of the White House, of pictures of Libyan soldiers shooting down helicopters. Despite these efforts, Johnson observed, the U.S. public was not convinced but had suspended judgment until the administration came up with more evidence. Meanwhile the administration continued to give "the highest official blessings to the widest circulation of the most sensational stories to reach the public in years." No opportunity was missed to attack Qaddafi. Even Presidents Carter and Ford had used their trip to Sadat's funeral to get at the Libyan dictator: Carter had called him "sub-human"; Ford had said Qaddafi was a "cancer" on that part of the globe and had openly spoken of U.S. action against him. It all reminded Haynes Johnson of the talk about Castro when the U.S. government was planning the Bay of Pigs and had ordered Castro's assassination. One had to wonder if public opinion were being prepared for a military attack on Libya or Qaddafi.

Another skeptical view comparing European and U.S. assessments of Qaddafi appeared in the New York Times on November 28. To many Europeans, the Reagan administration's view of Qaddafi was a "deliberate oversimplification" based on what quite probably was "tainted" information supplied by other self-interested governments, such as Egypt or Israel. According to the Los Angeles Times, Israeli intelligence had supplied most of the sensational information about the assassination plot.(36) Moreover, the Europeans believed the Reagan approach would harm Western interests in Libyan oil and drive the Libyans even further toward the Soviet Union. In this view, Qaddafi is admittedly anti-West. However, he is not seen to be as dangerous as the Reagan administration believes and has often failed, as he did in Uganda and Chad. The Europeans also believed that Reagan's was a poor way to deal with Qaddafi. Washington has no communication at all with Libya, but there must be talks if Western interests are to be protected and Libya kept from growing closer to the Soviet Union. The Western oil interests in Libya provide a counter to Soviet military and political influence in Libya and earn a great deal of money for Western companies. Both advantages are worth keeping. Finally, the Europeans feel that Reagan has singled out Qaddafi as an arch-villain in response to domestic political considerations rather than foreign circumstances. The PLO, for example, is regarded as a terrorist organization by the Reagan administration, while in other countries the PLO is seen as a legitimate nationalist group.(37)

While one might, perhaps, quibble over the accuracy of this rendering of European opinion, it was undeniably what Secretary Haig encountered in Brussels when he pressed his NATO colleagues to join the United States in opposing Qaddafi. At a news conference after the Brussels meeting Haig criticized European governments for their double standard of morality that justified "business as usual" with Qaddafi. To the Europeans, Haig was inconsistent and wrong. Haig's remarks were inconsistent because at $610 million for the first nine months of 1981, U.S. exports to Libya had nearly doubled the total for the same period in 1980. This included many militarily important exports, such as heavy Oshkosh trucks, the microwave communications systems sold to Libya by such companies as Cortronic Systems International of Virginia; and Comtech Telecommunications Group of New York; or the high frequency two-way radio equipment sold by RF Communications of New York. Moreover, the United States continued to import large quantities of Libyan oil. The total amount imported had fallen in 1981 because of Libya's high price rather than U.S. government restrictions. Haig was wrong in European eyes because it was the wrong approach at the wrong time. The French in particular emphasized Qaddafi's withdrawal from Chad and asserted that Libya was no longer expanding into foreign countries. After the Brussels conference French Foreign Minister Claude Cheysson pointedly said "To isolate Libya, not to try to have relations with it, would be an error."(38) Gamely, the administration responded that it was the right time to increase the pressure against Qaddafi. His oil income was down. The worldwide glut of oil offered a perfect chance to cut even further into Libyan income by turning to other suppliers. Admittedly, there were specific U.S. concerns. As Libya's biggest customer, the United States in effect paid Qaddafi to harm U.S. and Western interests. "We are paying for his depredations," as one senior officer put it.

There was also the reputation of the United States as a strong ally of friendly Middle Eastern governments to consider. Many Arabs thought Washington was obsessed with Qaddafi and, as a result, was actually building him into a far more important figure than he would otherwise had been. The U.S. threats against Qaddafi – the Gulf of Sidra incident, Operation Brightstar – had even created sympathy for Libya as it was forced to deal with what one Kuwaiti newspaper called "cowboy diplomacy." No one in the Arab world regarded two million Libyans, many of whom had scarcely left their previous nomadic life as Bedouins, as a threat to the United States, regardless of how many Green Beret mercenaries and Soviet weapons Qaddafi bought. Qaddafi's Green Book was ridiculed in the Arab world, and his untried 50,000 troops were hardly a match for the combat-hardened Egyptian army of 361,000. "Just becaue Qaddafi claims to be a leader or a commander does not make it so," as an Arab diplomat in Beirut told the New York Times.(39)

But this coin had another side. To U.S. policymakers Qaddafi had to be taught a lesson precisely because he was so unimportant. If the United States was unable to stop "a known murderer, terrorist, and invader," in the words of the ubiquitous "senior U.S. official," would Saudi Arabia believe that the United States would come to its aid? "The fact that a country as weak as Libya can get away with as much as it does is a signal to the rest of the Arab world about our willingness to use military power."(40)

Despite the skepticism about the reports of Libyan assassination squads, the administration had its defenders in the press. Joseph Kraft argued, not altogether convincingly, that "Machiavellian foreign policy calculations" played no part in the release of the intelligence reports about Libyan hit-squads entering the United States to kill President Reagan. Instead, Kraft said, the political exploitation didn't begin until after Qaddafi attacked Reagan on television. The administration then was presented with a target of "incomparable unpopularity." At that point the decision was made to inflate the Libya-U.S. confrontation. The results had not been all that satisfying from the U.S. point of view. Even so, "nothing like a concerted campaign has been under way" against Qaddafi. There were no anti-Qaddafi propaganda broadcasts being beamed into Libya, Kraft said. Requests from friendly Arab governments for help against Qaddafi had been brushed aside. In opposing Qaddafi in Chad, the United States had followed the French lead and relied heavily on the African nations opposed to Qaddafi. The leaks about the assassination teams could upset such delicate diplomatic maneuvers. Implausibly, Kraft insisted that just because of Qaddafi's televised attack on Reagan, the president had convened two meetings of the National Security Council and had allowed his subordinates to suggest that the United States would make a strong response to Libya.(41)

Kraft's goodwill and his desire to restore a sense of due proportion to the whole affair are evident and commendable. But his version of events doesn't hold water. First, Qaddafi didn't appear on television and call Reagan names until December 6. By that time the controversy was raging. "Top Federal law enforcement officials" told the New York Times on December 3 of reports that a Libyan hit-team had entered the United States. "Senior intelligence officials" had already blamed Qaddafi for the attack on Christian Chapman in Paris and the attempt on Ambassador Rabb in Italy.(42) There were countless other stories given by officials to the media before Qaddafi's appearance on David Brinkley's show: stories about the informant, about the validity of his reports, about the extra protection given high officials. Above all, the president himself had publicly said on several occasions that he took the threat seriously.

As late as December 17, when other members of the administration were trying to minimize the affair the president was still asserting that "the threat was real," and that he had "complete confidence" in the veracity of the reports.(43)

William Safire offered a more plausible explanation of the administration's handling of the assassination threat. Disclaiming any specific inside information Safire argued that the very willingness of the Reagan administration to contradict Qaddafi publicly demonstrated its total confidence that it would never be embarrassed later if the whole story came out. Therefore, Safire concluded, there was a Libyan plot to kill the president. The interesting question was whether or not it was a good idea to publicize it. Safire, in other words, believed the "leaks" had been authorized more or less from the beginning. Constructing an imaginary policy debate inside the administration, Safire suggested that the White House and State Department had probably favored publicity. The White House argument might have been as follows: if there is no publicity and an attack occurs, there will be heavy criticism of the administration for laxness and incompetence; if there is publicity and an attack occurs anyway, then the public basis for a severe reprisal will have been laid. The Secretary of State, Safire felt, might have argued in favor of publicity in order to "escalate the war of nerves with Qaddafi."(44) In what was also a generally favorable view of the administration's handling of the affair, a Washington Post editorial suggested that the furor over the assassination teams had started with an "unauthorized leak not an authorized one." The distinction was important, the Post argued. If the leak were officially sanctioned, the administration had displayed a foolish willingness to compromise its intelligence sources and a "disconcerting readiness" to raise public expectations of an official reprisal against Libya. An unauthorized leak, as appeared to have happened, meant "merely" that the Reagan administration had been unable to control the "public play," that is the immense controversy that burst out when the Libyan threat against the president became known.(45) The whole truth about the Libyan assassination teams may never be known. It is clear, however, that the administration exploited the public outcry and used it to smooth the way both for the imposition of further sanctions against Qaddafi and the strengthening of the U.S. position in North Africa and the Gulf.

Immediately after the president ordered Americans to leave Libya, the administration began to play down the assassination squads and, implicitly, the drastic military responses that had been mentioned so casually to reporters as appropriate punishments for a nation plotting to assassinate the president of the United States. The whole thing had been exaggerated, FBI officials told reporters. "It's been blown way out of proportion," one said. There was a serious threat, the Secret Service and intelligence officials told Philip Taubman of the New York Times, but the unauthorized release of the reports about the assassination squads had led to "unplanned reactions and exaggerations" by the administration and the press. The first reports of a Libyan assassination plot had come in September, after the air combat. They were dismissed as too reckless. But then there was the plot against Ambassador Rabb and the shooting at Chapman in Paris. Concern mounted. Then came the informer's bombshells in November. It was not, therefore, just a question of responding to information from one defecting terrorist but of putting a stop to a campaign of calculated violence directed against the government of the United States.

On December 17, Senator Majority Leader Howard Baker told reporters that the threat from the Libyan hit-squads had "diminished some." Although this was immediately denied by a White House spokesman, perhaps because the president had just announced that the "threat was real," the direction of the administration was clearly away from confrontation. On Christmas Day, "U.S. analysts with access to the latest top-secret information" told reporters that the Libyan hit-squads had "suspended their operations." This was confirmed two weeks later by "senior American officials" who said Qaddafi had "postponed" or "cancelled" plans to kill the president.(46) From beginning to end, as George Wilson of the Post observed, the affair was "shadowy" and the evidence "mushy." A kind interpretation that may be accurate was offered to Philip Taubman of the Times after the dust had settled. A "senior Administration official familiar with National Security Council deliberations on Libya" told him that the administration had purposely exploited the hit-squad stories. However, the sanctions against Libya had been under consideration for several months. "He said the assassination threat gave the Administration a dramatic basis for imposing [sanctions] last week. It wasn't artificial; just lucky timing."

Even if one accepts this generous view of the affair, the administration's handling of the assassination-squad reports raises a number of disturbing questions. Was this the best way to protect the president, or did it actually draw the attention of terrorists to him and thus increase his vulnerability? What foreign policy purpose was served by the publicity? Admittedly Qaddafi's reputation may have been further tarred, but at the price of what loss of administration credibility? Didn't the reports of an informant "defecting" to the United States from what, purportedly, was a highly sensitive, secret position in the Libyan government, focus attention on the possibility of U.S. infiltration of the Libyan government, thereby endangering other covert agents of the United States still in place there? What of the readiness to threaten the massive use of force against Libya and its striking display during Operation Brightstar? Most troubling of all was the disproportion between these hypothetical and displayed threats and the step actually taken by the administration: the recall of Americans from Libya. If Qaddafi had actually set on foot a plot to kill the president, a much more serious punishment than this was warranted, even if it had to wait until after the withdrawal of Americans had been completed. No such punishment ever came. Three months later the administration ordered a boycott of Libyan oil and the embargo of the export of high technology equipment to that country. The oil boycott had little meaning because imports of Libyan oil had fallen very low. The technology would be missed by Libya, but only for a relatively short while. Neither punishment was commensurate to a threat to murder a president.

It is tempting to regard the leaks that surfaced in August 1981 about the existence of a CIA plan to overthrow Qaddafi as part of the administration's campaign against Libya. When the leak came the Libyan government was certainly alarmed and concerned to learn that such a plan had apparently been approved by the CIA director, William Casey, and his deputy for covert operations, Max Hugel, and that Hugel had presented the plan to the Congress for approval. The Reagan administration was determined to produce alarm and concern in Tripoli about some kind of drastic U.S. action against Libya as a means of forcing Qaddafi to withdraw from Chad and refrain from other foreign interventions. Therefore, it is quite possible that the leak was intentional and meant as a warning to Qaddafi. At the same time, the circumstances in which the leak appeared made it difficult to give a categorical judgment about the reasons why the plan to overthrow Qaddafi became public. The first public suggestion that the administration was considering a plan to bring down Qaddafi came in an article in the New York Daily News in mid-May, not long after the closing of the people's bureau in Washington. "A secret administration plan existed," the Daily News said, "to topple Qaddafi using Arab states friendly to this country." The State Department denied that such a plan existed.(47) The public heard of an anti-Libyan plan again three months later, under quite different circumstances.

William J. Casey, a flamboyant businessman and former member of the OSS, the precursor of the CIA, had been Reagan's nominee to be director of Central Intelligence. Casey in turn named Max Hugel, a fast-lane business executive without any espionage experience whatsoever, to be the CIA's chief of covert operations, or a nation's "chief spy," in the words of Senator Barry Goldwater, chairman of the Senate Select Committee on Intelligence. Hugel resigned in July because of criticism of his past business practices. Casey himself was under attack for alleged improprieties committed on behalf of Multiponics, Inc., an agricultural business in which he had an interest. Casey was eventually cleared of having acted illegally in his work for Multiponics, but not before submitting to an extensive investigation by the Senate Intelligence Committee.(48) The inquiry into Casey's business record was conducted in a non-partisan spirit. It was Republican senators, such as Barry Goldwater (Ariz.), Ted Stevens (Alaska), and William Roth (Del.) who called for

Casey's resignation and not Democrats such as Henry Jackson (Wash.) who urged his colleagues not to prejudge Casey, or Daniel Patrick Moynihan (N.Y.), deputy chairman of the Intelligence Committee, who announced he would play the Casey investigation "straight down the middle."

However, there were ideological and partisan elements to the controversy. In keeping with its tough overall foreign policy the Reagan administration wanted to "unleash" the CIA, that is, to amend its charter in order to enable the organization to conduct more aggressive covert operations. This was opposed by many members of Congress, liberals and Democrats, for the most part, and apparently by Admiral Bobby Ray Inman, deputy director of the CIA who, as former head of the National Security Agency, was a career intelligence officer. Inman was not popular at the White House and soon resigned because of policy differences. During the controversy over Casey's business dealings and after Goldwater urged Casey to resign, White House officials felt it would be prudent to tell reporters they had begun to look for a replacement for Casey. Inman's name was not on the list. Thus, the leaks about the plan to overthrow Qaddafi occurred against a background of serious ideological and partisan differences within the Congress and major policy disagreement inside the executive branch. It could well be that the leaks were the result of the clash of ideologies and bureaucratic political maneuvering rather than a desire to intimidate Qaddafi.

During the investigation into Casey's taxes and business activities, reporters were told by "Congressional sources" and perhaps by others, as well, that Casey's judgment and not his corporate ethics was the subject of greatest concern. Then came the leak. In its August 3 edition, issued in late July, Newsweek reported that Casey and Hugel had approved a "large-scale, multiphase, and costly scheme" to overthrow Qaddafi and perhaps to kill him. The plan had three stages, according to Newsweek: a "disinformation program designed to embarrass Qaddafi and his government . . . the creation of a 'counter government' to challenge his claim to national leadership [and] . . . an escalating paramilitary campaign, probably by disaffected Libyan nationals, to blow up bridges, conduct small-scale guerrilla operations and demonstrate that Qaddafi was opposed by an indigenous political force."(49) The cost was large enough to force the CIA to obtain Congressional consent to carry out the full operation, Newsweek was told, although it could have been launched without Congressional consent. Hugel presented the plan to the House Intelligence Committee. Alarmed and skeptical, its members took the unusual step of sending "a strongly worded letter of protest directly to President Reagan."

It is difficult for an open, democratic society to control secret intelligence agencies without sacrificing their vital contribution to national security. This has resulted in the creation of complex and awkward procedures in the United States, particularly when the public and Congress have lost confidence in the judgment and competence of the executive branch. At present there are a major piece of legislation and an executive order that control the nation's intelligence agencies. In addition Congress and the president together also authorize the agencies' budgets and spending, which is a powerful instrument of control. The major piece of legislation is Public Law 96-450 which sets guidelines for Congressional oversight. Passed in 1980 when Congress failed to write a new intelligence charter, PL96-450 significantly eased the legal restraints on U.S. intelligence agencies. It changed the procedures for notifying Congress of covert operations; reduced the number of congressional committees that must be informed of covert operations from 8 to 2 – an intelligence committee in each chamber; required the executive to give full and current information on intelligence activities to the committees; determined that the committees may not block intelligence operations; allowed the president to limit prior notice to the chairmen and ranking minority members of each committee, and even to forgo prior notice altogether, although he is obliged to explain his postponement of notification.(50) In addition, the Congress passes and the president ratifies the budgets of the CIA and other intelligence agencies. Any major new expenditures of funds as was apparently necessary in the anti-Qaddafi plan, or any reprogramming of funds for covert operations and away from expenditures for programs already approved by the Congress would require new legislative approval. Casey approved such "hare-brained" schemes too easily, "Congressional sources" said. Although Casey denied the CIA planned to kill Qaddafi, the House Committee, in the words of another source, "just doesn't trust Casey" and took its misgivings directly to the president. Ultimately, the leaks and the misgivings of influential senators failed to force Casey out of office. However, the public discussion of the anti-Qaddafi plan undoubtedly alarmed the Libyan government, even if that was not the primary intention of the leakers.

13
SHOWDOWN

The decision of the Reagan administration to put military pressure on Qaddafi was taken months before Sadat's death. It took the form of a carefully prepared air and naval challenge to Libya's claim to sovereignty over the Gulf of Sidra and, after Sadat's assassination, the dramatic use of U.S. strategic bombers in an expanded military maneuver – Operation Bright Star – in which the United States, Egypt, Sudan, Somalia, and Oman took part. The heightened military pressure deeply alarmed Qaddafi and his associates and undoubtedly contributed to their decision to withdraw from Chad.

At the time of the air clash over the Gulf of Sidra on August 20, 1981, the Reagan administration had already decided to do everything it could feasibly arrange to "tie up" the Libyan dictator.(1) The very first "interdepartmental foreign policy study" ordered by the new administration was an exploration of ways to oppose Qaddafi. Before long, "authoritative sources" were telling journalists that the administration had drawn up a plan intended at the least "to make life uncomfortable" for Qaddafi. Virtually from the moment he took office Secretary of State Haig denounced Qaddafi for his "policy of international terrorism and subversion" and declared that the United States would change it. Haig was said in news reports to have rejected an early policy review about Libya which emphasized the dangers to Americans and oil interests in Libya if a policy of confrontation were followed; he wanted a "tougher more positive" approach. As described earlier, the administration then closed the people's bureau, stopped private travel to Libya, warned the 2,000 Americans there to leave, and offered to aid all nations willing to oppose Qaddafi, while continuing the barrage of criticism of Libyan terrorism and subversion. The United States had also sought the help of Egypt and Western Europe in condemning and isolating Libya, and had greatly increased military aid to Libya's neighbors. On July 14 the Wall Street Journal reported that the administration had given U.S. oil companies repeated warnings to get their American employees out of Libya. Clearly, the Journal said, something drastic was being prepared against Libya.(2) Part of that something drastic turned out to be a U.S. naval exercise in the Mediterranean that in a calculated challenge to Qaddafi brought U.S. warships and jet fighters into the Gulf of Sidra, claimed by Libya as territorial waters since 1973.

The basis in international law for the U.S. challenge to Libya's claims to the Gulf was the 1958 Convention on the Territorial Sea and the Contiguous Zone, accepted by the United States in 1964. Under the 1958 convention governments are allowed to claim as territorial waters all of any coastal bay less than 24 miles wide at low-water at its natural entrance. The Gulf of Sidra, which touches about one-third of Libya's coastline, is some 275 miles wide where it meets the Mediterranean. The United States has never recognized Libya's claim to the Gulf.(3)

After warning mariners and airmen routinely on August 12 and 14, the United States sent sixteen warships toward the Gulf. The task force included two aircraft carriers, one of which was the huge Nimitz, and hundreds of aircraft, among which was the elite "Black Aces" squadron of F-14s, the Navy's most sophisticated and potent fighter aircraft. Ostensibly the exercise was intended to train the ships' crews in the use of naval missiles and to assert the U.S. claim that the Gulf of Sidra was an international waterway. While those objects were achieved, the primary purpose of the exercise was to challenge Qaddafi directly and bring him under the threat of U.S. military might. The exercise began on Tuesday, August 18. Two U.S. warships and a number of aircraft went into the Gulf, below the 32° longitude, 30' line at its mouth. From the start the Libyan air force was active and made repeated flights toward the U.S. ships. Each time, when intercepted by U.S. aircraft the Libyan pilots turned back. But early in the morning of August 19 two Libyan Su-22 fighters flew toward the task force. Monitored from the moment of takeoff by the task-force electronic surveillance aircraft, the Libyan jets appeared on the radar screens of two F-14s from the Black Aces squadron, flying some 60 miles off the Libyan coast, at about 7 A.M. After spotting the Su-22s on radar at a range of 30 to 40 miles, the U.S. pilots saw the two planes when they were 5 to 6 miles away. They did not turn back. When the Libyan and U.S. jets were just hundreds of feet apart, one Libyan pilot fired a Soviet Atoll air-to-air missile at the F-14s, while the other Libyan pilot maneuvered to attack. The Atoll missed. Turning hard across their tails, Commander Henry Kleeman and his wingman pursued their attackers and destroyed them with Sidewinder missiles. The Libyan pilots ejected from their crippled planes and apparently were rescued.

The United States called the Libyan action an "unprovoked attack" and warned Libya through the Belgian embassy that any further attacks would be resisted by force. Initially, Libya called the attack "a provocation that endangers world peace." The fight occurred while Qaddafi was in South Yemen preparing to sign a tripartite alliance joining Ethiopia, South Yemen, and Libya. Qaddafi then went to Ethiopia and on August 21, during a news conference in Addis Ababa, he admitted that Libya had fired first. But his version of the incident differed substantially from the U.S. report. According to Qaddafi, the Libyan jets had gone out to meet what they thought were two U.S. jets to order them out of Libyan airspace. When the U.S. pilots refused to leave, Qaddafi said, a Libyan pilot fired and shot down an F-14. The two Libyan planes were then "ambushed" by eight F-14s. In the skirmish that followed the two Libyan Su-22s were lost. The United States emphatically denied the loss of any U.S. planes.(4) There were five more uneventful encounters between Libyan and U.S. warplanes over the Gulf before the exercise ended at 1 P.M. on August 20.

According to U.S. sources this was the first time Libyan fighters had fired on U.S. aircraft since 1973, when two Libyan planes fired on a C-130 about 83 miles off the Libyan coast. There was no damage to the U.S. plane. In September 1980 U.S. Navy fighters drove Libyan jets away from an EC-135 electronic surveillance plane. Intercepts of Libyan radio transmissions suggested that Libyan fighters may have fired on a similar plane a month later. From 1974 to 1981 the United States conducted four naval exercises in the Gulf of Sidra. The last exercise before the air fight came in 1979. In 1980 the Carter administration declined to send a task force into the Gulf because of its fear that a clash or even the appearance of a military intrusion involving an Islamic country would needlessly complicate the negotiations for the release of the American hostages held by Iran.

After the Libyan planes were shot down the Reagan administration clung to its official version of the incident: it was a routine assertion of international rights in the Gulf of Sidra; the American pilots had merely fired in self-defense as was consistent with routine rules of engagement for the U.S. armed forces. This was not untrue. It simply did not give the whole truth. The truth was that the naval intrusion into the Gulf of Sidra had been authorized as part of the administration's systematic campaign to heighten external pressure on Qaddafi.(5) The administration knew from past experience that Libyan fighters would challenge U.S. ships and planes during the exercise. They foresaw that there might be shooting. Accordingly, the entire exercise was meticulously planned. The exercise was discussed intensively within the Defense Department with other departments and agencies taking part. The plans were brought all the way up through channels and given final approval by President Reagan at a meeting of the National Security Council.(6) Even the follow-up publicity by the White House smacked of premeditation. The day after the destruction of the Libyan planes the president went on board the U.S. carrier Constellation. Standing before a cheering crew, with lines of F-14s at his back, the president declared in ringing tones that the brave performance of the Navy pilots and task force in the Gulf of Sidra should give notice to "friend and foe alike" that "the United States has the muscle to back up its words."(7) In short, there is no reason to differ with the prediction offered by the "Periscope" column in Newsweek a week before the incident. The maneuvers were the "first direct challenge" to Qaddafi by the United States after weeks of searching for ways to "neutralize" him. The point of the exercise, according to Newsweek, was to test Qaddafi's reactions and those of his friends in Moscow. Qaddafi's reaction was predictably belligerent, and the Soviets did nothing.

Because the United States anticipated trouble and prepared for it so meticulously and well, the naval exercise was a baited trap. Unaccustomed to such hard-headed behavior by the United States Qaddafi fell into the trap and was humiliated. That was the point. In the aftermath of his loss Qaddafi also felt all the more keenly the external pressure the administration was bringing to bear on Libya. Before the incident Libya had protested to the United Nations that the United States was preparing world opinion to accept an attack on Libya. The Libyan protest cited military aid to Libya's neighbors, a propaganda campaign against Libya, and the reports of plans to kill Qaddafi. It was now clear beyond doubt that the United States was prepared to use force against the Libyan dictator when the circumstances were right. It was a chilling realization. That was also the point of the exercise. The episode was a small but real success for the Reagan administration in two ways. First, the plans worked. Qaddafi was outwitted. The U.S. Navy emerged as a potent, effective force. Second, the objective of intimidating the Libyan government was achieved. As summer passed into fall Libyan officials made very clear to American businessmen and European diplomats in Tripoli that their government was obsessed with the threat from the United States. This was exactly the state of mind that Reagan wished to foster in the Libyan capital.

Initially, only the Middle Eastern allies and clients of Libya condemned the United States: Syria, Iran, South Yemen, the PLO, and Palestinian factions. Several days later the Gulf Cooperation Council — Saudi Arabia, Kuwait, United Arab Emirates, Qatar, Oman, Bahrain — criticized U.S. behavior as a "provocative trap and medieval piracy on the high seas." There was prompt and lavish praise for the United States from the Sudanese government, and U.S. commentators had a grand time. George Will's stern delight is representative of most comment on the right: Qaddafi got what he had coming, Will wrote, for the Libyan dictator is "a mad dog on the streets of the world, a peculiar and perhaps psychotic dictator who has funded terrorism from the Philippines to Northern Ireland." Commenting on the flap over the failure of aides to awaken President Reagan with immediate news of the fight, Will said there was no need. He then reached into his larder of invective and found a particularly overripe specimen: "When the tail of a stallion whisks away a fly, the fly has a crisis, the stallion does not." The president's explanation was a cute quip: Libyan not American planes were lost; I'd expect to be awakened only if it had gone the other way. Caught up in the spirit of the skirmish, George Will allowed himself to be carried away. Everything about the fight was good for the United States, he claimed. It sent the right message to Moscow about U.S. willingness to use force. Soviet clients and the enemies of the United States had been made to realize their vulnerability, and Arab moderates had been reassured to see that radicals run genuinely dangerous risks.

Closer to the political center, former Secretary of Defense James Schlesinger spoke for most Americans when he said "Good show." The downing of the Libyan planes protected the interests of the United States, Schlesinger argued, and upheld the dignity of the country. Although Qaddafi had repeatedly said he had no intention of interfering with the operations of U.S. oil companies in Libya, Schlesinger believed he would shut off the flow of oil to the United States. Schlesinger apparently shared Wills's doubts about Qaddafi's mental health, for he managed to combine pessimism about Libyan oil with a dig at the Libyan leader's supposed psychosis. "Qaddafi is not likely to be constrained," he wrote, "by normal calculations of economic rationality."

A few observers expressed reservations about the military encounter and about the nationwide indulgence in chest-thumping that had followed it. The military outcome of the fight was meaningless, suggested former Senator J. William Fulbright, for it was no more than the destruction of two inferior Soviet planes. Who doubted that the Navy's best pilots in the United States' most formidable jet fighters would always bring down opponents in older, slower, less well-armed aircraft? As a demonstration of how the United States uses its power the fight was full of wrong meanings. Above all, it could prove nothing worthwhile about the United States. "The validity of our conception of a good society," Fulbright concluded, "can not be proved by military means."(8)

Qaddafi reacted with bluster and threats. In a speech at the celebration of the September 1 revolution he declared that if the United States "attacked" the Gulf of Sidra again, Libya would launch assaults on the nuclear depots of Western countries around the Mediterranean, such as those in Sicily, Turkey, and Crete. Libya would not hesitate to "cause an international catastrophe," he cried.

Libyans would turn the Gulf of Sidra red with blood. It was quite a show: the long lines of Soviet weapons, groups of natty teenagers shouting "Rubbish on America" and "Reagan is a cowboy," and Qaddafi on the reviewing stand flanked by Yasir Arafat of the PLO and Goukouni Oueddei of Chad.(9)

The United States also brought severe pressure on Libya by strengthening its military cooperation with Egypt and Sudan. Egypt, Sudan, and the United States took three kinds of military steps together. They agreed to major increases in U.S. military assistance, they stepped up their overt military cooperation with one another, and Egypt and Sudan sought and received promises of military protection from the United States. In Egypt's case some of the more spectacular elements of the closer relationship with the United States were muted after Sadat's assassination. There has been much less talk, for example, of Egypt as the United States' strategic partner in the Middle East. One must keep in mind that the preservation of U.S. interests in Egypt and Saudi Arabia is the main object of U.S. policy toward the Arab world. Libya is a secondary concern by comparison. This is not always apparent because of the publicity attracted by Qaddafi, and because officials in Washington, Cairo, and especially in Khartoum readily use the specter of Libyan subversion and intervention to justify initiatives or commitments they wish to make for other, more important reasons. Thus, closer U.S. military cooperation with Egypt is of interest to U.S. policymakers primarily because it helps protect a friendly regime in Cairo, thereby avoiding a major war in the southeastern Mediterranean, and because in time it may help the United States move its forces to the Gulf to protect Saudi Arabia. Sudan can never be the political and military treasure that Egypt is, but its geography is vital to both Egypt and Saudi Arabia, and its importance to the United States lies in this. At the same time, steps taken to achieve the larger aims of U.S. or Egyptian or Sudanese policy bear on the relations of all three with Libya. Understood and executed as they were during the Reagan administration they become mutually reinforcing. Closer U.S. military cooperation with Egypt, for example, seriously inhibits Qaddafi's international freedom of action, while it reduces the likelihood of war in the southeastern Mediterranean. Foreign policy in this area operates in two intersecting planes. The most important involves Egypt, Saudi Arabia, and the United States. Libya and Sudan are in a secondary plane, but the two intersect and developments in each plane affect developments in the other.

Closer military cooperation between the United States and Egypt began to develop during the summer of 1981. On July 23 in a speech celebrating the anniversary of the Egyptian Revolution, Sadat laid out his general conception of the new relationship. "I will give the United States every facility," Sadat declared, "so they can reach any Arab country on the Gulf, so they can reach any Islamic country anywhere, so that the tragedy of Afghanistan is not repeated." Sadat discussed his plans with Reagan during a visit to Washington in early August. In essence, Egypt would be the "strategic pivot" from which U.S. forces would move to stop threats to Moslem states in Africa and the Middle East. Sadat made clear he was offering the use of facilities, not the command of permanent bases. He was said by the Egyptian delegation to have given Reagan a "letter of under-standing" on the use of the facilities and to have argued for strategic "parity" for Egypt with Israel. Egypt was also seeking speeded-up deliveries of U.S. arms, particularly of F-16 fighters. It wanted three times more F-16s than it had received and substantially more aid, as envisioned in a five-year aid plan the two countries were discussing. In addition, the United States was to build a major air and naval base at Ras Banas on the Red Sea. The Reagan administration had asked $106 million for this for fiscal year 1982. Although Congress did not act until December and then appropriated less than one-tenth of what had been asked for the base, it did accept a commitment to build the base. Ras Banas is located directly across the Red Sea from the Saudi port of Yanbu, the outlet for the new oil pipeline built by the Saudis to escape total dependence on their Gulf ports. Iraq has also been given the right to build a pipeline from Basra to the Red Sea. If U.S. forces were able to move freely in and out of Ras Banas the task of protecting friendly governments in the Gulf area would be enormously simplified. Sadat and his delegation argued in Washington that Egypt was better able to aid the United States than Israel. Other Arab states would more readily accept U.S. troops if they were deployed from Egypt than from Israel, it was said. There were problems, though, with the strategic partnership Sadat proposed. The fate of the shah haunted U.S. policymakers who were reluctant to endanger Sadat by too close an American embrace. As the experience of the Soviets and the British before them showed, there is an intense dislike in Egypt of any kind of foreign military presence. Moreover, relations between Saudi Arabia and Egypt were cool, and this reduced the usefulness of the partnership. The Egyptians were not deterred by the lack of warmth between Riyadh and Cairo. It was not necessary to agree on everything, Egyptian officials pointed out, in order for nations to realize how much they needed each other.(10)

Sadat's proposal came in response to much rhetoric from the Reagan administration about the desirability of building a strategic consensus in the Middle East as the basis of U.S. policy toward the region. The idea was abandoned before the end of the second year of the administration, and after Secretary Haig's resignation would not be revived. But at the time it played a large part in the approach of the administration to the region and its problems. Sadat may also have been moved by a desire to outbid and even preempt the Israelis, who had been trying for years to obtain an overt strategic partnership with the United States, and who were undoubtedly as prepared as he was to respond to the administration's emphasis on strategic cooperation. In this he was correct.

A few days before Sadat was assassinated the Israelis offered themselves as strategic partners for the United States. It was not clear at the time whether this meant that the partnership with Egypt was off or that the Israeli partnership would be added to it. The plan that was made public in October called for the United States to store large amounts of equipment in Israel where it would be picked up by U.S. troops en route to an emergency in the Gulf. Israel, like Egypt, could defend the stockpiles against seizure by other nations. Moreover Israel could provide all the vital services of an advanced society, from hospitals near the theater of operations to the maintenance of sophisticated military hardware. Israel's goal, according to Defense Minister Ariel Sharon, was to become part of "an extensive American network of deterrence to the Soviet Union." The advantages for Israel were also large. The stockpiled equipment would be available to Israel in case of war, and thus eliminate both the need for emergency resupply from the United States and the vulnerability to outside manipulation that came with it. If Israel became an explicit part of U.S. containment of the Soviet Union, Israeli officials believed that this would create a real U.S. stake in Israeli survival. Israel's proximity to the Gulf compared well with that of Ras Banas. According to studies conducted at the beginning of the Reagan administration, 11 days would be required to move 70,000 tons of equipment for one mechanized division from Israel to Saudi Arabia, assuming one-half the existing U.S. strategic airlift were used. It would take 10 days to make the move from Ras Banas. By comparison it would take 8 days from Oman, 14 days from Somalia, 22 days from Kenya, 27 days from Diego Garcia, and 77 days from the United States. Oman was within range of Soviet aircraft operating from Afghanistan and unable to defend itself against attack from South Yemen.(11)

Sadat's death took Egypt out of the strategic partnership, at least for the immediate future, and the administration thereupon swallowed its fears of anti-Israeli sentiment among its Arab allies and struck a strategic bargain with Israel in December. The administration was vague in public about the terms of the deal. As described by Secretary Weinberger and others it provided for the provision of military assistance by Israel and the United States to one another with the goal of coping with threats to the "security of the entire region" by the Soviet Union or "Soviet-controlled forces." Apparently other questions such as stockpiling in Israel and direct use by Israel of U.S. satellite intelligence were not resolved. Both sides agreed to the conduct of joint military exercises, which had the effect of giving Israel strategic parity with Egypt, with which exercises had been staged for two consecutive years. If it is true that the sticky questions were put off, there was obviously no time to resolve them, for the entire agreement was revoked by the

United States following Israel's annexation of the Golan Heights in the spring of 1982.

The next step in increased military cooperation between Egypt and the United States came in early October 1981 during the visit of Vice-President Hosni Mubarak to Washington. At the time the public knew only that Mubarak had come with a "very urgent" message for President Reagan from President Sadat on the tense situation between Libyan and Sudanese forces on the border of Chad. Mubarak asked, it was said, for more arms, and particularly for antiaircraft weapons for the Sudan. On the eve of Mubarak's visit the Sudanese government had charged that Libya had bombed Sudanese towns along the border for nineteen days. The Egyptian defense minister, Lt. General Mohammed Abdul Halim Abu Ghazala, told reporters that he believed the Soviets and Libyans were going to do something through the border of Chad in order to divert attention from what they were about to do in Poland. Egyptian sources accompanying Mubarak to Washington said that the vice-president had urged the United States to take a stronger role in the Middle East and to speed military assistance to the Sudan. He also asked, according to news reports, that the Reagan administration take steps to reassure its friends elsewhere in the Islamic and Arab world. He had in mind the AWACS deal for Saudi Arabia, and aid and reassurance for Oman and Somalia. In leaks given reporters after Sadat's death and in interviews conducted by the author with former U.S. policymakers a crucial added element to the Mubarak visit emerged. Sadat and Nimeiry were apparently ready to strike at Libyan forces in Chad, either by air or air and ground attack. They recognized that this might mean war with Libya and if Libya appealed to the Soviet Union for help, as Qaddafi surely would, it could bring a joint Soviet-Libyan attack on Egypt in the Western desert. While Sadat had no doubts that his armed forces could defeat Libya, they were no match for the Soviet Union. Accordingly Sadat, through Mubarak, sought and obtained from the Reagan administration a U.S. promise to protect Egypt against Soviet attack in the event of war between Egypt and Libya. According to "official sources" this commitment was given "in definitive form" to Mubarak during his visit.

This was not the first time the United States had given this promise to Sadat. The Egyptian president made the first request in 1976 after the explosion of a bomb in a train station in Alexandria. The Egyptians blamed Qaddafi, and Sadat publicly vowed to punish Qaddafi, even if it meant resorting to war. To protect Egypt's long exposed supply lines across the Western desert Washington was told that Egypt was considering war against Libya and needed protection against Soviet attack. The Ford administration agreed to deter Soviet intervention against Egypt. When the Carter administration took office and learned of the commitment they revoked it for several reasons. First they believed that it gave Sadat too much encouragement and left the United States with too little control over a situation that could lead to a dangerous confrontation with the Soviet Union. Moreover, unless the Egyptians were instantly successful their invasion would almost certainly bring the Soviets into Libya in much greater strength than ever before. From the Carter administration's point of view, the United States would thus have gotten a bad result all around. Qaddafi would not have been overthrown, the Soviets would have been ever more deeply entrenched in Libya than before, and Libya accordingly less independent than before, and the Egyptians would have been angry at the United States because it had not stopped the Soviet Union from rescuing Qaddafi.(12)

In late September and early October in order to prepare the way for the request to the Reagan administration to renew the protection, Sadat and Nimeiry exaggerated the seriousness of the incidents along the Chadian border and Libyan complicity in subversion inside Sudan. Mubarak thus arrived in Washington amid a kind of war hysteria emanating out of northern central Africa that proved to be a figment of Egyptian and Sudanese propaganda created, apparently, to justify an attack on Libyan forces in Chad. News reports indicated that Mubarak asked in a more subtle way. Would the Reagan administration deter Soviet intervention if Libya attacked Sudan and then, in response, Egypt "went after" the source of the problem in Tripoli. This gave a semblance of U.S. control, because it suggested that only a Libyan attack would trigger Egyptian intervention. The Reagan administration assured him that the United States would deter Soviet intervention against Egypt. But the hope of maintaining U.S. control of a crisis was an illusion, for Sudan and Egypt had been complaining of Libyan aggression against Sudan for weeks. They would have no trouble finding a suitable incident to justify a strike into Chad. Then, if Libya still refused to withdraw from Chad, an Egyptian attack on Libya would follow. If a confrontation between the United States and the Soviet Union developed, it would have come at the instigation of Egypt and Sudan, yet another example of the tail-wagging-the-dog diplomacy so common in the Middle East.

The funeral of Anwar Sadat brought Secretary of State Haig to Cairo, along with former Presidents Carter, Ford, and Nixon, and many other heads of state, including President Nimeiry of Sudan. As is customary, the political leaders and diplomats used the occasion to advance their own interests and policies. On the U.S. side there was tough talk. Before he left for Cairo Secretary Haig told reporters that there were no signs of external involvement in Sadat's assassination. However, he added that the United States "would view with great concern" any attempt by an outside power to exploit the assassination for its own advantage. He had particularly stern words for the Libyan government which, in a colossal display of bad taste, had welcomed Sadat's death with gloating and cheery "I told you so's" in its public statements and propaganda. Haig also mentioned a build-up of Libyan forces along the border of Sudan, and administration "sources" told reporters that U.S. intelligence had evidence of a Libyan plot to kill Nimeiry. On October 7, the day of Haig's news conference, the Sudanese government announced the formation of an anti-Qaddafi front headed by the Libyan exile Mohammed Mogaryef. The move was seen as a Sudanese response to the call for the assassination of Nimeiry issued by Qaddafi after the assassination of Sadat. In Khartoum Magaryef said that there had been seven coups attempted against Qaddafi, and that the latest had occurred only five months earlier. Administration officials said that in May rebels in the Libyan air force had tried unsuccessfully to shoot down Qaddafi's plane as he returned from a visit to Moscow.

Sudanese authorities kept up the tension with a series of alarming reports about Libyan-inspired subversion and military aggression. On October 8, for example, the Washington Post reported that officials in Khartoum were saying that a "Libyan-organized secret underground army" had been uncovered as it was preparing to attack the Nimeiry government. The plot had been scotched, Sudanese officials said, by the arrest of thousands of people, perhaps as many as 24,000, if one takes a rough average of press reports. Particularly suspect were the thousands of Sudanese coming home from Libya. The Sudanese news agency SUNA stated that Qaddafi had established a "Salvation Army for the Liberation of Sudan" and had found recruits for it by pressing workers into military camps. Mubarak had told the Reagan administration about the plot during his Washington visit, the Sudanese officials said, and had discussed contingency plans for the airlift of Egyptian troops to Sudan if they were needed to quell the rebellion. Sudanese and Egyptian leaders were said to believe that Qaddafi was working for a coup against Nimeiry using the Libyan presence in Chad and Sudanese and Chadian workers in Libya as commandos. The stories of Libyan support for the 1976 coup attempt were repeated.(13)

Throughout October 1981 there was intense military and diplomatic maneuvering. The lines of policy had been tangled by Sadat's assassination, and the initial reactions of a number of governments, particularly in Khartoum and Washington, worsened the mess. First there were the reports of crisis in Sudan. The internal and external dimensions of the crisis were linked. Libya, it was said, was attempting to overthrow the Sudanese government. Sudanese authorities painted a lurid and barely credible picture of how this would be done. Libyan assassination squads would enter Sudan from Libya or across the Chadian frontier and kill the top thirty members of Nimeiry's government. With Sudan decapitated a mobile legion of commandos organized and led by Libya would drive down to Khartoum from the northwest across 600 miles of desert and seize control of the capital and the country. The Sudanese minister of security and vice-president, Omer Mohammed Tayeb, described the plot for reporters on October 17. The main attack according to Tayeb was to be on Khartoum using agents infiltrated into the capital and Sudanese irregulars who had driven across the desert. A second front was to be opened along the border with Chad by Libyan and Libyan-trained troops who would seize western Sudan. After the top twenty to thirty Sudanese leaders had been killed, Libyan paratroops would be airlifted to Khartoum, where they would join forces with the rebels and, in this way, forestall any U.S. or Egyptian response. To support his argument, Tayeb said that Libya had begun concentrating troops on the Sudanese border two weeks earlier. In the last three months, he added, some 11,000 Sudanese had returned to Sudan from Libya. The Sudanese government had arrested a number of suspects and had found ten to fifteen ring-leaders who had been assigned the responsibility of organizing revolutionary committees for the rising. It was the arrest and interrogation of the returning Sudanese that uncovered the plot. Tayeb refused to say how many had been arrested, but the number was evidently very large judging from press reports. Once they became aware of the plot, Tayeb added, the Sudanese government was able to stop its realization. "But they will try again," he said. "There has been a decision by Qaddafi to overthrow this govern-ment. . . . This is a series of plots."(14) Several days before Tayeb's statement on the plot to overthrow his government, the Sudanese government had asked the United States for assistance in strengthening its internal security. The administration was said to be receptive to the aid and was discussing it with the Sudanese.(15)

It is hard to know what to make of the Sudanese alarms. They appear to have been sounded initially to provide a pretext for an Egyptian-Sudanese strike against Qaddafi in Chad. Attacks on Sudanese territory and attempts to subvert the Sudanese govern-ment would have provided ample justification for a counterstrike. They won, as has been seen, a promise of U.S. aid against Soviet intervention on Libya's side. When Sadat was killed the Egyptian-Sudanese military reprisals were probably scrapped. But the Sudan-ese complaints and accusations continued. This may have been an attempt by Nimeiry to speed and increase the amount of aid the United States would send to Sudan.(16)

The Reagan administration reacted in two ways to the concerns of the Sudanese government. A large increase in U.S. military aid to Sudan had been requested before Sadat's death. After the assassination, Nimeiry was apparently given a promise that the United States would defend Sudan against an attack by Libya. "As part of this commitment," in Nimeiry's words, Sudan would be included in Operation Brightstar. There was no public comment by the U.S. side on Nimeiry's claim to have a defense commitment from the United States.

The inclusion of Sudan in the military exercise was part of another of the Reagan administration's reactions to the death of Sadat. Direct U.S. military involvement in the region was to be made more visible and potent. This was done by sending two AWACS aircraft to Egypt, by enlarging Operation Brightstar, and by speeding the shipment of military aid to Sudan. Drawing equipment from U.S. army stocks the administration proposed to ship to Sudan twenty M-60 tanks, tank transporters, a dozen 155-mm howitzers, and two F-5 fighter trainers as the first of a dozen F-5s to be delivered. Redeye antiaircraft missiles were to be included in the accelerated shipments, as well. The purpose was to strengthen Sudan and contain Libya. "We don't necessarily want to kill Qaddafi," one administration official said, "we just want to tie him up." It was more difficult to accelerate shipments to Egypt because they involved much larger amounts of equipment. The AWACS arrived in Egypt on October 15 and immediately began patrolling the border with Libya.

The announcement of the enlargement of Brightstar was accompanied by a number of stories about the use of B-52s in the exercise. The United States Strategic Air Command has set aside two fleets of B-52H bombers to use conventional bombs against targets at extremely long ranges, such as the Gulf. The name of the unit was the Strategic Protection Force or SPIF. Its motto, according to press reports, is "Anytime Anywhere." The planes are based in North Dakota; fourteen are at Grand Forks and fourteen at Minot air bases. They are armed with 750 and 500 pound conventional bombs. According to an administration official, the purpose of using the strategic bombers in Operation Brightstar was to protect the new Egyptian government and to attempt to deter attacks on the Gulf oil fields and governments friendly to the United States in the region.(17)

Operation Brightstar began on November 9 and officially concluded on November 24 in a spectacular display of air power involving the B-52s, which arrived exactly on time over the Egyptian desert after a nonstop flight from North Dakota. The giant bombers thundered across the battlefield at low altitude to drop their bombs, making their presence unmistakable to the large audience, which included a number of Soviet bloc military observers. Some 4,000 U.S. troops took part in the Egyptian phase of Brightstar, alongside a like number of Egyptians. In Sudan, 350 members of the U.S. Special Forces conducted training in counterinsurgency. In Somalia, engineering and medical untis conducted training exercises at Berbera before Somali observers. In Oman, 1,000 marines landed for one day near Salalah, capital of Dhofar province, which borders South Yemen.

There was little doubt that the United States had shown its commitment to its "regional allies," as administration officials put it, and had made a brave show of countering the Ethiopian-Libyan-

South Yemen pact. However, the expansion of the exercise and the extremely belligerent talk coming out of Khartoum had led the administration to emphasize the deterrent character of its activities and to lay to rest any ideas the Sudanese or anyone else might have had about invading Libya. Seen from Tripoli or Moscow the rhetoric and military preparations of the Americans, Egyptians, and Sudanese must have appeared as preliminary to an invasion. Libyan and Soviet broadcasts in mid-October charged that Brightstar was actually a cover for a Sudanese invasion of Libya and they quoted Nimeiry as having threatened to invade Libya. With these considerations in mind State Department officials emphasized the internal character of Sudan's problems in off-the-record briefings for reporters that, as intended, quickly found their way into print. The department also publicly sought to defuse the rising tensions in the Middle East. It stressed, for example, that U.S. military activities and the speeding of arms deliveries to Egypt and Sudan were merely a "telescoping" of long-laid plans. U.S. participation in Brightstar, the Department implied, was not a sign of approval for the invasion of Libya. The extension of U.S. military protection to Egypt and Sudan thus not only served to deter further Libyan aggression but it also removed the justification for an Egyptian and Sudanese attack on Libya, and in this way contributed to the stability of northwest Africa.(18)

From the beginning of its campaign against Qaddafi, the Reagan administration had not been of one mind about the need for economic sanctions against Libya. As they had with the other severe steps under consideration the advocates of a limited multilateral approach to Libya managed to delay the implementation of economic sanctions. Apparently the scare over the Libyan assassination squads reopened the internal administration debate and prejudiced the outcome in favor of the imposition of sanctions. The initial punishment – the recall of Americans from Libya – was mild, although in Libyan eyes it may have appeared as more ominous than mild. The departure of the U.S. nationals "cleared the deck" and in this sense could well have been the precursor of more drastic punishment. Indeed, the administration imposed an additional sanction on Libya within three months of the recall of U.S. citizens. However when it came it was unilateral and purely economic – a boycott of Libyan oil and prohibition of the export of high-technology equipment.

The decision to recall U.S. citizens from Libya came at a time of declining U.S. imports of Libyan oil, falling oil revenues for Libya, and a reluctance on the part of at least the major oil companies doing business in Libya to continue their operations there. In a sense this made the imposition of sanctions easier for the administration. It reduced the objections by the companies to the sanctions and it strengthened their hands in seeking to persuade the Libyan government to lower crude oil prices or reduce taxes or both. A month before the administration's recall of Americans, Exxon announced that it was withdrawing from all its operations in Libya. The oil company gave no reasons for the decision, but experts said it was largely economic. The price of Libyan oil was so high, at one time it had been $41/barrel, and then stood at $37.50/barrel (including a $4 premium above the OPEC price), the oil companies were losing money on the oil they pumped in Libya. The oil companies were also said to be under pressure from the administration and from Saudi Arabia to cut their Libyan operations. This was of special importance to Exxon and the other majors: their holdings were small in Libya and very large in Saudi Arabia and the Gulf, where Saudi influence was paramount. Exxon had produced 135,000 barrels/day in Libya during the first six months of 1981 and had exported no oil from Libya since that time. Mobil had halted its Libyan production of 110,000 barrels/day on November 1 and was said by reporters to be considering withdrawing from Libya. There were rumors in oil-industry circles that Libya had cut its price by $1/barrel in late November in an effort to keep U.S. companies in operation in Libya. JANA denied the cut but said that the Libyan government had offered Oasis a tax reduction of $1/barrel. Libyan revenues from oil were said to have fallen from a high of $22 billion to perhaps as little as $10 billion for 1981. This was thought to be enough to cover Qaddafi's ambitious $12 billion development plan but little else. Libyan reserves were given in the press as approximately $12 billion.(19)

A week after the first public reports on the Libyan assassination squads the Reagan administration was reported to be planning "some form of economic sanctions against Libya." Reporters were told that two National Security Council meetings had been held on December 7 and 8, but that no conclusions had been reached. The administration would brief the Congress within a day or two, it was said. But when Senator Gary Hart introduced a sense of the Senate resolution saying that the Senate would favor and support an oil boycott of Libya the White House chief of staff, James Baker, asked the Senate Majority Leader to persuade Hart to withdraw his proposal. Senator Baker complied and told Hart the president needed more time before acting. Hart acquiesced and withdrew his resolution. The recall of Americans was announced by Deputy Secretary Clark on December 10, the day after the appearance of the Post article.

The U.S. oil companies in Libya reacted by announcing they would obey the president's call. However, they indicated they would replace their U.S. employees with other nationals rather than close their operations. Senior U.S. officials continued to refuse to say if a comprehensive boycott of Libyan oil would follow the recall. The withdrawal of Americans called further attention to Libyan oil production and U.S. imports of Libyan oil. In response to inquiries from reporters the American Petroleum Institute stated that overall Libyan production was down to 700,000 barrels/day from 1.8 million in 1980. Of this the United States took 270,00 barrels, down from

400,000 barrels/day at the start of 1981. This was 5 percent of total U.S. imports and 2 percent of total U.S. consumption. The French government's reaction was an implicit condemnation of the president's decision. France no longer considered the attitude of the Libyan government to be one of "external destabilization" the announcement said, and France intended gradually to resume normal relations with the North African country.(20)

In its response Libya refused to penalize its U.S. oil companies or to embargo oil shipments to the United States. Instead, Qaddafi instructed his oil minister, Abdessalam Zagger to ask OPEC to embargo oil shipments to the United States and to blacklist all U.S. companies that obeyed the recall order. Although Iran took Libya's side, OPEC decided that the issue was political and therefore not suitable for its intervention.(21) During the OPEC oil ministers' conference in Abu Dhabi the Libyan oil minister called the U.S. decision an "act of aggression" and said it would hurt Libyan oil production. He denied the "hit-squad" charges and said that U.S. oil men were free to leave Libya and would be safe if they stayed.

Several weeks went by in relative calm and then, at the end of February, the administration decided to move to what Secretary Haig called "Phase II" of its campaign against Qaddafi. On February 25 the National Security Council (NSC) approved a boycott of Libyan oil shipments to the United States and a ban on the export of equipment that might have a military use or contain high technology components, such as oil and gas drilling equipment. Administration officials briefed reporters hurriedly on February 25 immediately after the NSC decision because the Middle East Policy Survey, a Washington-based publication, for February 26 would carry the story. Reporters were told that the boycott and export prohibitions would be instituted within the coming month, after talks with U.S. allies, oil companies, and members of Congress were concluded. The administration stressed its view that the sanctions had not been triggered by any new development but were part of a "long-term program of opposing Qaddafi," as one reporter put it. The administration regarded Qaddafi as a supporter of international terrorism and a surrogate of the Soviet Union.(22) A General Accounting Office study was released on February 26 which indicated that there might be a "small short-term revenue loss" for Libya as it found new customers for its oil, but no other effect, either on Libya or the United States. The GAO study warned that U.S. companies might be expropriated. Most oil-industry experts contacted by the press, such as John Lichtblau of the Petroleum Industry Research Foundation, doubted that the boycott would have much impact on Libya.(23) The administration hoped that Libya would have to cut its oil price in order to attract other buyers, and that this might cause a further drop in Libyan oil revenues. Libya then might be forced to draw even more heavily than it had on its reserves, which had fallen from $14 billion to $9 billion in the previous twelve months.(24)

On March 10 the administration dropped the other shoe and formally announced the boycott on the importation of Libyan oil and the export prohibitions. The presidential order banned the importation of Libyan oil; required a license for all exports to Libya except agricultural products and medical supplies; and stated the intention not to allow the export of oil and gas technology, of equipment that could affect national security, or of any other equipment that contained high technology and could be put to military use. The administration offered more of a rationale for the decision than it had two weeks earlier. "Libyan efforts to destabilize U.S. regional friends have continued," the State Department spokesman said. There had been "no lasting change" in Libyan behavior. This last was meant to deal with the apparent inconsistency of imposing the boycott and export ban a few months after Libya had withdrawn from Chad, a withdrawal that had persuaded the French government, at least, that Libyan foreign policy was no longer in an expansionist phase. Administration officials were anxious to dispel any notion of inconsistency. U.S. opposition to Qaddafi required the boycott. A desire to make U.S. policy consistent was the most important reason for the action. The United States couldn't oppose Qaddafi's subversion and terrorism and continue to import billions of dollars of Libyan oil. Qaddafi hadn't changed, they argued. True, he had withdrawn from Chad, and called off the hit-squads in Europe and the United States. But these were tactical shifts, taken in part because he wished to be president of the OAU. Despite these steps he continued to subvert Sudan, Somalia, and Oman to support radical movements in Central America and the Caribbean, and had as recently as November tried to kill hundreds of Americans at a social club in Khartoum by booby-trapping stereo speakers with dozens of pounds of explosives. Fortunately the explosives were discovered and disarmed in another country through which the speakers were sent en route to Khartoum.

Reporters learned that the boycott had been tentatively decided in December. It had been postponed to allow time for the recall of Americans to take effect and to enable the administration to consult with its European and Japanese allies and with other friendly governments, such as Egypt. Administration officials said, the allies opposed Qaddafi but would not take substantive steps against him. Greece, Turkey, Italy, and West Germany were the major users of Libyan oil. Meanwhile, the U.S. community in Libya had fallen from over 2,000 to about 350 and this group was regarded as essentially "indigenous Libyans" who would not leave and probably would not be harmed in case of trouble.

The administration recognized that the boycott would not have a severe effect on Libya. It might cut Libyan oil revenues if Libya had to lower prices to find new customers. Of much greater importance in lowering Libyan income was the ready availability of oil on the international market. A Gulf Oil Corporation study showed that

Libya needed to export 1.3 million barrels/day to cover its expenses. It had produced 2.1 million barrels/day in 1979. According to the U.S. Department of Energy Libya was currently producing 800-900,000 barrels/day. As for U.S. exports, although 70 percent of the $578 million in goods sent to Libya in the previous year would have required licenses, only about 2 percent of them contained high technology.(25)

Administration spokesmen openly spoke of a campaign against Qaddafi, of which the boycott was a part. They reviewed for reporters the various steps in the campaign, from the break in relations through the air battle in the Gulf of Sidra to the strengthening of friendly governments around Libya. As the State Department spokesman put it, the boycott was "necessary to complement other measures for dealing with Libyan behavior, such as support to regional states and efforts to reduce the underlying instability which Libya exploits."(26) The goal of the boycott and of the campaign against Qaddafi was to "modify Libyan behavior around the world." The administration expected Qaddafi to respond by improving his relations with his neighbors rather than ending his training of terrorists, of which he had trained 5,000 in 1981, officials said.

Qaddafi's immediate response was to go to Austria. The trip was hastily arranged and politically embarrassing to Austrian Chancellor Bruno Kreisky. Although Austria seems a strange choice at first, there are a number of reasons for the journey. Moreover, by obtaining a reception in Vienna and the attendant international news coverage, Qaddafi undoubtedly achieved his purpose, which was to demonstrate to the world that the Reagan administration had not completely isolated Libya. When Qaddafi arrived in Vienna he was greeted at the airport by a crowd of Libyans chanting "Arab unity! God is Great! Down with America!" And denunciation of the United States from a Western European vantage was clearly one of Qaddafi's purposes. Reagan was a "destructive person," he told a news conference on March 10 in Vienna, and a "terrorist." Libya would never submit to U.S. pressure. He told radio interviewers that Libya might be attacked by the United States, and that a U.S. conflict with Libya could escalate into a world war. Qaddafi was so vehemently anti-United States and the outcry against the visit in Austria so great that Kreisky was compelled to say at a banquet for Qaddafi that Austria was a close friend of the United States. If Qaddafi's reasons for coming to Vienna are clear so are Austria's for accepting his visit. Austria was seeking fat industrial contracts to offset its oil bill to Libya. In 1981 Austria's trade balance with Libya was in deficit by $84 million, nearly all of it because of oil. Austrian trade with Libya had risen 300 percent in five years, and an Austrian company, Voest-Alpine, was the leader of a European and Japanese consortium to build a $5 billion steel complex near Tripoli.(27)

Qaddafi might use the podium given him by Chancellor Kreisky in Vienna to denounce the United States and the sanctions it had imposed against Libya, but he could not alter the decision. On March 26, U.S. Customs officers seized a $1.7 million shipment of equipment for water purification and oil and gas drilling on the docks in Brooklyn. Eventually the water purification manufacturer, Ionics, Inc. of Massachusetts, was offered a license to ship part of the shipment worth $300,000, although this was of little help to the manufacturer. The decision could not be altered, and it was increasingly difficult to get around the economic sanctions by illegal means. A week before the seizure of the cargo in Brooklyn, customs officials announced that they had uncovered a plot to steal fifteen U.S. Cobra helicopters and sell them to Libya for more than $125 million. Seven men were indicted on March 16; five had been arrested, two in California and three in Texas; two were still at large. Customs officers said it was the largest plot discovered in the history of the United States. And the helicopters were merely the first installment. Later shipments were to have included missiles, tanks, automatic weapons, virtually everything in the U.S. arsenal except nuclear weapons. A bank account in the Cayman Islands had been established to receive laundered Libyan funds. The Cobras were to have been stolen in March and transferred to 747s by a Texas air cargo company.(28)

In addition to its systematic campaign to embarrass and isolate Qaddafi and reduce his economic resources, the Reagan administration in June 1981 announced its determination to aid all nations attempting to oppose Libyan "interventionism." Before his confirmation by the Senate, assistant secretary of state for Africa, Chester Crocker, told a foreign policy conference at the State Department on June 2 that although Chad was an African problem and Libya was an African country, the United States would support "those states that wish to resist what Libya has done in Chad and it will continue to do so." Crocker repeated this administration position a month later in testimony to the Senate Foreign Relations Committee. The United States, he told the senators, would increase its aid to countries opposed to Libya.(29) The administration chose to do this almost exclusively through sudden, dramatic increases in military aid to Sudan, Tunisia, Oman, and Morocco.

There were several reasons why military assistance was so heavily emphasized by the Reagan administration. First, there was a military dimension to the threat Libya posed to its neighbors, as shown by the raid on Gafsa, Tunisia, the weapons aid for Polisario in its war against Morocco, and the invasion of Chad. Second, the recipient nations sought U.S. weapons to modernize and strengthen their armed forces. In addition, the Reagan administration consciously chose to accord a great deal of importance to military aid. As Reagan's undersecretary of state for security assistance, James Buckley, put it, arms transfers were an essential element of the global defense posture and of the foreign policy of the Reagan administration.(30) Restrictions imposed by the Carter administration were replaced by an emphasis on flexibility. Concern for human rights gave way to a greater concern for U.S. national interests. Discouragement of U.S. arms salesmen abroad gave way to active help. A ceiling on arms sales was dropped, U.S. financing of arms sales was increased, and terms were eased for certain especially important customers such as Sudan. Last, Congress was asked to repeal the various restrictions it had imposed on arms sales.(31) As one authority put it, "A cornucopia of arms sales seemed to mark the beginning of the Reagan Administration. . . . Arms sales had become a major component of the American government's approach to the competition with the Soviet Union on a global basis, perhaps the major instrument for action overseas, short of the direct use of U.S. armed forces."(32)

The striking efforts of the Reagan administration to strengthen the Sudan have already been mentioned. President Nimeiry in the course of twenty-seven international press interviews in Cairo during the funeral of Anwar Sadat even claimed that the United States had promised to defend Sudan against attack by Libya. This was denied by both Haig and Weinberger in the course of appearances on U.S. television. Haig suggested that Nimeiry's statement had been "somewhat overdrawn," but added that threatened nations must know of U.S. concern and willingness to give aid. Weinberger, appearing on the same program, said he knew of no commitment to defend Sudan.(33) U.S. military aid to Sudan was increased from $30 million for fiscal year 1981 to $100 million for fiscal year 1982. In 1979 Sudan had received $5 million in military assistance from the United States.

The Reagan administration planned an even more drastic increase for Tunisia, from $15 million to a requested $95 million for 1982 and $140 million for 1983. During an official visit to Washington in late April 1982 Tunisian Prime Minister Mohammed Mzali tried to downplay the significance of the major increase in U.S. credits for arms sales. For years, he told reporters, the Tunisian government had ignored the country's military requirements to concentrate on building the economy. As a result Tunisia's armaments were aging and obsolete. It was time to replace them with U.S. M-60 tanks and F-5 fighters. The prime minister added that for the present Qaddafi had apparently stopped trying to subvert Tunisia and was seeking improved relations between the two countries. Although neither Mzali nor Reagan said so, this was undoubtedly a success for the administration's policies. By his conciliatory behavior Qaddafi was clearly attempting to reduce the size of U.S. arms imports and slow the development of closer relations between Tunisia and the United States.(34)

Mzali's remarks were directed at critics of the arms sales to Tunisia, such as Claudia Wright, who argued that the Reagan approach placed impossible burdens on the Tunisian economy and encouraged violent anti-Americanism among Bourguiba's internal opponents. The Reagan policy, she wrote in the New York Times, offers "nothing but arms and debts — and mounting insecurity."(35) To the additional arms sales Reagan added a public commitment to Tunisia's security. "I have told the Prime Minister," he said during Mzali's visit, "that he can count on us as Tunisia faces the external threats that have emerged in the past few years." All the weapons for sale on easy terms in Washington and the huge loans to Egypt and Israel simply written off at taxpayers' expense encouraged everyone to ask for more. Among those who did was Youssef Alawi, minister of state for foreign affairs for Oman. His country wanted a grant of $200-250 million for weapons, he told David Ottaway of the Washington Post during an interview in Muscat, in addition to the $1 billion the United States would spend for improvements to the military facilities Oman had made available for U.S. use.(36)

A similar increase in military aid was planned for Somalia. The Somali leader, Siad Barre, once displayed his picture alongside the other stars of the Marxist universe, Marx and Lenin. Now "Comrade" Barre's picture hung alone in Mogadiscio, and in March 1982 he journeyed to Washington and announced that a "new chapter of closer cooperation" with the United States had opened. In 1980 Barre had agreed to allow the United States to use Somali military facilities during an emergency in the Middle East or Northwest Africa. In return the United States had increased its military aid to Somalia. The Reagan administration wanted to increase it by one-third, from $78.5 million in 1982 to $90-95 million and maybe more. Officials suggested that Somalia was concerned about the threat from Libya, but Barre disagreed. The United States has talked too much about Libya, he said. This only served to enhance Qaddafi's prestige. The real threat to Somalia came from the Soviet Union, Cuba, and East Germany. Libya had only money.

By far the most ambitious new arrangements were concluded with Morocco. Toward the end of 1981 and throughout 1982 the Reagan administration went out of its way to demonstrate its attachment to the regime of King Hassan. A cluster of high U.S. officials paid formal visits to the North African kingdom, including Secretary of Defense Weinberger, the deputy director of the CIA, Admiral Bobby Inman, and the assistant secretary of defense for international security affairs, Francis J. West. Former President Richard Nixon got into the act, as well, stopping in Morocco on the way home from Sadat's funeral, and returning at the invitation of the king for a vacation and policy discussions the following March. Secretary of State Haig visited Morocco in February 1982 to confer with the king and his ministers and to initiate serious negotiations over the acquisition by the United States of the right to use

Moroccan military bases. The king was scheduled to visit Washington in the spring. The United States had maintained strategic air bases in Morocco until 1963 when they were closed at the insistence of the Moroccan government. The revolution in Iran, the Iran-Iraq war, the death of Sadat, and the resultant possibility of upheaval in the Gulf had persuaded the United States of the need to acquire the facilities necessary to stage a rapid movement of sizable U.S. forces to that region. Morocco, about half-way there, was willing to make the bases available for U.S. use, provided certain conditions were met. In a sense, it was a classic swap: bases for aid. One of the first decisions of the Reagan administration after taking office was to offer to sell 108 M-60 tanks to Morocco. However, with only $34 million in U.S. military aid for 1982, Morocco declined to pay for the new weapons. At this writing the tanks still have not been sold. The solution of the Reagan administration was to triple military aid for Morocco to $100 million. Congress was wary of the war in the Western Sahara and might not provide all that was requested, but the intent of the administration was plain. Reporters with Secretary Haig's party in Marrakesh in February were told that the United States was seeking the use of two bases: one at Kenitra, south of Tangier, and the other at Sidi Yahia, west of Marrakesh. Both were near the Atlantic coast.

But more than aid and bases were involved. As part of its entente with the Moroccan monarch the administration decided to come down forcefully on his side in the war with Polisario. Haig told reporters that the United States supported the Moroccan position over the Western Sahara. In that conflict, he added, Morocco was endangered by "the actions of Libya, the high level of armaments provided by the Soviet Union, and the recurrence of these arms in various destabilizing actions."(37) At the end of his talks with the king, Haig announced that the two governments had agreed to establish a joint military commission and to take steps that would lead to the use of Moroccan bases by U.S. forces in times of emergency. The point, he said, was to draw Morocco into the strategic consensus the United States was building in the region among friendly governments opposed to the actions of the Soviet Union and its "surrogates" in the region.

This gave a clue to the other political basis of the new Moroccan-U.S. relationship. Morocco's opposition to the grant of membership in the OAU to Polisario at Addis Ababa had continued and had acquired a decided anti-Libyan twist. The closing session of the foreign ministers' conference at Addis was disrupted by the boycott of nineteen delegations, protesting the seating of Polisario. This was more than the one-third absent necessary to deprive the meeting of a quorum. The motion by Morocco to halt the meeting because of a lack of quorum was defeated on a technicality. Undeterred, Morocco continued its protest. On March 7, for example, the Moroccan government appealed to all African governments to reverse the Addis decision. It was a serious crisis for the OAU. As Abdelhaq Tazi, Morocco's secretary of state for foreign affairs indicated, unless a solution was found, the OAU could break apart. Tazi also indicated that unless the decision on Polisario was reversed, Morocco and its supporters would try to ruin the summit at Tripoli in August. Until there was a return to "legality," as Tazi put it, "there won't be a summit at any level." This was a direct blow at Qaddafi, who hoped to assume the presidency of the OAU at the summit in Tripoli in August 1982. As it turned out, Morocco's campaign was stunningly successful. When the OAU meeting opened in Tripoli only sixteen nations were represented. Qaddafi had been humiliated.(38)

In May during the king's visit to Washington, Morocco and the United States officially concluded the deal. The terms of the agreement were not made public. This undoubtedly meant that Morocco retained a veto over when the bases might be used by U.S. military forces, and that the United States was required to obtain Moroccan consent before using the bases. This was certainly the impression conveyed by Moroccan spokesmen, such as Foreign Minister Boucetta who advised reporters that Moroccan facilities would never be used against any Arab state.(39) A week before the king arrived, the House Foreign Affairs Committee voted to limit military aid to Morocco to $50 million and to prohibit U.S. advisors from going into the Western Sahara. On the same day Hassan left Washington, the State Department announced a five-year $200 million U.S. aid program for the improvement of dry-land farming in Morocco. This would mean a large addition to the existing $13.5 million already allocated for development assistance. On May 27, 1982, the United States and Morocco agreed formally that the United States could use Moroccan bases in emergencies. The identity of the bases was not given, nor were any other terms of the six-year agreement made public.

The decision of the Reagan administration to work closely with France in ousting Qaddafi from Chad was at once natural and paradoxical. France and the United States are allies, and contrary to initial worries in Washington the conservative Reagan administration found it easy to find common ground with the aggressively socialist Mitterand regime. The two allied governments shared a number of policies, including their opposition to Soviet intervention in Poland, the desirability of a Soviet withdrawal from Afghanistan, the need for a negotiated settlement in Southwest Africa, the importance of a settlement to the Middle East crisis, and the appropriateness of a major strengthening of Western, and particularly U.S., nuclear and conventional strength. This congruence of policy was registered and made public during meetings between French Foreign Minister Claude Cheysson and Secretary Haig in early June. Vice-President Bush visited Paris later that month, and Prime Minister Francois Mitterand and President Reagan held consultations in the United States on the occasion of the two-hundredth anniversary of the victory over Britain at Yorktown. There were disagreements, as well, especially over Central America, high U.S. interest rates and, in general, the tendency of the Reagan administration to see North-South issues primarily as they relate to its concern over Soviet expansionism in the Third World. This difference of view applied to Libya and in particular to the Libyan presence in Chad. As will be seen, France's method of dealing with Libya, of obtaining Libyan withdrawal from Chad, and of handling its relations with other African nations differed considerably from the United States.

The differences were both superficial and profound. The surface differences arose because of U.S. support for Egypt and Sudan in their backing of Hissene Habre's rebellion against Goukouni Oueddei's GUNT and the Libyan occupation of Chad. France under Mitterand re-entered Chad by supporting Goukouni, initially, at least, against Libyan attempts to overthrow him, and by sponsoring the introduction of an African peacekeeping force into Chad, whose arrival removed the last shred of plausibility from Libya's presence in the central African country. Even while it supported Habre, the United States backed these French initiatives and announced itself as "reluctantly accepting" of the other French decisions, such as the fulfillment of existing Libyan orders for arms, embargoed by Mitterand's predecessor Giscard d'Estaing in February. This apparent inconsistency could be reconciled by larger consistency in French and American policy: both were determined to force the Libyans out of Chad.

However, there are deeper differences of method and conception which are revealed by French and American cooperation and disagreement over Chad. The essence of the French approach was to oppose Qaddafi through the desire of other African states to end the Libyan occupation of Chad. Following this approach, the French government publicly renounced intervention in Chad's internal affairs and restricted its military activities in connection with Chad and elsewhere in Africa to the provision of "regional security" and protection of French nationals. At the same time, once Qaddafi withdrew from Chad and completed the repairs to the French embassy in Tripoli the Mitterand government was willing to resume normal relations with Libya. In this manner the idea of a Libyan contribution to African affairs and even the legitimacy in principle of such a contribution was recognized, although France reserved the right to oppose other Libyan initiatives in the future. France certainly agreed with the reluctance of Francophone governments to deal with Qaddafi; for example, their refusal to attend the Tripoli summit of the OAU. Nor did the French approach to Qaddafi put Libya's close relationship with the Soviet Union directly at issue. In a sense, by managing to draw Libya to a point at which normal relations could be resumed in a manner consistent with France's commitments to its African allies, Mitterand was then in a position to try to dilute the influence of the Soviet Union in Tripoli.

There were no such nuances in the U.S. approach. The Reagan administration had decided on total opposition to Qaddafi. In the administration's view Qaddafi was a surrogate of the Soviet Union and an international outlaw and, on both grounds, had to be opposed implacably. The withdrawal from Chad thus appeared to the administration as a tactical retreat. Since it represented no fundamental change in Qaddafi's outlook it could not be rewarded in any way. Since Libya's ties to the Soviet Union remained as close as ever it was impossible to think of restoring normal relations between Washington and Tripoli. So total was the administration's opposition that it was difficult to imagine how normal relations might be restored until Qaddafi was overthrown or killed.

The initial meetings between Haig and Cheysson and Reagan and Mitterand were relaxed tours d'horizon as two allied governments became acquainted.(40) Then a series of developments in Chad speeded the pace of French policy and began to expose the areas of cooperation and disagreement between France and the United States over the conflict in that sad, bleeding African nation. Through the summer and fall of 1981 the French government had tried both carrot and stick in its dealings with Qaddafi. On July 15, for example, Mitterand lifted the embargo on arms sales to Libya for contracts concluded before the invasion of Chad. The oil deal between Libya and ELF-Aquitaine was also allowed to go forward. It provided for the exploration of 5,770 square miles and an offshore concession. The French arms to be delivered included helicopters, thirty Mirage F-1 fighters, and ten fast patrol boats. Only after Libya withdrew from Chad and repaired the damage to the French embassy in Tripoli would it be possible for France to resume normal relations with Libya. In a move to blunt criticism of the opening toward Qaddafi, the French government pointed out that the United States still allowed U.S. oil companies to handle most of Libya's oil trade, despite its outspoken opposition to Qaddafi.(41)

In September Oueddei visited Paris, and apparently persuaded the French government to support him against the Libyans. The French promised, for example, to help in the reconstruction of Ndjamena even before the Libyans withdrew. There were other signs as well of increased French involvement on the side of GUNT. In an interview with the Washington Post the French minister of economic corporation and development, Jean Pierre Cot, repeated that France could not have normal relations with Libya until Qaddafi ceased to pursue an aggressive policy in Africa. But he also revealed a number of other steps the French government had taken. France was training a pan-African force that would be able, he said, to replace Libyan troops within a year. By that time, he added, France would have "helped free" Chad or have shown that Libya was there as an occupying power against the wishes of the Chadian people. The

8,000 French troops elsewhere in Africa would no longer be involved in internal politics but would attempt to maintain regional security and to protect French citizens. France would now become much more actively involved in Chad, he said, and was prepared to help Oueddei "reconstruct a sovereign and unified Chad," to win recognition by the OAU, and to rebuild N'Djamena. Despite his avowal that France would stay out of internal politics, Cot admitted that France was helping Cameroonians train Chadians to form part of the French contribution to a pan-African peacekeeping force for Chad. Asked about Qaddafi, the French minister commented that the Libyan leader had "an enormous capacity for bluff," more than Adolf Hitler, as he put it. Qaddafi's strength, Cot suggested, came not from terrorism or real power, but from "an extraordinary tactical intelligence and understanding of the governments around him."(42)

Strengthened by the French aid and the movement within the OAU to send a peacekeeping force to his country, Oueddei resisted Libyan demands to complete the merger proposed by Qaddafi a year earlier. In late October several articles given to reporters by French government sources stressed the possibility that the Libyan occupation might be prolonged. There was fighting between the factions of GUNT, between Ahmat's and Oueddei's troops at Mongo in central Chad, for example, as well as between GUNT and Habre's forces. It was possible, the French sources said, that the Libya-Chad merger might even be completed. When Qaddafi said in an Italian television interview that as long as the Sudanese government supported Habre he would "unfortunately" be unable to withdraw Libyan forces from Chad, the French became alarmed. Prime Minister Mitterand sent a cable to OAU President Moi from the summit at Cancun urging the dispatch of a peacekeeping force to Chad "without delay." Foreign Minister Cheysson followed this move with a statement that leading elements of the force should be in Chad within a week. To strengthen Oueddei the French government announced that they had begun to send light arms and ammunition to his forces in N'Djamena. French government sources now said that earlier in October Qaddafi had threatened to withdraw his support for GUNT and give it to Ahmat unless Oueddei completed the merger with Libya. Secretary of State Haig strongly endorsed Mitterand's proposal from Cancun and said the United States would support it diplomatically and possibly financially.(43)

An article in the New York Times on October 28 indicated that the French air force was preparing to airlift Senegalese and Nigerian troops into Chad. Keeping in step with the French, the State Department announced on October 27 that the United States was reviewing its policy and might stop or cut aid to Habre. The same day a UPI report from Paris said that sources at the French foreign ministry had stated that Jalloud and Ahmat had attempted to overthrow the Chadian government to forestall a demand by Oueddei for Libyan withdrawal. They had failed. Ahmat and Jalloud had arrived together by plane, apparently from Tripoli. Ahmat had moved some of his troops into N'Djamena and the Libyans had flown in reinforcements for their troops in the capital as part of the preparations for the takeover. Jalloud left N'Djamena the next day. On October 30 Oueddei asked Libya to withdraw its forces from Chad immediately. As the annual summit of French African nations opened in Paris on November 2, Habre announced that he was suspending his military operations against GUNT and the Libyans. As he arrived at Orly airport for the meeting, Oueddei told reporters that he expected Qaddafi to leave Chad by December 31.(44) The Libyan commander in Chad, Colonel Radwan Salah, received direct orders from Qaddafi to leave immediately, according to Agence France Presse.

In the end only three African nations — Senegal, Nigeria, and Zaire — contributed a total of 3,700 troops to the peacekeeping force in Chad, the first ever put in the field by the OAU. They were assisted in transport, food, and medical supplies by the United States and France. But the Western governments refused to pay the entire costs of the peacekeeping enterprise, and the members of the OAU were no more willing to meet the expenses, estimated by OAU officials to run some $160 million a year. Nor was it possible to take the financial difficulties of the force to the UN, for the GUNT refused to request UN financial assistance, and a request by the host country was necessary before the UN could act. After such a promising start, nonetheless, the new OAU and French initiatives failed to bring peace to Chad. The Libyan withdrawal was carried out without incident, but the peacekeeping force could not stop the fighting which, when it was renewed in 1982, steadily turned in favor of Habre. By the spring of that year Oueddei's forces were on the defensive and before long he and his GUNT were driven out of the country, which passed under the control of Hissene Habre. The outcome of the civil war had been completely reversed in less than eighteen months. Everyone could claim victory, except Qaddafi and GUNT. It remained to be seen whether Habre would be any more amenable to the wishes of his Egyptian, Sudanese, and American supporters than Oueddei had been to the dictates of his Libyan benefactor.

14
U.S.-LIBYAN RELATIONS SINCE THE BREAK

Qaddafi's decision to withdraw from Chad was only the beginning of a series of defeats and embarrassments that he would have to endure for the next eighteen months. He had only himself to blame. By late 1981 the Libyan dictator had united the United States and so many African, Arab, and European governments against him that he had lost all his international leverage. In its isolation Libya was compelled to suffer manipulation and punishment at the hands of others. There was nothing else Qaddafi could do but wait and endure the humiliations. Eventually, he knew, developments in the Middle East and Africa and the divergent interests of his opponents would split the fragile coalition against him. Then, but only then, would he be able to escape the international strait jacket he had so laboriously fitted for himself.

It is a measure of the soundness of Qaddafi's tactical judgment that, grasping this, he cut his losses and waited for the next round. His opportunity came as a result of Arab reaction to the Israeli invasion of Lebanon and the introduction of U.S. and European expeditionary forces around Beirut. The invasion and the European-U.S. intervention blunted the enthusiasm of all Arabs for close overt cooperation with the United States. It wasn't much, but through this small opening Qaddafi again sent his tanks, troops, and planes into Chad. He gained only a brief return to center stage, for the vigorous response of the United States, Egypt, Sudan, and France quickly stalemated his move. But the recapture of even a limited freedom of maneuver must have been very satisfying.

Before he could recover in this way Qaddafi suffered a second and then a third major defeat. He was denied the presidency of the

Organization of African Unity (OAU) – a post not withheld from Idi Amin – and the government of Goukouni Oueddei in Chad was overthrown by Hissene Habre, acting with the strong support of Egypt, Sudan, and the United States. The OAU decision to designate Tripoli as the site of its 1982 meetings would normally have brought the presidency of the organization to Qaddafi. It was not to be. When OAU Secretary General Edem Kodjo ruled that the membership of the Saharan Arab Democratic Republic (SADR) in the OAU could be decided "administratively" because a majority of member states supported its entry into the organization, he triggered a revolt against his decision and against Libya that wrecked Qaddafi's claim to the presidency and nearly destroyed the OAU. To protest Kodjo's decision, nineteen members quit the Council of Ministers meeting at Addis Ababa on February 22, 1982. The sitting President, Daniel Arap Moi of Kenya, viewed the protest and spreading boycott of the Tripoli meetings as "the most serious challenge to the survival of the OAU in its 19-year history." He sought but failed to find an acceptable compromise at a meeting of the previous bureau of the organization in Nairobi April 22-23.(1) He then urged all members to attend the Council of Ministers meeting, but by July 26 only twenty-eight states had sent delegations to Tripoli. This was five short of the thirty-three states required for a two-thirds quorum. When SADR refused to accept anything less than full membership (Nigeria reportedly suggested sitting only with the ministers and not the heads of state), the Council meeting dissolved.

Stung by the defeat, Qaddafi lashed out at the United States and France. The Libyan leader accused the United States of bribing African heads of state to boycott the OAU summit, previously set for August 5-8. When no quorum appeared in Tripoli, Qaddafi urged those present to forget the absentees and go ahead without them. Finally, on August 7, Abdullah Obeidi, head of Libya's Foreign Liaison Committee (foreign office) publicly admitted that the summit was a failure. A number of states remained in Tripoli for an ad hoc summit, where they passed a series of anti-U.S., anti-Israel, and pro-Palestinian resolutions.(2)

While the controversy over SADR's membership prevented the first set of Tripoli meetings, a second issue arose and proved to be nearly as troublesome for Qaddafi. The seat for Chad was claimed by two delegations: the representatives of the new government of Chad, led by Hissene Habre, and those of Qaddafi's protégé, Goukouni Oueddei, whose government had just lost control of that country. Neither was seated. But when delegations from forty-four states convened in Tripoli on November 15 for a Council of Ministers meeting the Chad question appeared again and could not be resolved. In a sense, the SADR controversy was repeated in reverse image. A majority of the members wished to seat Habre's delegation. The others argued that if the seat were not filled it would be easier for Habre and Oueddei to reach a peaceful settlement of the war in Chad. Nigeria again took the role of mediator, with a proposal to seat the Habre group pending a final decision by the OAU on which contender it would recognize as the government of Chad. The core of delegations supporting Habre weren't satisfied and walked out. Their departure deprived the Council of a quorum and the meeting ended in stalemate.

The contending governments held to their positions after the Tripoli Council failed to meet. There was no quorum for the heads of government session in Tripoli on November 23. Yet another compromise was tried: Habre could have the seat if he would agree not to send a delegation to take part in the meeting, on the understanding that no other delegation would be given Chad's place. When Habre's foreign minister, Idriss Miskine, rejected this proposal, the summit meeting collapsed. To keep the OAU alive President Moi and Secretary General Kodjo agreed to stay in office until a summit could be held. Libya, Ethiopia, Mozambique, and Madagascar then repudiated the compromise offer to seat Habre without seating him. Another ad hoc session was held, and another round of resolutions was adopted. These supported armed struggle in Namibia and criticized South Africa and U.S. friendship for South Africa. In addition, the Ethiopian head of state, Colonel Mengistu Haile Mariam, announced on November 26 that the nineteenth OAU summit would be held in Addis Ababa.

After the debacle, the Libyan government attempted to salvage something of its position. According to Obeidi, the failure of the summit meant that the previous OAU resolutions on Chad, which were in support of Oueddei's transitional government, were still in effect. In his view, Habre's regime had not been accepted by the OAU as the legitimate government of Chad. Nor was there any relief on the Western Sahara question. According to its foreign affairs minister, Ibrahim Hakim, SADR planned to continue to act as a full member of the OAU. Morocco's response was to declare that the failure of the Tripoli summit nullified SADR's admission to the OAU and left the question where it had been when defined by the OAU call for a referendum in June 1981.(3)

Despite its brave words Polisario yielded, and SADR withdrew from the OAU "voluntarily and temporarily." Freed of this controversy, the OAU could gather a quorum, and the nineteenth summit of the organization opened in Addis Ababa on June 8, 1983, with Qaddafi among the heads of state in attendance. When the Ethiopian head of state, Colonel Mengistu Haile Mariam, was elected president, Qaddafi left Addis Ababa. The secretary general, Edem Kodjo, was removed and an acting secretary general, Peter Onu of Nigeria, was chosen to replace him temporarily; delegates had not given a preponderance of votes to either of the candidates for the post from Gabon and Mali. It had become essential to replace Kodjo, because his country, Togo, had withdrawn its confidence in him after his decision to admit SADR.

It seems likely that SADR's decision to relinquish its membership in the OAU had been eased by the promise of a favorable resolution on the Western Sahara dispute. Several delegates told reporters that Morocco had agreed not to oppose a revival of the call for a referendum on the Western Sahara if Polisario withdrew. At first, Moroccan representatives denied such a deal had been made, but later admitted they had worked out much of the resolution on Western Sahara with Algeria before the vote was taken.(4) Other delegates feared that Qaddafi's defeats — Mengistu's election in his place and the loss of SADR's membership — would spur him to launch another invasion of Chad.(5) These concerns were not eased by the remarks of Oueddei's deputy, Mohamed Nur, to a New York Times reporter after Polisario's concession. "We will march on Ndjamena," he vowed.(6)

As dawn neared on June 11 the OAU was able to agree to a common position on the Western Sahara. Naming Polisario — but not SADR — officially for the first time, the resolution called on Morocco and the guerrillas to begin face-to-face negotiations. A peacekeeping force was to be constituted by the OAU and UN acting together. Although the resolution stipulated that voting should occur in an atmosphere free of "administrative or military restraint," there was no reference to the tens of thousands of Moroccan troops behind a 400-mile fortified barrier holding the northwestern corner of the territory claimed by Polisario.(7)

These were not the only omissions. The character of the administration of the territory during the vote was not agreed on, nor was the number of eligible voters settled. Neither Polisario nor Morocco accepted the OAU figure of 230,000 voters. One authority has suggested a "working estimate" of 120,000 to 150,000 for the entire population.(8) Apparently these matters, along with the question of the Moroccan troops, were to be arranged by a seven-member implementing committee whose members were: Guinea, Kenya, Mali, Nigeria, Sierra Leone, Sudan, and Tanzania.(9) Although Polisario had achieved a breakthrough of sorts in its mention in the resolution, the outcome decidedly favored Morocco. King Hassan had "agreed" to a referendum two years earlier.(10) He lost nothing in agreeing again, particularly when there was no mention of a withdrawal of his troops, and SADR had been denied its seat in the OAU. Although they supported the resolution, the Moroccan delegates made plain that they had not agreed to direct negotiations with Polisario.

The Israeli invasion of Lebanon and the forced evacuation of the PLO from Beirut were defeats for Qaddafi. He had long given money and arms to some of the uncompromising factions of the PLO there, and he had joined Syria and Iran against Iraq. To be sure, Hafez Assad of Syria and the PLO lost more in Lebanon, but the Libyan leader had taken their side and could not avoid sharing in their defeat. The Lebanese invasion and its aftermath shamed and angered Qaddafi. Day after day of Israeli victories without a telling Arab response; thousands of Arab dead and wounded; the PLO herded like sheep onto U.S. boats; the unanswered eleven-hour Israeli bombardment of West Beirut; the Reagan Plan for Palestinian confederation with Jordan; the massacres at Sabra and Shatila refugee camps; the intervention of the U.S.-European military force in Lebanon; the Fez resolutions by Arab heads of state, which offered the most yet to Israel; the U.S.-led negotiations for peace among Israel, Syria, and Lebanon.

These were bitter times. Whatever their feelings about the Lebanese or the PLO, all Arab leaders must have felt sadness as they watched the events in Lebanon unfold; they must have known anxiety as they wondered what was to come. Qaddafi hated what was happening in Lebanon. He also feared that the developments increased Libya's isolation and therefore its vulnerability to pressure from the United States and regimes friendly to it in the Middle East. But Libya was "impotent" as he recalled a few months later, and could not intervene.

Qaddafi pondered what he saw as a disaster, even as he tried to muster whatever influence he could to prevent Lebanon, the PLO, and Syria from concluding peace agreements with Israel. As 1982 ended he resolved to go on the offensive again. He would arrange for Libya and the Soviet Union to strengthen Syria even further, he would foster unrest and turmoil in Arab states friendly to the United States, and he would invade Chad. A victory for Libyan arms in Chad offered a number of attractions. It would be a fitting response to Israel and the United States. It would show the rest of the world, and particularly the other Arab states, the proper way to deal with "Zionists and imperialists." While the rest of the Arab world was shattered and demoralized, ready to make peace with Israel and accept an ever-larger U.S. presence, Qaddafi would attack and win greater territory and influence.

These decisions would cause a direct conflict with the United States. Qaddafi recognized this in advance. He knew there would be risks, but he was confident that he could control the danger and perform the kind of symbolic acts of sacrifice and leadership he regarded as essential after the catastrophe in Lebanon. Disciplined, perhaps, by the Israeli victories in Lebanon and his failure to win the OAU presidency, Qaddafi was at his most rational and cautious as 1983 began. At the same time his policies were more belligerent and uncompromising than they had ever been.

An important clue to his state of mind and intentions came during a meeting of Arab dissidents in Tripoli in early February. These were the people to carry out that part of his strategy which required the fostering of unrest in countries friendly to the United States or likely to be drawn into the peace process. Among those present were Lebanese, Jordanians, Sudanese, Iraqis, Somalis, Syrians, Hungarians, the president of the People's Democratic

Republic of Yemen, and Ahmed Jibril, head of the Popular Front for the Liberation of Palestine – General Command. Assembled at Qaddafi's invitation, the "Pan-Arab meeting of the opposition and popular movements in the Arab homeland" brought, by Libyan count, some 350 people representing 135 dissident organizations and movements to the Libyan capital from February 1-5. According to the official Libyan news agency (JANA), the purpose of the conference was to "draw up a new strategy of struggle capable of facing the military and psychological reality of the Arab world." The Libyans left no doubt about the nature of that reality. The point was to confront "the Arab defeatist reality."(11)

Qaddafi addressed the opening session of the conference. He gave one of the most brilliant speeches of his career. His intention was to inspire the dissidents to return home to commit acts of defiance and protest against their own governments, against Israel, and against U.S. plans for peace. During the speech he used his own feelings of pain and humiliation to anger and rouse the audience to act as he proposed. After the destruction of the Palestinian resistance in Beirut, he asked, what Arab regime can boast of being steadfast and having dignity and integrity? We watched Beirut burn as if we were scouts around a bonfire. Trying to sting them into action, he spoke eloquently of what had been lost in Lebanon:

> Destruction and unprecedented humiliation now exist. What more can happen to us if we fought America? . . . We are defeated . . . torn apart . . . expelled . . . . Our land is occupied. . . . Our honor is tread upon. . . . Our dignity is injured. . . . Our houses are demolished over our heads. . . . Like the sheep in a boat, the Palestinians were dispersed. . . . Our armies surrendered. . . . They lowered our flags and raised instead of them the Israeli flags. . . . They plant them now over Arab land. . . . There is no greater loss than this. They occupied, annihilated, and insulted us. We are the most despicable and contemptible nation on earth.(12)

Qaddafi brought more than a scourge to the dissidents. He offered a rationale for his alliance with Syria and Iran. It was not betrayal for Syria to decline to fight against Israel. Syria did not fight because it would have been destroyed. Qaddafi said that he had sent a personal message to Hafez Assad during the fighting. "Preserve the Syrian army from destruction and Syria from occupation. Another opportunity will arise."(13) Libya was not against Iraq or Saddam Hussein, he added, but the Iranian revolution stands against Israel and the United States, and no Arab should oppose it. "Even if this revolution espoused blasphemy, it is one that is opposed to America and Zionism." Moreover, Iraq made a peace treaty with the shah, friend of Israel and an ally of the United States. Why didn't Iraq fight the shah? It was not Syria and Iran that should be opposed but all the Arab regimes who were traitors to Arab nationalism and Arab unity.

The Egyptian opposition must come out and force Egypt to abandon Camp David. The whole world was saying that Israel had destroyed Camp David by its war in Lebanon. It would be no dishonor now for Egypt to abandon the accords. If the opposition doesn't act, then what was done to Egypt and then to Lebanon will be done in Syria and then Libya with Israeli troops under the U.S. umbrella and with the help of "Arab capitulation."(14) Why hasn't the opposition in Syria refused to service the plane and hotel of Habib? Qaddafi asked. Violence is not necessary. Boycotts, embargoes, sit-ins, demonstrations. All will breathe defiance and courage into the Pan-Arab liberation movement. Prove me wrong by rebellion against these regimes, he urged the audience. "Show me that you have the power to rescue the Arab nation from extermination."(15)

The statement adopted by the meeting reflected Qaddafi's views. It went further than the public text of his address in advocating armed struggle. Otherwise the positions taken were identical with Qaddafi's. The Pan-Arab liberation movement was in a grave crisis, the participants stated. Imperialism and Zionism are opposed to the aims of Arab liberation. "There is no option but to have a confrontation with them." The invasion of Lebanon had exposed "the reality of the tragic Arab conditions from the ocean to the Gulf." This included: the treachery of the reactionary regimes, the impotence of [Libya and Syria], the failure of dissident movements to confront Israel and the United States. To overcome the defeats, the opposition movements must adopt a program of armed struggle, increased funds from progressive states for liberation movements, widespread popular struggle (sit-ins, demonstrations, boycotts), and an increase in the "combat programs" of revolutionary opposition forces in various Arab states.(16)

Taken together, Qaddafi's rousing speech and the statement of the dissidents charted a course of defiance and military opposition to Israel, the United States, and the Arab regimes friendly to the United States. Of particular importance in discerning Qaddafi's intentions in his repeated insistence that a confrontation with Israel and the United States couldn't be avoided and that so much had been lost in Lebanon that nothing remained to lose, even in battle with the United States. Both the speech and the statement are startingly realistic in their recognition of the weakness of those who sought what Qaddafi called "Arab and unity goals." Qaddafi and his friends were weak. No one could doubt he knew that after his speech and the dissidents' statement. But as Qaddafi proposed again and again, weakness must not lead to surrender or compromise. At most, it counselled caution and a search for means to become stronger. The one power able to help Libya in this way is the Soviet Union, and Qaddafi would not wait long before turning to Moscow.

To summarize, in early February Qaddafi was preaching that because of the Lebanese disaster the Arab world faced a desperate struggle for its very existence. To escape destruction by Israel and the United States, the Arabs must launch defiance, rebellion, and armed struggle against Israel, the United States, and its friends in the Arab world. Collisions with the United States are inevitable, he warned, and not to be feared. With this in mind, no one should have been surprised at the crisis that blew up between Libya and the United States in mid-February.

Qaddafi wasted little time in renewing his defiance of the United States and its Arab friends. A few days after his speech at the dissidents' conference and his final rebuff by the OAU, Western diplomats and Chadian officials told reporters that Qaddafi had decided to attack Chad.(17) These complaints appeared in the press on the same day as news that President Reagan had sent four AWACS plans to Egypt in order to be able to help Sudan defeat a Libyan plot against its government.(18) Two days earlier the United States had moved the carrier Nimitz toward the Libyan coast. It is difficult to assess the accuracy of the reports about the plot against Sudan. The United States reacted as if they were true. The Reagan administration not only sent the AWACS to Egypt, but increased its pressure on France to react to Qaddafi's support for the Chadian rebels. The Egyptian government accepted the AWACS but responded to the Libyan moves very much more quietly than it had a year earlier, a result, perhaps, of its dislike of Israeli and U.S. behavior in Lebanon.

The story of the strong U.S. response developed in a peculiar way. Before the commotion ebbed, as much had been revealed about the strains in U.S.-Egyptian relations as about the Reagan administration's opposition to Qaddafi. During the weekend of February 12-13 the United States sent the four surveillance aircraft to Egypt and ordered the Nimitz to sail toward the Gulf of Sidra. The AWACS were sent, according to news reports, in response to the concern of the Egyptian government over signs that Libyan forces were concentrating to the south near the Sudanese frontier in order to support a coup against Sudan. The story in Newsweek spoke of a warning by "a trusted CIA agent" that Qaddafi would attempt to overthrow President Nimeiry of Sudan on February 18.(19) Officials at the Pentagon told reporters that Egyptian President Mubarak had requested the AWACS in order to determine exactly what Qaddafi was up to. Reporters were also told that U.S. reconnaissance satellites had spotted a build-up of Libyan warplanes at Kufra, a base on Libyan territory to the west of the Sudanese frontier.

According to U.S. intelligence reports Qaddafi planned to attack Khartoum from the air as Sudanese rebels attacked military and government objectives on the ground. The presence of the Nimitz near Libyan waters was confirmed by two Libyan fighters who broke off their approach when challenged by two F-14s. The dispatch of the Nimitz was meant to force Qaddafi to divide his air force. If Qaddafi had actually attacked Sudanese targets, the AWACS would have been used to direct Egyptian F-4s in battle against Libyan planes.(20) On the surface, the story seemed to be straightforward enough. Qaddafi was at it again – trying to overthrow Sudan. A swift harsh reaction by the United States and its allies wrecked the plot. "Qaddafi is back in his box where he belongs," as Secretary of State Shultz told David Brinkley on ABC television. But there were other parts of the story that suggested much more was involved than misbehavior by Qaddafi. Although President Nimeiry confirmed the existence of a coup plot in a joint news conference with his Egyptian counterpart, Mubarak spoke only of a Libyan violation of Egyptian air space, a problem, he added, that had been dealt with by a telephone call to the Libyans.(21)

There was also the question of the manner in which the public learned of the missions of the AWACS. The Pentagon correspondent for ABC television news, John McWethy, broke the story about movement of the AWACS and Nimitz on Wednesday, February 16. ABC broadcast the report despite a plea from the president's national security advisor, William P. Clark, to postpone it for twenty-four hours. Clark's story to the ABC bureau chief in Washington was that the immediate release of the information that U.S. forces had been shifted in order to defeat a Libyan plot would endanger the lives of unspecified persons. "They wouldn't be specific about lives being lost," said ABC President Roone Arledge. This left it unclear whether Clark meant the lives of the servicemen on board the Nimitz and the AWACS or the lives of intelligence agents in Libya who might have disclosed the plot to Egyptian or U.S. officials. Lacking a specific explanation of the danger to human life, ABC broadcast the story. The broadcast caused questions in the president's news conference. President Reagan replied with a cover story: the AWACS had been moved as part of a previously planned exercise, he said, and added: "There's been no naval movement at all."(22) The president's denial of naval movements started the media troubles for the White House, because other administration officials were telling reporters that the Nimitz had been moved, not into Libyan waters but from Lebanese to Egyptian waters as a diversion for the AWACS. The same officials were also saying that the reconnaissance planes had been sent at the request of the Egyptian government, which was worried about a Libyan coup against Sudan.(23)

Given the ingrained resentment in the U.S. media left by Watergate and Vietnam, any attempt to conceal government action greatly heightens interest in whatever might have been done. This is exactly what happened with the AWACS and Nimitz movements. Indeed, to those with post-Watergate sensitivities, it might appear that the president had done something and then lied about it. Not only was the administration contradicting itself, but the shoot-out in the Gulf of Sidra a year earlier was still fresh in the public memory. The administration never succeeded in coordinating its stories, assuming it intended to try to speak with one voice. At the White House, a senior spokesman for the administration, presumably Judge William Clark, tried to calm reporters and editors and said the media had incorrectly given the impression of a crisis. The senior spokesman said that the AWACS had been sent to Egypt because of Libyan behavior, but was adamant that the Nimitz's movements had nothing to do with the dispatch of the reconnaissance planes. The credibility problem for the administration was increasing, because the same stories that gave the White House spokesman's statements would also carry a direct contradiction of them from officials at the Pentagon and expressions of incredulity from others at the State Department. "Anonymous Administration officials," as the Los Angeles Times put it, "with ties closer to the Pentagon continued to report Thursday [February 17] that the Nimitz was sent to the area to discourage any aggressive Libyan action."(24)

The administration's cover story was in shreds. Perhaps it was not surprised to get into trouble with the Egyptians as well. The administration admitted that the AWACS had been sent to Egypt to conduct joint exercises because of a threat from Libya against Sudan. The Egyptian government said, in effect: "What exercises?" The United States and Egypt were not holding joint exercises of any kind. Servicemen from the two countries were training "in the use and operation of electronic equipment of American reconnaissance aircraft."(25) Throughout the hubbub, Egypt assumed a distant, cool attitude toward the United States.

Administration spokesmen also told reporters that the AWACS move had been part of a quiet signal to Qaddafi to leave Sudan alone. The hope was that Qaddafi would notice the presence of the planes and stop plotting. The Egyptians had insisted that everything be done without publicity in order to avoid any suggestion of Egyptian dependence on the United States. As described in the New York Times: "The cover story, agreed to by both sides was that the AWACS were sent as part of joint training exercises."(26) One problem was that the Egyptians refused to support the cover story. But there was little doubt that the administration intended to warn Qaddafi against an attack against Sudan and, by implication at least, a move against Chad. On February 18, a senior Pentagon delegation arrived in Cairo to discuss U.S. military assistance. It included the assistant secretary of defense for international affairs, Francis West, and the commander of the Rapid Deployment Force. Another senior U.S. official, Vernon Walters, former deputy chief of the CIA and then assigned to the State Department, went to Khartoum. Walters's visit was "entirely coincidental," a White House spokesman said. With front-page stories headed "Qaddafi Threatens War" and "U.S. Ready to Help Allies Meet Any Antagonist," the administration had ample reason to try to undo the atmosphere of crisis that had developed. But the story died hard. As the U.S. military delegation arrived in Cairo reporters were told of the run-in between Libyan MIGs and U.S. F-14s from the Nimitz over the Mediterranean near Libya. The U.S. fighters had "chased" Libyan planes away from the Nimitz, reported the New York Times.(27)

The crisis ended as abruptly as it had begun. On Saturday, February 19, the day after the aircraft encounter, the administration ordered the AWACS to leave Egypt and directed the Nimitz back to Lebanese waters. Officials in the Pentagon insisted that both moves had come after strong urging by Egyptian President Hosni Mubarak. The Egyptian leader "put much more stock in the intelligence reports about the planned coup than did the U.S. intelligence community," the officials added. The U.S. sources of this account of the crisis emphasized that the United States responded as forcefully as it had because of Mubarak's and Egypt's great importance to U.S. strategy. In particular they mentioned the use of the Egyptian base at Ras Banas on the Red Sea by the U.S. Rapid Deployment Force. The U.S. doubts about a Libyan coup attempt proved to be correct, the sources added, but: "With Qaddafi you just never know, and the President didn't want to take a chance once Mubarak had asked for our help."(28) One version of the U.S.-Egyptian plan was to put the AWACS and Nimitz quietly in place. Then, if Libya attacked Sudan, Egyptian and U.S. warplanes would destroy Libya's air force. If Libya did nothing, the allies would claim they had deterred Qaddafi's attack.(29)

Secretary of State Shultz was the first administration official to allow himself to be quoted saying that the United States had acted to counter a Libyan threat. "As far as we know," he said on the CBS television program "Face the Nation," "the threat that was clearly present had receded."(30) The planes were to leave in two days, a State Department official said. The Egyptians reacted in what had become a standard fashion. The Egyptian news agency announced that Egypt had "never asked the United States to conduct military moves in the Mediterranean or elsewhere." Egypt, the agency added, was "not an adherent to any country's strategy and has nothing to do with any moves by the United States or any other country."(31) Not to be outdone, the Egyptian defense minister announced in Cairo that he knew nothing of a Libyan plot against Sudan. Twenty-four hours later he added that the AWACS had come to Egypt for training and would leave when Egyptian authorities had decided the training had been completed.(32)

Libya reacted with threats. Qaddafi promised to turn the Gulf of Sidra into a sea of blood. The resolutions of the General People's Congress, whose meetings coincided with the crisis, were equally defiant. Libya would use its oil wealth, the delegates vowed, to arm the Libyan people and "all the revolutionary forces in the Arab and Islamic worlds." It would also create "suicide squads," a resolution stated, to attack Israelis in occupied Arab terrritory and Arabs friendly to the United States, "the leader of world terrorism."

The crisis ended without any shooting. Sudan continued to accuse Libya of plotting and massing military forces against it. The Egyptian government pledged its support of Sudan, and the AWACS and Nimitz were withdrawn. The whole affair left a curious impression. Qaddafi may have gained an advantage internally by being able to point to an external U.S. threat. President Reagan had acted quickly and decisively and, because there were no casualties, may have shown evidence of strength and resolution to Congress and the United States' allies, despite his curious handling of the cover story.(33) However, this appearance of strength was surely diluted by Egypt's determined coolness about the dispatch of U.S. reinforcements. If the Pentagon refused to stick to the cover story, at least officials there declined to be identified. In Egypt, the defense minister publicly denied that Libya had made threatening moves of any kind, thus explicitly contradicting Secretary Shultz.

This disturbing facet of the crisis went beyond a tactical Egyptian desire not to appear dependent on the United States. Plainly, Egypt was using the event and the U.S. handling of it to signal a deeper dissatisfaction with U.S. policy. The unanswered questions remain: Why were the anonymous Pentagon officials so talkative? Why were the Egyptian denials so emphatic? Most important of all: Was Qaddafi misled by the open Egyptian-U.S. disagreement into assuming he had gained the freedom of action he needed to attack Chad?

The next step in Qaddafi's offensive was to increase the support of the Soviet Union for Libya and Syria. This was the purpose of Jalloud's visit to Moscow March 16-18. There is no evidence in the public domain as to what was actually agreed to by the Libyan and Soviet representatives during the meetings. However, there are a number of clues that may be drawn from the responsibilities of the individuals Jalloud took to Moscow, the positions of the Soviet leaders they were reported to have met, and the coverage given the visit and the communique by the Soviet and Libyan media.

Based on this evidence, on the Soviet decision to send SS-5 and SS-21 missiles to Syria, and on Qaddafi's subsequent invasion of Chad, one would conclude that Qaddafi sought at least three major agreements during his trip. First, he asked and undoubtedly received an assurance from the Soviet government that it would provide whatever additional military supplies the Libyan armed forces needed to carry out the invasion of Chad. Second, Qaddafi asked for an alliance with the Soviet Union, or for at least a "friendship and cooperation" agreement similar to that between Moscow and Damascus. He was unsuccessful. The most that could be arranged was "an understanding in principle" (printsipialnaya dogovorennost) that Libya and the Soviet Union would conclude a friendship and cooperation treaty. Third, Qaddafi offered to pay for some or all of the cost of a major military strengthening of Syria by the Soviet Union. This was to take the form of the dispatch of highly advanced Soviet missiles to Syria, together with the thousands of Soviet military and technical personnel required to operate them effectively. Of the three suggestions, this is the most difficult to substantiate.

The Libyan delegation was composed of some of the most senior and important individuals in the Libyan government. They met with Soviet officials of comparable rank. Little more could have been done by either side to lend importance to the visit short of having Qaddafi and Andropov themselves attend. On the Libyan side, in addition to Jalloud, there was Abu Bakr Yunis Jabr, commander in chief of the Libyan armed forces; Abdul Ali Obeidi, the Libyan foreign secretary; Abdul al-Majid al-Qaud, secretary for atomic energy; and M. Shaban, Libyan ambassador (secretary of the people's bureau) in Moscow.

The Soviet leaders who met with the Libyans included Nikolai Tikhonov, a member of the Politburo and chairman of the Council of Ministers (prime minister) of the Soviet Union; Andrei Gromyko, foreign minister; Dimitri Ustinov, minister of defense; and N.V. Ogarkov, first deputy minister of defense and chief of staff of the armed forces of the Soviet Union. The Libyans also brought a number of secretaries with trade and economic responsibilities who met with their Soviet counterparts. But the most important participants on both sides were political, diplomatic, and military. An agreement for economic and technical cooperation was concluded between the two governments during the visit, but its negotiation would hardly have required the participation of heavyweights such as Gromyko or Ustinov on the Soviet side and Jalloud or Jabir on the Libyan side.

The coverage of the visit by the Libyan and Soviet media also suggested much about the nature and importance of the talks. The visit was covered simultaneously in Libya and the Soviet Union, and this allows a comparison of the treatment given to it by the two different government-controlled news organizations. In general the Libyans treated the visit sketchily. JANA did not publish a full text of the communique, and its other coverage was less complete than that offered by Moscow. Accordingly, the interpretation here is based largely on the Soviet version of the meetings. The Libyan vagueness, in the author's view, was intentional. Qaddafi felt obliged to disguise the weakness of his position, and to cloud his role as petitioner. The Soviet coverage of the visit, and especially the communique, give the clear impression that Libya adopted all major Soviet international positions, that the Soviet Union did not repay this embrace in kind, and in return – almost as an afterthought – the Soviet Union conceded an agreement in principle to conclude a friendship treaty with Libya.

The silences of the Soviet and Libyan coverage are eloquent. No recognizably Libyan positions receive a Soviet endorsement, while numerous exclusively Soviet formulations are endorsed by the Libyans. If anything, the two governments went out of their way to stress what they called "the proximity and coincidence" of their foreign policies. In such circumstances it is the smaller country – Libya – that is conforming to the larger – the Soviet Union – and not the other way around. Meanwhile, from the Libyans came repeated pleas that, as Jalloud put it in his response to Tikhonov's toast at dinner, the Israeli and U.S. attack on the Arab people made it "vitally important to coordinate actions" between Libyan and the Soviet Union.(34) The Soviet news agency TASS reported that Obeidi and Gromyko had stressed the importance of "stepping up cooperation" against Israel and the United States. They, too, confirmed the "closeness and coincidence" of Libyan and Soviet positions on all important international questions. There were also frequent references in press reports and in the communique to Libyan and Soviet agreement on disarmament in Western Europe and on the worldwide peace policies of the Soviet Union. However, no comparable Soviet endorsement of Libyan policies can be found.

Perhaps the most striking Libyan embrace of a Soviet position concerned Afghanistan. During his 1981 visit, Qaddafi had made great efforts to stress his disagreement with the Soviet intervention in Afghanistan. In March 1983 the formulation agreed by Jalloud and Tikhonov must have suited the Soviets perfectly. Libya and the Soviet Union supported the Democratic Republic of Afghanistan, the communique read. They backed a political settlement that would forbid imperialist intervention in that country's internal affairs.(35) There was even a reference to Israeli withdrawal to the 1967 borders as the only basis for a just and stable peace in the Middle East. This had long been the position of the Soviet Union. Qaddafi had never accepted it, but he was willing to tolerate its inclusion in the communique. If the Soviets had been willing to back Qaddafi against the United States, the logical place to have shown that backing would have been by a stern warning to the United States to refrain from threatening Libya. But when reference was made in the communique to the U.S. AWACS in Egypt and the movements of the Nimitz, the Soviet Union ducked the opening and agreed to issue only a routine condemnation of the "aggressive actions of the United States against Libya."

The message from the Soviet leaders to Libya was clear. We are willing to allow Libya to endorse Soviet foreign policy, but that endorsement will not win a commitment from the Soviet Union to defend Libya against the United States. There is precious little here for Qaddafi. Only the references to the "coinciding viewpoints" of the two sides on "the need for increased efforts" against Israel and the United States suggest that Qaddafi received anything at all from the Soviet leaders. Here was some evidence that the Soviets were willing to resupply Qaddafi after the invasion of Chad.

A broadcast in Arabic from Moscow by the Soviet commentator Alexander Timoshkin supported this interpretation. Speaking on the day Jalloud left for Tripoli, Timoshkin stressed that the military aid which the Soviet government gave to Libya "is not directed against any third party following an independent, patriotic policy."(36) Libya was an ally in the Arab struggle against imperialism, Timoshkin added. Strengthening Libya was in the general Arab interest. Further, Timoshkin assured his listeners, Libya "makes a great contribution to the consolidation of the steadfastness of Syria" against Israel and the United States. Presumably this refers to Libyan financing of Soviet arms for Syria. The Soviet commentator also repeated Jalloud's refrain: that the attacks on the Arab people created a "vital necessity" for coordinated actions between "the forces of national liberation" and the Soviet Union. This is the standard Soviet conception of its foreign policy in the Third World: all unite with the Soviet Union against the West, and particularly against the United States. But what was its relation to Libya in the early spring of 1983? Had Qaddafi agreed to pay for the Soviet missiles that would be sent to Syria? Had he promised to launch the war in Chad as a way of relieving the pressure on Syria? Both?

The emphasis on coordinating the actions of the Soviet Union and Libya suggests that there was a connection between the behavior of the states in the coming months. Unfortunately, the evidence is too slim to justify a firm conclusion. In the absence of more evidence of direct links between the two, a persuasive case can be made that the policies of the Soviet Union and Libya were simply running in parallel and, for that reason, offered mutual support. Qaddafi's alarm over the plight of the Arabs was genuine enough, and his determination to lash out at the United States was equally firm. The Soviets were content to resupply Libya after the invasion of Chad. After all, Qaddafi paid cash, and the intervention might distract the United States from its deepening involvement in the Middle East. In return Soviet leaders brought Qaddafi closer in line with Soviet policy and strengthened the rather tattered group of Arab states willing to coordinate their policies with the Soviet Union.

However, even if the milder, second version of the nature of the coordination between the Soviet Union and Libya is the correct one, it is consistent with the much more ambitious agreements sought by Qaddafi. The Soviets simply would not follow him as far as he would have liked them to. It must also be added that Jalloud's achievements in Moscow strengthened Libya, even if not as significantly as Qaddafi might have wished. At least the French would be moved by the threat to sign an alliance with the Soviet Union. In fact, French Premier Francois Mitterand took this line in his handling of the Chadian affair. France's goal, he avowed, was to prevent the extension of the superpower rivalries into the heart of Africa. In addition, the Soviet commitment to resupply Libya's armed forces was essential to the success of the invasion of Chad. Finally, if Jalloud was able to enhance Soviet military assistance to Syria, this was a success for Libyan policy.

In addition to drawing closer to the Soviet Union, Qaddafi showed his determination to confront the United States in a way that hit close to home and was particularly galling to the Reagan administration. He simply began shipping large amounts of arms to the Sandinista government in Nicaragua. The shipments were discovered on April 16, 1983, when four Libyan transports landed for refueling in Recife in northern Brazil. The planes' documents described their cargo as medical supplies, destination Nicaragua. Acting on a tip from U.S. intelligence, Brazilian authorities searched one of the aircraft, a C-130 Hercules, which remained in Recife for repairs while the others, three Soviet-built Ilyushins, flew on to Manaus.(37) They found tons of Soviet weapons on the Hercules and more of the same when they searched the Ilyushins in Manaus. Altogether the planes carried 52 tons of rockets, small arms, and two dismantled Czech-made jet trainers.

The sensational discovery was an intelligence coup for the United States. Because the Libyans had falsely listed the shipments, Qaddafi appeared to have subversive intentions in Latin America. A number of Latin governments were concerned by the weapons delivery. Venezuela had denied overflight rights, and this had forced the pilots to follow an awkward flight plan in the first place. The defense minister of Colombia, General Fernando Landazabal, told reporters that he had received foreign intelligence reports that the weapons aboard the C-130 had been destined for Colombian rebels.(38)

The discovery of the Libyan arms also came ten days before the president was to address Congress on the external threat to U.S. security in Central America: a wonderfully appropriate moment for the Reagan administration. It was a "tremendous gift" for President Reagan, as one administration official put it. "If you wanted to design a gift for Reagan, you couldn't find a better one." Qaddafi's initial reaction was to apologize for what he called the "dishonesty" of a Libyan aviation official, who had not correctly listed the cargo.(39) Later, when the Brazilians refused to allow the plane to continue to Nicaragua, Qaddafi resorted to name-calling. Brazil, he said, displayed "a complete subservience to American imperialism and an open hostility towards the Nicaraguan people and the Latin peoples who are struggling for liberty."(40) A spokesman for the Nicaraguan embassy in Brazil chimed in with a statement to reporters in which he called the arms a "military gift" from Libya to Nicaragua for use against the United States.(41)

Qaddafi's clumsy deceit and his interference in Central America had offended the Brazilian government and ran counter to Brazilian policy. The Brazilians chose to make a public issue of the shipments

— and risked cancellation of the large arms contracts between Libya and Brazil — for these reasons. They had no objection to Libyan arms shipments to Latin countries for purposes and in ways agreeable to Brazil. During the Falklands War, Libyan planes with accurate documents had delivered a number of arms shipments to Argentina by way of Brazilian airports.(42) Brazil's military leaders wanted the arms shipped back to Libya by independent means, with the four airplanes returning empty. For a time it appeared that Alitalia would accept the weapons on its jumbo 747s. This arrangement collapsed when, perhaps for political reasons, Italian airline officials insisted that each shipment be so small as to make the return of the weapons in this manner prohibitively expensive. Ultimately, a plan designed in the Brazilian foreign ministry was adopted. The arms were moved by land to Rio where the Libyan planes were loaded one at a time; each was allowed to depart only after Brazilian officials had determined that the previous flight had landed in Libya. The last plane left Rio for Libya on June 14.(43)

All these maneuvers by Qaddafi — the plot against Sudan, the coordination of policy and resupply arrangements with the Soviet Union, and the arms shipments to Nicaragua — fitted the Libyan leader's plan to confront the United States and to strike blows against its interests wherever possible. In a way, even the discovery of the arms on the Libyan planes in Brazil contributed to the image of militancy which Qaddafi wished to convey to the world and, particularly, to the governments of the Middle East.

But the centerpiece of Qaddafi's new offensive was the invasion of Chad. Beginning in May GUNT launched major attacks against the Habre government's forces in northern Chad. According to the Habre government they were supported by Libyan troops, armor, and aircraft. It seemed to be a replay of the 1981 invasion. However, there was one important difference. Qaddafi has never admitted that Libyan forces intervened in Chad in 1983. This clouded the whole question of the fighting for a time. Moreover, because the war was going on in an extremely rugged and remote area, and the front was fluid and capriciously dangerous, it was extremely difficult for the Western press to obtain independent confirmation of the Libyan intervention.

Before long there were reliable eyewitness reports from Chad that confirmed the presence of Libyan forces. Still Qaddafi stuck to his story. He was lying. The possible reasons for the deception are clear, although which was persuasive to Qaddafi is not so obvious. By denying that Libya had intervened directly, Qaddafi may have hoped to lull his opponents into complacency long enough for him to overturn the Habre government, or so to reduce its control of the country as to be in a position to compel its replacement. By avoiding a formal, public commitment to GUNT's campaign, Qaddafi also minimized the consequences of a defeat. He could far more readily back away from the fighting if he had never admitted being a party to it in the first place. It also enabled Qaddafi to insist that the rebel Chadian factions be included in any negotiations to restructure the government of Chad.

Beginning in May, the fighting built toward a crisis in August 1983. At that point, with Habre's forces deteriorating and Libyan pressure increasing, the United States and France intervened and brought the conflict to a stalemate. The government of Zaire, at U.S. urging and with U.S. aid, responded to the Libyan intervention by dispatching several thousand troops to Chad. Their presence freed more of Habre's armed units for combat against GUNT and the Libyans. France, with a large military force in Chad, sought negotiations between the parties, but without success. Throughout July, a thread of tension – a kind of subcrisis – ran between the United States and France. Mitterand assumed a position above the fray, suggesting that the Reagan administration was obsessed with Qaddafi, and that the basis of French policy was to prevent the division of Africa between the superpowers. The Reagan administration pushed the French hard to intervene militarily against Qaddafi and went so far as to implicitly threaten to displace France unless Mitterand acted. Qaddafi had again succeeded in exposing the conflicting interests of the coalition arrayed against him. But the French and U.S. interventions stabilized Chad, and the subcrisis in Franco-American relations passed. The Libyans reinforced their position in northern Chad, and the French, who disposed their troops along an east-west line drawn at the fifteenth parallel through Arada-Abeche-Ati-Salal, settled down for a long wait. The French moved the line north to the sixteenth parallel in late January 1984 after defeating a new rebel attack. At least most of the fighting had stopped for a time.

The main events leading up to the crisis in August began with the capture of Faya Largeau by the Libyan-backed rebels on June 25. The rebel column then moved south and attacked Oum Chalouba on July 2. Three days later Chad publicly requested French aid, and France refused to intervene. The French defense minister, Charles Hernu, cited France's 1976 agreement with Chad, whose terms limited aid to the provision of supplies and equipment. The village of Abeche fell briefly on July 10 and was then retaken. A French journalist stranded overnight in Abeche reported he had seen Libyan supply planes during the fighting. On July 25 the first shipments of U.S. military equipment arrived. The United States had agreed to provide $10 million in military aid, later raised to $25 million. On July 31, the Habre government reported that its forces had retaken Faya. They held on for about two weeks. But at this point, according to Western diplomatic sources, the Libyans dramatically increased the weight of their attacks against Habre's forces. The sources mentioned low-altitude attacks by jet fighters and helicopter gunships and concluded that Qaddafi was trying to break Habre before the newly delivered French and U.S. antiaircraft weapons could have an effect on the fighting.(44)

To prevent this from happening, the United States took four strong steps against Libya. First, on August 3 the Reagan administration announced it had ordered the aircraft carrier Coral Sea to joint the Eisenhower on station off the Libyan coast. A day later it sent two AWACS to Egypt ahead of their regularly scheduled arrival for maneuvers. On August 5, the United States announced that it had a vital interest in preventing a Libyan success in Chad. Important allies in the area, the announcement stated, must be able to count on U.S. aid against Libya. Then on August 6 the United States sent two AWACS and eight F-15s to Sudan to support Chad. An additional 700 troops were dispatched from Zaire at this time, to join the more than 1,600 already in Chad. Finally, to pressure the French the United States first leaked reports in Ndjamena that the United States was taking the lead in Chad with aircraft carriers, antiaircraft missiles, and advisors. President Reagan then sent Vernon Walters from the State Department to confer with President Mitterand in Paris. The visit by Walters was confirmed by Mitterand in an interview in Le Monde on August 25 after the crisis had passed. The U.S. official had come on an "urgent" visit, Mitterand said, on the day the AWACS were sent to Sudan.

The French government was annoyed by the U.S. tactics. In particular it resented having its hand forced in a way that made its actions appear to be subordinate to U.S. objectives. On August 8, for example, French officials accused the United States of having failed to consult them before sending the AWACS. There were other considerations. Mitterand had campaigned against neocolonialism during the presidental elections. On the other hand, the French worried that Washington would try to take their place in Central Africa. And they feared that not offering support would harm their position in Africa.

Although they were annoyed, the French took action. On August 9, amidst press reports of Libyan tanks and troops moving toward Faya Largeau, Charles Hernu announced that France would send 180 paratroopers to Chad "as instructors." They would have no combat role and were going under the terms of the 1976 agreement. He added that Libya, not France, had internationalized the conflict, and he warned Qaddafi against further attacks. "What Libya did, we'll do." French Foreign Minister Claude Cheysson warned that France "cannot be indifferent" to the Libyan intervention. Washington continued its sniping. A Pentagon source said that the AWACS wouldn't be used unless France deployed jet fighters to Chad. "The AWACS can do only half their job," he said, "if there are no attack aircraft." In addition, the United States announced that it would fly 800 more Zairian troops to Chad.(45)

On August 10, less than twelve hours after the announcement of the dispatch of the French paratroop-instructors, Qaddafi attacked Faya Largeau. Western sources said he had committed three armored columns in a pincer attack from the north, east, and west.

Habre lost control of the town the next day. Some of his troops were trapped, but most managed to escape to the south. France then tripled the number of troops it was sending, raising the total to 500 instead of 180. In Washington, President Reagan held a news conference as Libyan troops consolidated their hold on Faya Largeau. There were no foreseeable circumstances in which the United States would intervene, he told the reporters. The U.S. role would be restricted to airlifting African troops from those countries that wanted to help Chad. In any case, he added, Chad "is not our primary sphere of influence. It is that of France."(46) Although these words undoubtedly removed any doubts in Paris that the United States intended to replace France in Central Africa, they did not ease France's burden in Chad in any way.

Libyan and rebel Chadian troops continued their attacks to the south, as Habre's troops withdrew to Salal, an oasis 200 miles north of Ndjamena. Qaddafi again denied that Libyan soldiers were in Chad. "It is not true," he told the U.S. Cable News Network. France matched the deceit by continuing to call its paratroops "instructors". On April 13 France sent 150 of these "instructors" and 3 Puma helicopters to Abeche. A pattern had formed which would hold throughout the remainder of 1983. Libyan and rebel troops held the northern third of the country. South of them, on a rough line from Oum Chalouba to Salal, were Habre's forces. Behind them were the French "instructors." But the number of French troops was growing rapidly. On August 15, French officials in Chad said it had reached 700 to 800.

While they were building their military strength in Chad the French took pains to conduct themselves in a way that would allow a negotiated settlement of the conflict. On August 17, Mitterand told Le Monde that he would not seek the overthrow of Qaddafi and did not share the obsession of Chad's neighbors and the United States. "What interests us is Chad," a French official told the New York Times. What he meant, of course, was that France had an interest in holding the southern part of Chad as a glacis to protect its main interests to the south and west. By August 17 the French presence in Chad had grown to some 2,000 troops. On August 19 the French appointed an experienced general officer, Brigadier Jean Poli, to command its detachment in that country, whose strength was headed for 3,000, according to press reports.

These moves by France had drastically changed the circumstances in Chad. From about August 13 until early September an undeclared cease-fire existed in the country, as the Libyans chose not to engage the French force and, instead, to build up their positions around Faya Largeau. The French refused to give an official figure for their troop strength in Chad. French news reports put the total in the last week of August at between 2,000 to 3,000. There were, according to the Christian Science Monitor, around 3,000 Libyan troops and an equal number of rebels in the north under the nominal command of Goukouni Oueddei. To the south there were, in addition to the French, 2,000 Zairians, and 4,000 troops loyal to Habre. Bernard Gwertzman of the New York Times gave 1,000 as the number of French troops in Chad, with another 1,500 in the Central African Republic as a reserve.(47) The president of Zaire made an impromptu visit to Ndjamena on August 20 to publicize his support of Habre. On August 21, perhaps in response to reports that Libyan troops were massing for an attack, the French sent in 8 jet fighters – 4 Jaguars and 4 Mirages – and at least one KC-135 air tanker, which greatly extended the range of the French fighters. Qaddafi's jets had no in-flight refueling capability and were, consequently, outranged by the French planes.(48)

With a military stalemate firmly in place, the French turned to diplomacy. Mitterand sent a personal representative to Qaddafi and official representatives to Habre and Mengistu, president of the OAU. Qaddafi received the French emissary, but continued to refuse to admit that Libya had intervened in Chad. On the other hand, he firmly stated that French troops would have to withdraw. Nor was he any more helpful about negotiations: "One cannot envision in the short term a solution to the Chadian question."(49) Habre was equally opposed to negotiations with GUNT, although he welcomed negotiations for the withdrawal of Libyan forces. Of the two, the French would presumably find it easier to persuade Habre to move, although he had not been amenable to pressure from the outside in the past. Although the cease-fire broke down in early September, the French were able to scatter the attackers by sending their fighters over the battlefield at low altitude without firing. There the situation stuck.

Given the ins and outs of French policy, and the maneuvers of the Reagan administration to thwart Qaddafi in Chad, an apt way to close this chapter in Libya-U.S. relations might be in the words of a retired French truck driver who was interviewed outside Paris by an enterprising U.S. reporter during lunch one day in late August. "At one time or another," the elderly gentleman said, "we've defended both these guys who are fighting, the one who's in and the one who's out. It gets very complicated at times."

15
EPILOGUE

The record of Libyan-U.S. relations since 1969 is an instructive one. By constant close attention, by a willingness to resort to stern measures, and, above all, through a willingness to cooperate with friendly and allied governments, the United States can limit Qaddafi's ability to damage U.S. interests. The list of governments whose cooperation is needed is long, and the coordination of all the conflicting interests consequently becomes exceptionally difficult. They would include: Egypt, Sudan, Chad, Morocco, France, Tunisia, Nigeria, Zaire, and Saudi Arabia. France has its own group of allies in Central and West Africa to consult, and this at least doubles the list. However, what is lost in neatness and instantaneous response is more than regained in credibility and firmness over the longer term. The United States very nearly got too far ahead of its allies in 1983, as the cold reactions of the Egyptian government and the hesitations of the French revealed.

In general one must conclude that the policy of calculated hostility and stern retribution adopted by the Reagan administration is more effective in curbing Qaddafi than the previous approaches of the U.S. government, which were based on friendship and indifference. Qaddafi can cause too much harm to be ignored. The only real choices, therefore, appear to lie between the all-out hostility of the Reagan administration and a policy more akin to that of the French — downplaying areas of disagreement, not throwing the survival of Qaddafi's regime into question, stressing a willingness to return to business as usual after each collision. The French approach was clearly displayed during Libya's intervention in Chad in the summer of 1983. Mitterand made it clear to Qaddafi that within limits France was prepared to accommodate Qaddafi's desire, in the French president's words, "to guarantee, if not expand, at least its southern border." At the same time the French demonstrated by the deployment of their own troops just what the permissible limits of that expansion might be. Mitterand had no illusions about Qaddafi's motives. If Libya could easily advance further south, he pointed out, "it would not miss that chance."(1) A Socialist president of France with Communists in his government was not prepared to give Qaddafi that chance.

The difference between the Reagan and Mitterand policies would therefore appear to be one of style and not substance. Both were obliged in the end to resort to force and alliance politics to contain Qaddafi. Mitterand's approach may have made it somewhat simpler to start negotiations after the collision, but Qaddafi preferred, at least for the foreseeable future, to try to wait out the French rather than to negotiate. The gains from a different style therefore seemed illusory.

One could do worse than regard the experience of the U.S. government with the terrorist entrepreneur Edwin Wilson as a metaphor to summarize the Libyan-U.S. relationship since 1969. U.S. authorities finally arrested Edwin Wilson on June 15, 1983. He had been tricked into leaving Libya for the Dominican Republic, where he was allegedly to have been given refuge and a free hand to carry out his "business" activities. The United States had arranged for him to be detained at the airport in Port-au-Prince and then put on a plane for New York City. When he arrived on U.S. soil he was arrested by federal agents and taken to jail. Wilson was indicted in Houston and Washington on charges of illegally shipping explosives and arms to Libya and convicted in both trials. He received a prison sentence of 15 years and a fine of $145,000 in the explosives case, and a sentence of 17 years and fine of $200,000 in the arms shipment case.

What is astonishing — and what makes Wilson's case symbolic of the Libyan-U.S. relationship — is that from his jail cell, Edwin Wilson tried to arrange for the murder of his prosecutors, the chief witnesses against him, and a business contact he felt had wronged him. Wilson offered $250,000 to an FBI agent he thought was a professional killer for the deaths of the prosecutors, Lawrence Barcella and Carol Bruce, and $50,000 apiece for the deaths of seven others who were instrumental in his arrest and conviction.(2) Wilson was convicted in October 1983 for attempting to murder the prosecutors and witnesses.(3)

Edwin Wilson and the United States were on a collision course. It was beyond the power of the United States to deter or persuade him to behave differently. Even imprisonment failed to alter Wilson's determination to continue his destructive operations. The lesson is apt for Libyan-U.S. relations. Qaddafi is now restrained by strong bonds of national self-interest that unite a dozen governments and stretch from Morocco to Egypt and from Zaire to France to the United States. These shackles will no more change Qaddafi's determination to carry out his plans than physical jailing affected Edwin Wilson's murderous greed. Indifference and friendship were no more successful in containing Qaddafi than rehabilitation will be in making Wilson a good citizen. It remains to be seen whether Qaddafi's present confinement can be maintained.

REFERENCES

NOTES FOR CHAPTER 1

(1)   Memorandum of conversation between Ambassador Newsom and King Idris, August 30, 1967, Tripoli, A-61, September 7, 1967. Declassified under the Freedom of Information Act.

(2)   Interview with senior official in the Carter administration.

(3)   Interview with senior official in the Carter administration.

(4)   Oriana Fallaci, New York Times Magazine, December 16, 1979, pp. 121-22.

(5)   Edward Said, Covering Islam: How the Media and the Experts Determine How We See the Rest of the World (New York: Pantheon, 1981), pp. 51 ff.

NOTES FOR CHAPTER 2

(1)   Adrian Pelt, Libyan Independence and the United Nations, A Case of Planned Decolonization (New Haven: Yale University Press, 1970).

(2)   See U.S. Congress. Senate. Committee on Foreign Relations, Subcommittee on United States Security Agreements and Commitments Abroad, Morocco and Libya, Hearings Pt. 9, 91st Cong., 2d sess., July 20, 1970.

(3)   Facts on File, May 10, 1975, p. 312.

(4)   Interview with U.S. intelligence officer.

(5)   Among the general works I consulted in the preparation of this book some of the most important were: Omar I. El Fathaly and Monte Palmer, Political Development and Social Change in Libya (Lexington, Mass.: D.C. Heath, 1980); Ruth First, Libya: Elusive Revolution (New York: Africana publications, 1975); Robert O. Freedman, Soviet Policy Toward the Middle East Since 1970, rev. ed. (New York: Praeger, 1978); Michael C. Hudson, Arab Politics: The Search for Legitimacy (New Haven, Conn.: Yale University Press, 1977); Majid Khadduri, Modern Libya: A Study in Political Development (Baltimore, Md.: Johns Hopkins University Press, 1963); Harold Nelson, ed., Libya: A Country Study, 3rd ed., Department of Army Pamphlet 550-85 (Washington: Government Printing Office, 1979); William Quandt, Decade of Decisions: American Policy Toward the Arab-Israeli Conflict, 1967-1976 (Berkeley,

Calif.: University of California Press, 1977); John Wright, Libya: A Modern History (Baltimore, Md.: Johns Hopkins University Press, 1982).

(6)   Interview with John Cooley, former Middle East correspondent, Christian Science Monitor, Washington, D.C., January 15, 1981.

(7)   Peter R. Odell, Oil and World Power, 5th ed. (New York: Penguin, 1979).

(8)   Interview with John Cooley, Washington, D.C., January 15, 1981.

(9)   First, Elusive Revolution, p. 71.

(10)   See Robert Shaplen, "Profiles (David Newsom)," The New Yorker, June 2, 1980, p. 68.

(11)   Cooley interview. See also First, Elusive Revolution, p. 114.

(12)   See Rodney Tasker, "The Moros: A Butterfly in the Oily Spider's Web," Far East Economic Review, January 6, 1978, pp. 41-42.

(13)   Author interview with David Newsom, Los Angeles, California, February 12, 1981.

(14)   Ibid.

(15)   Ibid.

(16)   Ibid.

(17)   Ibid.

(18)   Ibid.

(19)   Ibid.

(20)   Author interview with John Cooley, Washington, D.C., January 15, 1981.

(21)   Patrick S. Seale and Maureen McConville, The Hilton Assignment (London: Temple Smith, 1973).

(22)   Author interview, Los Angeles, California, February 12, 1981.

(23)   Ibid.

(24)   Author interview with Blakeley, Washington, D.C., April 1981.

(25)   The principal sources consulted were: M. A. Adelman, The World Petroleum Market (Baltimore: Johns Hopkins University Press, 1972); Sheikh Rustum Ali, Saudi Arabia and Oil Diplomacy (New York: Praeger, 1976); James A. Bill and Robert W. Stookey, Politics and Petroleum: The Middle East and the United States (Brunswick, Ohio: King's Court Communications, 1975); John M. Blair, The Control of Oil (New York: Pantheon, 1976); Henry Kissinger, White House Years (Boston: Little, Brown, 1979); Robert B. Krueger, The United States and International Oil (New York: Praeger, 1975); Peter R. Odell, Oil and World Power (New York: Penguin, 1979); Anthony Sampson, The Seven Sisters: The Great Oil Companies and the World They Shape (New York: Bantam, 1976); Frank C. Waddams, The Libyan Oil Industry (Baltimore: Johns Hopkins University Press, 1980). U.S. Congress. Senate. Committee

on Foreign Relations. Subcommittee on Multinational Corporations. Hearings on Multinational Petroleum Corporations and United States Foreign Policy, Pts. 4-9; and Report on Multinational Corporations and U.S. Foreign Policy, 93rd Cong., 2d sess., 1974, 1975.

(26) P. Odell in his Oil and World Power, advanced the view that the U.S. government simply folded in Tripoli and Teheran in order to hurt the European nations and Japan by raising their energy bill. Unfortunately for his argument he cited only the consequences of the price rises, which undoubtedly hurt Europe and Japan more than the United States. Specifically, Odell argued: ". . . given the fact that the U.S.A. was fed up with a situation in which the rest of the industrialized world had access to cheap energy (and which the U.S.A. itself could not have because of its underlying belief in a policy of autarky in its energy policy), it deliberately initiated a foreign policy which aimed at getting oil-producing nations' revenues moving strongly up by talking incessantly to the producers about their low oil prices and by showing them the favorable impact of much higher prices. It was, of course, assured of the co-operation of the largely American oil companies in ensuring that these cost increases, plus further increases designed to ensure higher profit levels for the companies, were passed on to the European and Japanese energy consumers, so eliminating their energy-cost advantage over their competitors in the United States. And, in as far as the U.S.A. itself would be affected by the higher foreign-exchange costs of the increased amount of foreign crude that it expected to have to import, even this, it was argued, would be offset entirely, or to a large degree, by the greatly enhanced abilities of the U.S. oil companies to increase their earnings and, thus, their remittances of profits back to America.

"Thus, within the framework of a re-evaluation of how their best interests could be served and the consequential establishment of what might be termed a somewhat 'unholy alliance' between the United States, the international oil companies and the O.P.E.C. countries, the stage was set for changing the international oil-power situation as it had evolved over the previous fifteen years." (pp. 215-16).

(27) Author interview with David Newsom, Los Angeles, California, February 12, 1981. See also James E. Akins, "The Oil Crisis: This Time the Wolf Is Really Here," Foreign Affairs, April 1973, pp. 462-90.

(28) U.S. Congress. Senate. Committee on Foreign Relations. Subcommittee on Multinational Corporations, testimony of George Schuler, Multinational Petroleum Corporations and U.S. Foreign Policy, Part 6 (Appendix to Part 5), pp. 1-2.

(29) The reductions in production and the increases in payments to the Libyan government in 1970 are well described in Frank C. Waddams, The Libyan Oil Industry (Baltimore: Johns Hopkins University Press, 1980), ch. 12.

(30) John M. Blair, The Control of Oil (New York: Pantheon, 1976), p. 218.

(31) Ibid., p. 220.

(32) Quoted in Blair, The Control of Oil, p. 225.

(33) Ibid., p. 227.

(34) First, Elusive Revolution, p. 71; Odell, Oil and World Power, pp. 215-16.

(35) See U.S. Congress. Senate. Schuler's remarks, Multinational Petroleum Corporations and U.S. Foreign Policy, Part 5, pp. 75-143; Part 6, pp. 1-222.

(36) See especially U.S. Congress. Senate. Committee on Foreign Relations, the testimony of the vice-president of Standard Oil of California, Hearings on Multinational Petroleum Corporations, Pt. 7, pp. 426-27.

(37) The shah's words to U.S. Ambassador MacArthur are given in Blair, Control of Oil, p. 225.

(38) Hearings on Multinational Petroleum Corporations, Chronology of the Libyan Negotiations, 1970-71, p. 4.

(39) See Robert B. Krueger, The United States and International Oil: A Report from the Federal Energy Administration on U.S. Firms and Government Policy (New York: Praeger, 1975), pp. 61-75, especially, p. 66. See also U.S. Congress. Senate. The testimony of the oil company attorney, John T. McCloy, Hearings on Multinational Petroleum Corporations, Part 4. McCloy disagreed that the U.S. government had forced the collapse of the single negotiation strategy. Instead, he told the Church committee, the industry had made the best deal it could and had for its own reasons agreed to split the negotiations.

(40) Blair, The Control of Oil, pp. 233-34.

NOTES FOR CHAPTER 3

(1) Facts on File (hereafter FF), January 7-13, 1973, p. 20.

(2) See Keesing's Contemporary Archives (hereafter KCA), March 5-11, 1973, pp. 25, 762-64; September 17-23, 1973, pp. 26,105-6; FF, June 17-23, 1973, pp. 262, 526.

(3) Quoted in Claire Sterling, The Terror Network (New York: Holt, Rinehart and Winston and Reader's Digest Press, 1981), p. 304.

(4) Ibid., p. 259.

(5) Ibid.

(6) Bryan Crozier, "Libya's Foreign Adventures," Conflict Studies, no. 41 (December 1973); cited in Sterling, Terror Network, ch. 14, note 5. Sterling accepts Crozier's findings and regards the key break with the Palestinians as consistent with Qaddafi's engagement with European Fascists.

(7) Sterling, Terror Network, p. 118.

(8) Ibid., n. 19, pp. 321-22.

(9) KCA, March 18-24, 1974, p. 26,417.

(10) Sterling, Terror Network, p. 140.

(11) Quoted in ibid., p. 140.

(12) Ibid., p. 141.

(13) Ibid., p. 265.

(14) Ibid., p. 145.

(15) On the PFLP denunciation of Qaddafi on August 18, 1973 see FF, August 19-25, 1973, p. 699.

(16) See KCA, July 1-7, 1974, p. 26,603.

(17) KCA, August 2-8, 1973, p. 25,806.

(18) KCA, April 30-May 6, p. 25,865.

(19) Ibid.

(20) Interview Figaro, April 20, 1973, cited in KCA, July 2-8, 1973, p. 25,968.

(21) Sterling, Terror Network, p. 161, and n. 19, p. 325.

(22) Ibid., p. 161.

(23) KCA, April 30-May 6, 1973, p. 25,868.

(24) Ibid., March 18, 1974, p. 26,417.

(25) Ibid.

(26) See FF, Feb. 18-25, 1973, p. 136; Feb. 25-Mar. 3, 1973, p. 160.

(27) Sterling, Terror Network, p. 265 and n. 18, p. 338.

(28) Ibid., p. 265.

(29) New York Times, Sept. 13, 1975. See also Walid Khalidi, Conflict and Violence in Lebanon: Confrontation In the Middle East. (Cambridge, Mass.: Center for International Affairs, 1981), pp. 85-86.

(30) Sterling, Terror Network, pp. 261-64.

(31) See Jeune Afrique, February 13, 1980.

(32) Claire Sterling, "Terrorism! Tracing the International Network," New York Times Magazine, March 1, 1981, pp. 24, 59.

(33) Ibid., pp. 19, 55.

(34) Sterling, Terror Network, p. 295.

(35) See John W. Amos II, Palestinian Resistance: Organization of a Nationalist Movement (New York: Pergamon Press, 1980), ch. 10.

(36) Ibid., p. 246.

(37) Ibid., p. 217. My comments on the social-technical and Palestinian roots of terrorism follow Amos, Palestinian Resistance, p. 217 ff.

(38) Ibid., p. 227, and Appendix 12.

(39) Ibid., p. 245.

(40) Ibid., p. 251.

(41) Segre and Adler, "The Ecology of Terrorism," Survival, quoted in ibid., p. 234.

(42) Amos, Palestinian Resistance, p. 234.

(43) Ibid., p. 246.

(44) Ibid., pp. 246-47. It is always difficult to evaluate the truth of these stories. In this case, for example, the name of the

Palestinian Red Army would hardly have appealed to a fervent Muslim like Qaddafi.

(45) Ibid., p. 219.

NOTES FOR CHAPTER 4

(1) Keesing's Contemporary Archives (hereafter KCA), Jan. 31-Feb. 7, 1980, p. 23,809. See also Facts on File (hereafter FF), Dec. 25-Dec. 31, 1969, p. 851; New York Times (hereafter NYT), Jan. 22, 1970.

(2) NYT, Jan. 22, 1970.

(3) See ibid., Jan. 24, 1970.

(4) Ibid., Feb. 10, 1970.

(5) For details of the arms transfers to Libya during this period, see World Armaments and Disarmament: SIPRI Yearbooks 1968-69, 1969-70, 1972, 1973, 1974, Stockholm International Peace Research Institute (New York: Humanities Press, annual).

(6) NYT, Nov. 19, 1973.

(7) Ibid., Nov. 21, 1973.

(8) Ibid., Nov. 22, 1973.

(9) See Robert O. Freedman, Soviet Policy Toward the Middle East Since 1970, rev. ed. (New York: Praeger, 1978), pp. 72, 79.

(10) See ibid., p. 87.

(11) Quoted in KCA, July 8-14, 1974, p. 26,609.

(12) Ibid.

(13) Freedman dates the beginning of large Soviet arms shipments to Libya as "soon after" Kosygin's visit to Libya in May 1975. See his Soviet Policy, p. 200.

(14) Pravda, May 15, 1974, quoted in ibid., pp. 160-61.

(15) Ibid.

(16) Ibid., p. 277.

(17) Ibid., p. 200.

(18) Pravda, May 15, 1974, quoted in ibid., p. 160.

(19) Roger F. Pajak, "Soviet Arms Transfers as an Instrument of Influence," Survival 23 (July/August 1981): 170-71.

(20) Yearbook (Stockholm: Stockholm International Peace Research Institute, annual); The Military Balance (London: International Institute for Strategic Studies, annual).

(21) FF, September 20, 1975, p. 678.

(22) NYT, April 10, 1975.

(23) KCA, September 1-7, 1975, pp. 27,313-14.

(24) FF, September 20, 1975, p. 680.

(25) Ibid., Dec. 31, 1975, pp. 995, 1,025.

(26) KCA, May 28, 1975, p. 27,755.

(27) KCA, January 7, 1977, p. 28,128.

(28) Washington Post, March 15, 1976.

(29) Excerpts from the Pravda article and the Soviet-Libyan communique are in KCA, January 28, 1977, pp. 28,165-66.

(30) FF, December 25, 1976, pp. 964-65.

(31) See ibid., April 9, 1977, p. 249; for deterioration of relations between Sudan and Ethiopia see KCA, July 1, 1977, pp. 28,422-23.

(32) Interview with David Newsom, Los Angeles, California, February 12, 1981.

(33) Wall Street Journal, September 26, 1977.

(34) KCA, June 17, 1977, p. 28,379.

(35) NYT, March 29, 1978.

(36) FF, February 4, 1978, p. 61.

NOTES FOR CHAPTER 5

(1) For a discussion of the Carter administration's policy see P. Edward Haley, "Carter's Lonesome Road to Peace: The Effects of Negotiating Strategy on Policy," (Los Angeles: Center for International and Strategic Affairs, 1981).

(2) Interview with senior official in the Carter administration.

(3) For two informed Israeli views on this crucial matter see Moshe Dayan, Breakthrough: A Personal Account of the Egyptian-Israeli Peace Negotiations (New York: Knopf, 1981); and Ezer Weizman, The Battle for Peace (Toronto: Bantam, 1981).

(4) See Facts on File (hereafter FF), October 15, 1977, p. 769; and October 22, 1977, pp. 792-93.

(5) Ibid., December 3, 1977, p. 909.

(6) Ibid., December 10, 1977, p. 929.

(7) See ibid., November 26, 1977, p. 896.

(8) Keesing's Contemporary Archives (hereafter KCA), April 22, 1977, p. 28,307-8. Habre's role in Madame Claustre's captivity was deeply resented in France and contributed to France's reluctance to aid Habre during the second Libyan intervention in Chad in 1983.

(9) FF, November 12, 1977, p. 852.

(10) KCA, January 28, 1977, p. 28,156.

(11) FF, March 3, 1978, p. 139.

(12) Texts of the agreement may be found in ibid., September 22, 1978, pp. 711-12; texts of letters exchanged among the three parties are in ibid., September 29, p. 731.

(13) Ibid., September 29, 1978, p. 730.

(14) Ibid., October 27, 1978, p. 803.

(15) Text of the communique is in KCA, June 8, 1979, pp. 29,659-60.

(16) FF, December 31, 1978, p. 993.

(17) John Amos, Palestinian Resistance: Organization of a Nationalist Movement (New York: Pergamon Press, 1980), Appendix 16, pp. 344-45.

(18) Ibid., p. 230.
(19) Foreign Broadcast Information Service, Daily Report, vol.5, no. 061, Middle East and North Africa, March 28, 1979, p. I1. (Hereafter: FBIS, date, page.)
(20) Ibid., March 30, 1979, p. A1.
(21) For the text of the PLO working paper see ibid., March 28, 1979, p. A4.
(22) See, for example, the remarks of the chairman of the conference, Dr. Sahun Hammadi, quoted on Baghdad radio on March 29. Ibid., March 20, 1979, pp. A1-A2.
(23) For a summary of Hussein's address see ibid., March 27, 1979, pp. A2-A3.
(24) Ibid., March 29, 1979, pp. A1-A2.
(25) The text of the Arab League Council resolution passed at Baghdad on March 31 may be found in ibid., April 2, 1979, pp. A1-A8. The resolution has two appendixes which name the specialized Arab agencies from which Egypt was suspended.
(26) FBIS, December 7, 1979, p. 12.
(27) See New York Times (hereafter NYT), December 11, 1979, and FF, December 14, 1979, p. 937.
(28) FBIS, December 3, 1979, pp. 13-14.
(29) Ibid., December 7, 1979, p. A5.
(30) Ibid., December 10, 1979, p. I1.
(31) Ibid., p. 15.
(32) Ibid., December 11, 1979, pp. A3, A4.
(33) Ibid., p. A5.
(34) Ibid., December 13, 1979, p. A2.
(35) Ibid., December 17, 1979, p. A4.
(36) Ibid., December 18, 1979, p. A3.
(37) Der Spiegel, December 17, 1979, pp. 26-29; quoted in ibid., December 19, 1979, p. A6.
(38) See ibid., December 21, 1979, p. A1.
(39) Ibid., December 26, 1979, p. 12.
(40) Ibid., December 27, 1979, pp. A2, I1-I2.

NOTES FOR CHAPTER 6

(1) Keesing's Contemporary Archives (hereafter KCA), May 12, 1978, p. 28,977.
(2) Quoted in ibid.
(3) Ibid.
(4) International Herald Tribune, March 25-26, 1978.
(5) London Times, July 5, 1978; Facts on File (hereafter FF), July 28, 1978, p. 572.
(6) FF, July 28, 1978, p. 561.

(7)   See, for example, the statement to the press on June 8 by Tanzanian President Julius Nyerere. KCA, August 11, 1978, p. 29,131.

(8)   FF, December 31, 1978, p. 999; KCA, October 13, 1978, pp. 29,256-57.

(9)   KCA, April 14, 1978, p. 28,928.

(10)   Ibid., p. 29,307.

(11)   Ibid.

(12)   For the French paper's chart comparing the numbers of Cuban and French military personnel in Africa see KCA, August 11, 1978, p. 29,129.

(13)   There were, in addition to FAN and FAT, Goukouni Oueddei's Forces armees populaires (FAP) of Frolinat; Mouvement populaire pour la liberation du Tchad (MPLT or Third Army); Forces armees occidentales (FAO); Front populaire de liberation (FPL); Premiere armee Volcan (or First Army); Conseil democratique revolutionnaire (or New Volcano); Frolinat (Front de liberation nationale du Tchad) originel; Frolinat fondamental; and l'Union nationale democratique (UND).

(14)   Ibid., January 12, 1979, p. 29,399.

(15)   Ibid., February 1, 1980, p. 30,065.

(16)   The Council members were: Frolinat: Goukouni Oueddei (Chairman and Information); Sayyid ash-Shaykh Bin Omar (Education and Labor); FAN: Mahamat Nouri (Public Works, Transport, Communications); Mahamat Saleh Ahmat (Finance and Planning); FAT: Lt. Colonel Wadal Abdel Kadar Kamougue (Agriculture, Armed Forces); Barma Ramadan Omer (Foreign Affairs); MPLT: Aboubakar Mahamat Abderaman (Interior); Idriss Adoum Mustapha (Health).

(17)   Ibid., February 1, 1980, p. 30,066.

(18)   International Herald Tribune, June 22, 1979. The five claimants were: Acyl Ahmat, Conseil democratique revolutionnaire (New Volcano Army) supported by Libya in the extreme north and southeast; Abdoulaye Adoum Dana, Premier armee Volcan (First Army), supported by Sudan in the northeast; Abba Siddick, Frolinat originel; Mohammed Abba Said, Front Populaire de liberation, in central Chad; and Hadjero Senoussi, Frolinat-fondamental.

(19)   London Times, July 5, 1978.

(20)   KCA, February 1, 1980, pp. 30,066-67.

(21)   FF, May 4, 1979, p. 329.

(22)   Ibid., p. 30,067.

(23)   KCA, June 22, 1979, p. 29,671.

(24)   Ibid., p. 29,673.

(25)   New York Times, April 1, 2, 1979.

(26)   Ibid., April 6, 1979.

(27)   Ibid., April 15, 16, 1979.

(28)   KCA, June 22, 1979, p. 29,674.

(29)   Ibid., April 27, 1979, pp. 29,565-67.

(30)   Ibid., September 21, 1979, p. 29,841.

(31) The text of the peace agreement may be found in John Damis, Conflict in Northwest Africa: The Western Sahara Dispute (Stanford, Calif.: Hoover Institution Press, 1982), pp. 150-51.

(32) KCA, November 9, 1979, pp. 29,917-20, 29,925.

(33) Ibid., July 6, 1979, p. 29,700; FF, April 20, 1979, p. 277.

NOTES FOR CHAPTER 7

(1) New York Times (hereafter NYT), January 29, 1980.

(2) Ibid., February 1, 1980.

(3) See also Jeune Afrique, February 13, 1980.

(4) Washington Post (hereafter WP), February 5, 1980.

(5) Le Monde, January 31, 1980.

(6) Ibid.

(7) NYT, February 1, 1980.

(8) WP, February 1, 1980.

(9) NYT, February 1, 1980; WP, February 5, 1980.

(10) French Domestic Radio, Feb. 5, 1980, Federal Broadcast Information Service (hereafter FBIS), February 7, 1980, p. 17.

(11) FBIS, February 5, 1980, p. 14. See also Tripoli radio report, ibid., pp. 16-17.

(12) Ibid., February 5, 1980, p. 112.

(13) Agence France-Presse interview in FBIS, February 11, 1980, pp. 12-15.

(14) Ibid., February 3, 1980, p. 11.

(15) Ibid., February 4, 1980, p. 15.

(16) Ibid., February 11, 1980, p. 15.

(17) Interview in Le Figaro, February 9, 1980, in FBIS, February 19, 1980, p. 16.

(18) The text of the Council resolution is in FBIS, February 29, 1980, p. A4.

(19) FBIS, February 29, 1980, p. 14.

(20) See NYT, February 1, 1980; FBIS, January 21, 1980, pp. 14-15; February 1, 1980, p. I1.

(21) NYT, May 21, 1980.

(22) FBIS, January 23, 1980, p. 16.

(23) Ibid., January 28, 1980, p. A13.

(24) Seymour M. Hersh "The Qaddafi Connection," New York Times Magazine, June 14, 1981, p. 52.

(25) FBIS, January 9, 1980, p. I1.

(26) On closer relations with the Soviet Union and the break with Fatah see FBIS, January 1980, passim; Los Angeles Times, January 18, 1980.

(27) NYT, May 15, 1980.

(28) WP, September 14, 1980.

(29) Text of the declaration of the revolutionary committees is in FBIS, February 7, 1980, p. 19.

(30) WP, April 18, 1980.
(31) NYT, April 11, 1980.
(32) Ibid., April 26, 1980.
(33) In June 1981 Terpil was convicted in absentia on the New York City charges and given the maximum sentence of 17-53 years in jail.
(34) Ibid., April 25, 1980.
(35) Hersh, "The Qaddafi Connection," p. 58.
(36) Ibid.
(37) Ibid., p. 56.
(38) Ibid.
(39) NYT, May 5, 1980.
(40) Ibid., May 8, 9, 10, 1980.
(41) WP, May 4, 1980.
(42) NYT, May 11, 12, 1980.
(43) Neue Zuricher Zeitung, May 14, 1980.
(44) NYT, May 22, 1980.
(45) Ibid., May 23, 1980.
(46) WP, June 14, 1980.
(47) This discussion is based in large part on Bernard Nossiter's excellent articles on the case. See especially NYT, May 26, 27, and July 16, 1981.
(48) Ibid., May 26, 1981.
(49) Ibid., May 26, 1981.
(50) See ibid., August 23, 1981; Newsweek, November 30, 1981.
(51) Quoted in Hersh, "Qaddafi Connection," p. 56.
(52) NYT, July 23, 1981.
(53) Ibid., June 23, July 3, 1981.

NOTES FOR CHAPTER 8

(1) Mulcahy would be found dead in his car six years later, apparently killed by the effects of prolonged abuse of drugs and alcohol.
(2) Seymour M. Hersh, "The Qaddafi Connection," New York Times Magazine, June 14, 1983, p. 53.
(3) Ibid., p. 56.
(4) Ibid., p. 58.
(5) Ibid., p. 72.
(6) Ibid., p. 66.
(7) Ibid., June 21, 1981, p. 34.
(8) Ibid., p. 44.
(9) Ibid., p. 34.
(10) Ibid., p. 42.
(11) Ibid., p. 48.
(12) Ibid., pp. 48-49.
(13) Ibid., pp. 42, 44.

(14) New York Times, January 7, 1982.
(15) Ibid., October 24, 1981.
(16) Ibid.
(17) Ibid.
(18) Newsweek, November 30, 1981, p. 42.
(19) Ibid.
(20) Ibid.

NOTES FOR CHAPTER 9

(1)   New York Times (herafter NYT), February 16, 1979.
(2)   Ibid., February 15, 1979.
(3)   Ibid., February 27, 1979.
(4)   Ibid., March 3, 1979.
(5)   Ibid., March 30, 1979.
(6)   Ibid., April 16, 1979.
(7)   Ibid., April 19, 1979.
(8)   Ibid., May 3, 1979.
(9)   Ibid., May 25, 1979.
(10) Ibid., June 19, 1979.
(11) Ibid., September 2, 1979.
(12) Ibid., September 17, 1979. The author has not been able to identify the black group that visited Tripoli. Following the forced resignation of Andrew Young as UN ambassador a delegation of the Southern Christian Leadership Council visited Lebanon to open a dialogue with the PLO about this time, but no mention was made in press accounts that the SCLC delegation had also stopped in Tripoli.
(13) Author interview with David Newsom, Los Angeles, California, February 12, 1981.
(14) NYT, September 30, 1979.
(15) Ibid.
(16) Ibid., October 12, 1979.
(17) Ibid., July 15, 1980.
(18) Ibid., July 16, 1980.
(19) Ibid., July 24, 1980.
(20) Quoted by William Safire, Ibid., July 21, 1980.
(21) Ibid., July 18, 1980.
(22) Ibid., July 19, 1980.
(23) Ibid., July 20, 1980.
(24) Ibid.
(25) Ibid.
(26) Ibid., July 23, 1980.
(27) Ibid.
(28) Ibid., July 24, 1980, Pt. IV, p. 1.
(29) Ibid.
(30) Ibid., July 24, 1980.
(31) Ibid., July 24, 1980.

(32) Ibid, p. 19.
(33) Ibid., July 25, 1980.
(34) Ibid.
(35) Ibid., July 26, 1980.
(36) Ibid., July 26, 1980.
(37) Ibid.
(38) Ibid.
(39) Ibid.
(40) Ibid., July 28, 1980.
(41) Ibid.
(42) Ibid., July 27, 1980.
(43) Text of the statement is in ibid., July 30, 1980.
(44) Ibid., July 30, 1980. The president was asked to submit all relevant documents and tapes.
(45) Ibid., July 30, 1980.
(46) Ibid., July 31, 1980.
(47) Ibid.
(48) Ibid.
(49) Text in ibid., August 1, 1980.
(50) Ibid., August 1, 1980.
(51) Ibid., August 2, 1980.
(52) Ibid.
(53) Ibid., August 3, 1980.
(54) Ibid., August 10, 1980.
(55) The documents are U.S. Congress. Senate. Committee on the Judiciary. Subcommittee to Investigate the Activities of Individuals Representing the Interests of Foreign Governments. Inquiry into the Matter of Billy Carter and Libya. Hearings, August 4, 6, 19, 20, 21, 22; September 4, 5, 9, 10, 16, 17; October 2, 1980; 3 vols.; Interim Report, September 1980; Report together with Additional Views, October 2, 1980. (Washington, D.C.: U.S. Government Printing Office, 1980). (Hereafter: Bayh committee.)
(56) See U.S. Congress. House. Permanent Select Committee on Intelligence. In the Matter of Billy Carter. Report No. 96-1269. 96th Cong., 2d sess., August 28, 1980.
(57) See Newsom's replies to Senator Bayh, Bayh committee, vol. 1, pp. 49-51.
(58) See Philip Taubman's article, "Libya Using U.S. Trucks to Haul Soviet Tanks," NYT, January 21, 1982.
(59) Ibid.
(60) Ibid.
(61) Ibid.
(62) See Bayh committee, August 4, 1980, vol. 1, pp. 6-57; September 16, 1980, vol. 2, pp. 1,259-89.
(63) See especially Bayh committee, September 16, 1980, vol. 2, pp. 1,260-61.
(64) See statements by the Libyan desk officer W. Alan Roy, Bayh committee, vol. 2, pp. 1,284-85.

(65) NYT, August 2, 1980.

(66) Bayh committee, Interim Report, p. 45.

(67) Ibid., p. 1,285.

(68) There were also questions about allowing the shipment of jeeps with four-wheel drive. See ibid., pp. 1,288-89.

(69) See the testimony of Robert L. Keuch, associate deputy attorney general, Bayh committee, vol. 1, pp. 187-88.

(70) Federal Broadcast Information Service (hereafter FBIS), August 8, 1980, pp. I1-3, quoted in Bayh committee, vol. 1, pp. 23-25.

(71) Ibid., p. 23.

(72) See Bayh committee, Interim Report, pp. 1-45.

(73) Bayh committee, vol. 2, p. 1,291.

(74) Bayh committee, Interim Report, p. 12.

(75) Bayh committee, Interim Report, p. 20.

(76) See the testimony of the head of the Criminal Division, Assistant Attorney General Philip Heymann, Bayh committee, vol. 2, pp. 685-87.

(77) Bayh committee, vol. 1, p. 530.

(78) See Bayh committee, vol. 1, pp. 251-52.

(79) Ibid., vol. 3, pp. 1,503-5.

(80) McGregor testified to the Bayh committee that Billy and he had first discussed a Libyan oil deal "in March or April 1979." Ibid., vol. 1, p. 418.

(81) See the informative article by Linda Snyder Hayes, "How Charter Co. Saved Carey Energy and Got Instantly Rewarded," Fortune, October 8, 1979, quoted in Bayh committee, vol. 1, pp. 491-97.

(82) Ibid., p. 492.

(83) See the testimony of Louis Nasife, president, Charter Crude Oil Co., in Bayh committee, vol. 2, pp. 452ff.

(84) McGregor's version of this is "We were well on our way, it was felt, toward negotiating a resolution of those problems [with NOC] in late January 1979, but were not at all certain there would be an approval [by NOC] of whatever negotiated settlement might emerge." Ibid., p. 425. Linda Snyder Hayes in her Fortune article quotes Edward Carey as saying to everyone looking to take over Carey Energy that "they first needed to come to some sort of agreement with the Libyans." Ibid., p. 494.

(85) See Billy Carter's testimony, ibid., pp. 506-7; and Randy Coleman's testimony, ibid., pp. 216-17.

(86) Ibid., vol. 1, p. 453.

(87) Ibid., pp. 418-19.

(88) See Nasife's testimony, ibid., p. 455, 464, 467-68.

(89) A copy of the agreement is in Louis Nasife's testimony, ibid., vol. 1, p. 454. Nasife also instructed Billy as to the credit terms he should seek and the oil fields from which Charter would like to buy the crude oil.

(90) Ibid., pp. 460-61.

(91) See Randy Coleman's testimony, ibid., pp. 217-18.

(92) See Brzezinski's statement in the president's report to the Bayh committee, vol. 3, pp. 1,532-41.

(93) See ibid., vol. 3, pp. 1,609-37.

(94) Ibid., vol. 3, pp 1,539-46.

(95) Ibid., vol. 2, p. 703.

(96) See Heymann's testimony, ibid., vol. 2, p. 707.

(97) See Brzezinski's statement in the president's report to the Bayh committed, ibid., vol. 3, pp. 1,541-42.

(98) Ibid., vol. 2, p. 1,365.

(99) Ibid., pp. 1,364-65.

(100) Ibid., p. 1,148.

(101) Ibid., p. 1,092.

(102) Ibid., p. 707.

(103) Ibid., vol. 2, p. 695.

(104) Heymann statement to Bayh committee, ibid., vol. 2, p. 709.

(105) The text of the consent agreement, dated July 24, 1980, is in ibid., vol. 3, pp. 1,647-51.

(106) Ibid., Interim Report, p. 143.

(107) Ibid., pp. 144-81.

(108) Ibid., pp. 180-81.

(109) Bayh committee, Report with Additional Views, October 2, 1980.

(110) Ibid.

(111) Ibid., Interim Report, p. 148.

NOTES FOR CHAPTER 10

(1) New York Times (hereafter NYT), February 17, 1980.

(2) Ibid., March 24, 1980.

(3) Members of FAC included the Front populaire de liberation and Premiere armee Volcan of Abdoulaye Adoum Oana.

(4) Keesing's Contemporary Archives (hereafter KCA), February 6, 1981, p. 30,693.

(5) Ibid.

(6) Ibid., February 6, 1981, p. 30,694; Le Monde, December 5, 1980.

(7) Facts on File (hereafter FF), December 19, 1980, p. 965.

(8) NYT, November 6, 1980.

(9) Ibid., November 7, 1980.

(10) Ibid., December 4, 1980.

(11) KCA, February 6, 1981, p. 36,695.

(12) NYT, December 13, 17, 1980.

(13) KCA, February 6, 1981, pp. 30,695-96; FF, December 31, 1980, p. 979.

(14) Quoted in London Times, January 17, 1981.

(15) Federal Broadcast Information Service (hereafter FBIS), January 5, 1981, p. I1-I3.

(16) Ibid., January 7, 1981, p. I1.

(17) Ibid., January 5, 1981, p. I2.

(18) Ibid., January 7, 1981, p. I1.

(19) London Times, January 8, 1981.

(20) Ibid., January 9, 1981.

(21) FBIS, January 7, 1981, p. I1.

(22) London Times, January 17, 1981.

(23) Ibid., January 10, 1981.

(24) Agence France Presse, January 7, 1981, reported in FBIS, January 8, 1981, p. 14.

(25) Quoted in FBIS, January 8, 1981, p. S1.

(26) The communique was published by ATP (Chadian News Agency) and reported by Agence France Presse (AFP), January 15, 1981. Text is in FBIS, January 15, 1981, p. S1.

(27) AFP in FBIS, January 22, 1981, pp. D5-6.

(28) Ibid., January 28, 1981, p. S1.

(29) Ibid., January 8, 1981, p. D1.

(30) January 9, 10, 1981 reported in FBIS, January 12, 1981, pp. D1, D2.

(31) FBIS, January 12, 1981, p. D6.

(32) FBIS, January 19, 1981, p. D5.

(33) KCA, October 30, 1981, p. 31,162.

(34) Ibid., January 14, 1981, p. I3; January 19, 1981, p. I5.

(35) Statement by Sudanese Foreign Minister Mohammed Mirghani Mubark in Jidda en route to the Islamic Conference at Taif, January 20, 1981, FBIS, January 22, 1981, p. I5; KCA, October 30, 1981, pp. 31,159-60.

(36) KCA, October 30, 1981, p. 31,157.

(37) Ibid., October 30, 1981, pp. 31,157; 31,162.

(38) Ibid., October 30, 1981, p. 31,157.

(39) Ibid., p. 31,160; see also FBIS, Western Europe, January 8, 1981, p. K1.

(40) London Times, January 16, 1981; KCA, October 30, 1981, p. 31,160.

(41) FBIS, January 9, 1981, pp. S1-S2.

(42) Ibid., January 8, 1981, p. T1; January 19, 1981, p. T4.

(43) Ibid., January 13, 1981, p. T1.

(44) Ibid., January 19, 1981, p. T6.

(45) Ibid., January 14, p. S1.

(46) See the statement by U.S. Assistant Secretary of State Chester Crocker to the Senate Foreign Relations Committee of July 8, discussed in NYT, July 9, 1981.

(47) FBIS, January 14, 1981, p. Q1.

(48) According to a report by AFP, the drafting committee at Lome was composed of reprsentatives of Senegal, Niger, Nigeria,

Libya, CAR, and Sierra Leone. FBIS, January 15, 1981, p. Q1. The Nigerian draft may be found in the same place. The text of the Lome communique is in KCA, October 30, 1981, p. 31,160.

(49) KCA, October 30, 1981, p. 31,163.
(50) Ibid., September 4, 1981, p. 31,055.
(51) FBIS, January 14, 1981, p. I1.
(52) Ibid., January 15, 1981, pp. I1-2. See also Jalloud's remarks at the second session of the Libyan People's Congress, January 16 in FBIS, January 19, pp. I1-2.
(53) Ibid., January 19, 1981, p. I3.
(54) London Times, January 17, 1981.
(55) FBIS, January 21, 1981, p. Q1.
(56) Ibid., January 21, 1981, pp. I8-9.
(57) Le Monde, January 22, 1981, printed in ibid., January 23, 1981, p. I2.

NOTES FOR CHAPTER 11

(1) Keesing's Contemporary Archives (hereafter KCA), April 18, 1980, pp. 30,197-99.
(2) See ibid., July 1980, pp. 30,379-80.
(3) The Carter Doctrine and much of the text of the State of the Union address appear in ibid., May 16, 1980, p. 30,246, and generally 30,245-47. The other developments are covered in ibid., May 9, 1980, pp. 30,229-43.
(4) Ibid., July 25, 1980, p. 30,378.
(5) Excerpts of Komer's speech are in ibid., July 25, 1980, pp. 30,378-79.
(6) Ibid., November 28, 1980, p. 30,596.
(7) Ibid., April 11, 1980, p. 30,193.
(8) Ibid., May 2, 1980, p. 30,223.
(9) Ibid., February 15, 1981, p. 30,714.
(10) Ibid., February 13, 1981, pp. 30,714-16.
(11) Ibid., December 12, 1980, p. 30,613.
(12) Washington Post, September 18, 1980.
(13) Ibid., September 16, 1980.
(14) The text of the October 16 message is in ibid., October 21, 1980, p. A19.
(15) New York Times (hereafter NYT), October 24, 1980.
(16) In 1977 Libya began training a team to assassinate Ambassador Eilts. The United States had an agent in the camp who was able to monitor the assassins' progress and to keep U.S. intelligence informed about plans and training. When it became clear that a potentially effective operational plan was being developed — for example, the ambassador's daily schedule and habits were being carefully plotted — the United States withdrew its agent, and took the matter to President Carter. The president chose to send

Qaddafi a handwritten letter warning that he would hold Qaddafi "personally responsible" if anything happened to Ambassador Eilts. In order to make the letter credible, the president revealed some of the detailed knowledge of the plot available to the U.S. government. The letter was given to Ambassador Kikhia for delivery to Qaddafi. Shocked by the contents of the letter Kikhia took it to Libya. In his response, Qaddafi denied an assassination team or plot existed – the men accused of this were "agricultural workers," he said, but gave his promise that nothing would happen to Eilts. (Interview with senior official in the Carter administration, May 20, 1982.)

(17)   NYT, December 3, 4, 1979.

(18)   Ibid., December 6, 1979.

(19)   See Bernard Gwertzman, "Passions and Perils: An Anxious Washington Studies the Fever in Islam," ibid., December 9, 1979, section 4.

(20)   New York Times Magazine, December 16, 1979, p. 40.

(21)   Ibid.

(22)   Ibid., p. 121.

(23)   Ibid., pp. 121-22.

(24)   Ibid., p. 122.

(25)   Ibid., p. 127.

(26)   Ibid., p. 128.

(27)   Edward Said, Covering Islam: How the Media and the Experts Determine How We See the Rest of the World (New York: Pantheon, 1981), p. 26.

(28)   Ibid., p. xv.

(29)   Ibid., p. 51.

(30)   Ibid., December 11, 1979.

(31)   KCA, February 13, 1981, pp. 30,710-11; September 11, 1981, p. 31,076.

(32)   Ibid., August 28, 1981, pp. 31,049-52.

(33)   Ibid., August 28, 1981, p. 31,051.

(34)   Ibid., February 20, 1981, p. 30,728.

(35)   Ibid., February 6, 1981, pp. 30,703-4.

(36)   Ibid., November 7, 1980, pp. 30,558-59; February 13, 1981, pp. 30,714-16; February 27, 1981, p. 30,737; May 22, 1981, p. 30,871; July 31, 1981, p. 31,001-4.

(37)   Ibid., September 4, 1981, pp. 31,053-56.

NOTES FOR CHAPTER 12

(1)   This analysis of the change in U.S. policy toward Libya is based on interviews with senior U.S. officials conducted in 1980, 1981, and 1982.

(2)   Washington Post (hereafter WP), March 21, 1981.

(3)   New York Times (hereafter NYT), March 1, 1981, p. 1.

(4)   Ibid., March 11, 1981.

(5) For a layman's explanation of the ways Iraq could and apparently did try to escape the safeguards, see the article by Thomas O'Toole, WP, June 28, 1981, p. A-15.

(6) NYT, June 20, 1981.

(7) Ibid., March 13, 1981.

(8) WP, April 28, 1982.

(9) See Foreign Broadcast Information Service (hereafter FBIS), Soviet Union, International Affairs, April 28, 1982, p. H4.

(10) NYT, April 29, 30, 1981.

(11) FBIS, Soviet Union, International Affairs, April 30, 1981, pp. H2-H7.

(12) NYT, August 31, 1981.

(13) WP, May 13, 1981.

(14) This account of the closure of the people's bureau and the worsening of Libyan-U.S. relations is based on articles in the NYT, May 7, 8, 15 and June 20, 1981; WP, May 6, 7, 8, 14, 15, 19, and June 20, 27, 1981.

(15) See NYT, May 24, 27; July 26, 27, 28, 29, 30; September 6, 19, 25, 30; WP, March 22, 24; May 30, 1981. A partial list of newspaper stories about the activities of U.S. nationals in Libyan pay compiled by the author shows that starting in late June 1981 the articles appeared every 5 to 10 days with occasional breaks of several weeks. They appeared more frequently in September and October and then a rush began in November and December that carried over into January and February 1982. NYT: July 26, 28, 29, 30; September 6, 19; October 22, 23, 24, 26, 28; November 1, 2, 3, 6, 9, 10, 12, 13, 19, 20, 26, 30; December 3, 5, 9, 17, 26, 1982; January 6, 7, 11; February 1, 3, 14, 1982. WP: June 26, 29, 30; July 27, 28; September 10, 12, 16, 28; October 10, 24, 26; November 1, 3, 6, 30; December 1, 14, 1981; January 6, 1982.

(16) NYT, May 24, 1981.

(17) Ibid., May 7, 1981.

(18) Ibid., May 27, 1981.

(19) WP, May 7, 1981.

(20) NYT, September 30, 1981.

(21) Interview with senior Carter administration official, Washington, D.C., January 1982. See also Newsweek, October 19, 1981, p. 83.

(22) WP, October 10, 1981.

(23) Ibid., October 13, 1981.

(24) Newsweek, October 19, 1981, p. 43.

(25) NYT, November 1, 1981.

(26) Newsweek, November 9, 1981.

(27) NYT, November 13, 1981.

(28) See the statement by Said Hanifa, head of the Libyan people's bureau in France, WP, November 14, 1981.

(29) See WP, November 22, 1981.

(30) Ibid., November 28, 1981.

(31) NYT, December 4, 1981.
(32) WP, December 5, 1981.
(33) NYT, December 4, 1981; WP, December 3, 4, 5, 1981.
(34) Ibid., December 10, 1981.
(35) Newsweek, November 14, p. 51; December 21, p. 49.
(36) Los Angeles Times, December 12, 1981.
(37) NYT, November 28, 1981.
(38) Newsweek, November 30, p. 51; December 21, 1981, p. 19.
(39) NYT, December 9, 1981.
(40) Newsweek, November 30, 1981, p. 52.
(41) WP, December 10, 1981.
(42) NYT, December 4, 1981.
(43) WP, December 5, 1981; NYT, December 18, 1981.
(44) Ibid., December 10, 1981.
(45) Ibid., December 9, 1981.
(46) Ibid., December 25, 1981; NYT, January 14, 1982.
(47) See NYT, May 18, 1981; WP, May 19, 1981.
(48) For details of the Senate Intelligence Committee's findings criticizing but exonerating Casey, see Congressional Quarterly Almanac, vol. 37, 1981 (Congressional Quarterly, Inc.: Washington, 1982), pp. 156-57. Casey had failed to disclose $250,000 in assets and $500,000 in debts and had not listed some 70 legal clients at the time of his confirmation hearings. A brief discussion of Hugel's problems may be found in the same place.
(49) Newsweek, August 3, 1981.
(50) See Congressional Quarterly Almanac, vol. 36, 1980 (Congressional Quarterly, Inc.: Washington, 1981), pp. 66-71. Executive Order 12333, issued by President Reagan on December 4, relaxed restrictions on intelligence activities that had been established during the Carter and Nixon administrations, particularly in regard to the domestic operations of the CIA. Congressional Quarterly Almanac, vol. 37, 1981, p. 150.

NOTES FOR CHAPTER 13

(1) See article by Don Oberdorfer, Washington Post (hereafter WP), August 20, 1981.
(2) Ibid.
(3) New York Times (hereafter NYT), August 20, 1981.
(4) WP, August 24, 1981.
(5) See the article by Don Oberdorfer, WP, November 8, 1981.
(6) Ibid., August 20, 1981. See Secretary Haig's conference on August 23, , reported in ibid., August 24, 1981.
(7) Ibid., August 21, 1981.
(8) Articles by Wills, Schlesinger, and Fulbright appeared on the opinion page, ibid., August 23, 1981.
(9) Ibid., September 2, 1981.
(10) Ibid., August 20, 1981.

(11) NYT, October 2, 1981.

(12) Interview with senior Carter administration official, Washington, D.C., January 1982. See also the article by Don Oberdorfer in WP, November 11, 1981.

(13) Ibid., October 8, 1981.

(14) Ibid., October 18, 1981.

(15) NYT, October 14, 1981.

(16) See the articles on October 17 in the NYT and WP on the economic rather than political or military basis of Sudan's difficulties. See also the fascinating eyewitness report by Alan Cowell of the Times from El Geneina on the Chadian border, NYT, October 29, 1981. Cowell found no evidence of significant Libyan military operations against Sudan.

(17) WP, October 11, 1981. See also the interesting article on the AWACS as the new "gunboats" of modern diplomacy: ibid., October 18, 1981.

(18) Ibid., October 15, 1981; NYT, October 16, 1981, particularly the article by Bernard Gwertzman.

(19) See WP, November 13, 1981; NYT, November 23, 1981.

(20) WP, December 11, 12, 1981.

(21) Ibid., December 12, 1981.

(22) Don Oberdorfer, in ibid., February 26, 1982. See also NYT, February 26, 1982 and the critical editorial on March 7, 1982.

(23) NYT, February 26, 1982.

(24) Ibid., March 11, 1982.

(25) Ibid.

(26) Ibid.

(27) Ibid., March 11, 12, 1982.

(28) Ibid., March 21, 1982.

(29) Ibid., June 3, July 9, 1981.

(30) James L. Buckley, "Arms Transfers and the National Interest," Current Policy, no. 279, Department of State, May 21, 1981; cited in Andrew J. Pierre, The Global Politics of Arms Sales (Princeton: Princeton University Press, 1982), p. 62, no. 20. See also Congressional Quarterly Weekly Report, 1982, pp. 722-24, 797-802.

(31) Pierre, Arms Sales, pp. 63-65.

(32) Ibid., pp. 65, 68.

(33) WP, October 13, 14, 1982.

(34) Ibid., April 29, 1982.

(35) NYT, March 8, 1982.

(36) WP, April 7, 1981.

(37) NYT, February 12, 13, 1982.

(38) See ibid., February 23, 28, March 1, 8, 14, 25, 28, April 5, 10, 23, 1982.

(39) Boucetta made this statement at the end of the king's visit during a news conference at the offices of the Carnegie Endowment for International Peace in Washington, attended by the author, May 20, 1982.

(40) NYT, June 7, October 19, 1981.

(41)   WP, July 16, 1981.
(42)   Ibid., October 2, 1981.
(43)   Ibid., October 25, 27, and NYT, October 25, 28, 1981.
(44)   NYT, October 28-30, and WP, October 28-29, November 3, 1981.

NOTES FOR CHAPTER 14

(1)   Bureau members of the eighteenth OAU Assembly of Heads of State were Angola, Congo, Gambia, Kenya, Lesotho, Libya, Tanzania, Uganda, and Upper Volta. Only Angola was absent from the Nairobi meeting.
(2)   Algeria, Angola, Benin, Burundi, Congo, Ethiopia, Ghana, Guinea Bissau, Lesotho, Libya, Madagascar, Malawi, Mali, Mauri-tania, Mauritius, Mozambique, Rwanda, Sao Tome and Principe, Seychelles, Swaziland, Tanzania, Uganda, Zambia, Zimbabwe.
(3)   This account of the deadlock in the OAU is based on John Damis's Conflict in Northwest Africa; The Western Sahara Dispute (Stanford, Calif.: Hoover Institution Press, 1982), pp. 72-76, 80-82, 92-93, 99-103, 146; New York Times, 1982; Keesing's Contemporary Archives, 1983 (hereafter KCA), pp. 31,935ff. See also Virginia Thompson and Richard Adloff, The Western Saharans: Background to Conflict (Croom Helm: London, 1980), p. 282.
(4)   New York Times (hereafter NYT), June 9, 1983, p. 12.
(5)   On Qaddafi's supprt of Polisario see Damis, Conflict in Northwest Africa, pp. 108-112.
(6)   NYT, June 10, 1983.
(7)   Ibid., June 12, 1983. For a thorough description of the Moroccan fortifications across the Sakiet El-Hamra see Damis, Conflict in Northwest Africa, pp. 97-98.
(8)   The OAU estimate was too high for Morocco and too low for SADR, which has claimed a population of 750,000-850,000. Damis, Conflict in Northwest Africa, p. 9.
(9)   NYT, June 12, 1983.
(10)   See Damis, Conflict in Northwest Africa, pp. 100-103.
(11)   Federal Broadcast Information Service (hereafter FBIS), February 1, 3, 1983, pp. Q1, Q3.
(12)   Ibid., February 3, 1983, p. Q11.
(13)   Ibid., p. Q8.
(14)   Ibid., p. Q5.
(15)   Ibid., p. Q7.
(16)   For the text of the statement adopted by the meeting see FBIS, February 8, 1983, pp. Q1-3.
(17)   NYT, February 19, 1983.
(18)   Washington Post (hereafter WP), February 19, 1983.
(19)   Newsweek, February 28, 1983, p. 26.
(20)   Ibid., p. 27.

(21) Facts on File, February 25, 1983, pp. 123-24.

(22) NYT, February 17, 1983.

(23) Ibid.; see also Los Angeles Times, February 17, 1983. The L.A. Times report disagrees with that in the New York Times. The Los Angeles paper held that the AWACS were in Egypt as part of previously planned exercises. The New York paper reported they had been sent to help scotch the Libyan plot.

(24) Los Angeles Times, February 18, 1983.

(25) NYT, February 18, 1983. See also Los Angeles Times, February 18, 1983.

(26) NYT, February 18, 1983.

(27) Ibid., February 19, 1983.

(28) Los Angeles Times, February 20, 1983.

(29) NYT, February 22, 1983.

(30) Ibid., February 21, 1983.

(31) Los Angeles Times, February 20, 1983.

(32) Ibid; NYT, February 21, 1983.

(33) See John Cooley, "Libya's Bizarre Power Play," Christian Science Monitor, March 6, 1983.

(34) FBIS, The USSR: International Affairs, p. H2.

(35) Text of the communique may be found in ibid., March 21, 1983, pp. H2-5. The Libyan version is in FBIS, March 21, 1983, pp. Q2-6.

(36) Ibid., p. H-6.

(37) The U.S. disclosure that it had tipped the Brazilians is in WP, April 21, 1983.

(38) WP, April 23, 1983.

(39) Ibid., April 21, 1983.

(40) NYT, June 15, 1983.

(41) WP, April 21, 1983.

(42) See ibid., April 27, 1983.

(43) NYT, June 15, 1983.

(44) Ibid., August 3, 1983.

(45) Ibid., August 9, 1983.

(46) Transcript of the president's news conference is in ibid., August 12, 1983.

(47) Christian Science Monitor, August 22, 1983; NYT, August 23, 1983.

(48) NYT, August 21, 1983.

(49) Christian Science Monitor, August 21, 1983.

NOTES FOR CHAPTER 15

(1) Washington Post, August 25, 1983.

(2) New York Times, February 6, 1983.

(3) Ibid., October 22, 1983.

INDEX

ABOUT THE AUTHOR

P. EDWARD HALEY is currently Director of the Keck Center for International Strategic Studies, Professor of Political Science, and Chairman of the International Relations Committee at Claremont McKenna College. Dr. Haley received a bachelor's and master's degree from Stanford University and a Ph.D. from Johns Hopkins University, School of Advanced International Studies. An International Affairs Fellow of the Council on Foreign Relations, he has served on the staffs of members of the Senate and House of Representatives. He is author of Congress and the Fall of South Vietnam and Cambodia, Lebanon in Crisis: Participants and Issues, Revolution and Intervention: The Diplomacy of Taft and Wilson with Mexico, 1910-1917, which was awarded the Premio Sahagun by the Mexican National Institute of Anthropology and History, and numerous articles and reviews on United States foreign policy and international politics. Dr. Haley and his wife, Elaine Seagrave, live with their daughters, Laura and Catherine, in Claremont, California.